Doing Your Own Research

Doing Your Own Research

Eileen Kane & Mary O'Reilly-de Brún

MARION BOYARS
LONDON · NEW YORK

First published in the United States and Great Britain in 2001
by MARION BOYARS PUBLISHERS
24 Lacy Road, London SW15 1NL

www.marionboyars.co.uk

Reprinted in 2005
10 9 8 7 6 5 4 3 2

Distributed in Australia and New Zealand by
Peribo Pty Ltd, 58 Beaumont Road, Mount Kuring-gai, NSW

A CIP catalogue record for this book is available from the British Library
A CIP catalog record for this book is available from the Library of Congress

ISBN 0-7145-3043-3 Paperback
13 digit ISBN 9780714530437

Printed in England by Mackays of Chatham plc, Chatham, Kent

To our beloved
Paud Murphy
and
Tomas de Brún
models for so many of our characters

ACKNOWLEDGMENTS

The authors would like to thank everyone who helped us, particularly Louise Vimmerstedt, whose careful reading of the original manuscript has saved us more gasps than we would otherwise have had when reading the book in future years. We also thank her, Eliza MacLeod, and Barbara Rodes for their various contributions to Chapter 8. Elizabeth Thomas put order on Chapter 14. Leila Doolan identified and connected us to people whose expertise we needed, such as Lucy Daniels, who went to a lot of trouble to teach us much of what we know about life in London tower blocks. We also got some very good ideas from Fever, Inc, Dublin.

We are grateful to Mr John Lonergan, Governor, Mountjoy Jail in Dublin, Ireland, for the loan of his genial persona; to counselor Trish Murphy; and to inmates of various jails for their insights. The other characters are all fictional, although various people have lent their real names, such as Leland De Witt, who was seven years old recently, and Randy Anderson, who is charming and articulate in real life. Dr Brian O'Connell was good enough to acknowledge that we caught his speech 'to the life', but of course his actual life is far more interesting than the fictional one we gave his character here. We'd also like to thank the editorial staff at Marion Boyars, Ken Hollings, Brendan King and Julia Silk, and to take this opportunity to remember Marion Boyars, who asked us to prepare this second revised edition.

But above all we'd like to thank Paud Murphy and Tomas de Brún for all the good ideas they contributed, and for all their time, effort and cheerful support. As the Irish say, we won't see their like again.

CONTENTS

PART I

BEFORE YOU BEGIN

1 THE BOOK, THE PEOPLE, THE PLACES

This book makes two promises:

You will learn how to do basic social research.
You will get to travel, meet new people, practice your research skills, and be locked up in a local jail.

Few other research books promise this. Of course, for some people, a jail threat is almost trivial compared to the prospect of doing a piece of research. 'You have to go to university to do research,' they think, or 'only professional researchers can do proper research.' Many academics, however, will admit that although they were exposed to a lot of research, they were never really taught how to do a piece of research starting with the original idea and finishing with the final paper; they had to learn the process themselves.

Many first-time researchers run into all kinds of problems. They don't know where to begin; they don't know how long it will take; they use a particular research technique not because it is the best one for their problem but because it is the only one they know. They don't know how to record the information, unless they are using simple questionnaire forms. They don't know when they are finished — all they know is that they allowed themselves, or were allowed, two months to do the research, and, since the two months are up, they must be done. They are unable to analyze their material properly because they have it on hundreds of dog-eared bits of paper spread all over the floor. Household cleaning stops. After a while they cram it all in a box, put it in a cupboard and get a sinking feeling every time their glance falls on the cupboard. Eventually they start avoiding the room altogether. They feel guilty going on holiday or getting married. They really should get down to it and write up that research, they think.

Even if they escape these problems, first-timers can find that what they collect doesn't match their title. Then they have to figure out what they have and find a title to justify it. They may have to invent a whole new field of human knowledge to correspond to their meanderings through a range of human topics which had no logical connection, except for the fact that they accidentally happened to study them while confused.

Most people who are doing a thesis or a study will recognize these problems — indeed most live in the guilty secret belief that they are the only people to whom this has ever happened. Rest assured — you are not alone.

Who Should Use This Book?

This book is the result of thirty years of classroom experimentation and community research experience in Western societies and in developing countries. It has been used successfully by fourteen-year-olds and Ph.D. students, and some of their research, such as that done by a group of unemployed young people in a Dublin suburb, has been published (Portmarnock: A Closer Look, Wolfhound Press, 1985). Some of it, such as the approaches in Chapter 14, have been used successfully by people who cannot read or write. In this second edition, my co-author is Mary O'Reilly-de Brún, a former student, as was Professor Richard Scaglion, the author of Chapter 17.

The book is meant for people who:
- have little or no training in social research;
- need or want to look into a problem, situation or issue and don't know where to begin;
- will be working with small numbers of people or local issues, and will not be trying to carry out regional or national surveys;
- have time and budget constraints and may have little, or no, assistance;
- might like to use the results as the basis for some kind of action, such as a group or community initiative.

Perhaps you are:
- a member of a community association who wants to learn more about the community's attitudes toward setting up a drug program;
- a teacher concerned that girls may not be participating in the classroom as much as boys;

- a home-owner worried about how development has affected your neighbourhood;
- a person working in a local government department who's just been told to write a report on how a proposed by-law will affect local environmental issues;
- an employee who wants to tell senior management that the new work shifts have reduced productivity and requires some evidence to strengthen the claim;
- a staff member of a small charitable organization that can't afford to hire a researcher but still needs to study the impact of its programs;
- a member of a voluntary organization working in development: community, rural or developing countries.

Or, though the book isn't really intended for this purpose, perhaps you are in a waking nightmare: a desperate student who was told five months ago to do a research-based report, forgot about it, and now it's the end of the term. For you, although you don't deserve it, we suggest you go to an Internet site such as **www.researchpaper.com/questions/society/contemporary-issues/**. You will have to narrow the topics offered there (see Chapter 4) and you would be well-advised at this late stage to stay away from anything with the word 'cause' in it (see Chapter 5). You'll still have to read the book to learn how to do research on the topic.

If you are in any one of these kinds of situations, this book will help you to do a modest piece of research which is valid and credible. You will be able to stand over it. It will not turn you into a professional researcher, so hold on to the day job, or stay in school.

There's a final category of people who will find this book useful: those who simply want to be informed consumers of other people's research. Too often we are at the mercy of special interests who use research to further their agenda. We see newspaper headlines that announce 'Study Shows Dandruff Prolongs Life'. We read books that tell us that intelligent women are, basically, men (Anne Moir and David Jessel. 1992. *Brain Sex*. New York: Dell). We see statistics which seem to prove that driving further away from home is safer than driving nearby ('Study Shows Most Accidents Occur Within Five Miles of Home'). People who can't judge the quality of research that supports such statements end up spluttering 'I don't believe it — I don't care what the research says.' In the cut and thrust of debate, this is about as useful as stamping your foot.

Finally, there's a good reason why more people should know how to do social research. Historically, decisions about what information was important, who gathered it, and how it was used have been determined by the powerful for the less powerful. Elites and people of higher social standing study the poor, men study women, the industrial world studies the developing world. Even today, most research is 'of the privileged, by the privileged, and for the privileged' on the less privileged. Learning how to do basic social research enables people who traditionally have been left out of this process to contribute and to bring different perspectives and insights to bear.

About the Book

This book will help you to:

- understand the basics of social research
- get valid, relevant information
- do the research in a relatively short time
- use the research for a practical end
- meet folks who make your uncle look normal

The techniques in the book are drawn from a wide variety of social science disciplines, but the spirit comes from anthropology, sociology, rapid rural appraisal, participatory research, educational evaluation and dog training.

Some features of the book:

- Because the book is meant to be a practical guide, the chapters are presented in the order that you are likely to use them if you are carrying out a complete project, starting with the planning stage, and ending with some kind of report, or action. Figure 1–1 shows the general plan.
- This is a book for beginners, but you should be able to use it to carry out a useful piece of research. When you feel confident enough to move on, you can use more specialized books to pursue the ideas and techniques which interest you. At the end of each chapter, you'll find a list of books and articles under 'References and further readings'. These will take you at least one step beyond what is presented in the chapters here.
- You can certainly carry out research on your own, but you may find it enjoyable to work with a group or team. Then again, after working with the team that we have created for you in this book, perhaps not. But in any research you need to have an orderly plan, a standardized way of recording your information, and a systematic approach to making sense of what you have collected. This is even more important when you are working with a team. Chapters 9 and 14, which explain research that can involve teams, will help to keep everyone on the same track.

- Chapter 2 is a special case. Even though you do not need to read Chapter 2 to do your research, it will help you to understand that there are different ways of looking at the world, and that these different ways lead to different kinds of research. But it is possible to skip the chapter. Come back to it when you have time and want a better understanding of why you did what you did, or why other researchers did.

Figure 1–1 An overview of the chapters in the book

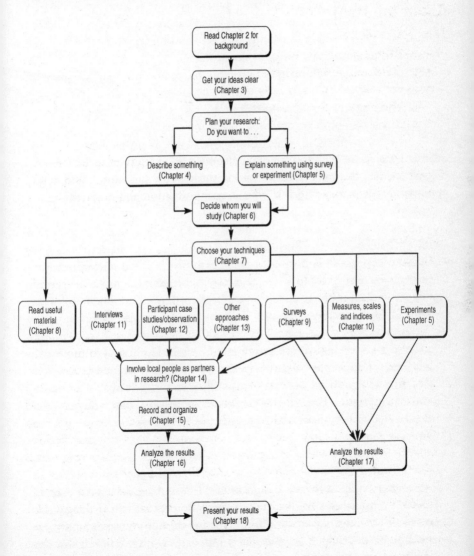

About the People and the Places in the Book

You will be working as part of a team in two places. As the book opens, you are working in Hope And Glory, Ohio, a tiny rural speed trap where people will welcome you, more or less. Your fellow researchers are Sharon Darwin, Brixton, London; Pius Gallagher, Dublin; Jean-Luc Peillon, Paris; and Tiffani Shapiro, New York.

In the second half of the book, you go to Hancock Towers, London, a high-rise block of public housing, where you will work with Sharon Darwin and a motley crew of Towers residents. A couple of people from Hope And Glory will come along, too. What you learn in these places can be applied to almost any research situation.

Finally, the people and places in this book are not real. We have to say that.

We begin in our first research community, Hope And Glory, Ohio…

In the early morning, gentle freshets of cool air drift across the little town, smoothing the cheeks of the sleeping here, whispering half-dreams there, blowing feathery wisps of hair across voluptuous white pillows. Soft old sheets caress their bodies as they slumber on, sighing, knowing, for a few moments, the innocence of Eden.

That's in the early morning. Later in the day, up, washed, and wary, they will be issuing writs, shooting one another's dogs, looking into one another's affairs, and believe it or not, doing some social science research, for it is we who created them and we shall make them do it. But not without a struggle. In their sleep, the people of Hope And Glory, Ohio, are gentle, mild, kind, genial, tender, and considerate. Awake, they are cranky, peevish, and testy.

We will be working as a research team here in Hope And Glory for the next while, using what we learn in this book to find out more about the place and its people. They, of course, will be doing the same — there isn't a small town anywhere in the world where people don't observe their neighbors, question them, and read their police records if they can get their hands on them.

Septus McCardle

Researchers, huh? Well, as a matter of fact I don't have a police record, but I think I must be one of the few here who don't. That fellow that sold me one of those new combination ironing board-trouser press contraptions last week down at Winkle's — those little bitty eyes — don't tell me he don't have a record. And the damn thing don't even work — I was ironing away and it snapped shut and prettineer baked my arm flat. Got a good crease in it though.

What I wanted to tell you about this place is you don't want to believe everything you hear. Bert Whump'll tell you I had 45 dogs over at my house, and gambling and women and the Lord knows what all. Well, I did have 45 dogs, but not all at once, no more than 28 at any one time, and I was tossing coins for a good reason. No gambling, I don't hold with that. And women? My wife Laurinda. She makes enough noise and trouble for ten — that's probably what got him going. Let me give you a piece of advice. If you're going to talk to her, shave that beard off. Don't blame me if she tries to plaster a bag on your face. My own face is raw from shaving, I can tell you. If I had enough money for a lawyer, I'd be shut of her. As it is, I got to get me a lawyer anyway because Whump served me with a writ over those dogs.

Randy Anderson, mayor

I'm real glad I arranged for you folks to come here to look into the state of affairs, cause they've come to a pretty pass.

Squabblin' and wranglin' is second nature to the people here: we got guys shooting each other's animals, we got some folks behind the boiler factory that nobody in town talks to, we got a mayor without a driving license, and we got a chief of police with an IQ in the red numbers. He's turned this place into such a speed trap that all we get is foot traffic — you could play hopscotch on the highway. I lost my license after four tickets: the last one was for going 19 miles-an-hour in a 13 mile-an-hour zone. He and Judge Quinn are in this together. The judge wants some anti-speed signs around the town, right above the welcome signs, so he sentenced me to write some slogans. Either that or 120 hours community service. What the hell does he think a mayor does, if it ain't community service? Anyhow, I said I'd give it a shot. He didn't like the first one much. Marked it all up in red and wrote 'Can do better' across the top:

If you want to live
to tell the story
Don't try to drive
in Hope And Glory
Welcome to Our Town
Pop. 1780

But I got better at it, and for the last one I got me a star. You can see two of them out on Route 123 and over at Beaver Dam Road.

Anyhow, I was trekkin' out to my place on Route 123 the other day and prettineer got flattened by some fool going 50 miles-an-hour. I knew who it had to be. He says to me, he says, 'I see yer scampering along real smart there, Mayor. Why don't ya get a horse?' Next thing, he puts on the siren and zooms over to Winkle's Party Pak and Live Bait for lunch. The eats is swell there. It's real provoking when you can't think of a quick comeback to a fool comment like that, but my mama always said 'Never miss a good chance to shut up' so maybe it's just as well. Acourse that ain't a bad idea, actually: I just might get me a horse. Anyhow, welcome to Hope And Glory. Anything you want, you just let me know. And I know a nice place the five of you can stay.

Laurinda McCardle

The first thing you need to know about me is that I'm a career woman. I used to work with my mother over at the Precious Lambs Daycare Center. She owns it, but I objected when she started giving rifle lessons to the pre-schoolers. She was only giving them to the boys, and I said 'Whoa! That's gender discrimination' and I left. Now I'm a wiener demonstrator over at the supermarket. You know, you have a little table with cocktail sausages on it and you ask people would they like a taste. Nights, I play the pie-anna over at the Party Pak.

But I'd love to be a researcher like you, hon. What I would do, I would look at breasts and beards. I know I can talk to you about this, you being a lady scientist. The thing is, when I was in school we learned about the primary and secondary sex characteristics. It seems the breasts and the beard are both secondary. The primary…well, we know what *they* are, and they don't concern me. Not here, anyhow. You can probably see where I'm going, right? How come breasts have to be covered up in public, and beards don't? They're both secondary, right? How is it that males don't have to wear their beards in little bags is what I'd like to know. Now if I could learn how to do a questionnaire, I'd ask people their opinions, and then see could I get it put on the ballot. They say we only walk this way but once, and when my time comes I'd like to be able to point to something and say: 'Maybe it's not much, but I did that.' I'd be real pleased.

Juanetta Wilcox

My father was the police chief here, and thank God he ain't alive today. Well, for one thing, he'd be over 120. I don't think I want to live that long. Drooling and all, it ain't attractive. However, not much chance of that, with all the grief I have. My daughter's gone crazy. There's a study for you: ungrateful children and how they love to persecute their parents. She's got some notion about beards — you a doctor? A Ph.D.? No, she needs a real doctor, I'd say. But you watch yourself, honeybunch, a good-looking Irish fellow like you. She's got some kinda power over men. She had the mayor and the police chief fighting over her all through school, and there's still bad blood there, even though she didn't marry neither one of them. She married Septus. Anyhow, looky here, what I really want to say is that we got a crowd of no-goods living over beyond the boiler factory — dozens of them. There ain't but half of them can read and write, I bet. I don't know where they come from. I don't think they're even Methodists.

She won't say nothing about that teeny beard of yours, except maybe to snigger. She's pretty big-breasted, herself. No manners to speak of, though.

Bert Whump

That Septus, I tell you. Dogs here, there and everywhere. You fellows English? I hear the English won't tolerate cruelty to animals, no sir. But this here mess was pitiful. One night raccoons got into my garbage. You ever seen a raccoon? They look like bandits. No, not the bandits behind the boiler factory. Anyhow, them's just poor people. My daughter's married to one of them fellows. Raccoons got furry faces, like a fox with a mask over the eyes. Anyhow, there I was sleeping. It was one of those kinds of sleeps you have maybe two, three times in a lifetime. The sheets felt like clouds. The breeze…the pillows…man! Then three of Septus's dogs got after the raccoons. Old lady Wilcox come out shouting. They all went for her. I woke up with the commotion, and I threw water on them. They was snarlin', and old lady Wilcox was waving a umbrella and whatnot, so I got out my gun and blasted the whole lot to Kingdom Come. Not old lady Wilcox, acourse. But she was a fearful sight. Didn't neither one of us recover for days. All because Septus lets his dogs — I believe he's got about 28 — run wild. It's against the law. There's also something else going on over there. Hard to say what, with all the carry on.

So I phoned the police and reported it, and they gave me all this guff about being sensitive to his needs, and reasoning with him, and I don't know what. I said if they wasn't going to be any more use than that, I'd just give him a few broken teeth myself. Then they started on about his body being a temple and all. Turned out, of course, I had the presbytery, not the police. One line different in the phone book.

Leland De Witt

You know what keeps this town going? You're looking at him. I'm chief of police here. If it wasn't for me, the place would be bankrupt. The mayor and the council, they have all these fancy ideas: macramé classes, bird sanctuaries, flowers all year around the Tomb of the Honorary Veteran — that's Randy's father. Chicken John, we called him. Where's the money supposed to come from? Me. I put more in the town coffers every year than the whole lot put together. And then dudn't a day go by but they sneer at me because I don't have much education. It's true. I give up after eighth grade. I remember I got whomped by Mr. Rawley when he give me a famous proverb to memorize. It started out 'All the world's a stage...' I didn't think it was so hot, so I said to him 'OK, then where's the audience sit?' Them teachers have a lot of learning, but no sense. You ever seen the school principal at the gas station? Has the same car for fifteen years and never once has he drove up and got the tank opening and the gas pump on the same side. Has to pull the pump around and still gets it wrong. Was me, I'd be embarrassed. The mayor and the council's the same. Mud thinks faster.

Don't you worry about being French, boy. But I do got to ask you one question. Where in hell was you folks during the war?

The Hope and Glory Vindicator

Volume 182 Issue 4   May 19, 2001

Mayor caught in police trap

In a new development in the ongoing war between the mayor and the chief of police over the use of speed traps to fund the town, Mayor Randy Anderson has been cited by Police Chief Leland De Witt for failure to display a rear light on a moving vehicle.

Witnesses say that Mayor Anderson was riding his horse Trigger down Robbers' Lane last evening when he was stopped by Chief De Witt, who issued a ticket for failure to have a rear light on the horse.

'A horse is a moving vehicle,' he told the mayor. 'You know the rules as well as I do.'

Witnesses stated that the mayor handed the chief a flashlight, saying 'There's an opening beneath the tail, if you want to install it yourself.'

A fracas ensued. Witnesses differ on what happened, but this morning the mayor's lawyer, Bert Whump, announced that the mayor was slightly injured in the melee and was pressing a charge of assault and battery.

Team to visit Hope and Glory

A five-member research team will study various aspects of life in Hope And Glory, according to Mayor Randy Anderson, who issued a statement from his hospital bed last night. The team, slated to arrive in Hope And Glory next week, consists of social scientists from Paris, France, London, England, New York and Dublin, Ireland. Mr. and Mrs. Meryl 'Bob' Matthews, 125 Garfield Street, visited Dublin, Ireland last year, and Mrs. Meryl Bob is thinking about taking her daughter this year.

According to the mayor, the research team is part of a Federal Disaster Relief Program. Hope And Glory is the first community to receive this type of assistance. Police Chief Leland De Witt, in a separate statement, said: 'I never heard the like. Other towns get money, food parcels, what have you, and we get a research team? And where's the disaster?'

The team, which includes Ms. Sharon Darwin from Brixton in England, Ms. Tiffani Shapiro from New York, Mr. Jean-Luc Peillon from Paris, and Mr. Pius Gallagher from Dublin, and a fifth researcher whose name we didn't catch, will be staying in the Anderson Motel out on Highway 123.

National survey gives the real low-down

A national survey of 1,000 women has shown that 72% wear their panties under their tights, 15% wear them over, and 13% don't know.

INSIDE THIS ISSUE

2 SOCIAL RESEARCH: THE BIG DEBATE

Summary

Sometimes people who want to do a piece of social research are afraid that their research will not be 'scientific'. Often, these fears are based on misconceptions about what science is.

Paradigms are patterns or models for understanding. For several centuries, science was based upon certain paradigms, but it has changed considerably in recent years. Other paradigms also exist. Three are explored in this chapter. Each of them offers different answers to such questions as: Is there such a thing as reality? How can we understand the world? What is the relation of the researcher to what is being researched?

The first two paradigms, *positivism* and *postpositivism* are the basis of traditional science. These paradigms are based on the belief that there is an 'objective' real world which is orderly and predictable. Nature can be understood much as we understand a machine. The aim of research is to discover its causes and effects.

Phenomenology, another paradigm, holds that there is no such thing as objectivity. Instead, there are many, changing perspectives on reality. In doing research, getting the whole picture, context and meanings are what is important. In other words, understanding. The observer is part of the picture, not separate from it.

In *critical theory*, there is an objective world which the observer can stand apart from. But whose world is it? Elites have had charge of the research agenda, setting the questions, funding the research, interpreting the results. The purpose of research is to empower people to set their own action agendas.

Is social science a science? Modern science is moving closer to some of the perspectives of the social sciences.

It's obvious that there are a few hidden agendas in Hope And Glory. There are hidden agendas in research, as well. In this chapter, we will be looking at some idea systems that are the foundation of all research — the 'agendas' behind all inquiry. They are not usually discussed in books for beginners, so why are they here?

First, they will give you a little advantage as a novice. Many professional researchers aren't aware of the debate, or don't fully understand it, or have decided that it doesn't apply to their work. It does. Since you are learning from scratch, why not start out with some fundamentals which are often skipped? And the best part is that when someone who has been doing research for years tells you that your study is not 'scientific' or 'objective' or has no 'hard data' you can temporarily immobilize them with words like 'phenomenology' while you rush off to some of the works listed at the end of the chapter for more ammunition. If you already have a traditional research background, this discussion will give you some insight into the newer approaches to research. It will also help those people who are still worried about how 'scientific' their research is going to be.

In this debate, some important questions are: 'What is the nature of reality and of human knowledge?' 'How do we go about getting at it?' and 'Where does the researcher fit in?' Some of the best near-popular writing of the past decade or so has been done by scientists and social theorists trying to deal with these questions. Look at the work, for instance, of Richard Feynman, James Gleick, and Stephen Jay Gould.

Although science was once thought of as the model for all research, it has been on a credibility roller coaster for the past decade or so. Great discoveries, like cold fusion, have been announced; great counter-attacks of research fraud and near fraud have emerged soon after. Chaos and complexity theory, questioning our ideas about the way the world works, have appeared, and some scientists have begun to doubt some of the assumptions we have made in the past about science itself.

Philosophers and social critics have joined the debate and are reasserting the idea that there are alternative ways of knowing things, other than the purely 'scientific' way which most of us had assumed was the ideal. As a result, science and social theory have become more accessible, interesting, and transparent; people who fled science in school are buying books in airports about chaos, final theories, and debates in natural history; people who are not particularly immersed in literature, philosophy, or social theory are using labels like 'postmodernist' to describe the local bus station. An introduction to some of these issues will help you to understand that there are various ways of getting knowledge, or doing research. At some point in your research journey, you should learn more about these ideas.

But one of the nice things about studying a book on your own is that you can ignore the author's ideas about the order in which you should read the book. The rest of this chapter is theoretical; it contains no practical instruction on how to do research. And perhaps you have an urgent practical problem: the powers that be are going to build a major road where your garden now stands, which happens to be a nesting place for the great-crested grebe. You want to show that in other high traffic areas the great-crested grebe has disappeared. Or perhaps your university instructor is crouched and ready to pounce, suspecting, correctly as it turns out, that you have done no work on your research paper. If you find yourself in these kind of circumstances, you may want to move along to the next chapter. Indeed, it is not necessary that you read the rest of this chapter at all in order to use the rest of the book, but it will help you to get a deeper understanding of why you are doing what you are doing. And at parties, it will let you make a change from talking about how long it takes your car to go from zero to sixty. So read on, or proceed to Chapter 3.

How Do We Know About the World?

Well done! Here's a star (★) for continuing to read on!

Today, all thinking about the way we understand the world, including science itself, is undergoing a profound change. Traditionally, two techniques have dominated social research: surveys, which have been the most commonly used; and participant observation, or watching what people do and asking them about it. Sociologists, economists, educators, agricultural scientists, and health workers, among others, are the most frequent users of surveys. Anthropologists are more likely to use participant observation. Surveys are often described as quantitative, that is, they process their findings numerically, and produce results in number form, while participant observation is qualitative, and produces results in words. More recent approaches, such as rapid assessment techniques and participatory approaches (see Chapter 14) often combine both, with a heavier emphasis on the qualitative. But this quantitative-qualitative distinction is a somewhat simplistic, shorthand way of summarizing a much more fundamental debate.

The debate

What is reality? Does a single, absolute reality exist, or are there many, changing perspectives on reality? Can reality be known at all? How? Some of these questions are the kind that creep up on people in the middle of a sleepless night. Other people think about these things in the daytime as well, for example, people who are avoiding a particularly boring task. But professionally, it is the work of specialists in the philosophy of knowledge, who ask: 'What is the nature of reality?' 'What is the nature of human knowledge?' 'How do we go about finding knowledge?' Philosophers have tried to answer these questions for at least 2,000 years, and the debate continues today. Unfortunately, the literature on these subjects is about as user-friendly as a tangle of wire coat hangers, as you will probably guess from some of the words that come up later in the chapter.

But it is important for beginning researchers to understand the different answers to these questions, because they lead to different ways of doing research and different ideas about what is acceptable evidence. As you do your research, the choices you will make about what to study and how to study it, even those choices you think are 'only common sense' or 'natural', will probably be based on one of the approaches we will be discussing.

You should be familiar with the features, strengths, and weaknesses of each approach. You should also realize that there is no single way to acquire knowledge. There are many paths to knowing things, and this discussion presents four of them.

The answers that philosophers have offered to these questions form sets of assumptions called paradigms. A paradigm is a set of underlying beliefs or assumptions about the way things are. These have certain consequences. For example, the way people behave in relation to the supernatural reflects a paradigm. If you believe that you are subject to the will of the supernatural, you will behave in a prayerful and beseeching way. This is usually called 'religion'. On the other hand, if you believe that under certain circumstances you can control the supernatural, you will try to use the correct formula or ritual to get what you want. This is usually called 'magic'. Both are based on a respect for the supernatural, but are two different ways of dealing with it.

The approaches discussed in the rest of this chapter are paradigms about how to understand the world we live in. None can be proved or disproved as right or wrong.

Paradigm 1: positivism

In research, one paradigm has been dominant for more than 300 years: positivism, and its successor, postpositivism. For many of us it is the only one we know, because it forms the basis of modern science. Among researchers, pure positivism — a belief that only observable, objective, provable hard facts count — was fading even in the 1950s, but generally, the person in the street is still a hide-bound positivist.

Positivism is based on the assumption that reality exists: it is 'out there'. Nature is like an orderly machine, a great clock that operates according to unchanging universal laws. We can find out the way things are, what is really happening. We can unlock the secrets of nature if we ask the right questions, just as we can understand the workings of a clock if we take it apart and study it carefully. The 'facts' we discover are true if they correspond to 'objective reality'. The relationship between the researcher and nature is dualistic. The researcher does not have to be part of nature. The researcher can stand apart from nature and observe it objectively.

In this paradigm, the world is stable, consistent, predictable, and orderly. Things occur in a single-line order of cause and effect: A causes B. Causes in both the natural and social worlds can be studied in the same way, through experimental procedures. The researcher singles out and examines the relationships between variables, or separate aspects of reality, just as one might take apart and examine the relationships between parts of a clock. This is called deduction: determining in advance what is important to study and selecting only those elements for examination, for example, only looking at certain parts of the clock. The examination is done through empirical (based on the senses) observation and tests, such as experiments or statistical analysis. Because measurement is standardized, that is, carried out in the same way each time, using the same instruments, such as questionnaires or tests, on all the people in the study, one can repeat the same procedures with other groups and make comparisons.

In positivistic research, much time and effort goes into developing the instrument. If it is a questionnaire, the questions are carefully thought out to make sure they address the variables that interest the researcher, the questions are pre-tested on people to see if they produce the required information, and the people administering the questionnaire are trained in exactly what to say and do. Much depends on the instrument. With other paradigms, as you will see, this is not as important.

If our research can identify laws of cause and effect and the conditions under which they apply, we can explain past events and predict future ones provided, of course, that our explanation is correct and the conditions are the same. Our study has great breadth. Given that reality is absolute and nature is orderly, our findings will be true anywhere in which the same circumstances exist.

However, this can present a problem. Because positivistic research is often carried out under experimental conditions rather than in natural settings, it is unlikely that you will come across the same conditions except in a similar experimental setting. Real life, of course, is not an experimental setting. As a result, we say that our results have high internal validity (are valid in that setting), but not necessarily high external validity (valid in other settings), because the experimental setting is artificial. If the boiler factory in Hope And Glory gives half of its workers an extra ten-minute break each day and finds they have less absenteeism than the other half who did not get a break, we might conclude that extra breaks improve attendance. Perhaps the researchers who did the experiment carefully controlled the situation so that the workers in both groups have exactly the same conditions, so that we are satisfied that it is the break itself that made the difference. But in real life will the break have the same effect on workers whose surroundings will not be as carefully controlled? Will other kinds of treats or privileges work too? Your experiment does not answer these questions.

The research techniques used in the positivistic approach are usually, but not always, quantitative, because the variables are clearly defined, can be measured, and the results can be converted to numbers. Suppose you are still studying the boiler factory in Hope And Glory. Now the management wants to do a new study to see if there is a relationship between 'worker participation' and 'higher productivity' in the industry. The organization might define 'worker participation' this way: 'eighty per cent or more of the workers are members of the company's worker-participation committees'; and 'higher productivity' as being 'at least twenty per cent above the industry average for that activity'. Using these definitions, it will be easy to count the organizations which qualify as having 'worker participation', and to compare their results with the industry average. The term 'quantitative' is often used to refer to the entire paradigm we have been discussing, when, in reality, it is simply a description of the most common way of handling the data.

If you can isolate what you consider to be the causes and effects of something, positivistic strategies are good for finding out why something has happened, or for predicting that under certain circumstances certain things will happen. Perhaps you can begin to see that this kind of prediction is not the same as prophecy. Science cannot predict the future except in very limited circumstances.

Some of the strengths of the positivistic approach, such as breadth of coverage and the possibility of making comparisons, are also the source of its weaknesses. Suppose we are writing a paper on female adult literacy and health and want to show that, in countries where literacy is high, and where women have relatively high rates relative to men, people — both men and women — live longer.

Let us say that we then look at 'The State of the World's Children 1999', and assemble a chart. Part of it looks like this (Figure 2–1):

Figure 2–1

Place	Adult literacy % Males	Females	Life expectancy at birth
Europe			
Croatia	98	97	72
Moldova	98	99	68
Slovenia	100	99	73
Africa			
Swaziland	78	76	60
Malawi	72	42	41
Sierra Leone	45	18	37
and so on…			

Such figures can be very useful, but also have some limitations: one is the obvious fact that institutions such as educational systems may be structured in different ways across countries, or records may not be kept the same way in each country. But surely a person is either literate or not, you think, and an adult or a child, so your task should be easy.

Not so. For example, in some countries literacy may be defined as the ability to sign a marriage license; in others, it is based on performance in a test. Sometimes literacy assessments are based solely on the person's declaration that he or she is literate when the national census is taken, but in other cases national authorities simply provide national estimates. It may also be the case that people with no schooling are classified as illiterate, whether they are or not, and in other cases, some part of the population, such as nomads, may be excluded, because it is too much trouble to find them. Who is considered an adult also varies. Sometimes the term refers to people as young as nine; in other cases it refers to those fifteen and older (Greaney, 1994, p. 222). Reports such as 'The State of the World's Children' or the World Bank's 'World Development Report' will tell you what is meant by each term used in the report, but that does not necessarily mean that countries supplying information for the reports have always collected the information according to such definitions.

Suppose that we were trying to use similar kinds of data to relate 'health' in general to literacy, and we find a chart which presents both. A fundamental disadvantage when you are dealing with social information is that people in different countries or cultural groups may define concepts like 'health' in different ways, making comparisons difficult, and sometimes meaningless. In some places, you are a paragon of health if you still have all your teeth at the age of twenty. In others, you're not healthy unless you have produced eight or ten children. Words like 'unemployment', 'wealth', 'a good wife', and many others differ so much from one place to another that comparisons may be meaningless. Another problem is that the categories chosen for study reflect the variables that the researcher considers important to study. Other variables and definitions of variables are therefore omitted. For example, you may have decided to measure 'health' in terms of 'life expectancy at birth', 'births attended by health staff', 'maternal mortality', and 'immunization rates for common childhood diseases'. 'Access to contraceptive measures' and 'fertility' may also be important to aspects of health, but the organization you are working for doesn't believe in family planning, so you are leaving those out. In fact, maybe it never occurred to you: you have worked so long for the organization that you don't even think of family planning issues. You can see, therefore, that you need to know a lot about a situation before choosing the variables to study and defining what you mean by them, and if you are trying to use them on different groups of people they should have some meaning for those groups. Eventually, however, you must choose so that you can decide what to look at and what to ignore, and also so that you can make clear to others, perhaps people who are working with you on your research or those who will read your study, what exactly you were looking at.

Paradigm 2: postpositivism

The paradigm we have just been discussing is the one that most people still think of when they think of science, but for some time now, scientists have recognized a number of problems with it, and a modified version, postpositivism, has emerged. The postpositivist position is that although a real world does exist, imperfect humans cannot fully comprehend it. Gone also is the idea of the independent, value-free observer, because observers cannot stand apart from nature. In fact, the entire research process is shaped by the interaction between the observer and the observed. How do we get around this problem? Postpositivists say we must not give up the struggle for objectivity. We must still aim for it despite these messy 'human' problems. To do this, observers must be honest and forthcoming about their methods and assumptions, and other scholars must carefully scrutinize their research. Also, we should take a more thorough research approach. We should use as many researchers, methods, theories, and sources of information as possible so as to strengthen the findings. We should use natural as well as experimental settings, and qualitative as well as quantitative methods.

Most people's misconceptions about science and research arise from misunderstandings or misapplications of the positivistic paradigms. For example, we tend to believe that when we give a single name or label to what is actually a culturally defined bundle of behaviors or ideas, like 'intelligence' or 'personality' or 'sex appeal', those things really exist in some standardized form and therefore can be measured. We assume that tests measure what they claim to measure, and that the Sex Appeal Test you took in a newspaper really does measure your sex appeal. Once measured, the results can be converted to numbers (0.01, you are disappointed to discover from your own results). And of course, anything in numbers is seen as more 'scientific' than anything in words, and because we also confuse precision (exactness) with validity (soundness), anything in extremely precise numbers, like 9.037, is better yet. We believe that using instruments, such as a questionnaire, is more scientific than using a human (perhaps even the human who designed the questionnaire). Instruments have the added advantage of putting distance between the observed and the observer, thus guaranteeing 'objectivity'. But as one expert points out, all that it really guarantees is distance (Patton, 1990). A questionnaire, therefore, is commonly thought to be more 'objective' and 'scientific' than an interview in which exactly the same questions are asked.

Unconsciously, some people also think that the more a body of material is processed, the more scientific it is: a sample is drawn, a questionnaire given, the answers are marked off in boxes, the results are coded in numbers, the numbers are fed into a computer, and the computer results are grouped and statistically analyzed. Thus, our vague 'yes' to a badly-conceived question written by someone who finds it hard to tell one end of a pencil from the other passes into the system and comes out with the weight of 300 years of science behind it.

Finally, the source of material is important: some people think information from official sources such as government ministers or documents is more 'objective'; information from people on your own street is 'subjective' even if they are commenting on something they know more about than the officials do; and the researcher who argues for the value of the local perspective is accused of 'being soft in the sciences'.

Paradigm 3: phenomenology

The phenomenological paradigm argues that positivism may give facts, but it does not give meaning or understanding. Phenomenology denies the existence of an objective reality: what is important is reality as people perceive, experience, and interpret it. If you have ever been involved in a large family dispute, you may have seen that each person saw things in a different way, and that each person may have been 'right'. So phenomenologists believe in multiple realities, each of which is a social construction of the human mind. There is no bare, absolute reality. People use models — cultural, historical, group, and individual — to organize, interpret, and reconstruct their perceptions. That is reality. Knowledge is the result of an interaction between people or, in the case of the physical sciences, between people and objects. Facts are created in this process, not discovered. The researcher is part of this construction, not independent of it. The researcher's task is to interpret or make sense of these constructions rather than to predict.

The perspective of the phenomenologist is holistic: the whole of the situation, individual, organization, or project is greater than its parts. Phenomena can only be understood in this total context, not through the neat variables that the positivistic researcher has selected for study. You, for example, may have snaggle teeth, a wart, and a bump on your nose. On you, they look exquisite. On someone else, the same features are ghastly. The observer is seeing the features, in both cases, in their total context.

Phenomenologists take a naturalistic approach, rather than an experimental one: researchers study the actual situation as it develops naturally. They do not attempt to identify the variables before the research begins or to manipulate the research setting; the variables emerge or unfold from the research like the features of an ancient city under the archaeologist's brush. This is called induction. Unlike an archaeological site, however, the situation is seen as dynamic and changing. Descriptive data, which we might get from participation, from observation, and from interviews, allow us to get an insight into the complex web of interaction, which may not be understandable in a simple, single-line, cause and effect way. People who take this approach argue that theories and facts are not objective, but are value laden from the start. The very act of choosing one variable to study rather than another — and the definition of that variable — reflects values: investigators often study the causes of single motherhood, for example, or of homosexuality; they do not study the causes of wedded motherhood or heterosexuality, both of which are considered the 'natural' state.

The techniques phenomenologists use are usually, but not always, qualitative. They might include, for example, interviews and participant observation. The validity of their results is based on the skill of the researcher rather than on the careful development and administration of the instruments. Indeed, the researcher is the instrument. Phenomenologists analyze their material through content analysis and case studies. The advantage of the phenomenological approach is that one comes to understand the context of the situation and appreciate the complexity and interdependence of the various aspects of the situation. Studies are thought to have greater depth. For example, in the field of participatory learning approaches (see Chapter 14), 'well-being' ranking is a commonly used technique: local people, often drawn from a variety of occupations and statuses and from both sexes, are asked, either individually or in groups, to rank all the people in the community by well-being. They sort a pack of cards with the name of each person in the community on a card and create several piles. These piles reflect shared local conceptions of well-being. In Hope And Glory, well-being means having a second pick-up truck for the wife, being able to afford cable television, and having a relative in the chief of police's office. In Hancock Towers, it might mean having a regular job, a few bob for a drink on Friday night, and burial insurance.

Obviously, using this method will give you a good picture of local ideas, but another community might have very different ideas about well-being, so you cannot assume that your findings will apply to it. Comparing people's level of education by their well-being across a number of groups using this approach would be difficult if each has a different idea of well-being. If you used a positivistic approach, however, you could make comparisons by developing one set of common categories such as owning one's house, ability to take an annual family trip, owning a car, and the means to send one's children to university. The problem is that they might not mean much to some (maybe even most) of the groups involved. The first two would not mean a lot to nomads, for example, who would have very different notions of what constitutes well-being, and the last two would be irrelevant to the Amish people of Pennsylvania, who don't drive cars and don't believe in higher education.

Phenomenological studies can take a long time (though in fairness, designing, administering, and analyzing a large survey can also take a long time). If you are looking for funding for your research, you should know that many sponsoring agencies and funding bodies will expect you to provide a clear-cut statement of your research problem, to spell out the variables to be studied, and to submit a budget and a timetable before the research begins. By now, you should be able to see that phenomenological approaches do not easily fit into this pattern (for advice on this problem, see Dobbert, 1990).

Paradigm 4: critical theory

A final paradigm, critical theory or ideologically-oriented inquiry (Guba, 1990, pp. 23–25) shares with postpositivism the idea of an imperfectly understood, but still quite definite, reality 'out there'. But the important question asked is: 'Whose reality are we talking about?' Because values shape every aspect of the inquiry (the paradigm, the questions selected, the researchers, the methods, the findings, the recommendations, and so on) it is important to ask whose values are being used. Critical theorists say that in most research projects, the values are those of an elite — whether it be males, capitalists, the powers-that-be, the dominant ethnic group, the Western world, or others — who choose the questions to be asked and use the results of the research to support their interests and to oppress others. In Hope And Glory, Juanetta Wilcox describes the people behind the boiler factory as 'no-goods'. Bert Whump sees them just as 'poor folks trying to feed their kids'. And we have not yet heard from the people themselves, but we can be almost certain they have another perspective. Juanetta would work on how to make them more responsible, even though maybe they just don't have enough money to meet their obligations; Bert might look at the causes of their poverty, such as single motherhood, even though there is a higher percentage of single mothers among the rest of the population in Hope And Glory; and they themselves might suggest a totally different angle. Since we know nothing about them yet, it would be a waste of time to guess what that might be. But in each case, the research is driven by the perspective. Juanetta and Bert may have more money and power, so it is their version of the research which is likely to be carried out. Thus, we will learn why the boiler factory folks are irresponsible and poor, when in fact they may not be at all.

By contrast, critical theorists interact with participants in the research, rather than manipulate them, to enter into a dialogue and create a 'true consciousness'. This allows the oppressed, in theory, to transform their world. The researcher's intent is not simply to collect information and work with people to get an understanding of their current situation; it is to encourage the group to go further and plan action for change. The participants do not just ask 'what is?' They ask 'what can be?' As two 'militant' sociologists, Roseca and Miguel Darcy de Oliveira, say, it is the researcher's task to show people that 'today's reality is not the only possible reality' (1981, p. 47). Indeed, this was the life mission of the Brazilian educator Paulo Freire, who argued for 'conscientization' — the process of helping people, through literacy programs, to break through their 'culture of silence', understand the injustices which oppress them, and take action (Freire 1972a, 1972b, 1985).

The strengths of this approach (or rather, these approaches, because feminism, neo-Marxism, Freireism and some of the participatory approaches fall under this heading) are that historically unquestioned biases are identified and exposed. Other perspectives and approaches are seen as valid. But a weakness of many critical theorists is that they often assume that it is only other people who need consciousness-raising, empowering, and liberation. They do not ask the people they study to help them become more liberated. Some 1970s and 1980s social workers fell into this category — sandalistas who warbled on at conferences about 'empowering the people', 'validating people's experiences', etc., but when they appeared at your front door in their free-range yak-hair handknitted sweaters, there was little real exchange; they simply gave you advice on how to run your life like theirs. To take a less irascible example, for years, people in the Western world have been concerned about the conditions of women in 'less developed' societies. They also assumed that in the process of improving women's lives, their status might be raised to that of Western women. But having an easier, healthier, more productive life and status are not necessarily related, as social scientist Martin King White (1980) has shown. In a study of 93 societies, he found that the higher the level of complexity — technological, political, economic — in a society, the lower the status of women relative to that of men. Western women do not necessarily have higher status, even though they live in more complex societies. So the lesson is that we all need our consciousness raised.

However, critical theorists have made a real contribution by making us look at the world from perspectives other than that of the establishment. They have questioned the basis of research ideas and means and ends, arguing that historically they have marginalized the less advantaged. This can be seen clearly in various feminist arguments, for example, which show how male-centered research selectively limits or ignores women's roles and experiences (see, for instance, Harding, 1987).

Is Social Science a Science?

Some researchers in the 'hard' sciences such as biology or chemistry often dismiss the social sciences as not being sufficiently scientific. (Only relatively recently have social scientists charged the hard sciences with not being sufficiently social.) Probably the only time you'll really care about whether social science is a science is when someone who doesn't like the sound of your project or the results of your research attacks it as unscientific. As you become more familiar with the paradigms on which human inquiry is based, you will probably feel that this issue is not as clear-cut as some think.

Today we are experiencing a second scientific revolution. 'Old' science, which has been based on the physics of the sixteenth and seventeenth centuries, argued that there were absolute, certain laws of cause and effect, neatly located in time and space, that the whole was best understood by breaking it up into parts and looking at those parts separately, and that the observer and the subject were separate. This was the objective way: anything else was subjective. Even philosophers, social theorists, and social scientists, from Hobbes to Darwin to Freud, drew inspiration from this model. Auguste Comte (1798–1857) the father of sociology, even called his subject 'social physics'.

However, a 'new' science has emerged in the twentieth century that includes relativity theory, quantum mechanics, chaos theory, and complexity theory, all coming from the hard sciences. Although different, each shares a paradigm: that the whole is greater than the sum of its parts; that things are ever-changing, uncertain, and unpredictable, so that new forms are emerging all the time; that the universe is moving toward increasing complexity; and that observers participate in what is being observed (they help to make the reality that is being studied). Does some of this sound familiar? Some social scientists had been thinking along these lines for quite a while.

You may have formed some views on these ideas now, but it is important not to fall into the trap of over-simplistic dualism. Some of the dualisms that you might be tempted to create from the paradigms discussed in this chapter are shown in Figure 2–2:

Figure 2–2

'hard' sciences	'soft' sciences
experimental strategies	naturalistic strategies
deductive approaches	inductive approaches
quantitative techniques	qualitative techniques

Even though four paradigms are presented here, the most common debate is between postpositivists and phenomenologists: postpositivists think phenomenological approaches are soft or subjective; phenomenologists think there is no such thing as objectivity. Positivist-oriented purists group together, as natural strategies, the items in the left-hand box, and phenomenological-oriented purists those in the right. But is it as clear-cut as that?

Some researchers argue that while these approaches and techniques are mutually exclusive as ideas, they do not have to be exclusive in use. That is, in a particular research project you can use each of these paradigms and the techniques associated with them, sometimes to support each other, sometimes as separate stages in a project, getting both explanation (why?) and understanding (how?). Educator Michael Quinn Patton (1990) describes this as a 'paradigm of choices'. Other researchers reject this. Egon Guba and Yvonna Lincoln (1989, p. 11), supporters of a phenomenological approach, argue that paradigms cannot be mixed or used together because their underlying assumptions are not just opposite, or even complementary, but fundamentally different.

In practice, however, many positivists seem to be warming to qualitative research and soon will probably be claiming that they invented it. At the same time, few phenomenologically-inclined researchers actually take a completely consistent phenomenological approach in their work. As for critical theorists, those of us who are concerned about social issues and action research are all indebted to them for making us less self-satisfied about some of the perspectives that we once took for granted.

But we are not going to solve these debates here. Indeed, as research experts Miles and Huberman (1994, p. 20) have said: 'If the debate is unlikely to be resolved during your lifetime, it is probably best to get on with your work, clarifying for yourself and your readers in which camp you are nestled.' Certainly, those who just want to know what people in their community think about the need for a preschool do not have to sort the matter out before going down the road with a questionnaire. But it is good to remember that it was not God who said that questionnaires are the best way to get information. It was a decision that some people made, and that some others dispute. In that spirit, this book presents a variety of strategies for planning and carrying out your research, and shows how you might, in practice, mix them and use appropriate techniques. It is true that the strength of each approach lies in its own internal logic and integrity, so mixing them prevents the full realization of their power, but otherwise, as one sociologist says, 'Nothing bad happens if you do this' (Denzin, 1989, p. 9). Your research won't explode.

Where Does Theory Fit In?

Most research is guided by theory, just as someone seeking to get to an unfamiliar place is guided by a map or a set of directions. The theory may be clearly specified or it may be a set of unquestioned assumptions so general as to be the foundation of an entire discipline, but it is there, nonetheless. In sociology, for example, Emile Durkheim (1858–1917) theorized that social phenomena follow social laws in the same way as physical phenomena follow physical laws, and the same logic of investigation can be used for both. (As you may recall, this is the foundation of positivism.)

You may feel that you are just trying to get on with the job and get a little bit of useful information. You are: but what is useful social information, how it relates to the issue you are trying to understand, how you go about gathering it, what it 'proves', and, if you are collecting it to further a cause, what good it is going to do are all shaped by theories, no matter how invisible they may seem. You don't have to know what theories are to do simple descriptive research, but if you want to make your research more powerful by being able to relate it to bigger ideas and to the work of other researchers, you should think about theory. It's most likely that you will be drawing on existing theories.

A theory is an organised, testable set of concepts, which attempts to explain or predict a social phenomenon.[1] Theories can be arrived at in two ways: you can do the research first, i.e., making empirical observations which are then used to construct a more abstract explanation or prediction. This is called inductive theory. On the other hand, you can create the theory first, that is, use an abstract explanation or idea as a kind of blueprint for selecting what you want to examine or test. This is called deductive theory. Theory can thus range from 'grounded' (Glaser and Strauss, 1967), that is, derived from prior observation of real life, to 'grand', abstract, philosophical, and rather removed from real life, to anything in between. Deductive theory is the form most traditionally associated with science and positivism, and inductive theory with phenomenological approaches, although in practice theories are usually constructed using a combination of the two approaches, developing an idea, using empirical research to examine it, refining the idea as a result of the research and so on.[2]

An alternative to theory is pure empiricism: the assumption that the material speaks to the senses for itself, that it needs no interpretation. This, in fact, is a theory itself. You may recall from our earlier discussion that

[1] For a discussion of the requirements of theory, and an example of the analysis of a theory, see Cohen, Bernard P. *Developing Sociological Knowledge*, Chicago: Nelson-Hall, 1989, Chapters 10–11.

[2] An important work by Thomas Kuhn (1962, 1970) argues that 'normal' science proceeds not through the rules of deduction *or* induction, but is guided by hidden assumptions (paradigms) arising out of the current culture of scientists. It is not empirical evidence which

phenomenological approaches allow variables to 'emerge' from research rather than determining them in advance; however, interpretation is still the aim. But all that 'facts' give us is observation, and for observation to be organized enough to carry out it needs to be guided, and for it to be useful it requires explanation, both of which are the function of theory. Usually, people who feel that they have let the facts speak for themselves are guided by quite transparent theories: 'There have been more male composers than female in history, the facts speak for themselves.' Yes, but what do they say?

Hypotheses

Researchers, pondering the possible consequences of a theory, create hypotheses, or specific deductive predictions which can be tested. The prediction is a relationship of cause and effect, or some form of association, between two constructs (ideas, abstractions, concepts): thus, A causes B in a certain group under certain circumstances. A theory, in itself, cannot be tested, because in order to say anything generally useful, it must deal in abstract concepts, rather than 'observables'. For example, in the statement, 'Girls have better verbal ability than boys,' verbal ability cannot be observed: it must be converted into something which can. Therefore, the researcher will also state the form in which this will be observable, such as 'Performance on the Blank Test is a valid indicator of verbal ability.'

A hypothesis, then, contains a statement of relationship between constructs and a practical translation from the realm of ideas (the concepts of the theory) into the world of the observable (variables to be examined or measured). It is based on a proposition or statement about a relationship between two or more variables. Propositions can take a variety of forms, one of which is the hypothesis. The following are some propositions which can be made sufficently precise to test.

'Nobody wants you when you're down and out' is a general statement — a hunch, an opinion, a proposition — but it can be made more precise and testable. For example: 'Street people in Washington DC are more likely to be moved on more quickly from seating areas in fast food restaurants than people who appear to be living in housing.'

Similarly, the statement 'You can't teach an old dog new tricks' could be made sufficiently precise to test some version of it, as could 'Investment in

causes the direction of science to change, or new paradigms to emerge, but rather 'scientific revolutions' brought about by a new generation with a different agenda. This statement, shocking to the tender research novice, and accurate as it may be in the natural sciences, refers to the history and culture of science and doesn't affect the need to consider how to plan a specific project. It also has less bearing on the social sciences, which have, as we have seen, at least three paradigms in common use, sometimes by the same people.

female adult literacy in New York leads to reduced child mortality.'

People often say 'I have a hypothesis' about something when they mean that they have a hunch, or an intuition. A good hypothesis has certain characteristics: 1) in order for science to be cumulative, a hypothesis must be drawn from or related to a theory or theories, rather than simply arising out of something you happen to find interesting; 2) it must be conceptually clear, that is, the important concepts can be defined, preferably in a way which states exactly how to decide whether something falls within that concept, or doesn't. This is called 'operationalizing'[3] — for example, defining 'child mortality' so that it refers to a specific age group; 3) it does not contain moral judgements — for example: 'Women are better at caring for children than men' or 'Christians have been persecuting Jews for centuries'; 4) it must be specific enough to be tested (the two previous examples are not); and, finally, 5) it must be technically possible to test it — that is, the appropriate research techniques must exist, or be capable of being created, in order to carry out the test.

Theories contain statements of cause and effect, but research itself, even experimental research, cannot 'prove' causation. It can show that two or more things go together in an orderly way (covariation) — height and weight, for example, tend to go up or down together. It can also show that one thing happens after another (temporal sequence). But 'proof' is impossible in any kind of research for several reasons. First, as mentioned before, to be useful, theories and statements derived from theories are general. They deal with broad concepts, and make broad, often universal claims: 'Boys have better spatial abilities than girls because they have more testosterone.'

Even when such a statement is 'operationalized', that is, made concretely researchable in the form of a hypothesis — as in 'In school A, boys do better on standardized tests of spatial ability than girls' — a finding consistent with the statement does not prove the larger statement, which refers to all boys and girls everywhere back and forward in time. Even doing the study many times in many places will not suffice: induction (reasoning from the particular to the general) cannot be used as proof. Proof applies only to deduction (reasoning from the general to the particular). For the same reason, a theory cannot be disproved, either, since the hypothesis which we are using to test it is one specific instance of the theory; if a hypothesis is disproved, we don't know which element in the chain between the general theory and the 'spelling out' of the specific hypothesis is false. It may be that if we spelled the theory out in another way, the results would be different. Thus, we would

---

[3] This is not necessarily the same as *operationalism*, an assumption of positivism which states that all *constructs* (ideas, concepts, abstractions of interest) can be measured or observed (see Judd, 1999: 45).

have 'proof' and 'disproof' of the same theory, which is not possible.[4]

For example, we might take as our theory 'Males feel threatened by female competence.' Think of all the hypotheses this theory could generate, such as 'In classrooms where girls do better on examinations, boys will be more disruptive' or 'Male factory workers will rate women who are less productive as "friendlier", ' etc. Another hypothesis we might spell out is as follows: one instance of female competence is intelligence: one instance of intelligence is extensive reading: one instance of extensive reading is wearing glasses. We will take 'feeling threatened' to mean not treating women as desirable, and not treating women as desirable to mean not approaching them with invitations and suggestions. Thus, we have: 'Men don't make passes at girls who wear glasses.' When we set up an experiment with specific groups, in specific places, and our findings support the hypothesis, we haven't proved the theory that males feel threatened by female competence (all the other possible hypotheses haven't been proved). Also, our hypothesis might not be supported in other settings, and even if it were, there may be better explanations for it: glasses are not considered attractive at the moment; men don't want to pass on poor eyesight to future offspring; women who wear glasses are more competent, and thus better able to see passes coming and prevent them; and so on.

These explanations of why research cannot prove are drawn from logic and apply to experimental as well as non-experimental research. This may surprise people who have come to believe that experiments 'prove' things. The more 'practical' reasons why they don't are discussed in Chapter 5, where we look at what experiments do, and what requirements you must meet in order to perform experiments. In this book, we will be looking at only the simplest kinds of hypotheses. To read more about this subject, you might like to look at some of the books listed below.

References and further readings

Patton's work contains a very good introduction to the issues. Some other excellent works which deal with the issues, at various levels of difficulty are:

Bailey, Kenneth D. 1994. *Methods of Social Research*. 4th ed. New York: The Free Press.

Bernard, H. Russell. 1994. *Research Methods in Cultural Anthropology*. 2nd ed.

---

[4] For an extended discussion of why this is the case, see Cohen, Bernard K. *Developing Social Knowledge*, 2nd ed. 1989. Chicago: Nelson-Hall. Chapters 4 and 13 in particular). For a completely different interpretation (i.e. theories must be capable of either being corroborated or refuted by empirical data) see the work of a major advocate, Karl Popper (*The Logic of Scientific Discovery*. London: Hutchinson, 1959).

Newbury Park, California: Sage.

Darcy De Oliveira, Rosica and Miguel Darcy de Oliveira. 1981. 'The Militant Observer: A Sociological Alternative.' In Budd Hall, Arthur Gillette, and Rajesh Tandon, eds. 1982. *Creating Knowledge: A Monopoly? Participatory Research in Development.* New Delhi: Society for Participatory Research in Asia (45 Sainik Farm, Khanpur).

Denzin, Norman K. 1989. *Interpretive Interactionism.* Newbury Park, California: Sage.

Dobbert, Marion Lundy. 1990. 'Discussion on Methodology.' In Egon Guba, ed., *The Paradigm Dialog.* Newbury Park, California: Sage.

Freire, P. 1972a. *Pedagogy of the Oppressed.* London: Penguin Books Ltd.

—— 1972b. *Cultural Action for Freedom.* London: Penguin Books Ltd.

—— 1985. *The Politics of Education: Culture, Power and Liberation.* Trans. Donald Macedo. London: Macmillan.

Glaser, B.G. and A.L. Strauss. 1967. *The Discovery of Grounded Theory: Strategies for Qualitative Research.* Chicago: Aldine.

Glaser, B.G. 1998. *Doing Grounded Theory: Issues and Discussions.* Mill Valley, California: Sociology Press.

Greaney, Vincent. 1994. 'World Illiteracy.' In Fran Lehr and Jean Osborn, eds., *Reading, Language and Literacy: Instruction for the Twenty-First Century.* Hillsdale, New Jersey: Lawrence Erlbaum Associates.

Guba, Egon G., ed. 1990. *The Paradigm Dialog.* Newbury Park, California: Sage.

Guba, Egon G. and Yvonna S. Lincoln. 1989. *Fourth Generation Evaluation.* Newbury Park, California: Sage.

Harding, Sandra. 1987. *Feminism and Methodology.* Milton Keynes, U.K.: Open University Press.

Kuhn, T.S. 1962. *The Structure of Scientific Revolutions.* Chicago: University of Chicago Press. Second edition, 1970.

——. 1970. *The Structure of Scientific Revolutions,* 2nd ed. Chicago: University of Chicago Press.

Miles, Matthew B., and A. Michael Huberman. 1994. *Qualitative Data Analysis,* 2nd ed. Thousand Oaks, California: Sage.

Patton, Michael Quinn. 1990. *Qualitative Evaluation and Research Methods,* 2nd ed. Newbury Park, California: Sage.

UNICEF (United Nations Children's Fund). 1989. *The State of the World's Children.* Oxford, U.K.: Oxford University Press.

White, Martin King. 1980. *The Status of Women in Pre-Industrial Societies.* Princeton, New Jersey: Princeton University Press.

PART II

GETTING READY TO DO RESEARCH

The Hope and Glory Vindicator

Volume 182 Issue 5   May 26, 2001

Rev. Wayman sentenced

The Rev. Dwight Wayman, pastor of the Word of God Church on Muddy Branch Road, received sixty days' house arrest today for reckless endangerment of life at the Word of God Summer Bible School. The Rev. Wayman developed a miniature electric chair that delivered shocks to children aged 3–6 who answered Bible questions incorrectly. Mr. Wayman told Judge Dick Quinn that his Empowerment Program was simply an attempt to spark the children's interest and he had not intended any harm. Judge Quinn ordered the Rev. Wayman to wear an electronic ankle tag, saying that he had wanted to try one of these for a while now.

Other current church news

Church buys property

The House of Peace Sanctuary Temple has bought Stacia Darnell's little house on three acres out on Highway 123. Mrs. Darnell said that she understood that the Temple was proposing to use the house for a small office. Mr. Stephen Barker, president of the congregation, said when contacted by a Vindicator reporter last night that, 'generally, this is the plan.' The property is sited beside the home and motel of Mayor Randy Anderson. Mrs. Darnell says she is thrilled at the sale because she was fed up looking at her kitchen linoleum. She wants all brand new next time, and has her eye on a starter castle out at Ye Olde Robinwood Estates.

Kiddie Corner: Essay Contest Prize Winner

The following essay won first prize for Miriam Whump, aged 10, in our Kiddie Contest. Miriam attends President William Henry Harrison Elementary School

How I spent my vacation

The Mescoito Indians are a very interesting tribe. They do not have many tribal ways such as wearing cloths but they have music. There are about 18 people. They are vegeter-rians and for their work they clean chimbleys. They live behind the boiler factry. I talked to a man called Hard Spirits and he told me their ancient name of Mescoito means people who live behind the boiler factory. They are very interesting.

Court Notes

Mrs. Laurinda Wilcox McCardle, who goes by her maiden name, has petitioned the court to change her name to 's or Apostrophe s. According to Mrs. McCardle, women are frequently lumped in with their husbands when being referred to, as in The John Brown's. 'I am always receiving invit-ations addressed to 'The Septus McCardle's' she said. 'I might as well make it legal.'

INSIDE THIS ISSUE

3 WHAT WILL YOU STUDY?

Summary

All research requires planning. Some dimensions of research to consider are the following:

- Is it *basic* (knowledge for its own sake) or *applied* (to be used toward a practical end)?
- Is it *descriptive* (providing a picture), or is it *explanatory* or *predictive* (showing relationships, including cause and effect, between events in the past or the future)?
- Are you asking 'What do I see these people doing?' (research from your perspective) or 'What do these people see themselves doing?' (research from the perspective of those participating in the study)?
- Will your research be *extractive* (you determine the issues, choose the approaches, and and carry out the research), or will it be *participatory* (local people help to identify the problems and concerns and participate in gathering, analysing, and using the information)?
- What will it cost?

Some people think 'research' is simply immersing oneself in a topic and learning everything there is to know about it. 'I'll go to the library and make a lot of notes,' they say. The next step is a bit vague — perhaps some night the Report Fairy will come and assemble it all. These are the same people who believe that making a will is bad luck, that the stars are God's daisy chain, and that the government is here to serve us. You, of course, are not like that, which is why you are reading this chapter. A sad feature of

Box 3–1 Research stages

Research step	Chapter
Step 1: Get your research idea	Chapter 3
Step 2: Clarify the goals and purpose of your research	Chapter 3
Step 3: Choose your perspective	Chapter 3
Step 4: Develop a rough research idea and refine it	
• Non-experimental research	Chapter 4
• Experimental research	Chapter 5
Step 5: Create a research statement or hypothesis	
• Non-experimental research	Chapter 4
• Experimental research	Chapter 5
Step 6: Make decisions about sources of information	Chapters 6, 8
Step 7: Make decisions about information-gathering techniques	Chapters 7–14
Step 8: Complete the research design	
• Non-experimental research	Chapter 4
• Experimental research	Chapter 5
Step 9: Obtain/produce the information	Chapters 7–14
Step 10: Record and organize the information	Chapter 15
Step 11: The information	Chapters 16, 17
Step 12: Present the results	Chapter 18

modern life is that we don't have as many eternal verities as we used to have. But we still have one: if you don't plan your research, you will wander off the track, waste time and money, or abandon the project. Your research design is the overall plan that tells you what information you need to collect, what techniques to use, and where to get the information. If you have read Chapter 2, you know a little bit more about different approaches to research, but no matter what research paradigm, perspective, or approach appeals to you, you still must have a plan.

The planning and preparation stage of a research project can easily take up a third of the entire time you have allowed for your research. Box 3–1 shows the stages involved in carrying out your research. Generally, the remaining chapters in this book follow this order. However, as the box shows, Chapters 4 and 5 keep popping up. They each alert you to a number of important decisions you will have to make. Before you can make some of the decisions, however, you need to know more about your sources of information (Chapters 6 and 8) and how you will get the information (Chapters 7–14). Then you can take the decisions necessary to finish the design you started in Chapter 4 or Chapter 5.

This chapter deals with the first three stages.

Finding Your Research Idea

Where do you get research ideas? Your own interests and experiences or those of others may suggest ideas to you. Perhaps you are simply wondering about something — for instance, why some people object so strenuously when their house number, street name or community name is changed — what difference does it make? If you have a hobby, there are usually special-interest magazines which may contain articles on enthusiasts' concerns and problems. You might consult these for ideas but you are more likely to be reading this book because you have come across an immediate problem that needs to be better understood or that requires some action — for example, immigrant parents in your community are worried about their daughters losing their traditional values if they attend mixed-sex schools, yet all the state schools are mixed-sex. Or perhaps the members of your trainspotting group feel that the public has the wrong impression about them. What do the public think trainspotters do? What kind of people do they think become trainspotters? (If you live in a country where 'trainspotting' means nothing, you might find it interesting to study why grown people might think that writing down the identification numbers of trains is an interesting hobby. What motivates them? What are the rules? Is there a dress code?)

You can also get your ideas from research that other people have already done. If you are training or working in a particular discipline such as education or social work there are many professional journals — just reading the tables of contents of journals will give you some ideas. Professional journals are often written in specialized language and assume some background knowledge of the subject, and maybe of previous research done on the specific topic. Once you become familiar with the material, you might do your own research to see if:

- a theory being used in a professional article or book can be applied in a new setting, to different people, or to a new problem, or if a different

or better theoretical explanation is available for what the author found;
- the author's findings are valid in your setting;
- the research techniques used in the study could be applied to a different problem, or other research techniques could usefully be applied to the same problem;
- researchers with different characteristics, women as opposed to men, for example, obtain different results.

Another possibility is that an organization, a school, your employer, or your class instructor has asked you to carry out a piece of research. In this case, you will have to work closely, at all stages of the research, with whoever is in charge. You will not make some of the decisions about the steps at the beginning of this chapter by yourself. Be sure you all agree on the focus, the approach, the methods, the costs, the time, the interim reporting to the sponsors, whether you will be required to make recommendations, who 'owns' the raw data (preferably you), and what form the final presentation is to take (a talk? a report?).

A final possibility is that you are part of the team working in Hope And Glory, Ohio. There, almost every misadventure known to humankind awaits you — the challenge is to be selective, and not simply fasten onto the first calamity that piques your interest. Why, for example, are there four gun shops and no parks? Who is in the jail — it appears to be 98 per cent black, when the town is 98 per cent white. Why? What do local people think about the mayor's plan to generate revenue by letting New York City garbage collectors dump their garbage in Hope And Glory for a fee? Do local people even know?

Clarifying the Goals and Purpose of Your Research

Why you are doing your research? Your aims, your perspective, and the role which people who participate in your research will play all have a part in shaping your research.

Basic and applied research

What is your research going to be used for? The aim of *basic research* is to advance human knowledge with no particular application in mind. Usually basic research, which can be expensive, has no urgent public audience and therefore no one rushing to fund it. It is usually done by academics who hope to contribute to the development and refinement of theories. They or others may then apply these new insights to specific problems. Someone might be interested in pursuing the theory of 'limited good' (Foster, 1965).

This is the theory that certain groups of people — peasants in Foster's case — see all good things as existing in limited supply, so that if I have more — money, good luck, beauty — you have less. This leads to uncooperativeness, begrudgery and various unpleasant behaviours. Does this apply to other situations? For example, suppose the Hope And Glory teacher 'grades on a curve' rather than simply giving each student what he or she earns — this means that 11 per cent get the highest mark, 22 per cent the next highest, 33 per cent the next, 22 per cent the next after that, and finally the last 11 per cent get the lowest grade. Does this affect students' behaviour? Even if all the class did well, only 11 per cent will get the highest mark. Will students steal each other's books and engage in other acts of sabotage to get into the coveted top 11 per cent? On the other hand, if the class is poor, will some become complacent, knowing that no matter how weak they are they could still get high marks?

Applied research, by contrast, usually addresses a practical problem. You may want to find out how to accomplish a goal or why something has happened. An educator might ask: 'How can we make science classes more relevant to girls?' or 'What can we do to attract children to the local libraries?' In our 'curve' example we could ask: 'What can we do to make our school's examination marking system more constructive and reflective of the school's philosophy?' Applied research can take a number of forms — for example, *evaluation research* is common in the world of education and in many kinds of community development and social projects. Evaluation research can be used to assess a problem or need or to select a program or a project, monitor it as it proceeds, and assess it afterwards. The meaning of some of these terms varies from one field to another. In many community development projects the term 'evaluation' is reserved for assessing projects after they are completed. In the field of education, however, it refers to research on any stage of the project once it is under way. There is a rich literature on evaluation research — for an introduction, the work of Michael Quinn Patton is very readable, and the other works listed at the end of this chapter each present an important dimension of evaluation.

Another type of applied research is *action research*, which is done to get enough information to solve a problem and take steps to deal with it. It can be used for a range of activities, from simple troubleshooting within an organization or community to militant mobilization of a group of people. The people involved may be encouraged to determine the sources of their own problems or, if the researcher is committed to a particular ideology, such as feminism or Marxism, they may be encouraged to consider their problems within that framework. Action research often draws upon the people involved in the situation as active participants in the research process.

Descriptive, explanatory, and predictive research

Research can describe, explain, or predict. *Descriptive research* includes exploratory research to get a picture of a situation, behaviour, or attitudes before planning further research. It can encompass community studies, needs assessments, organizational reviews, and generally any research that presents a picture of a situation, place, activity, behaviour, or event. The basic question you are asking is 'what?': 'What is happening?' 'What has happened?' What do people think?' For example: 'What went wrong with the new program for increasing girls' mathematics scores?' or 'What do people think of having a bypass outside the town?' You are not trying to prove cause and effect, so your research will not be experimental. *Explanatory research* shows relationships after the fact: 'How did the introduction of the new incentive scheme affect absenteeism in my company?' 'Why did the introduction of single-sex schools lower girls' mathematics scores?' 'Has the presence of four new gun shops in Hope And Glory led to a rise in accidental shootings?' *Predictive research* states what will happen or how it will happen before the event: 'What effect will gender sensitization programs have on reducing sex harassment suits in local industry?' 'Will attendance at union meetings increase if we subsidize the cost of dues?' Feasibility studies are a type of predictive research.

There are many ways of explaining something. Draper (1988) shows that explaining can take the form of making something clearer, giving reasons, showing why a conclusion has been drawn, or making a causal statement. For cause and effect studies you will probably test a hypothesis, or a statement of the relationships between two or more things. You can do this in several ways: conducting an experiment, doing what anthropologist Russell Bernard calls 'thought experiments', or using survey questions. If you do an experiment, your research design will be shaped by the answers to the questions in Figure 5–2 in Chapter 5. If you are using a survey to test your ideas, you need to look at Chapter 4 to plan your questions, Chapter 5 to understand the fundamentals of experiments, and Chapter 9 to understand more about surveys.

Your research project may contain descriptive, explanatory, or predictive research, or all three. On a 'glamour' scale, these three types would appear in reverse order: most researchers would prefer to be able to predict than to explain and to explain than to describe. Except in a few fields such as anthropology, where researchers describe cultures, or in evaluation studies, where researchers describe what is happening in a project compared to what was supposed to have happened, not many researchers are interested in 'mere' description. Some people even argue that work that is purely descriptive is not research at all (see, for example, Leedy, 1989, pp. 4–5), but this represents a confusion between research and 'science' (see Chapter 2). Good descriptive research is fundamental to knowledge: you can carry out an elaborate piece of research to explain the causes or effects of something, only to find later that the situation you are explaining does not exist. 'Everyone knows' that the Irish have a higher rate of mental illness than most of their fellow Europeans. Suppose you were to do a large study explaining the reasons why, as someone once did. The only problem, as someone else might later show, is that it isn't true — the Irish are only average on the scale. In the meantime, however, organizations or government departments could easily be misled into spending scarce resources on heroic measures to curb mental illness, all because the basic descriptive research wasn't carried out before jumping to conclusions. As a first-time researcher you may be tempted to try to carry out large-scale predictive or explanatory projects that make cause and effect statements, such as 'Female-headed households are the cause of juvenile drug abuse.' You are unlikely to be able to do this for two reasons. First, as you will see in Chapter 5, statements at this level are unprovable. Second, you must meet rigid conditions when you are trying to prove cause and effect that can be extremely difficult to meet. But perhaps you can meet them. Consult Chapter 5.

Choosing Your Perspective

What viewpoint will shape your research? Your choice will have a practical impact on how you plan your research and the research techniques you choose. This is a complex subject. In this book for beginners we are going to reduce the questions of perspective to two. Do you want to know: '*What Do I See These People Doing?*' or '*What Do These People See Themselves Doing?*' For the moment, we are going to call these 'my perspective' and 'their perspective'. In the professional literature these terms are often referred to as etic (*ett-ic*) and emic (*ee-mic*), respectively, and are drawn from anthropology. These two approaches are not ordered on a quantitative–qualitative principle. Each can, in theory, provide both types of information, although emic research is less likely to produce material that would profit by quantitative analysis. Each is important, and they can both be used in the same project. 'My perspective', or the etic approach, is by far the most common and probably the most familiar to you. 'Their perspective', or the emic approach, though less common, is a powerful way of understanding a situation, and is becoming increasingly important in development-related research.

'My perspective': the etic approach

In 'my perspective', when you ask: 'What do I see these people doing?' you are the one who determines what is important in the way of information. You have decided that an objective reality exists. You determine the variables and create the questions or, in the case of experimental research, the conditions under which the variables are tested. People's experiences and behaviour are forced into your question-and-answer categories or your experimental conditions. You probably recognize this as a positivistic approach. Questionnaires, censuses, structured interviews, measures and scales, and experiments are all based on this approach.

If you know a lot about a situation, and if your respondents see and experience the world the way you do, this approach has many strengths and advantages. You can issue a questionnaire or hold some interviews, put the answers into neat categories, and count the answers or run them through a computer. You can compare one program with another, one school with another, one country with another. For example, you can develop a questionnaire for teenagers in youth centers to determine their attitudes toward a drug needle-exchange center in the community. You decide the issues which are important, and the answers you get back will reflect those areas. You will be able to use this questionnaire in several youth centers and compare the results.

One disadvantage, however, is that you might not ask the right questions. For example, suppose you ask the teenagers whether they understand the risks of dirty needles, how often they change needles if they use them, and where they get them from. You ask *why* they get them from that source:

a) they are cheap
b) the location is convenient
c) they can trust the source
d) the source also provides drugs

However, you don't ask about privacy, and that may in fact be the main reason why they get their needles from a particular source: their identity is protected. When you use this approach, people will try to fit their knowledge and experiences (truthfully or untruthfully, accurately or inaccurately) into the choices you offer them. If your respondents do not see the world the way you do, or if you have got the wrong angle, people have to rearrange their experiences and knowledge of life into your categories, and they will probably do it, because most people are pretty obliging. They may even be intimidated by your status, or by something as petty as the fact that the questions are typed, into thinking that your way of looking at things is the 'right' way. The trouble is that they then go on living and looking at things their way, while you are busily designing a project or preparing a report based upon your way. To the extent that you are aware of this, you may even conclude that your way is scientific and necessary if the project is to operate properly, and that their way is what caused their problem to begin with.

A second disadvantage of this approach is that if you are trying to compare very different groups, you may not be able to develop questions that are equally relevant and meaningful to each group. For example, people who abuse substances can fall into a range of categories — glue-sniffers, heroin addicts, people who are addicted to over-the-counter medicines, etc. To handle these differences, you might create separate questions for each group, but then you can't compare the results as you haven't asked the same questions.

'Their perspective': the emic approach

In 'their perspective', the participants tell you how they see things. You may have decided that no 'objective' reality exists from which to create categories of inquiry, so the participants create the categories. For example, is it 'objective' or an organizational expedient to distinguish classes of air travel as 'first class', 'business', and 'coach'? The underlying principle in this categorization is money. However, the humourist Robert Benchley looked at it another way: 'There are two classes of travel — first class, and with children.' In his system, coach without children could be first class, and first with children couldn't be, as many parents will confirm.

An emic approach is most useful when you know little about the subject, or when the people you are dealing with have very different idea systems. It is also useful when you are so familiar with a situation that you can't see the forest for the trees. It is particularly important, however, when you are concerned with relatively 'invisible' or less powerful groups, such as children, poorer people, women, the homeless, and non-traditional family forms because, as some critics would point out, many of the 'established' categories of information were created, and are used by, the more visible, the more powerful, the richer, and men. For example, how will we find out about the people behind the boiler factory in Hope And Glory? Will we use a survey with the usual questions: age, marital status, religion, occupation, etc.? We might want the answers to those, but we also want to find out their own perspectives on who they are, what they are doing, who's a member of the group, who's not, and why, what they see as their problems, and a lot of other things. They may be so different from us that we can't even think up the right questions to gain good insights, and that's where emic research comes in.

Figure 3–1 What teachers do in a particular school system
from the children's viewpoint

Pick on kids	Beat kids
	Smack kids in the face
	Push against wall
	Have a paddle
	Hit kids (Hit with books
	{Hit with yard sticks
	Slam kids' heads down on desks
	Yell
	Bitch
	Send kids to office
	Send kids to detention center
	Make whole class stay after (school)
	Pick kids out who misbehave
	Act mean
	Make fun of kids
	Pick kids out by ability
	Won't help kids
	Call kids stupid
	Lean on kids' shoulder
	Make kids put nose on wall
	Cut down kids
	Assume kids are guilty
	Keep kids after school
	Tie kids to desk
	Embarrass kids
	Shake kids
	Make kids sit in a certain seat
	Give extra assignments
	Give sentences (to copy out)
Talk a whole lot	
Run A.V. (audio visual) equipment	
Give tests	
Pile on the work	
Keep you in the book (make you study)	

(con't.)

Hand out assignments			
Catch kids	Catch kids fighting Catch kids in the hall Catch kids smoking in the can (toilet)		
Try to be cool	Keep cigarettes in shirt pocket Dress cool Crack dumb jokes Cut down kids Give detention		
Be nice to kids	Let do something special	Let be pet	Let touch drapes Let read orally Let write on blackboards Let run errand all the time Let put stuff on the bulletin board
			Let turn off lights for movie Let run projector Let off assignments Let run errands Let switch assignments
	Let off easy		Let off detention Let you sleep instead of smacking you to wake you up
			Give good grades Write a note to another teacher saying you are staying for her Don't yell Call you your first name

Source: Davis (1972, pp. 110–111)

When you use the 'their perspective' approach, you are trying to discover the idea systems that shape people's behaviour. You are looking for the equivalent of 'rules of grammar' that direct their lives and decision-making. Because these idea systems are usually somewhat peculiar to a particular group — whether it be boys in a local gang, or automobile fitters in your factory, or the First Communion class in the neighbourhood Catholic school — what you learn will be extremely useful in understanding that particular situation, but may not be transferable to another gang, or fitters in Detroit, or a First Communion class in Edinburgh. Sometimes, however, it is the local situation you need to understand, rather than what you might learn from comparing these people with some other group.

How people categorize mental illness provides a good insight into the etic versus emic distinction. For example, people are much more likely to be first diagnosed as being in need of psychiatric treatment by their family or community than by their doctor. How do the diagnostic categories (the community's versus the doctor's, say) differ? A Western psychiatrist might use the terms psychosis, neurosis, etc. These categories are used across countries by professionals to produce comparative tables, even though people in some places might not quite fit into the categories and might group the illnesses in different ways, even adding or subtracting a few.

We can look at the Irish again. Now that we know they are not particularly mad, we might want to look at this topic instead. Local people in a western Irish community have a completely different set of categories for people who are psychiatrically ill or 'not quite right': 'nervous'; 'not the full shilling'; 'a wee bit simple'; 'on tablets'; and 'religious' are each separate, well-defined categories. These are not 'baby' or folk terms for the 'proper' or doctor's words: the boundaries of these categories don't correspond to those of the terms which the doctor is using, and the rules that determine which category one falls into are different. These categories will give you great insights into how the community uses these rules to decide who should see a doctor, who needs institutional care, etc. The disadvantage, of course, is that the categories are probably not transferable to other regions of Ireland, and possibly not even to the next community.

Figure 3–1 presents a picture of what happens in a school from the point of view of the children in it. Note how different it would be from that of the teachers or administrators. Indeed, note how different it would be from your own local school.

In this school, the researcher did not set out to study conflict, but what emerged was a lot of conflict, not only between teachers and students, as you might have guessed from this figure, but also, in another part of the study, between the students themselves.

Robert Serpell (1982), in a study of parents and teachers in an African school, discovered that the aptitudes and skills measured on a standard IQ test completely missed some characteristics that rural Zambians thought essential to intelligence in a child. One was 'sendability': an intelligent child could be sent on an errand and trusted to alter the instructions given depending on the circumstances he or she encountered. Once again, this is not a 'baby' word for a skill that has an 'official' name. 'Sendability' includes a number of abilities that are examined on the IQ test, and some that are not on it at all. But local people evaluated their children on these and other locally important abilities, and then made decisions about children's potential for different kinds of education, employment, and so on. Plenty of people in Western countries also believe that schools are not teaching the kinds of things that they think are important to know. In Hope And Glory, Leland DeWitt's feeling that his education neglected the practical, common-sense elements of life led to his leaving school. A study of those feelings in your own community might prove interesting.

An extensive application of the 'their perspective' approach can be comprehensive and time-consuming, but it can also be used simply as one part of your research strategy. We will see how to plan such research later. Some of the techniques associated with the 'their perspective' approach — emic interviews, card sorts, and triads — are discussed in Chapters 4 and 15.

Combining the approaches

Most studies take an exclusively etic approach: researchers create the categories of inquiry. Few are exclusively emic, but some good examples of emic approaches to school studies are those by Davis (1972), Doyle (1972), and Parrott (1972). You may wonder if you can combine the approaches when doing a study. The answer is yes, you can. Here are two examples. You could study a school day according to etic categories that you had created: teacher–student interaction, reading skills development, recreational activities, civic training, and so on, looking at how much of the day is devoted to each, and describing each. You might then use an emic approach to see how the participants, such as teachers, students, and parents view the day (each group will be different). The teachers might categorize the day as you did (that doesn't make it more 'correct'). The students might break the activities up into 'work', 'fun', and 'arithmetic'. The parents, particularly if they do not approve of the curriculum or the teacher, might break it up into 'proper lessons', 'that new sex education', and 'doing errands the teacher should do herself'.

You could also use the two approaches in a sequence. In a study of the boiler factory in Hope And Glory, you could use an etic approach to get a brief description of the community: its geography, its history, and its groups — social, religious, ethnic, economic, and political. When you write your study, this will provide the reader with a background picture. Remember, the community might not have chosen these dimensions. The most important one to them might be 'local people' versus 'strangers' or 'respectable folk' versus 'poor white trash'. A good researcher will find this out and include it.

Then you might take an emic approach to the central focus of your study. Perhaps one of the things you want to know is what workers in the boiler factory do all day. Instead of creating questions such as 'How much time do you spend in getting your workstation ready?' 'How much in assembly?' 'How much in rest periods?' 'How much in "down time" when equipment isn't functioning, or there are other problems?' say 'Tell me about your day', and let the answers create the next question. They might say: 'We get our workstations ready, wait for the metal, do some assembly, fix the broken equipment, listen to stupid questions from the foreman, have dinner, do some more assembly, sweep, and wash up to go home.' Pursue each of these. Perhaps the workers consider 'rest periods' and 'repairing the equipment' the same thing, if they never get a break except when equipment is broken. A factory study called 'Banana Time' reflected this: workers routinely broke the machinery in order to have a rest, since they had no programmed rests and couldn't actually function at full speed non-stop (Roy, 1974). However, if you had asked them in a survey: 'Do you ever purposely break the machinery?' they probably wouldn't have told you, nor, probably, would you have thought to ask to begin with. Chapter 11 shows you how to carry out this kind of research.

Perspective and purpose

If you are doing descriptive research, you can choose either perspective or combine them. If you are doing explanatory or predictive research, you are likely to ask: 'What do I see these people doing?' There are two reasons for this. First, in proper cause-and-effect research you have to be able to spell out what you think is the cause and what is the effect before you begin the research. You cannot let the categories emerge as you go along. Second, because you probably would like your results to apply to other situations or groups and not just the ones you studied, you need to use categories that will apply to many situations or groups, rather than ones that represent only one group's unique perspective. This should not stop you from doing some preliminary research to see whether you can devise categories that not only suit your experiment but also have locally appropriate meanings. We will explore that later.

Finally, you should consider the stance you want to take in relation to the people involved. Will your research be *extractive,* that is, will you make all the decisions and simply extract the information from people? Or will it be *participatory,* that is, will the participants be partners in the research, deciding the agenda, the issues and concerns to be looked at; participating in getting the information; and working with you to interpret the results? This is not a question of whose perspective, but rather of the role the participants take in research decision-making and activities. You will not be able to answer this particular question until you know more about participatory research, but it is an important one. The whole of Chapter 14 is devoted to rapid and participatory approaches.

Once you have answered these questions about purpose and perspective, we can begin to develop the research plan. As you are developing it, remember that an important part of planning involves budgeting. This can include paying assistants and covering the costs of transport, food and accommodation for yourself and others; writing materials; paper and printing for surveys; stationery and postage; books and reports; equipment such as tape recorders; translators; workshops; entertainment and/or gifts where appropriate; photocopying; computer analysis and preparing and circulating materials, including your final presentation. Try to estimate these costs as carefully as possible. Research need not be expensive, but many projects have come to a standstill because the researcher ran out of money.

Where do you get this money if you need it? If you have not done research before, you will probably have to prove yourself before an agency or organization will give you any significant assistance. Start with a modest but useful project and see it through. Then you may find that a local organization will give you some form of help for your next project, such as a contribution toward transport. To get any kind of assistance, you need to be able to show clearly what you propose to do, why, and how. If you look for financial assistance, find out what obligations are placed on you, what level of control the sponsor has, and whether this is acceptable to you. Action research, for example, is often commissioned or funded by interested groups or organizations, such as a Parent Teachers' Association or local merchants. In such cases, it is important to understand the functions, intentions and powers of the people who have commissioned you, otherwise you could end up making recommendations that the group is powerless to implement, or perhaps even having your research misused.

References and further readings

Bernard, H. Russell. 1994. *Research Methods in Cultural Anthropology,* revised. Newbury Park, California: Sage.

Davis, Janet. 1972. 'Teachers, Kids and Conflict: Ethnography of a Junior High School.' James P. Spradley and David W. McCurdy, eds., *The Cultural Experience: Ethnography in Complex Society*. Chicago: Science Research Associates.

Doyle, Jean. 1972, 'Helpers, Officers and Lunchers: Ethnography of a Third Grade Class.' James P. Spradley and David W. McCurdy, eds., *The Cultural Experience: Ethnography in Complex Society*. Chicago: Science Research Associates.

Draper, S.W. 1988. 'What's Going on in Everyday Explanation?' In C. Antaki, ed., *Analyzing Everyday Explanation: A Casebook of Methods*. Newbury Park, California: Sage.

Foster, George. 1965. 'Peasant Society and the Image of the Limited Good. *American Anthropologist* 67:293–315.

Guba, Egon G. and Yvonna S. Lincoln. 1989. *Fourth Generation Evaluation*. Newbury Park, California: Sage.

Leedy, Paul D. 1989. *Practical Research: Planning and Design*, 4th ed. London: Collier Macmillan.

Parrott, Sue. 1972. 'Games Children Play: Ethnography of a Second-Grade Recess.' James P. Spradley and David W. McCurdy, eds., *The Cultural Experience: Ethnography in Complex Society*. Chicago: Science Research Associates.

Patton, Michael Quinn. 1990. *Qualitative Evaluation and Research Methods*, 2nd ed. Newbury Park, California: Sage.

Roy, Donald F. 1974. 'Banana Time: Job Satisfaction and Informal Internation.' In Joseph G. Jorgensen and Marcello Truzzi, eds. *Anthropology and American Life*. Englewood Cliffs, NJ: Prentice Hall.

Serpell, R. 1982. 'Measures of Perception, Skills and Intelligence: The Growth of a New Perspective on Children in a Third World Country.' In W.W. Hartrup, ed., *Review of Child Development Research*, vol. 6. Chicago: University of Chicago Press.

The Hope and Glory Vindicator

Volume 182 Issue 6   June 9, 2001

Group to build 2,000-seat House of Worship

The House of Peace has received city planning permission for a sanctuary which will hold 2,000 worshippers, a social hall, classrooms, an outdoor stadium for music events, a commercial kitchen and parking for 1,000 cars, according to Planning Officer Ruthann Hittman. Ms. Hittman said that in this county, religious institutions could build to any size. The development will be built where Stacia Darnell's two-bedroomed house stood.

Mr. Stephen Barker, president of the congregation, when con-tacted by a Vindicator reporter, said: 'that is generally the plan.' He said he looked forward to working with the community.

Mayor queries planning permission

In a special meeting of the City Council yesterday, Mayor Randy Anderson asked members how House of Peace plans had progressed so far without coming to the attention of the council. Mrs. Laurinda McCardle, acting chair of the council during Mayor Anderson's recent stint in the hospital, said that the matter had been discussed thoroughly at the last meeting, and that she would have told him if he would call her once in a while like he used to. Septus was away most evenings. In her opinion, Hope And Glory had such a bad reputation as a speed trap that the town was fortunate to attract any development at all. Even the proposed llama farm never materialized.

The mayor said the value of nearby properties would be seriously damaged by this development, and that the Word of God Church was good enough for him. He recognized that the pastor, Rev. Wayman, was currently hindered in his mission, what with the house arrest and the ankle tag and all, but that he had a powerful gift for the ministry and the mayor hoped he would resume work shortly.

Mayor charged under ancient law

In a startling development arising from Mayor Randy Anderson's assault suit against Police Chief Leland De Witt, the chief has charged the mayor with uttering a profanity under a 90-year old law which forbids cussing in the presence of women and children. According to the chief, the mayor made an excretory remark in the presence of Mrs. Laurinda McCardle after falling from his horse, Trigger, and getting a thwack to the head. The mayor's office denies the charge, and Mrs. McCardle has issued a statement saying that the mayor's right to free speech and her right to free hearing were being in-fringed, and where was the Supreme Court when a person needed it.

INSIDE THIS ISSUE

4 DO YOU WANT TO DESCRIBE SOMETHING?

Summary

There are many ways of planning descriptive research. This chapter looks at three:

- the research outline and the grid
- grand tour questions
- card sorts

If you are hoping to describe or explore something, such as a situation, or behaviour, or attitudes, your approach will be non-experimental. Then you have to decide which perspective to use — your own (etic) or that of the people you are studying (emic).

If you are hoping to explain what has happened in the past or predict what will happen in the future, either in cause-or-effect terms, or in terms of relationships, you will probably use either an experimental or a statistical approach. See Chapter 5 for help with this.

Within these two major categorizations, there are many variations, and some specific techniques, such as questionnaires, are used in both categories — for example, you can use questionnaires to describe and explore, but you can also use them to test explanations or predictions.

This chapter deals with research which describes.

Let us look at two ways of planning descriptive research: one asking 'What do I see these people doing?' (the etic perspective, discussed in Chapter 3), and one asking 'What do these people see themselves doing?' (the emic perspective, also discussed in Chapter 3). From now on, we will be using the terms etic and emic in our discussion.

Etic approach

When you are in a situation in which *you* decide what is important to look at, you might think that you could just get out there and start the 'real work' of collecting information right away. Unfortunately, the real work starts much earlier: you must figure out, in an organized way, what you want and need to know. Doing this is a bit like cross-examining yourself, so that everything is clear in your mind before you begin.

This chapter helps you to:

- clarify your ideas;
- narrow them enough so that they can be studied in a manageable way;
- work out exactly what you are looking for;
- determine from whom you will get your information and how.

Developing a Rough Research Idea and Refining It

You need to avoid two important problems when developing and refining your research idea. One is choosing an idea that is too big or vague (juvenile delinquency, poverty) and the other is choosing one that sounds fancy, professional, or scientific, but that is really not clearly spelled-out: 'A Deterministic Approach to Multi-level Equalization and Symbiosis: Dilemma and Dialectic', or, indeed, my own first publication, 'Nonunlineality in Oceania: Review and Alternate Hypothesis' (Kane 1967). If you know exactly what you mean by a title like that, fine. Perhaps you could drop me a note. If you have come up with it because it will dazzle people, you are in trouble.

Study things that are real to you. Don't be intimidated by jargon. If you follow the process described in this chapter, you should be able to avoid both these problems. If you are working with an organization, use the process to have its staff work out what they want.

Descriptive research topics can be found everywhere. For example, go into any bar or pub late at night, and you will find a wealth of theses, propositions, and motifs. 'Summers aren't what they used to be.' 'I'll bet none of them council members could beat a dog at chess.' 'How do "Keep off the grass" signs get there in the first place?' 'It's a known fact that most

kids from that side of town grow up to be axe-murderers.' Or 'Women —
now there's a study for you.' Some of these can be cleared up by sobriety
or a brief trip to the library. But let's take the last one. We are already into
problem Number One: it's clearly too big, so just for discussion, let's limit
it to 'The needs of working women', even though we can be fairly certain
that this is not the study our drinking companions are looking for. It is still
too big — look at the questions in Box 4–1, where we are using the
journalist's old trick of simply asking 'Who?', 'What?', 'Where?', 'When?',
'Why?', and 'How?' You could create hundreds of questions this way, which
would help you to see how big your idea is. You will have to work out in
your own mind what you really want to do, because no matter how much
time, money, and assistance you might have, you will never cover the entire
topic of all the needs of all kinds of working women everywhere.

Box 4–1 Is your topic too big?

- Who do you mean? All women? All ages?

- What do you mean by 'working'? At home? In formal employment? In the
  non-formal economy? All professions and occupations?

- What aspects of the work situation? Working conditions? Pay? Promotion
  opportunities? Legal issues? Policy issues? Child care? Educational/training
  requirements? Balancing work with domestic responsibilities?

- Where? Everywhere? The nation? The region? Your town? One company?

- When? Are you interested in past patterns? Possible changes in the future?
  How are working women's needs being met now?

- Why women's needs? How are they different from men's?

Begin again. You are concerned with the needs of women who are
starting their own small businesses. The boiler factory in Hope And Glory
closed down a while back; the women who were employed there have
been out of work, and many have decided to set up their own small
businesses. This cuts the topic considerably, but it is still too broad.
However, once you have a topic, you can narrow it easily by:

- Considering a special aspect of the problem that concerns you, for
  example, the start-up needs of women would-be entrepreneurs, or the
  main causes of failure.
- Defining the words more specifically, for instance, economic needs,
  marketing and design needs, legal needs, educational needs.

- Restricting the study to a particular group: women in the service industry, immigrant women, women who have been made redundant, women who have never worked in formal employment.
- Restricting it to one geographic area or institution.
- Restricting it to a particular time (or two or more specific times if, for example, you are comparing a group ten years ago with a group today) For example, you could look at the needs of women entrepreneurs today; you could look to see how they have changed over the past ten years, you could look at projected needs five years from now.
- Taking a sample. Study something broader, but with a smaller, carefully chosen group.

Using this process, you can cut an idea to the point where it is nonsensical. Obviously, you don't cut a topic simply for the sake of cutting. Underneath all your words you probably have a core idea which you are not prepared to sacrifice and using a process like this will help you to see what is dead weight and what parts are really important to you. So let's look at the situation and get to the heart of what you really need to know.

The women in Hope And Glory, employed and unemployed, are fed up with Hyland Beam and his workmen. They have the town by the throat in terms of construction, and the fellows who work for Hy are usually late by a matter of weeks, treat you like you were a nitwit, leave the place a mess, and wear their jeans way too low in back. Hy Beam is a near man with a dollar and charges too much. Some of the women ex-employees from the boiler factory have set up their own small repair/construction businesses, and the women of Hope And Glory are all behind them, except, of course, for Hy's wife Weezie. However, it hasn't been easy: the women don't have a lot of business experience, they encounter some discrimination and they need to manage their ordering and materials better. You work for an organization that provides advice to would-be entrepreneurs, but the idea of women running repair and construction businesses is rather new, and your organization has not managed to meet their needs. You want to know what these women's problems were so that you can prepare women better in future, and have decided to focus on women who set up a business any time in the past three years.

Creating a Research Statement or Hypothesis

Write out a sentence beginning 'I want to study X' or 'We want to study X' and fill it in. Using some of the narrowing techniques listed, let us say we have come up with the sentence: 'I want to study start-up problems in the repair/construction business among women entrepreneurs in Hope And Glory, 1997–1999.' Already you are probably feeling better — not only does it sound good, but you understand what it means, and how you got there. This is your research statement.

There's one more thing to think about. Whose perspective do we want? The women themselves? Business experts? Bear in mind that each group may come up with problems which have never occurred to the other. The business experts, for example, may see a need for better design of packaging. The women may have discovered that wholesalers don't readily offer them credit, but since this is illegal, it may not be known by experts. You could do a study which covered both these groups, and customers, as well: simply repeat the entire process for all three groups.

If there are a large number of women entrepreneurs in the repair/construction business, you may have to study a sample of them, rather than the whole lot. Sampling is covered in Chapter 6, but whether you use a sample or not, the process from here on is the same. Literary quality is not important in a research statement. What is important is that all the aspects you want to study are included and stand out clearly. When you have finished the narrowing process make sure that the statement still covers what you want to study.

Here is what you do:

a) Select the topic of interest by asking 'Who?', 'What?', 'Where?', 'When?', 'Why?', and 'How?' and using any other device that helps you to realize how many facets your topic has.

b) State what you want to study in one sentence, if possible. If your research has several phases, you may have to use more than one sentence to develop the ideas. Box 4–2 shows some possible situations that might interest you and how each might be converted into a research statement.

c) Define every major word in your statement so that you have a clear guide as to what you are looking at throughout your research. You can define a word any way you like as long as you tell the reader what you have done: we have used the phrase 'recent labor-market entrants' in Box 4–2 to mean women who have just left school and women who have not worked in paid employment outside the home for the past ten years. You may choose to define some of the words in your statement according to definitions used in the professional literature in your field. Non-formal education, for example, has a generally accepted meaning

Box 4–2 Possible research situations and appropriate research statements

Problem	Research statement
Excluding women in other new businesses may limit the insights you get.	Start-up problems in businesses among women entrepreneurs in Hope And Glory, 1997–1999.
Perhaps some of the women are not ex-employees of the boiler factory, but rather have never worked outside the home before. They seem to be having more trouble starting businesses than women who have worked in paid employment, and you want to know what the differences are.	A comparison of the start-up problems of formerly employed women and new labor market entrants in Hope And Glory, 1997–1999.
Perhaps women in other towns are not having nearly so much trouble – it might be useful to see what the differences are.	A comparison of start-up problems in business among women entrepreneurs in Hope And Glory and Three Other Towns, 1997–1999.
Perhaps the conditions for men and women are different, and support services have unwittingly been designed around men's problems.	A comparison of start-up problems in businesses among women and men entrepreneurs in Hope And Glory, 1997–1999.
Perhaps women with some formal education in repair/construction (an accredited repair/construction training program for example) have different problems from those who have non-formal education in repair/construction (they got a few sessions at the local community hall, for example).	A comparison of start-up problems in businesses among women with formal repair/construction education and women with non-formal repair/construction education in Hope And Glory, 1997–1999.

in the field of education, and unless you are challenging or refining that definition in some way, you will probably use it or explain why you are not. Repair/construction training in a particular country has even more specific terms, and you may want to use those.

Also remember that if you use words such as 'effectiveness', 'satisfactory' or 'frequently', you have to explain what you mean by them. You may say: 'I will define a program as "effective" if 80 per cent of the group that is entitled to participate is using it.' '"Satisfactory performance" means having fewer than three service-related complaints in one month.' As we mentioned in Chapter 2, even words such as 'literate' which you might expect to be clear-cut, differ considerably from one country to another: in some places, it is the ability to write one's name; in another it is the ability to read a paragraph. You should have a good reason for your definition, and it should be meaningful to the people involved. If you want to compare the results of your research with someone else's, or with official statistics, you should use the same categories. For example, if you are doing a school study, unless you have a good reason to do so, why group children into age categories four-through-nine and ten-through-fifteen if school records or the official census groups them as five-through-ten, and eleven-through-sixteen?

d) Rewrite your sentence, taking all these decisions into account.

You can see that by using this procedure you are taking a positivistic approach: you are determining the variables to be looked at and defining what each will mean. In the next step, we take the process even further.

Identifying the Sub-topics for Study

Now that you know what general topic you want to study, you have to break it down into sub-topics so you will know what specific information you need to collect. This will be your research outline. The easiest way to do this is to identify your variables. A variable is any characteristic or attribute that can take a variety of forms, for example, education, sex, marital status, religion, ethnic group, career aspirations and type of training can all take more than one form. You can have primary education, secondary education, or third-level education; you can be male or female; and you can be single, married, widowed, or divorced. Each major word or phrase in your research statement is probably a variable, or else a word or phrase that requires explanation to put the situation in context (as in 'Birmingham', 'Dublin', or 'the boiler factory' in the examples below). Here are three sample research statements, with their variables marked with Roman numerals:

(i)   (ii)   (iii)

Cost-effectiveness of worker education programs in the boiler factory.

(i)	(ii)	(iii)	

Resettlement problems among Romanian immigrants in Dublin.

(i)	(ii)	(iii)	(iv)

Examination results of girls in single-sex schools and mixed-sex schools in

(v)

Birmingham.

Let's assume we are happy with the statement we worked out in Step 5: 'Start-up problems in the repair/construction business among women entrepreneurs in Hope And Glory, 1997–1999.' Our variables are:

i.   Start-up problems
ii. Repair/construction business
iii. Women entrepreneurs
iv. Hope And Glory
v.   1997–1999

This research statement has five major words or phrases about which information must be collected. The easiest way to figure out what information we need is to take each word or phrase and consider what facets or characteristics it could contain: that is, break it down into all its possible parts. (Remember our discussion of positivism in Chapter 2, in which we compared reality to a giant clock that can be taken apart for examination?)

The word or phrase you begin with does not matter, but 'people' words or phrases and 'place' words or phrases are easier. For example, people always have certain characteristics: age, sex, height, weight, marital status, social class, residence, ethnic group, education. 'Women entrepreneurs' is a people phrase and will have these. Because these women are entrepreneurs, they will have some special characteristics, such as number of years in business, type of training (or lack of it), and so on. If you were studying immigrants, their special characteristics might include country of origin, length of residence in this country, language, etc., in addition to the ordinary 'people' characteristics. Athletes would have position on team, records, etc. So we will begin with the women entrepreneurs.

Women entrepreneurs

First, make a rough list of all the attributes you can think of for people, such as age, sex, marital status, height, weight, number of children, religion, health, political affiliation, occupation. Keep going. Some may have no bearing whatsoever on your research, but thinking of them and discarding them later is better than forgetting to include them and regretting it later.

Now write each on a separate scrap of paper, and see if you can group them in some way that makes sense to you or makes sense in the context of the project. There is no right way to do this. For some projects you might group them into characteristics people are born with versus those they acquire or achieve. For another project you might group them into physical versus social characteristics. You might make more than two groupings or just one long list.

Your groupings will make sense only in the context of a particular project. For example, age and sex are physical characteristics but they can also be the bases of social groupings. And you are born into an ethnic group, so if your sortings were based on groups people were born into versus those they acquired later, ethnic group would end up with age group, sex group, and so on. There is no magic to this. Do what makes sense for your project and the people you are working with.

Make another list of the characteristics the women entrepreneurs will have because they are entrepreneurs: specialization, training, number of years in business, previous occupation.

Now put all the attributes together in a list (see Box 4–3). Leave out any that you feel certain are irrelevant to your project. For example, collecting information on height is unlikely to be worthwhile for this project. It could be, however, in a study of sporting interests of boys in a school.

It would be easy to think of other topics that might be in/not in this outline if you were doing, say, a study of your own area or region.

You might think it is not politically correct to include 'domestic responsibilities' in a study of women entrepreneurs, but if you suspect that domestic responsibilities have seriously interfered with the ability of some to function in business, you will want to build advice on this into your organization's program, so it is no good ignoring it. If, on the other hand, domestic responsibilities are clearly not a factor (you know that all the women have heavy domestic responsibilities and all handle them equally well, but some still do well in their businesses and others don't), your time would be better spent looking at other things. A few of the topics listed earlier, such as political affiliation, have been left out of our imaginary project, but in some studies political affiliation might be an important determinant in whether one gets contracts, etc. This is why we said in Chapter 2 that in doing positivistic research, in which you determine the variables, as you are doing in this outline, it is important to be very familiar with the situation. This is another reason why local knowledge and insights are valuable.

Hope And Glory

We can now take a second variable, the place word, Hope And Glory. Places (and institutions) by their nature have certain characteristics, like a location, a history, a size, and so on. Bear in mind that you are not doing a detailed study of the town. You are getting enough information to put the place in context, in relation to the subject of start-up problems of repair/construction businesses among women entrepreneurs. Box 4–4 sets out the characteristics for Hope And Glory. As we are studying repair/construction businesses, note that we have two sets of characteristics: general characteristics and business-related characteristics.

Box 4–3 iii: Women entrepreneurs

1. **General characteristics**
   A. Age
   B. Area of residence
   C. Marital status
   D. Domestic responsibilities

2. **Work-related characteristics**
   A. Occupation
   B. Other employment
   C. Training—occupational
      1) type
         a) formal
         b) non-formal
      2) institution attended
      3) accreditation received
   D. Training—business
      1) type
         a) formal
         b) non-formal
      2) institution attended
      3) accreditation received

Repair/construction businesses

Now we need to look at 'repair/construction businesses', not because we are doing a study of such businesses, but we want to know a little bit about the industry generally, so that we can understand the meaning of the 'start-up problems' when we look at them later on. For example, if most repair/construction businesses have good advisory services from

Box 4–4 iv: Hope And Glory

1. **General characteristics**
   A. Location
      1) geographic
      2) economic (in relation to suppliers, markets, etc.)
   B. Size
      1) area
      2) population
         a) by age
         b) by sex

2. **Economy**
   A. Major economic activities
      1) industries
         a) manufacturing
         b) service
         c) building and construction
         d) sales — retail and wholesale
      2) labor force profile
         a) by age
         b) by sex
         c) by income
         d) by occupation
         e) by training
         f) other
      3) resources
   B. Small business-related characteristics
      1) historical development of small businesses
      2) current picture
         a) types
         b) sizes
         c) turnover
         d) numbers of employees
      3) structures
      4) start-up issues
      5) survival rates

professional associations, and the women list this as a big problem for them, we will want to know why other repair/construction businesses have access to such services and the women don't seem to. On the other hand, perhaps

Box 4–5 ii: Repair/construction businesses

1. **Characteristics**
   A. Types
   B. Sizes
      1) turnover
      2) numbers of employees
   C. Structures
      1) management
      2) financial
   D. Business supports
      1) financial
         a) banking and credit
         b) grants
         c) advisory
            i. professional associations
            ii. government advisory boards
            iii. commercial organizations

we will find that there aren't any such advisory services — men may have been running such businesses on a father-to-son basis for many years and never felt the need.

Start-up problems

Next we come to what we are really interested in: start-up problems. Although making a research outline is tedious, it can almost become a game. For any variable, you can keep thinking up more sub-topics, and, if you do not mind running around collecting unnecessary information, it is not too serious a mistake. But if you go astray now, that is dangerous, because the variables you select here for 'start-up problems' are going to be game. For any variable, you can keep thinking up more sub-topics, and, if you do not mind running around collecting unnecessary information, it is not too serious a mistake. But if you go astray now, that is dangerous, because the variables you select here for 'start-up problems' are going to be the basis of the questions you ask people. If you create a list of problems which sound relevant to you but turn out to have no real bearing on the situation, you might never discover your mistake. You will ask people, and, since they are generally obliging, they will answer. They may even make the mistake of assuming that since you are the 'expert' you know their reasons better than they do themselves. For example, you decide the five major start-up problems are that (a) women don't have a business mentality (b) they have to build up their muscles gradually for carrying lumber and other heavy materials (c) they put in shorter days because they have to cook in the evening (d) they would really rather be doing something else and (e) other. You ask your questions about these problems and you will be surprised at how many people will genuinely try to fit their views and experiences into these categories as best they can. Others will find that your reasons have so little relevance that they will choose 'other'. Out of 100 people you question, 75 may mark off the box called 'other'. Everyone, including you, will be baffled.

To avoid this you have to do enough preliminary research to break down the reasons into meaningful categories. There are many ways to do this: you could interview a variety of people to get possible problems; you could do a pilot survey in which you ask a selection of women entrepreneurs some broad, open-ended questions about problems they have had and leave plenty of space for the respondents to write in their own answers; you could look at other studies that have been done; you could look at business records; you could talk to customers; you could talk to business advisers, etc. Doing several of these preliminary activities is a good idea. However you have done it, let us now imagine that you have enough information to begin to break down the variable 'start-up problems'.

1997–1999

Finally we have the dates. You don't have to break this down — it is only to remind you that you are restricting your study to businesses which were started during that period. If you were comparing start-up problems ten years ago versus today, and your research statement was 'Changes in start-up problems among women entrepreneurs in repair/construction businesses, 1989 and 1999', then you do the entire outline for 1989 and then repeat it for 1999.

Putting the Outline in Perspective

We are finished for the moment. But we need to pause a moment and get a bit of perspective. Just because each section of the outline is broken down in considerable detail, it does not mean the sections are of equal weight in terms of your time and energy. For example, the reason you are looking at Hope And Glory is to be able to put your study into a geographic, historical, demographic, institutional, and administrative context. Everything you learn from this part of the outline may occupy only two paragraphs in your final report, if you need to write one. But what you

Box 4–6 i: Start-up problems

1. Getting advice
   A. Financial, legal, tax
   B. Professional and technical
   C. Marketing and pricing
2. Getting training
   A. Professional or technical training
   B. Small business and management training
3. Developing a business plan
4. Working with lending and grant institutions
5. Establishing relationships with
   A. Suppliers
   B. Contractors
   C. Potential clients
6. Meeting financial costs
   A. Initial financial costs of
      1) rent or purchase of premises, remodeling, refitting
      2) deposits
      3) equipment and vehicles
      4) staff salaries, insurance, etc.
      5) utilities
      6) production materials
      7) inventory
      8) fees (licenses, legal, insurance, consultants, trade memberships, etc.)
      9) design, marketing
      10) cash reserves for salaries, operations, etc.
   B. Recurring financial costs of
      1) rent, mortgage, maintenance
      2) equipment and vehicles
      3) staff salaries, insurance, etc.
      4) utilities
      5) production materials
      6) inventory
      7) fees (licenses, legal, insurance, consultants, trade memberships, etc.)
      8) design, marketing
      9) cash reserves for salaries, operations, etc.
   C. Meeting opportunity costs (lost income or value of unpaid work while starting up)

7. Organizational issues
   A. Legal structure of organization
   B. Management structure
   C. Financial structure
   D. Procedures
   E. Cash flow, payments
   F. Schedules
8. Human resource issues
   A. Hiring staff
   B. Getting in-service training
   C. Staff and office management
9. Production or service issues
   A. Meeting demand
   B. Insuring quality
10. Discrimination issues
   A. Attitudes of potential customers to women entrepreneurs
   B. Attitudes of staff
   C. Attitudes of suppliers, credit institutions, professional colleagues

learn may help you or others to compare your findings with those of other towns: for instance, Hope And Glory may have a local college with a business department, while another community may have none, but it may be much closer to major markets and have a local business and trade association. What you learn may also help you to come up with new lines of research to follow later: is there a better success record in communities with a business college? Would it be helpful to a community to form a trade association and link up with national groups in order to provide seminars and other help for beginners?

Figure 4–1 Putting the variables in perspective

Start-up problems	Women entrepreneurs	Repair and construction business	Hope and Glory

While allowing for the fact that something helpful may emerge from this section of your outline, you should remember that you are not doing an economic study of the town. You are trying to get a picture of the context in which women entrepreneurs are working. Try to diagram your research statement to see the 'heart' of your research and the marginal areas, as shown in Figure 4–1: heavy lines represent the more central parts of the research and thinner lines the information being gathered for context.

A second caution is that you should not use this particular outline to do a piece of research. There is nothing 'scientific' about it simply because it appears in a book. It was made up for a nearly imaginary place as an example of one way, out of many, to do an outline. Even if you were going to do a very similar study, you should make your own outline using your knowledge of the local situation to make the topics relevant and meaningful.

Not every research topic can be handled in this way, but many can. Suppose you have come up with: 'I want to study girls. Why don't they have more ambition?' All girls? More ambition than what? Boys? More than girls used to have? What do you mean by ambition? You have assumed that they have less. You had better establish your facts first, and, if you are correct, then look at the causes. Why not first see what ambitions girls have compared to boys or compared to girls ten years ago? Then your research statement may become: *'Career ambitions* among *girls* and *career ambitions* among *boys* in *Southend Middle School'*. You may wonder if you should phrase it: *'Girls' career ambitions* and *boys' career ambitions* in *Southend Middle School'*. You can, but it means that 'girls' and 'boys' are no longer variables. If there are age, social class, economic, or ethnic differences between the boys and girls, there is no place for that to be examined, unless you use the first research statement rather than the second.

Or perhaps you have *'Attitudes of Residents* in *Hope And Glory* to the *New Church'*. This could also be *'Attitudes* of *Hope And Glory Residents…'* but Hope And Glory is no longer a variable: if you want to look at the religious, social, economic history and makeup of the town, go with the first version. What do you do with 'attitudes'? Don't treat it as a variable and break it down. Attitudes are what you will get when you do the study.

If you can show that girls have less ambition (defined and measured in some way) than boys, then you are in a position to look at why. You may decide to look at why people (teachers, parents, and others) think they have less ambition. This is a descriptive study. Its research statement may be: *'Teachers' perceptions* and *parents' perceptions* of *reasons for low career ambitions among girls* in *Southend Middle School* as held by *parents* and *teachers'*. Another way of stating the same thing is *'Perceptions* of *reasons for low career ambitions among girls* in *Southend Middle School'* and break 'perceptions' down into '(a) teachers' and '(b) parents'. It doesn't matter which; the important thing is to get your variables stated clearly. If you think, in doing these studies, that you have a good sense of what was causing the low ambitions (perhaps there was no work for adult women in the area, or a lack of female role models in the school), you could set up an experiment in which you compared two schools, one that had female role models and one that did not, and see if girls' ambitions were higher in the first school. We will look at experiments in the next chapter.

A grid approach

No one likes research outlines. People who take a phenomenological approach think research outlines are rubbish, tools of the devil, and products of a small, picky mind. Even some positivists, who by rights should spend their evenings sipping fine wine and outlining variables, do not like to see the logical outcome of a positivistic approach laid out quite so baldly. The people who dislike research outlines the most, however, are those who are trying to construct one, because the process is about as much fun as scraping your fingernail on a blackboard. Nonetheless, if you are taking an etic approach, failing to prepare a research outline is like trying to find something with your toes in a muddy pool of alligators: God knows what you'll find but it's unlikely to be what you want, you'll waste a lot of time, and you'll probably be sorry you ever started.

Another way of figuring out what you need to know is to use a grid. You can use this technique for any subject, but we are going to use an action research example here. Suppose that you want to plan a project and need to assess the situation first. Perhaps your community wants to plan a cooperative for sharing garden and do-it-yourself tools. You know that other places have tried this, and sometimes it hasn't worked out that well, so you are going to look at it carefully.

List all the aspects of the situation that you think are important. Convert each idea to one word, or two at most. Write each word in its own block down one side of a large box and then write the same words across the top (Appendix). Locate any particular box, and reading across and down, create a question out of the two words that 'meet' in the box. For example, in Box F–5, where 'Resources' and 'People' meet, you might ask: 'What resources do the people involved have?' and 'What resources do the people involved need?' Not all boxes will produce sensible questions for your project, and because every combination appears twice ('Facts' and 'Reasons' is one combination, and 'Reasons' and 'Facts' is another), you may have questions repeated. This is really only a device to help you cover a lot of angles that you can then include in your research or reject. This grid approach also has other uses. As you will see in Chapters 11 and 12, you can use it to get questions for interviews or to choose situations to observe.

The grid which appears in the Appendix would be suitable for assessing a situation or for evaluating a project. To assess a situation, leave the grid as is. To evaluate a project, wherever the word 'situation' occurs, change it to 'project'. For example, Box F–4 'How do the people carry out the processes involved?' might help you to look at whether the current staff ('People') in a school are sufficiently trained to carry out a new, more culturally sensitive curriculum ('Process'). As you will see, the grid in the Appendix is thirteen-by-thirteen, with a total of 169 question cells, but a grid could be much smaller, say two-by-three. The size of your own grid will depend on the problem you are studying and the number of dimensions that seem important. Whatever the size, it is most unlikely that all the questions will be equally important or that you will use all of them.

Notice also that this grid asks questions that require judgments that you or your team will make in the process of doing your research. To make the process a participatory one (see Chapter 14), the people involved in the situation can take responsibility for getting the information that will allow them to make these decisions. For a discussion of participatory evaluation, see Uphoff (1991).

The examples here are instances of descriptive research, but the basic principle of making your variables explicit is important for explanatory and predictive research as well.

Making Decisions About Sources of Information

Soon you are going to be ready to assemble your entire research plan: the outline, your sources of information, and your research techniques. When you have finished, you will have a research design.

First, for each point in your outline, you are going to have to decide where the information will come from. People? Records? The professional literature? You will probably draw on all of these. In the case of people, you will have to decide what types of people, and maybe even who in particular. In our study, 'Start-up problems in the repair/construction business among women entrepreneurs in Hope And Glory, 1997–1999', we are interested in finding out what the problems are, but do we want to hear only from the women themselves, or do we also want the views of customers, business experts, etc.? For some points, such as location of Hope And Glory in relation to markets, we may name a category of person (mayor, trade association president, or even a specific person — 'Mayor Randy Anderson'). Finally, we will discuss this in Chapter 14, but the point cannot be made too often that you should not restrict yourself to 'important' people, or 'experts', or people who are easier to reach. The women themselves, even those with the most modest businesses, have insights into their problems which the president of the largest multinational cannot possibly have. Everyone's voice is important when you are trying to understand something.

You will probably also have to consult records and statistics. It often helps to do that before you begin to plan, because they may give you some ideas of what needs to be studied. But even after you have chosen the topic, you will probably need records and statistics to help you get a general picture of, say, the number of enterprises which are service providers versus those engaged in some form of manufacturing. Chapter 8 looks at some of the sources available and some of the problems associated with using them. Or you may also want to look at the professional literature to see what else has been written on your subject. Chapter 8 also lists some of the major social science and education journals. Getting access to them requires the services of a good public, school, or university library.

It is possible that you will not have to look at the professional literature at all. You are probably not trying to make a new contribution to theory or research methods. You may just want to know what is happening in your community or organization and do a piece of research that will help you to understand or solve a problem. Once you have made these decisions, you can begin to make a research design. For every point in the outline, the design will show the sources of information that you will use and the techniques for getting the information. Let's look first at sources. Box 4–7 shows the part of our outline that deals with discrimination issues that women entrepreneurs face. This point first appeared in our outline in Box 4–6 i. Start-up problems, point 10.

Box 4–7 Part of a research outline: point and sources

Outline point	Sources
A. Attitudes of potential customers to women entrepreneurs	Potential customers Women entrepreneurs Existing studies
B. Attitudes of staff	Staff Women entrepreneurs State and federal records

Chapter 6 on sampling and Chapter 8 on using what is already available will give you more information on choosing sources.

Making Decisions About Information-Gathering Techniques

For each point in your outline you also have to decide how you will get the information. Will you conduct a survey? Will you interview people?

Will you see what the records say? Will you watch to see what happens? Part III of this book discusses these and other techniques that you might use. For the moment, let us imagine that you have some ideas about your sources and know enough about research techniques to choose the ones you will use (Box 4–8).

Box 4–8 Part of a research outline: point, sources, and techniques

Outline point	Sources	Techniques
A. Attitudes of potential customers to women entrepreneurs	Potential customers Women entrepreneurs Existing studies	Surveys, focus groups, observation Surveys, semi-structured interviews Analysis of documents
B. Attitudes of staff	Staff	Surveys, semi-structured interviews, observation
	Women entrepreneurs	Surveys, semi-structured interviews
	State and federal records	Analysis of documents

This process is carried out for each outline point. Note that for your central topics you should be using as many techniques as possible to get sound information. The topic shown here is not a central one: it provides background and context.

Using your outline to plan your work

Look at the partial design above. Interviews are mentioned for several points. When you have finished your outline, look through it and note the points for which you intend to use an interview. Are any of the interview points to be put to the same people? Can you draw up an interview form using these points? For example, in the partial design we mention 'local business people' twice and, in each case, we intend to interview them. We can go through the rest of the outline and see if there is anything else we want to ask them, put all the questions on a sheet of paper and use them when we go to talk to the business people. We can do the same for each category of people or other kinds of sources. When we are planning to issue a survey, we should look through the outline to find where a survey is mentioned in the 'Techniques' column: is it to the same group of people? If so, write it down and you will have the major items you need in order to begin to write your questions.

Box 4–9 The complete research design for one point in the outline

Outline Point	Sources	Techniques	What will this tell me?	How will it contribute to my study?
A. Attitudes of potential customers to women entrepreneurs	Existing studies	Analysis of documents	What kinds of attitudes have been revealed in previous studies of this topic.	May help me to create questions for my groups; will tell me what other researchers found to be important.
	Potential customers	Focus groups	What a carefully selected group of customers say.	May help me to create questions for my survey; will tell me attitudes in depth.
		Surveys	What large numbers of customers say.	Will tell me how widely held the attitudes are and by whom.
		Observation	How people act.	I will see how people behave toward women entrepeneurs.
	Women entrepreneurs	Surveys	What a large number of women entrepreneurs feel about potential customer attitudes.	Will help me to construct semi-structured interviews; will tell me how widely the problems are experienced and by whom.
		Semi-structured interviews	Will help me explore the problem in depth.	Will flesh out the information from the survey.

Finally, as shown above, you can put all the parts of your research design together: the outline, the sources, the techniques, and two additional columns to help you keep a sense of perspective (Box 4–9).

The fourth column encourages you to think about whether you need a particular piece of information, and whether what you are planning to do will provide it. The last column reminds you that some parts of your research are more central than other parts.

Emic Approach

The emic approach involves an entirely different way of proceeding. Because you cannot determine the variables to be studied, you cannot prepare a research outline. This alone may be enough to convert you to the emic approach! You will be starting with a general topic that interests you, for example, how long-time residents of a community categorize the various groups of immigrants who are moving into the community, or how a group of prisoners rate the categories of criminals in the prison, but you will be using methods that allow the important dimensions of the topic to emerge, rather than deciding in advance what they are and asking questions about them.

This approach is very good when you know little about a subject, or when you think you know a lot but need to stand back and get some other angles on the subject. For example, as part of a development project in a village in Zambia in Africa, a group of women were asked about the causes of local poverty. Perhaps you might have guessed some of them, but you probably wouldn't have come up with the first and the last:

'**God's creation. That is how God created them, hence no matter how hard they struggle nothing will change.**'

'Laziness. One's heart is not desiring to work.'

'Poor planning.'

'Lack of initiative. Not using one's initiative and talents.'

'***Maanu ndibule*: Not mixing with friends because they think they know everything.**'

The two in bold letters are not categories that an outsider could guess based on 'common sense', but they are meaningful to local people. As the investigators in this case point out, straightforward questioning on these issues would have tended to produce simplistic results (Norton and Milimo, 1993). You probably won't find yourself in Zambia all that often and may wonder if this approach is really only useful with people or situations that are very different from your own experience. How will teenagers at the local disco respond when you try this out on them? First of all, if you are over twenty-five, they will think you are barking mad anyway, so you might as well give it a try. Secondly, they are very different from you: they live in a different world and follow sets of rules about clothing, hair, music, behavior, etc. which would make you feel more at home in Zambia.

What is the value of information like this? First of all, the last one, 'not mixing with friends', gives you a clue that people have to cooperate with one another to survive, and you should explore what that means. But the first item is interesting: people obviously think some poor people are beyond help — they were born that way. Maybe some of the poor agree. This would have repercussions for any project you might think of setting up. Without such information, you might create a project which seemed perfectly designed, but yet some people didn't participate. It would take a long time to figure out that they might be the ones who felt there was no point.

Emic research can be quite comprehensive and time consuming. The following discussion presents a general way of using the approach to complement other techniques. Emic research can be carried out in several different ways. Two examples are the grand tour question and card sorts.

The grand tour question

The grand tour question approach (Spradley, 1979) begins by asking the broadest possible question appropriate to the situation. To a factory worker: 'What happens here all day?' To university students: 'What kinds of professors are there?' To flight attendants: 'What kinds of passengers do you get?' The aim of the exercise is to learn how people categorize things and why. For example, you will probably find, when talking to flight attendants, that 'business class' and 'economy class' are not major categories — 'people who are terrified of flying', 'drunks', 'gropers', 'mothers with infants', 'people who want to put steamer trunks in the overhead compartment' might feature instead. However, someone should ask them instead of guessing, as I am.

Let us say that you are talking to a group of girls about the students in their school.

Q.   Will you tell me about the girls in this school?
A.   What do you mean?
Q.   Well, what kinds of girls are in the school here? Tell me something about them.
A.   Well, there are all kinds of girls here: the poor girls, and the rough and ready ones, and the really gorgeous girls, and the snooty girls, and then, of course, the ordinary girls. Oh, and the handicapped. And the girls from the west side.
Q.   Tell me about the poor girls.

A. The poor girls? We don't talk to them. They wear funny clothes and they carry their own lunches because they don't come from here. Sometimes they hit us.

Q. Tell me about their clothes.

A. They can't afford nice clothes so they wear icky stuff. We laugh at them.

Q. Tell me about them hitting you.

A. They hit us for no reason at all. We can't help it if they're funny looking.

Q. Tell me about the rough and ready girls.

A. They don't live around here. They don't have enough money to buy nice clothes and they hang around with really dodgy looking older boys.

Q. Tell me about going with the dodgy looking boys.

A. They go out with these boys and a lot of them get pregnant and have to leave school. The guys spend a lot of money on them — buy them nice clothes and stuff.

Q. Do the poor girls go out with these boys, too?

A. No. Boys don't like them. They look funny. I told you.

Q. Tell me about the gorgeous girls.

A. The gorgeous girls always have plenty of money for nice clothes and hair styles and manicures and shopping. It doesn't matter that their parents don't have a penny.

Q. Then where do they get the money?

A. Their boyfriends.

Q. Like the rough and ready girls?

A. Oh, no. The rough and ready girls don't have real boyfriends. They just go with boys to get nice stuff.

Q. Tell me about the ordinary girls.

A. Oh, all the girls from around here are ordinary; nice normal girls like us. We help each other. If one of us is taking an afternoon off because a boy is going to take her shopping, we'll tell the teacher she got sick.

Q. What about these boys? What are they like?

A. Well, they're not so great, but when you want nice clothes, beggars can't be choosers.

Q. Tell me about the snooty girls.

A. They think they're wonderful. They don't talk to us. They say their parents won't allow them to. We don't care, because they're spoiled.

Q. How are they spoiled?

A. Well, they're poor but they never have to worry about money or clothes or anything. Their mothers and fathers give it to them, even if they have to work extra hours at the chicken factory to get the cash. They go with boys because they want to. They don't need the clothes and stuff.

Q. Tell me about the handicapped.

A. They need special help or something and so they come here because the school is bigger and can put on programs for them. A lot of them are poor.

Q. Do they go with boyfriends or older boys?

A. No. And they dress funny.

Q. Tell me about the girls from the west side.

A. Oh, they're from the west side. What can you say? They're all poor people and they're always hanging around older boys. See, there's one over there, the one in a wheelchair.

When you recover from such an interview, you might notice several things. First of all, you created only one question of your own, the first one. You might go into more detail about something that interested you in an answer but basically you are always coming back to the categories the girls gave you in the original answer. Second, it is not your job to set these girls straight. You are trying to find out how they see things, so don't point out why the poor girls might be hitting them and, although you might be sorely tempted, don't mention that you were once a chaste, reasonably well-off west side girl. Finally, notice that these girls have clear-cut categories in their minds that might not seem so clear to someone else. For example, all the girls appear to be poor, including the 'poor girls', but in the case of the others something else puts them in a special group rather than the 'poor' group. The 'ordinary' girls seem to have worked out the same strategy for getting nice stuff as the 'rough and ready' girls have. The only difference is that the 'ordinary' girls are all locals. The west side girl in the interview was in a wheelchair, but she was not put in the 'handicapped' group. Apparently, in their eyes being a west side girl is her major characteristic.

So far, what we have looks like Box 4–10.

Card sorts

You can also get the kind of information that we just got from one person or from a small group in the school using a card sort. Put the names of all the girls in the class on cards and ask the girls you are working with to sort them into categories. If they are working in a group, you will be trying to get shared categories. You can test the categories by repeating the process with other individuals or groups in the school. Probably no two groups or

Box 4–10 'The girls in this school'

Category	Funny clothes	Money from dodgy boys	Money from boy-friends	Money from parents	Local	Handicapped	West side
Poor	x						
Rough and Ready		x					
Gorgeous			x				
Snooty				x			
Ordinary		x			x		
Handicapped	x					x	
West side		x					x

individuals will come up with exactly the same categories: some might produce five, some six, and so on, but you may be able to rearrange them into five common categories. You can then go back to the individuals or groups and see if they accept the new categories.

When you have the agreed categories, you can reverse the process and present a new group of students in the same school with the categories and the pack of cards with the students' names and ask them to sort them. If the new group finds that some people do not fit, or that one of the categories has no cards in it, you have to refine the categories. You can also test the categories by presenting a person or group with a pack of cards with each person's name on it and ask that they be sorted into piles of 'likeness'. When the piles are finished, ask what the people in each pile have in common that makes them different from the people in the other piles. You are hoping that their answers will correspond, roughly, to the categories you got from the interview. This card sort or pile sort technique will be explained further in Chapters 11 and 15, along with other techniques suitable for emic research.

Some issues and problems

When you are doing emic research, you will find that although people may categorize information in their heads in the ways shown in our sample interview, they are so unused to being interviewed through this seemingly vague sort of questioning that their first answer will probably be: 'What do you mean, tell you about the girls in this school? What do you want to know?' Also, they are unlikely to announce the categories as clearly as in our interview, particularly when the subject is more complex. You must train yourself to listen for them. Of course, they may not start out by discussing the dimensions of the situation that interests you. They might sort their piles into 'people I know versus people I don't know' or 'people who owe me money versus people I owe money to'. You have to keep at it. If you want social categories, you can point to someone passing in the school, and say: 'Tell me about her. How is she different from you? How is she the same?' then steer the interview in the direction of social categories. Finally, you can ask these questions in a more conversational manner. The interview does not have to sound as rote and mechanical as the sample conversation, which was constructed this way to show the process.

What if people don't agree on the categories? Usually the reason you are using this method is to discover shared idea systems, not individual perceptions. If there is no agreement, perhaps none of the people with whom you are working will see things the same way, which is itself interesting. Or possibly the subject means little to them, and no one has really thought enough about it to have developed any categories.

Don't forget that any area of culture consists of multiple perspectives and interpretations. People may agree on categorizations but attach different meanings to them. Or they may feel that groupings exist, but do not agree on what they are. (We might be safe in guessing that the 'rough and ready' girls, even if they agree that such a category exists, may not see themselves in it.) Also, the categorizations occur in a particular context. If you were discussing some other important issue related to girls with exactly the same people, they would come up with different groupings. Groupings also change over time, as do their meanings and the people or items in them.

Remember, you are using these techniques for a restricted purpose: to get ideas about the way people see things in certain circumstances. For example, people tend to treat other people according to how they perceive them. (This is a version of a famous theory put forward by Robert Park in 1928.) If some girls are leaving school early because of the way they are treated, they don't have to agree with the category they have been put into, but they might still leave. In the etic research approach, you prepared a research design showing the sources and research techniques you hoped to use for each point in your research outline. You have no points in emic research, just general topics you want to explore, so the decisions you make about how to get the information are simpler. You will use emic interviews, card sorts, triads, content analysis, and other techniques discussed in Part III of this book.

The type of source — people, records, and so on — can be worked out in advance, but you will probably find that as your research progresses, it will lead you on to other sources in a snowball effect. This leads to the interesting question of how you will know when you have finished, because a snowball can keep rolling and growing. You will have finished when the group with which you are working agrees that these categories are real to them, when you go to new people and they can offer nothing that you do not already know, and when you can group people, items, or events in the same way as the local people do. Then you understand the principles, and there is no point in pursuing the categories further.

Is this information scientific or objective? After reading Chapter 2, perhaps you see that this is not the issue. The question is whether this information is useful in helping you to understand what is going on. The teacher's categorizations of 'late developers', 'gifted children', and 'children performing at grade level' are performance categories; the administrator's categories of 'late fee payers' and 'accounts paid' are accounting categories. The ones the girls gave you undoubtedly have more bearing on how they interact with each other.

What will you use emic research for? In and of itself, it provides you with local insights. You can also combine it with etic research. Before you determine your categories in a research outline, you might want to see what local categorizations exist. Leave part of your research outline blank and explore it through an emic approach. For example, in a study of why some university professors are highly unpopular with students, it is pointless to group professors by rank, which is an official administrative or 'etic' category imposed by the university. It is more likely that students are staying away because the professor has used the same notes for the last thirty years, not because she is an associate professor. However, then you might like to see whether this emic category relates to the etic categories in any way: are they full professors, or part-time professors, or professors in the sciences? Maybe there is no connection — maybe they are just lazy.

If you are taking an emic approach, you still may need to outline part of your research. If you want to explain the local setting or the school structure and are not doing it emically, you should outline those parts of the research to keep yourself on track.

Chapters 7 and 9–14 will give you more specific help with choosing your information-gathering techniques.

Further readings to help you

Kane, Eileen. 1967. 'Nonunilineality in Oceania: Review and Alternate Hypothesis.' Proceedings of the American Ethnological Society, 209–220.

Miles, Matthew, and Michael Huberman. 1994. *Qualitative Data Analysis*,

2nd ed. Newbury Park, California: Sage.

Norton, Andrew and J.T. Milimo. 1993. 'Zambia Participatory Poverty Assessment Synthesis Report.' Washington DC: World Bank. Draft.

Park, Robert 1928. 'The Bases for Race Prejudice.' *The Annals* 140:11–20.

Spradley, James P. 1979. *The Ethnographic Interview*. New York: Holt, Rhinehart and Winston.

Uphoff, Norman. 1991. 'A Field Methodology for Participatory Self-Evaluation.' *Community Development Journal* 26(4):271–285.

Wolcott, Harry F. 1984. *The Man in the Principal's Office*. New York: Waveland Press.

The Hope and Glory Vindicator

Volume 182 Issue 9   June 30, 2001

500 march against House of Peace

The City Council was told last night that allowing a 2,000-seat house of worship on a site designed for a single family house would devastate property values, poison the sewer and water supply, damage the environment, and infringe the constitutional separation of church and state. Five hundred local people presented a petition after marching from the town center.

Countering the petition were 18 busloads of church members from neighboring towns and states. Many of the visitors appeared to be people unfamiliar with the issue who were signaled by their minister about appro-priate times for applause and hissing.

Mr. Stephen Barker, president of the House of Peace congregation, said the government now expected churches to administer many of its welfare and community-service programs, such as Weight Watchers, and building restrictions damaged their ability to deliver to these ministries.

Rev. Wyman lashes House of Peace plan

In a sermon on Sunday, Rev. Dwight Wayman, pastor of the Word of God Church, told congregants to be wary of flagitious, sinful people whose only mission was to entice money from just and honorable people and usher them straight to perdition. He said the House of Peace Temple was the devil's camouflage and its leaders should be routed like the dogs they were.

Researcher gives talk

Tiffani Shapiro, an anthro-pologist on the visiting research team, gave a luncheon talk yesterday to the Busy Bee Mothers' Group. She spoke on the Hermeneutics of Phenomenology, which is the subject of her forthcoming doctoral dissertation. Mrs. Meryl 'Bob' Matthews thank-ed her on behalf of the Busy Bees. Ms. Shapiro said she was delighted to be in Hope And Glory. She is hoping to work with the group living behind the boiler factory. 'This is so exciting — anthropologists have never heard of the Mescoito Indians before — they are, like, so undiscovered. I was, like, "Wow!" when I heard about them.'

Court News

Mayor jailed for potty mouth

Mayor Randy Anderson was sentenced to 30 days or 30 dollars by Judge Dick Quinn for cussing in the presence of a lady. The mayor didn't have his wallet on him so said he'd take the 30 days. In a speech from the court steps, he said that he was going to jail on behalf of the American people and all oppressed peoples everywhere whose God-given rights were being eroded. Only last month, he said, the chief of police had tried to force his resignation, charging that the mayor had uttered a racial slur when he accused the chief of letting Judge Quinn go scot-free after getting a parking ticket. The chief insisted that the mayor is a bigot, saying, 'I've discovered a chink in his armor.'

INSIDE THIS ISSUE

5 DO YOU WANT TO EXPLAIN OR PREDICT SOMETHING?

Summary

The experimental approach involves another way of planning research. First you must pick out the effect you are interested in. Then you must pick out what you think is the cause. Then you must work out what other things might cause such an effect, and ensure that they are excluded.

Experiments do not prove or discover. They are, however, good for ruling out possible causes. You may recall that in step 5 (Box 3–1) we can use a non-experimental approach and create a descriptive research statement, or we can use an experimental approach, as we do in this chapter.

Ex post facto research means trying to work backward to establish causes after the fact. We use this a lot in daily life.

An intervention or treatment is something you expose your group to: it is the *independent variable* or *supposed cause*. The *dependent variable* is the *effect*. The experimental group is the group that receives the intervention or treatment. The control group is the one that does not.

Non-randomized experiments can be done on one or more groups. Tests can be given to the group or groups before and after, or only after. Their major feature is that (a) either they involve only one group; or (b) if two or more groups are involved, people are not assigned to them randomly.

Randomized experiments involve two or more groups to which people are assigned randomly. Tests can be given before and after, or only after.

Most explanatory social science research is done through *analytical surveys* using *correlation research* or *quasi-experimental designs*.

Experimental research is possible in the social sciences, but meeting the requirements of the most rigorous forms of experiment can be difficult.

Even though most beginners have very little opportunity to do experimental research, it is useful for you to get a basic insight into experimental design in order understand what an experiment requires, and what it can and can't do. In explanatory/predictive research, you may be looking for cause-and-effect explanations or you may be looking for some other kind of relationship — correlation, for example, in which you are trying to find out if two variables go together, like income and voting pattern. In that case, you're not arguing that income causes a particular voting pattern (or vice versa), but you may be hypothesizing that they go together in some patterned way: for example, that people with higher incomes tend to vote for conservative candidates.

Statements that attempt to explain or predict by relating two or more phenomena are called *theories*. To qualify as a theory, a statement must be testable — if not in its present form ('Gender discrimination lowers performance', which is too vague) then in a more specific version ('Girls who have gender-biased physics textbooks perform more poorly on state physics examinations than girls who have gender-sensitive physics textbooks.'). Theories consist of *concepts* and *variables*. A concept is an idea, such as 'freedom' or 'equality'. Some concepts can take more than one form and are called variables. Sex is a variable, since it can take two forms; social class is a variable, since it can take a number of forms. In our statement above, 'textbooks' is a variable, since we can have two types, gender-biased and gender-sensitive. We looked at variables when we constructed our research outline in Chapter 4.

When we relate a set of concepts/variables in a sentence, we have a proposition — for example, we related gender bias and poor performance in our earlier statement. Propositions can take a number of forms — postulates, axioms, hypotheses. In this chapter, we will look only at hypotheses. A *hypothesis* is a testable statement that predicts a relationship between two or more variables.

Explanatory and predictive research can be used to clarify matters, to present reasons, to show relationships, and to show cause and effect. In the social sciences, the most common ways of offering an explanation or prediction are through qualitative research using methods such as those presented in Chapters 11–13, through so-called thought experiments (Bernard, 1994), and through surveys such as the one shown at the end of this chapter. These are non-experimental methods. Experimental methods are not used as frequently in the social sciences for a variety of reasons, such as the inability to meet the requirements of an experiment, ethical considerations, or a desire to study something under real conditions rather than laboratory-like conditions. These reasons will become more obvious later in this chapter as we look at how to conduct simple experiments.

Whatever approach you take, you still have to refine your ideas, as you did in steps 3–5 (Chapters 3 and 4), because explanatory research demands that you be crystal clear about what you mean by each of the words and concepts you use. For example, if you are looking at whether community development projects are more successful if they are run by local government or by a community association, you are going to have to define what you mean by 'community development', 'projects', 'local government', and 'community associations'. This will allow you to make decisions about how to categorize each project and agency and to decide whether they qualify to be included in your study. Then you can go on to an experiment or a piece of correlational research. So make sure you remember how to carry out step 4 ('Developing a Rough Research Idea and Refining It'), before going any further. This is important not only for clarifying the terms of your experiment but also for describing the context of the experiment: the setting, the background, and the characteristics of the participants or respondents, etc. The research outline approach in the previous chapter will help you to lay out this descriptive work.

Cause and Effect Studies

Those who believe that the social sciences should not ape the natural sciences are critical of the idea that the notion of causality can, or should be, applied to studies of human behavior (see May, 1993, pp. 86–87). They argue that the rigid requirements which must be met in order to do experiments like those carried out in the natural sciences cannot be adapted to the social sciences, and if they are adapted, usually through a meticulous battery of compensating and checking measures, people and their responses are crammed into categories determined by the researcher. Variation, change, and, in particular, meaning are lost in the process. (They apply these same arguments to some forms of questionnaires as well, as we will see later.) Others argue more basically that the experimental method, whether used on humans or not, can't do what many of its adherents claim for it (see Cohen, 1989: 239–264). Finally, others may recognize some of these problems but feel that, all in all, experiments tell us something which cannot be accessed in quite the same way by any other method. A basic introduction to pre-experiments and experiments will not really equip you to contribute to this debate, but it will enable you to see what it takes to do experiments and, if you decide to do one, what kinds are possible, given your circumstances.

Some warnings about experiments

The most rigorous, and to some minds the only, way of establishing cause-and-effect relationships is through the experimental method and, in particular, through the most exacting type of experiment: the classic experiment or true experiment. Before we look at types of experiments, note that:

1. Experiments do not 'prove'.
2. Experiments do not 'discover'.
3. When people say 'I carried out a little experiment,' they probably didn't.

Experiments are usually carried out in controlled, artificial environments — a laboratory is one example. Many social behaviors must be studied in their natural environment for ethical, practical or theoretical reasons. For example, an experimental study of the causes of domestic strife carried out in a laboratory would tell you little about what triggers it naturally, it would probably alter the way the participants behaved, and could pose ethical problems. Finally, 'translating' the results of experiments to real-life application presents a conundrum: the more carefully you control (and therefore narrow) the experimental conditions, the more likely you are to reduce the number of situations in real life where the results will apply. If all this is true, what good are experiments? For people who can't stand any sort of uncertainty, or who are wedded to a cement-like view of 'science', they are no good at all, but then neither is anything else in the research repertoire — what you want is religion. However, experimental research does have certain strengths which are less developed in non-experimental research:

1. Experimental methods are the best methods in the social sciences for establishing causal links (even though it is debatable whether such

links can actually be proven). Experimental research can also eliminate more alternative explanations for something than non-experimental research can.

2. Experimental research can be repeated more easily than non-experimental research because of its clear-cut structures and rules. In particular, the researcher has control over the environment or circumstances in which the experiment is carried out, the composition of the groups being used in the experiment, the independent variable (the intervention which is the supposed cause), and the tests that are used to measure the effect of the intervention.

3. Experimental research, again because of its structures and rules, can isolate single factors and examine their associations and effects in a way which is difficult in real-life cluttered situations.

4. Experimental research allows the researcher to study change over time, before and after an intervention is introduced. Some experiments may last only minutes, but others may run for months or years.

We'll see what these points mean, and raise them again at the end of the chapter.

Experimental Designs

If you were asked to come up with the steps for doing an experiment — that is, for gathering evidence that one thing caused another — you would probably be able to do it, for the logic of conducting an experiment is basically horse-sense. Let us say that you want to conduct an experiment to see if a new diet will cause you to lower your weight. The diet is your cause, or *independent variable*. Your weight is your effect, or *dependent variable*. You measure your weight before you begin: this is called the pre-test. You then go on the diet, which is your *intervention*. When you finish the diet, you weigh yourself again: this is the post-test. You try, while on the diet, to control other things which might confuse the picture — for example, sickness, liposuction, etc., so that if you do lose weight you will be pretty confident that it was the diet which did it. This is the basic logic of the experimental process, and you have probably followed something like it many times. As long as you can control everything perfectly (the intervention, the tests, the other factors which might cause weight loss), you can say that the diet caused you to lose weight. However, in most research situations we don't have perfect control and so we have to come up with special designs to try to counteract this. The following sections show some of the problems which can arise and some of the designs for dealing with them.

Ex post facto research: experiments in reverse

To begin with, let's consider how people usually try to figure out things for themselves. In daily life, people often engage in what is called ex post facto reasoning, that is concluding that something that occurs before something else must be the cause of it. We see that many tedious menial jobs are held by women and we conclude that women are better at tedious menial jobs. People in Hope And Glory see a UFO, and later some of the townspeople feel they are far more tired than they were in the past. They compare their symptoms with those of people over in the mountains of East Paradise which had no UFO visit and find that those people are still as fresh and energetic as ever. People start saying that the UFO weakened them. Maybe it did and maybe it didn't. It can't be proven under these simple 'after, therefore because of' conditions.

Sometimes, an *ex post facto research approach* is the only form readily available to a researcher. We go into the Sunset Assisted Living Community in Hope And Glory and find that most of the senior citizens living there are much more mobile than in other care facilities for older people. The admission regulations seem the same as in other places, and the only thing which appears to be different is that most of them do a twenty-minute program of weightlifting each day. We form a hypothesis, or tentative explanation, of what causes the increased mobility. We will try to relate the variable 'mobility' to something else. But we are looking at an after-the-fact situation over which we have no control: an experiment in reverse. We didn't have a chance to measure the level of mobility before the weightlifting program and we don't know if other factors may have been at work. Perhaps before the program began the residents had no other activities and little reason to leave their rooms. They are moving around now because they made new friends at the weightlifting sessions and can now slip out with them to places like Winkle's Party Pak and Live Bait for a snort. Maybe the excitement and novelty of the weightlifting program had energized them. But maybe they were even more active before, and the program is wearing them down. In this case, we would have to say that weightlifting programs for older people reduce mobility. The point is, with the facts we have, we don't know enough to draw any conclusions.

Our experience, however, might lead us to design an experiment that would allow us to rule out some of the explanations that occurred to us. We would have to start with a new set of older people and assign them randomly to two groups, perhaps picking their names from a basket and putting them into two piles. By doing this, we hope to reduce the chances of all the former athletes or hyperactive people ending up in one group. Then we expose one group to the program, observe them before the program begins and at some point afterward, then compare their before and after results with those of the people who were not exposed to the program. This is a *classic*, or *true* experiment and, in an ideal world, this is what we would use.

Let's look at the less than ideal world for a moment: your own. In between these two approaches, ex post facto approaches and true experiments, are many other ways of looking at relationships between things. We will divide them into two groups: randomized experimental designs and non-randomized experimental designs (sometimes called pre-experimental designs). Somewhere among them, you may find an approach that fits your conditions.

Non-randomized experimental designs

Researchers in the social sciences often use non-randomized experimental designs. The difference between these designs and randomized experimental designs lies, obviously, in the meaning of the word 'random'. In non-randomized experiments, you don't assign people to different groups randomly. Often, this is because you cannot control what you think is the cause of whatever you are studying. If, for example, you had a theory that thunder decreases children's concentration in school, you could not arrange for thunder (the supposed cause) and you could not assign children randomly to thunder and non-thunder groups.

Sometimes, you do not want to control what you think is the cause. If you think that exposure to loud noises at birth causes slow development in children, you are hardly going to set up an experiment in which delivery rooms have or don't have loud noises and assign the mothers-to-be randomly to the two places. You could, of course, try to find hospitals where loud noises are routine, and hospitals which are quiet, then look at the results, but the infants are not being randomly assigned: perhaps the 'loud noise' infants come from underprivileged families served by poor hospitals, and this could have an effect on their development.

It often happens that all the requirements that you have to meet to perform a randomized experiment are so strict that you end up creating a totally artificial situation, one that is not very useful because you will never find such conditions in the real world. In these circumstances, a non-randomized experimental approach, or *quasi-experiment*, might be the one to try.

Box 5–1 The symbols used in experimental designs

R means random assignment
O means an observation, a test, a measurement of some sort. O_1 means the first observation, O_2 the second, and so on
X means an intervention, i.e. something done to the experimental group

To read an experimental design:

Experimental group	R	O_1	X	O_2
Control group	R	O_1		O_2
	Random assignment	Pre-test	Experimental group gets intervention; control group gets none	Post-test

Let us take one project and follow it through all the experimental types.

One-shot case study, or single group, post-test-only design

You and the team have been working in Hope And Glory for a few weeks now. The mayor is still in jail for potty mouth and has asked the rest of the team to come over and sit with him a spell while the police chief is away on a junket. But you're tied up over at Septus and Laurinda McCardle's house, sitting on the front steps with a beer and some munchies, talking research.

'How come so many of them researchers got beards?' asks Laurinda. 'Even one of the girls has got something going on there on her chin.'

'Don't start,' says Septus, scratching a dog's belly. 'I'm trying to train this here dog. Found him wandering around behind the boiler factory. Sit!' he shouts at the old dog, who regards him briefly, then closes his eyes.

Septus has a pet theory: he *can* teach old dogs new tricks. But he spent half his vacation trying to train this particular one to catch a Frisbee, and all the dog did was chew on it. Laurinda says that the neighbor's dog was seen catching a Frisbee just the other day, and, if Septus had started training this dog years ago when he should have instead of spoiling it rotten, maybe now she could have a real vacation, rather than just watch him playing with dog toys. It is obvious, she says, that there is a question of now being too old and too dumb, and you are not even certain that she is still talking about the dog. Nevertheless, Septus feels that dog training (which is his *independent variable*, or cause) will produce new tricks (which is his *dependent variable*, or effect.) In other words, he is saying that learning is dependent upon training. The thing for Septus to do is carry out a proper experiment,[1] so that Laurinda will see that he is right. This is usually a far greater incentive than any call to contribute to science. And you will probably agree to help, because the alternative is being down at the jail with the other researchers, minding the prisoners.

In fact, Septus has already carried out the weakest kind of pre-experimental design: the one-shot case study. Using the standard symbols for experiments, we can show what we have done:

One-shot case study

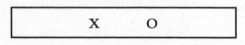

'X' stands for exposure to the independent variable, in this case dog training, and 'O' stands for the observation, measurement, or test that we make afterwards; not an observation like: 'That dog sure is as stupid as ever', but rather some kind of a test or measure of its performance. But since Septus didn't test the dog before the training, he can't be sure what effect the training has had. For all we know, the dog may have known how to catch a Frisbee before, and the training has confused him. Maybe the dog did actually learn something. We can't know, since we didn't test him first to see where he started from. Perhaps he didn't learn because something else was happening at the same time: the dog is off-color, maybe, or in a temporary slump. Even when we get a group of old dogs, which we will need anyway for the next approach, we still have exactly the same problems.

There is no point in doing things by halves, so we have to prepare ourselves properly. We are never going to be able to prove that we can teach an old dog new tricks: the idea is too vague to test. Instead, create a hypothesis that when exposed to a new and revolutionary training program, which Septus says he will develop in his spare time, old dogs exposed to the program will learn new tricks. Of course, we should make clear what we mean by 'old', 'new', 'tricks', and 'training program'. We hope we will be able to show that with this program, under these conditions, these dogs learned new tricks. This is more modest than: 'You can teach an old dog new tricks', but at least it is testable.

Single group, pre-test/post-test design
So we start again. Septus has a group of old dogs, assembled from the

---

[1] Although this is a book about *human* social research, we are using dogs in these examples. You could substitute people in each case, but they probably won't chase Frisbees for you, which is why we chose dogs.

neighbors, and this time we are going to test them first. We give them the training, and then we test them again. The advantage here is that we know how well the dogs did to begin with, and we know how well they did afterward (all this supposes that the test measures what we think it measures, see Chapter 10). The disadvantages, however, are considerable. Let's say the dogs learn something. We don't know that the training produced it. It could be that in the time between the first test, or observation, and the second one, other factors intervened: for example, the dogs are getting a better diet, or spring has arrived, or they have finally reached the point in life where they calm down and get some sense, or they were a bit depressed before the training — being homesick perhaps — but now they're back to their old selves.

Or perhaps the post-test shows that the dogs didn't learn anything. Once again, other factors may have intervened. Perhaps the pre-test had some effect on them: maybe they got fed up after it and decided they had done enough; or it could be that a short time into the training the smartest ones decided that the whole thing was rather monotonous and ran off, leaving you with the ones which have the I.Q. of a newt.

What you've done is this:

Single group, pre-test, post-test

$$O_1 \qquad X \qquad O_2$$

Time series design

We can tackle some of the problems by extending the process. Instead of observing the dogs, training them, and then observing them again, we could observe them many times, then train them, then observe them many times again. This, of course, means moving in with Septus and Laurinda, to give ourselves more scope. If the real explanation for the dogs' improvement was that they were just getting older and better, rather than learning from your program, the improvement would show as a progression that increased gradually each time we did an observation. If we were worried about whether the test itself was causing an effect, it should show up after each observation, not just the one after the training. There are a number of variations on this procedure (including using *two* groups and observing them over time but giving only one group the program), but the basic form looks like this:

Time series design

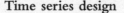

$$O_1 \ O_2 \ O_3 \ O_4 \ \ X \ \ O_5 \ O_6 \ O_7 \ O_8$$

What about something else which might be happening at the same time? How can we tell whether it, or our program, caused an improvement, if one occurred? If the other event was taking place gradually, it wouldn't explain any marked difference we observed right after our program. On the other hand, if it occurred as a single dramatic event at the same time as our program, separating the two might be more difficult. For example, Laurinda moved out right after the pre-test. The dogs might be more relaxed now. Maybe she made them nervous.

Figure 5–1 shows two possible outcomes: (a) that your program had an effect; and (b) that it didn't. Line (a) indicates that something happened at the point where you introduced your training (X). Line (b) shows that nothing happened at X, but something else was having an impact, because learning new tricks rose all through the period. Perhaps, as we suggested earlier, the dogs were gradually getting more confident as they matured.

Figure 5–1 Time series design: levels of participation

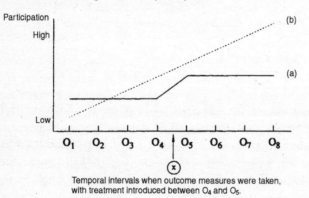

Temporal intervals when outcome measures were taken, with treatment introduced between O_4 and O_5.

Source: Judd, Smith, and Kidder (1991, p. 115)

Between-subject designs

Between-subject designs refer to experiments in which some individuals experience your program and others do not. Later, we will look at *within-subject designs*, in which the same individuals are observed to see how they perform with and without an experimental treatment.

Non-equivalent control group, pre-test/post-test design

One answer to your troubles might be to get another group of old dogs and compare the two. You will need to find homes for the first set, and start over with two sets of fresh dogs. Re-shape your hypothesis: now we are arguing that old dogs exposed to the training program will learn more tricks, or learn tricks faster, than dogs who are not exposed to the program. We will need to be clear about what we mean by 'more' and 'faster'. We might even have to define what we mean by 'dogs': no slipping some half-wolves into the untrained group, just to prove your point.

We are saying that increased learning is a result of, or dependent upon, training. Pre-test both groups. If the pre-test has some effect, it's likely to be similar for both groups. Train one group (the experimental group) but not the other (the control group) and test both groups again afterward. This approach is a slight improvement over the last one, because we have been able to manipulate the independent variable — the training — by giving it or not giving it. We also have a better basis for comparison, the control group, but we still have problems: the two groups may have been, unknown to you, very different from the beginning. One group may have been left in the local dogs' home by a passing circus, for example. Here is what we have, anyhow:

Non-equivalent control group, pre-test, post-test

Group 1	O	X	O
Group 2	O		O

How do you measure the effect of your treatment? Take the difference between the 'before and after' scores of the two groups, and subtract the score of the control group from the score of the experimental group. How do you know when the difference between the scores is large enough for you to be able to say that the treatment had an effect? This is a statistical issue, and you can learn more about it in Chapter 17.

Static group comparison

Now that you are more sophisticated, you may be worried about the effect of that pre-test. Maybe the pre-test itself taught the dogs something. Sometimes this is a valid concern, and the static group comparison is the only way to avoid it. But if we drop it and just train one group of dogs and not the other, then give them both a post-test, we could have another problem: maybe the trained group scored lower, even though the training worked, because the control group, which got a score which would nearly entitle them to enter Oxford, was better to begin with. A diagram of this approach looks like this:

Static group comparison design

Group 1	X	O
Group 2		O

Randomized experimental designs

So you probably don't need anyone to tell you what you have to do now. Get two new sets of dogs and a fishbowl. Find out all the dogs' names, put each name on a piece of paper, put the papers in the fishbowl, and draw them out, one by one, alternately putting them into two piles. A simpler method is to use a table of random numbers — see Chapter 6.

Round up all the dogs whose names are in the first pile of papers into one group, the experimental group, and put the ones whose names are in the second pile into the control group. Train the experimental group and post-test both. You've removed the effect of the pre-test and at the same time you're pretty satisfied that you've got two comparable groups. By randomly assigning the dogs, you've got around the problem of ending up with one group consisting entirely of half-coyotes. You are also not as concerned about the lack of a pre-test, since random assignment helps to reduce your worry that the two groups are unequal to begin with. Here's what we have, remembering that 'R' means random assignment:

Randomized control group, post-test only

R	Group 1	X	O
R	Group 2		O

But now that you're into the swing of things, we should consider another plan to ensure that the two groups are really comparable: the classic experiment. Randomly assign the dogs to the two groups *and* pre-test them, before we train one group and post-test both. The randomizing helps to ensure that the groups are equivalent, generally, and the pre-test tells us where each group is on the tricks scale. Incidentally, random assignment will not guarantee that the scores of the two will be identical on the pre-test. However, it should insure that any differences are caused by chance and not by other causes.

Randomized control group, pre-test and post-test

R	Group 1	O	X	O
R	Group 2	O		O

You can improve on this by adding a second control group, which receives no pre-test: this gets around the problem of the effect of the pre-test. The first control group will tell you the effect of the pre-test; the second will tell you the effect of the treatment, (X). By adding these two and subtracting them from the score achieved by the experimental group, we can estimate the effect of the treatment. This controls for the effect of the interaction between the pre-test and the post-test, that is, the subjects figuring out what the study is about and altering their responses on the post-test. Of course, if dogs could figure out what we wanted so easily, we wouldn't have had to bother with all this training in the first place. But in the case of human subjects, you can imagine that if people come to learn that you are measuring anti-Semitism in the pre-test, this may affect what they say in the post-test.

Solomon two control group

R	Group 1	O	X	O
R	Group 2	O		O
R	Group 3		X	O

How do you measure the effect your program had? Add Group 3's score, which shows the effect of the intervention, to Group 2's score, which shows the effect of the pre-test, and subtract this from Group 1's score. How do you get Group 3's score, when they had no pre-test? Since all three groups are randomly chosen, we assume that they started from the same point. Take the average of the two pre-test scores for Groups 1 and 2, and use that as an estimate for Group 3.

Finally, if you want to cover all possibilities — the effects of the pre-test, the effects of the training, random assignment among them — and also look at what has happened to a control group to which nothing has been done, we can combine the last two types of experiments. Get your dogs, randomly assign them (R) to four groups and pre-test and train them (or not) as follows:

Solomon four group design

R	Group 1	O	X	O
R	Group 2	O		O
R	Group 3		X	O
R	Group 4			O

This way, if the groups were simply getting older, or something happened between the pre-test and the post-test which had nothing to do with your experiment (fleas, for example), the effects of these, and nothing else, would show up in the final group.

How do you measure the effect of your interaction? Follow the instructions for the Solomon two control group, and in the case of Group 3 and Group 4 estimate their pre-test scores by taking the average of the pre-test scores for Groups 1 and 2.

Causation

Now that you have your results, you will want to analyze your findings. Chapter 17 shows how to do simple statistical analyses of data. But before we do that, let's look at some important issues. Does your experiment show causation? Many people make the mistake of assuming that because two phenomena 'go together' one causes the other. For example, single parenthood and poverty tend to go together. But does one cause the other, and if so, which one? Or does something else cause both? To make causal inferences, we have to have the following three things:

Co-variation: Co-variation means that two phenomena go together, and when one changes the other does. For example, gender and level of income co-vary in most places in the world — women tend to have lower incomes. To prove causation, we must show co-variation, but that in itself is not enough. We know, for example, that gender doesn't cause low income, nor does low income cause gender.

Non-spuriousness: If two phenomena go together without one causing the other, both may be caused by a third. If you had concluded that one caused the other, you would have made a spurious assumption. The usual example given here is the association between the number of firefighters at a blaze and the extent of damage caused by the fire. The greater the number of firefighters, the more extensive the amount of damage. Are the firefighters the cause of the damage? No, the size of the fire explains both. In a twist on this, however, in some parts of New York City in the late 1980s and early 1990s, you could have found a relationship between the number of police officers in a few areas and the number of drug deals and associated violence. In this case, however, it was the police officers (now ex-police officers) who were making the deals and creating the violence.

Time order. For one thing to cause another, the cause must occur first. You might think this is very obvious, as it would be in the case of an electrical shock causing death. In many cases, however, it's not so clear: are the British becoming more litigious, leading to an increase in the number of solicitors, or is an expansion in the number of solicitors encouraging an increase in the number of cases taken? Or, indeed, is something else causing both? Of course, time order alone is not sufficient to show causation, despite the old saying, 'Timing has a lot to do with the outcome of a rain dance.'

To deal with these kinds of problems, you need to do three things. First, you have to be able to *compare* the results, either within the same group before and after a treatment, or between two groups, one of which gets a treatment and the other doesn't. This will help you to see if two things co-vary — in your case, dog training and improved performance of tricks.

Second, you have to be able to *manipulate* the independent variable, that is, since you are arguing that your dog training program improved performance, you have to be able to set up the program and show that the improvement occurred afterwards. In non-randomized experiments this can be difficult or impossible to do. For example, you can't introduce a tornado in Hope And Glory to show that natural disasters encourage greater community solidarity. In true experiments, there are instances where you *can* manipulate the variable, but shouldn't, for example, wrongly tell people that their families have just suffered a bad accident to see how they respond to stress.

Third, you have to be able to *control* the research situation, so that you are ruling out other factors which might explain your findings. For example, if you give your experimental group both dog training and multivitamins, you won't know which one caused improvement in tricks performance.

If you don't, or can't, control the research situation, you will have problems of *internal validity*: you won't know whether your results are caused by your independent variable (your revolutionary training program, in this case) or by something else.

Some threats, or confounds, to internal validity are as follows (see Cook and Campbell, 1979, for a more detailed discussion):

1. *History*: The history confound is anything else that happens in the course of an experiment that may affect the results. You observe that in the spring a young man's fancy turns to love. You may conclude that spring causes this. Research now suggests that testosterone levels alter in cycles throughout the year. Which, if either, is the cause?

2. *Maturation*: Developmental changes in the research subjects over time may cause the change, regardless of your treatment: people get older and perhaps more conservative, wiser, decrepit, cantankerous, and so on. Let's say there's a lot of gender-based fighting among children in the Hope And Glory playground, and Laurinda decides that ten-year-old boys should be taught to be more aware of the need to cooperate with girls. She gets a grant from the Associated Federation of Associations and sets up a five-year training program for them. She shouldn't be surprised if the national press doesn't show up at the end of the program when they are now co-operating.

3. *Mortality, or attrition*: This doesn't necessarily mean that the participants die, although it can. It means that they drop out of the experimental categories, or out of one experimental category and perhaps into another. If there is any patterning to the dropouts, it may affect your research. For example, for years researchers have compared the health of drinkers of alcoholic beverages versus non-drinkers and found that moderate drinkers are healthier. But look at the non-drinkers: they might include former heavy drinkers who are now so unhealthy that they have had to give up drinking.

4. *Regression to the mean*: You may have caught participants who performed very well on your pre-test on a day when they were at their absolute peak, while those who did badly may have been at an all-time low. If you select these people because their extreme scores interest you, you may find that they have changed when you post-test. Is it your program, or have they just reverted to their *mean*, or average position? Sometimes, individuals are at such extremes that there is nowhere else for them to go but up or down on the post-test. For example, programs aimed at the poorest of the poor may seem to improve their lot, but it may be that they would have improved without the program, since they couldn't get any poorer.

5. *Selection interactions*: How you select the participants may interact with some of the other problems listed above and affect your results. For

example, *history* and selection can interact. Let us say the mayors in the region develop a program to encourage people to participate more in community organizations. The experimental group is Hope And Glory, but during the experimental period it loses funding for many of its organizations, largely as a result of a federal crackdown on corruption. When you discover that there is a decrease in participation in the experimental group after your program, you could conclude, perhaps wrongly, that the program isn't very good. Selection and *maturation* can also interact: one group of participants may change at a different rate than another: for example, people aged between twelve and seventeen years old change more, physically and socially, than people between thirty-two and thirty-seven years old.

6. *Testing*: People (and other animals) can be affected by tests. They can learn to perform better on them just by doing them; they can figure out what you are looking for; they can get bored, etc. Changes that you see in the post-test may be a result of these factors.

7. *Instrumentation*: This is a bit like changing the goal posts during the game. When you pre-test and post-test, the tests or measures have to be the same, and administered the same way under the same conditions. If you gave your dogs a difficult pre-test, and an easy post-test, you would probably show some improvement in scores, but it wouldn't tell you anything useful about the effects of the program. If someone is helping you and administers the tests in a different way, that, too, would confound the results.

8. *Diffusion of treatment*: This occurs when your program 'leaks'. People in a control group discover, one way or another, that you are working with an experimental group to see whether taking big doses of lemon juice gives one a lovely complexion. The control group would like lovely complexions, too, and they start taking lemon juice. Now you have two pucker-faced groups, radiant and glowing, perhaps, but no experiment.

You can probably see by now that pre-experimental approaches are far less successful at handling these problems than true experiments are, largely because they don't have a randomly assigned control group. For this reason, it is extremely difficult to use pre-experimental approaches to show causation. Table 5–1 shows the confounds associated with some of the approaches you used, arranged here from 'weakest' to 'strongest'.

Table 5–1 Experimental designs and some associated confounds

Type of experimental approach	Selection	Testing, e.g. 6	Extraneous variables e.g. 1,2,3,4	Interactive effects involving selection e.g. 1,2,3,4,5
Pre-Test–Post-Test O X O		–	–	–
Static group comparison X O O	–	+	+a	–
Non-equivalent control group O X O O O	+	+	+a	–
Randomized control group R O X O R O O	+	+	+	+

Note: A minus sign (–) indicates that the particular design has a weakness in regard to the particular confound, as explained in this chapter. A plus sign (+) indicates that the design is resistant to the confound, that is, it deals with it. A blank indicates that the confound is not applicable to that particular design.
(a) The static group and non-equivalent control group designs are resistant to the effects of extraneous variables to the extent that these variables affect both groups in the same manner.
Source: Adapted from Brim and Spain (1974, p. 18)

How can you try to get around these confounds? One method researchers use, particularly when dealing with small numbers, is *matching* the research subjects so that, for important characteristics, the participants in both groups are more alike. In pair matching, for every teenage high school dropout in the experimental group, you will have someone with the same characteristics in the control group. Each pair is matched on all relevant characteristics, such as age, sex, race. This is called *simple matching*, or *precision control*. This, as you can imagine, is a cumbersome process. Many people will have to be dropped from the experiment because they don't have a match. Another obvious problem with matching is that you might not be able to determine all the relevant characteristics which could have a bearing on your problem. (For an extended discussion of this and more complex problems associated with matching, see Judd, Smith, and Kidder, 1991, 118–123.)

Another possibility is to control for only one variable — age, for example. You can also work with averages rather than exact matches, so that each group has the same average age (also the same skewness and variance — see Chapter 17). This is called *frequency distribution control*.

The other precaution you can take to strengthen your design is random assignment, which helps to get around the problem of not being able to identify all the relevant characteristics in advance. This ensures that the distribution of any additional uncontrolled characteristics is governed by chance. You did this when you assigned your dogs randomly to the two groups, to avoid having two groups of dogs with two very different sets of characteristics. Suppose you found that the experimental group did learn more tricks, and then Laurinda points out that they were all males who had played Lassie on television when they were young, and the members of the other group were all three-legged females. What could you say? (Of course, if you didn't notice something odd about this particular situation to begin with, perhaps you shouldn't be working with dogs.) So now you combine pair matching with random assignment: pair your participants on whatever characteristic you think is important. You might pair your dogs by breed, then toss a coin for each pair, heads for Group 1 and tails for Group 2. Assign the first member of the pair accordingly, and the other member goes into the other group.

These aren't the only threats to the validity of your findings. Others arise with the researcher. For example, a researcher could affect the results by influencing the subjects in the direction desired, selecting only the experimental results which supported the hypothesis, or interpreting the results in a direction which favored it. Most researchers are ethical: these threats may occur without the researcher even being aware of it. For example, when researchers doing laboratory experiments were told that their lab animals were genetically superior or inferior (when in fact the two groups of animals were identical), the animals performed well or poorly according to the researchers' expectations.

Other threats arise with the subjects. People may not behave as they normally would if the conditions of the experiment are different from their ordinary experience; or they may figure out, or think they have figured out, what the research is about and therefore try to do the 'right' thing. People behaving in special ways because they know they are involved in an experiment is called the Hawthorne Effect, from a series of famous experiments in the 1920s and 1930s in which this happened.

When you have dealt with all these problems, you still have one more:

external validity. Can your results be said to be true for other dogs, who were not in your study? Most researchers aren't interested just in the groups they studied. They want to be able to generalize the results to a larger setting. In this context, you have three issues to deal with: how representative your group is of the larger population (all dogs in the world, in your case); whether your study's results will be mirrored in the larger population; and how 'artificial' your experimental conditions were.

Representativeness: If you are doing marketing research for a company that sells year-by-year personal planning diaries, and you want to see which of two diary types, long-term or short-term, works best for people, would you be happy to find out later that your participants were all members of The End is Nigh Society and felt there was no point in planning beyond May 12 two years from now? Or you only notice after making grandiose success claims in *Dog World* that all your dogs were Dalmatians? Your experiment might have high internal validity, but wouldn't have much general application.

Mirroring the larger population: The issue of whether your results will be mirrored in the larger population is related to representativeness. Let's say that you find that your training program works on all but 5 per cent of your dogs. Does that mean it will work on all but 5 per cent of dogs generally? Most experiments are not drawn on random samples of the entire population, and therefore there is no way to know the extent to which it will work in the larger group. It's possible to base an experiment on a random sample of the entire population (see Chapter 6) but since the aim of most experiments is to show cause and effect, or some other kind of relationship, this is not always a priority.

'*Artificiality*': A third problem is that the more carefully you control your study, the more likely you are to be moving away from real-life conditions, and therefore the less likely you are to have external validity. Are ordinary people going to feed their dogs exactly 12.5 ounces of expensive Doggo, as you did without fail in each experiment? If not, will they have the same results?

You have to balance internal and external validity. Of course, if your research has no internal validity, there is no point in worrying about generalizing the results to larger situations. On the other hand, if it's impeccably designed but meaningless in the real world, that isn't much use either. In the practical world there may be a case for sacrificing some internal validity for external relevance. You may not get published in a scientific journal but you may be able to get some sense of what works in a real situation.

Controlling variance

An understanding of the concept of variance is central to analyzing experimental results. Contrary to the popular image of 'Eureka!' experiments, the last thing you want in an experiment is a surprise. What you want to find is a nice variation (called *variance*) between two or more groups because of the variable(s) which you manipulated in your experiment. This is called *systematic between-groups experimental variance*, which, although cumbersome as a phrase, says it all. The best way of maximizing your chances of achieving this is to be careful in your handling of the independent variable, in the dog's case the training, so that the two groups really do experience two different conditions.

There are other kinds of variance which you don't want:

(a *Systematic between-groups extraneous variance*. This is caused by other factors which you didn't anticipate, or can't control, making one group different from another. The reason you don't want it is that you are not in control of something which may be causing a confusing variation in the results. This is particularly nasty since certain statistical tests can be used to tell whether there is a significant difference between the results of two groups, like the different test scores of your trained and untrained dogs, but they cannot tell you whether this variation is caused by experimental variance, as outlined above, which is what you want, or by this extraneous difference. To avoid this problem, you need to do two things: make sure that the groups experience no differences other than your program (no watching sheep–dog trials on television by one group, for example); and make sure that the groups are as similar as possible before you begin. You can do this by working out what differences might cause trouble, like sex or height, and picking dogs who are similar in these respects; or by actually inserting the difference that you are worried about into the experiment itself — if it's sex, trying the entire experiment with males and with females (discussed later under 'factorial designs'). Finally, something which would work in certain kinds of other experiments but not in your dog training experiment: use the same participants, if possible, and present them with two variations of the treatment (discussed under 'within–subject design', later). The reason, of course, that it wouldn't work in your experiment, or ones like it, is that you can't expose a group to a program, then test them, then not expose them and test them, since the effect of the program, if there is one, has already occurred.

(b A second kind of variance which you want to be aware of is that caused by *non-systematic within-groups error*. This refers to unanticipated differences *within* individuals – for example, some of your dogs are not at their best today. On the other hand, some are probably at their peak. Normally, the assumption is that these more or less cancel each other out, so that their effects are not systematic. However, error variance, like extraneous variance, can lead to difficulties in showing that your results really do result from the experiment. One way of handling this is to use a within-subject design, so you are using the same participants. Sometimes error comes not from differences within the subjects as such, but from the fact that you are measuring them differently; using a reliable test, administered the same way each time, is important. Quantitative analysis of experimental results is discussed in Chapter 17.

Within-subject designs

So far, in our experiments involving two groups, we've looked at *between-subject* differences — that is, some dogs got the training and others didn't, and you looked at the differences between the two groups. But you might want to try two different programs on the same group. This is *within-subject differences*. Mrs. Bert Whump over at President William Henry Harrison School in Hope And Glory has only one class of children to work with and she wants to know whether they do better with their math homework if she draws a happy face on the worksheet. One day she gives them a happy face worksheet; the next day she doesn't. However, other factors might intervene: she might not be wearing a happy face on one of the days, and that might affect the results. Since she can't assign the students randomly to a treatment and a control group, she could, instead, give each student a number and assign them all randomly to two groups. On the first day, she gives one group the happy face papers and the other the plain ones; the next day, she reverses the process with the two groups. That way, even if she looked like a troll on one of the days, both groups would be equally affected, presumably, and the results of both groups would reflect it. Even if she could manage to control her facial expressions, something else might intervene, like noise or thunderstorms, and this is a good way to ensure both groups share exposure to the same variables.

Within-subject experiments can be either randomized or non-randomized experiments. However, the approach has its limitations, just as between-subjects approaches do (remember the tornado variable which you couldn't manipulate?). Sometimes common sense will tell you if the treatment has a continuing effect. Let's say Mrs. Whump taught her class something one day, to see if it had any effect, and didn't teach them the next day; they would still retain the knowledge they acquired the day before. This is called a *sequencing effect*. Or, if she wanted to see whether the happy faces worked better with boys or girls, she would have to do a between-subjects experiment, because she couldn't change the students' sex.

Let's look at another situation. Suppose, instead of looking at the effect of your training program (the independent variable) on learning tricks, you were trying to find out whether the breed of the dog (the independent variable) affected the success of the training program (now the dependent variable) and you had four breeds to work with: they become Groups 1, 2, 3 and 4. You no longer have 'training' and 'no training' groups because you are not examining the effect of the training but rather the 'effect' of the breed.

This example raises another point: when 'training' was your independent variable, you could *manipulate* it, that is give it to some dogs and not to others. When we start talking about breeds, however, we cannot manipulate them — in short, one is a dachshund or one is not. The same is true of gender, as in the happy face example, as are race, height, etc. These are *subject* variables, which cannot be manipulated and cannot be used in within-subject experiments. Also, all of these examples have involved only one kind of treatment or independent variable. Experiments that involve two or more independent variables are called *factorial* designs. Suppose that, after all this, Laurinda said that because you had been giving the dogs vitamins, they were generally more alert and that had a big impact on their learning new tricks. You could perform two separate sets of experiments: one in which you did what you've already done, that is give two groups of dogs training/no training; and another one in which two groups got vitamins/no vitamins. You could compare the results. Another way, however, would be to create one experiment, with all the possibilities included:

Factor X: training	Factor Y: vitamins	
	vitamins	no vitamins
training		
no training		

By assigning your dogs randomly to each of the four groups, you can see whether one factor varies with, or depends on, the other. If, on the other hand, you were lucky enough to find that dogs who had vitamins and no training were as poor on their post-test as dogs who had no vitamins and no training, you know what you could say to Laurinda. This is called a two-by-two design, but you can have more levels of the variable, creating three-by-two designs (say high level of training, low level and none) or even more independent variables, adding, for example, age at three levels — old, very old, and just barely ticking over — to get a three-by-two-by-three factorial design. The analysis and interpretation of factorial designs is more complicated than single variable designs: there are more possible outcomes and more possible chances for threats to validity to occur.

Choosing Your Experimental Design

A boxer cannot prove he is the best in the world. All he can do is refute the claims of others that they're better, and, until he is proven wrong, we are more or less content with calling him the world champion. Something of the sort is true for the claims we make for our experiments.

Notice that we didn't attempt to prove the theory that you can teach an old dog new tricks, because to do so we would have to examine all old dogs and all kinds of new tricks everywhere, past, present, and future. A theory is usually a very general statement. In creating our hypothesis, and therefore making our idea testable, that your new program will teach the dogs you had on hand, you have already limited the scope of your statement considerably. You cannot then leap back to the general statement and argue that you have proved it. (This is called *induction*: proving the general from the particular.) But we haven't proved our hypothesis, either. Despite all the precautions we may take, our research may contain errors or be biased. The most our hypothesis can do is to withstand disproof by someone.

Experiments don't disprove theories, either. Any theory can be converted into a large number of different hypotheses. You have tested only one specific version. If you say that your experiment has proven the theory, it is like saying that because you have a piece of elephant hide, you have an elephant. And if you find that you cannot support your hypothesis, you won't know why: experiments do not tell you that. All you know is that, for some reason, it didn't work the way you expected. Any part of the process — the way you defined 'new tricks', for example — may have affected the results. The theory may still be true.

Maybe you don't care about theories — you are only worried about the one situation you are studying. Have you proved that your program taught your old dogs new tricks? To answer that, you have to satisfy yourself that you have tested all possible alternative explanations for what you found and ruled them out, which, in practice, is impossible. Could it be that just giving dogs more attention, or more air, or exposure to your own inimitable personality, accounts for the difference? Finally, experiments as such don't discover things: discovery is an inductive process whereby something is found in one instance which turns out to be true in all cases. Experimental research is deductive, proceeding from the general (the theory) to the particular (the hypothesis). In this respect, we might say that experiments are 'rigged' from the beginning: certain conditions, certain circumstances, certain procedures are specified, and the outcome we expect happens, or doesn't happen. This is not the same as discovery. Theories deal with cause and effect, but actual research can only show that two or more things go together and one comes before the other. No matter what precautions you take, an experiment is a simplified practical version of the theory, containing a lot of assumptions and articles of faith — for example, that the threats to validity have been controlled and that randomization has had the desired effect in that you haven't ended up with a group of Airedales and a group of half-coyotes. The chances of this happening are small, but they are there. So what experiments do is support theories or claims and, through repeated application by other researchers, give us more confidence in our line of thinking and suggest new ideas to be examined.

Finally, we never answered our original question: Can old dogs learn new tricks? Well, did you learn anything about?

Analytical Survey Designs

Surveys, whether in the form of questionnaires or structured interviews (see Chapter 9), can take two forms: descriptive surveys, in which the aim is simply to present a picture, and analytical surveys, in which you are trying to show a correlation between two things, such as a father's level of education and the income of his offspring. Correlational research cannot be used to show cause-and-effect relationships. It shows that two things, A and B, go together. The possibilities for causation seem to be simple: A causes B, B causes A, or something else (C) causes both. Surely common sense should be able to help you. But consider this example from research experts Graziano and Raulin (1993). You find that students' reading abilities and mathematics abilities go together. Does one cause the other? It is unlikely that high mathematics ability causes high reading ability, but it might be that high reading ability causes high mathematics ability, because reading development occurs first, and students learn some of their mathematics through reading.

You can ask a student: *John goes to the market and buys five tomatoes. If the tomatoes sell for $3 per dozen, how much change should John receive if he gives the clerk $5?* This question will measure simple arithmetic, but it also measures something else. Look at this question: *Jean va au marché et achète cinq tomates. Si les tomates coutent $3 la douzaine, combien de monnaie Jean doit-il recevoir s'il donne la vendeuse $5?* This is the same question in another language: if you do not know French well, it is more difficult to answer, yet the arithmetic skills involved are the same as in the English question. The lesson is that reading skills are required to perform well on most tests, therefore you would find a high correlation between reading skills and most other abilities (Graziano and Raulin, 1993, pp. 155–156). A final consideration is that something else causes both A and B, but what? It could be any one of thousands of things, none of which may have been examined in your study.

Despite these comments, analytical surveys are useful for showing correlations, as the following 'experiment' shows (adapted from Cole, 1980, pp. 31–41). Suppose we did a survey of a sample of 1,000 people in Hope And Glory: adults of all ages, living in the town and in the countryside, with all levels of education represented. Half the people were voters and the other half never bothered. In our survey, one of the things we asked was: 'Do you intend to make a financial contribution to the Police Association in their next fund-raising campaign?' When we looked at the replies, we were surprised to find quite a difference between those who lived in the town and those who lived in the countryside.

That is, 72 per cent of the 500 town dwellers and 48 per cent of the 500 country people intended to contribute.

Table 5–2 Percentage of people who intend to contribute to the Police Association by area of residence

Area of Residence	Percentage of respondents intending to contribute	Number of respondents
Town	72	500
Countryside	48	500

Notice the way the table is laid out. You put the independent variable as the first column and the dependent variable across the top, so that the table shows the percentage of the independent variable that is reflected in the dependent variable. In this case, residence is seen as the independent variable: residence 'determines' people's intentions to contribute to the Police Association. It is unlikely that you will try to argue that intention to contribute to the Police Association determines where people live. This is not just fussiness. The figures will be different if you do the table the other way around:

Intention to contribute	Percentage who are living in the town	Number of respondents
Yes	60	600
No	35	400

So throughout this exercise you must be certain that your tables are correctly laid out. Back to our survey. We also found that:

- More poor people said yes.
- More people who have never got a speeding ticket said yes.
- More voters said yes.

We can simply report what we found (description), or we can try to figure out why we found what we did. Why, for example, would more town dwellers say yes? Is there something about living in town that encourages people to contribute to civic causes? If that is the case, we should try to find out more about the tradition and see if similar ideas can be encouraged in other groups But let us say we know the town dwellers and the country people well, and they both place a high value on civic responsibility. So it is not town dwelling, as such, but rather something associated with being a town dweller. But what? Maybe more of them are voters? But when we sort our town dwellers and country people by voting, we find the results shown in Table 5–3.

Table 5–3 Percentage of people who vote

Area of residence	Percentage who vote	Number of respondents
Town	50	500
Countryside	50	500

Thus we see that it cannot be that more town dwellers said yes because more were voters. So we consider wealth, thinking that country people are living by farming and may be poorer these days, but town dwellers have paid employment and are more likely to be able to contribute. However, when we sort the groups by residence and by income, we find they look more or less like the table above. Let us form a hypothesis: remember the stories in the newspaper about people being arrested in speed traps? Hope And Glory is a small town, and the people who live in it walk most places. The people affected by the speed traps are usually tourists and those living outside the town who have to drive. Could it be that town dwellers are more likely to say they are going to contribute to the Police Association because they have not been caught by the police chief in speed traps, and people who have not been caught in speed traps are more likely to contribute to the Police Association?

We have to find information in our survey to support four statements:

1. Town dwellers are more likely than country people to say they will contribute to the Police Association.
2. Town dwellers are more likely not to have received speeding tickets.
3. People who don't have speeding tickets are more likely to contribute to the Police Association.
4. Town dwellers are more likely to say they will contribute to the Police Association because they don't have any speeding tickets.

We have already shown in Table 5–2 that statement 1 is correct. Now we need to look at statement 2. We sort our two groups by whether or not they have received a speeding ticket (Table 5–4), and find that fewer town dwellers have speeding tickets.

Table 5–4 Percentage of people who have speeding tickets by residence

Area of residence	Percentage who don't have speeding tickets	Number of respondents
Town	85	500
Countryside	40	500

For statement 3, we need to do a different kind of sorting: of the people who don't have speeding tickets, how many intend to contribute to the Police Association? (Table 5–5)

Table 5–5 People intending to contribute, by speeding tickets

Have speeding tickets	Percentage intending to contribute	Number of respondents
No	80	625
Yes	26.7	375

Thus, of the 625 people who don't have speeding tickets, 80 per cent intend to contribute, and of the 375 who do have speeding tickets, 26.7 per cent intend to contribute.

The last statement, that town dwellers are more likely to say they will contribute to the Police Association because they haven't received speeding tickets, is not based on any grand theory, although the last proposition in a set of statements like this often is. In our case, it is a simple fact of proximity to work and shops: town dwellers in Hope And Glory don't need to drive as much as country people. We look at our two groups and pick out the people who are intending to contribute. How many of these don't have speeding tickets and how many do? Notice that you are now dealing with three variables: residence, intention to contribute, and reception of speeding tickets, all in one table (Table 5–6).

Table 5–6 Percentage of people intending to contribute to the Police Association by residence and speeding tickets

| | Percentage intending to contribute | |
Area of residence	No speeding tickets	Speeding tickets
Town	80 (425)	26.7 (75)
Country	80 (200)	26.7 (300)

Note: The figures in parentheses show the number of respondents

Thus, 80 per cent of the 425 town dwellers who have no speeding tickets and 80 per cent of the 200 country people (340 + 160) who have no speeding tickets intend to contribute, while 26.7 per cent of the 75 town dwellers who have tickets and 26.7 per cent of the 300 country people (20 + 80) who have tickets intend to contribute. Clearly the deciding factor is not town dwelling or country residence but possession of speeding tickets, and vengefulness. This is the process we have followed:

We find an independent variable that is associated with the dependent variable; we then find a test factor that might explain the relationship between the dependent and independent variables. To see if we have found the correct test factor, we examine the relationship between the independent and dependent variables, which remain constant throughout one analysis, separately within each category of the test factor. If the test factor is the right one, the percentage difference should be less in each category than it was in the original two-way table (Cole, 1980, p. 41).

In our case, in Table 5–2, the percentage difference between town dwellers and country people is twenty points, and in Table 5–6 the percentage difference between them in each category of the test factor is zero. In real life for you to get a finding as neat as a zero difference is unlikely. If the difference was large, you would start looking for something else as an explanation, but if it was small, although greater than zero, could you be happy with your results? Look at the section on statistical significance in Chapter 17. To do research of this sort, your survey has to be comprehensive enough to include questions covering the likely factors, but the possibility still exists that some other fact covered in your survey explains the findings just as well as speeding tickets. What you have done here, as you would with an experiment, is to rule out factors, not prove.

References and further readings

Bailey, Kenneth D. 1994. *Methods of Social Research*, 4th ed. New York: The Free Press.

Bernard, Russell. 1994. *Research Methods in Cultural Anthropology*. Newbury Park, California: Sage.

Brim, John A. and David H. Spain. 1974. *Research Design in Anthropology: Paradigms and Pragmatics in the Testing of Hypotheses.* New York: Holt, Rinehart and Winston.

Cohen, Bernard P. 1989. *Developing Sociological Knowledge: Theory and Method*, 2nd ed. Chicago: Nelson–Hall.

Cole, Stephen. 1980. *The Sociological Method: An Introduction to the Science of Sociology*, 3rd ed. Chicago: Rand McNally.

Cook, Thomas D. and Donald T. Campbell. 1979. *Quasi-experimentation: Design and Analysis Issues for Field Settings.* Skokie, Illinois: Rand McNally.

Graziano, Anthony H. and Michael L. Raulin. 1993. *Research Methods: A Process of Inquiry*, 2nd ed. New York: HarperCollins.

Judd, Charles M., Eliot R. Smith, and Louise H. Kidder. 1991. *Research Methods in Social Relations*, 6th ed. Fort Worth, Texas: Holt, Rinehart and Winston.

May, Tim. 1993. *Social Research: Issues, Methods and Process*. Buckingham, England: Open University Press.

The Hope and Glory Vindicator

Volume 182 Issue 12　　　　　　　　　　　　　　　　June 21, 2001

Rev. Wayman supports new church

Rev. Dwight Wayman, formerly one of the major opponents of the proposed House of Peace Sanctuary, said in an open council meeting last night that there had been some public confusion about his position. 'I welcome the Sanctuary as an important move forward in the ecumenical development of this community. They are holy servants whose message resonates and articulates with the pastoral needs of this community. As a minister of religion, it is my responsibility to empower this righteous group to bring our community closer to God.'

Council to investigate signs

Angry council members demanded last night that the person responsible for the large signs which have appeared in Hope And Glory be apprehended and punished. Deputy Mayor Laurinda McCardle said the signs, which appear at four different entry points to the town, are obviously the work of a 'dim-witted pervert'. She cited two, in particular:

If you speed
or try to pass
Chief De Witt
Will nail your ~~xxx~~ driver's
licence

Another reads

Rich or poor,
car or truck
Chief De Witt
~~Don't give a~~

Mrs. McCardle said that even though the last line was nearly painted out, it still gave a bad impression. 'They look like they were writ with a kid's red crayon.'

The mayor agreed the person responsible for ordering the signs should certainly be identified, and perhaps even jailed. 'Mercy me,' he said, 'we have enough impediments to development in this town without adding more.'

INSIDE THIS ISSUE

6 WHO WILL BE IN YOUR STUDY?

Summary

Some of the words in this chapter have popular as well as statistical meanings: population, universe, sample, random. The statistical meanings are the ones that matter here.

You can study the *population* or *universe*, that is all the people or items in a group, or you can take a sample and study some of them.

Sampling can be divided into two types. In *probability sampling* everyone has a chance of being selected, but in *non-probability sampling* some people have no opportunity to be included.

There are several types of probability sampling. In a *stratified random sample*, you can make certain that subgroups you think are important are not left out. You can use *cluster sampling* when you cannot get a list of people to choose from.

You use non-probability samples when you cannot meet the conditions of probability sampling or when you do not need to. *Purposeful sampling* means deliberately choosing people because they have some characteristic that interests you. *Quota sampling*, while not a probability sample, is like stratified random sampling in that it allows you to make certain that groups you think are important are not omitted.

To take a sample, identify the population from which you want to take the sample, get a list of their names or get some other way of identifying them, and select the sample.

Sample size is determined by a specific formula rather than by choosing an absolute number or by taking a proportion of the population.

This chapter gives you more help with step 7: making decisions about sources of information. Are you going to study everyone within the group that interests you or only some of them? How do you decide? If the answer is only some of them, how do you choose which ones?

When it comes to statistics, most people have a combination of deep mistrust (what, for example, are 2.3 children?) and deep reverence (when flying in a plane). Consider the following, for example, which manages to sound 'scientific' and dodgy at the same time: 'Ten per cent of men in Great Britain are colour-blind. Sixty per cent of men have painted the interior of their homes in the last twelve months. [Therefore] one house in six is the wrong colour.' (*Observer Magazine*, January 24, 1992, page 10)

When you study an entire group, whether the study is of the attitudes of all supermarket owners in a town, of all the children in a pre-school, or of all the public parks in a county, you are studying the *population* or *universe* — that is, all of whatever there is. Strictly speaking, you are studying some of the characteristics of these people, and it is these that constitute the universe. If, for example, there are 25 public parks in your county, that is all there are. There are, of course, more public parks in the rest of the country, but you are restricting yourself to one county, so 25 constitutes the universe. If the number of people or items studied is sufficiently small and accessible for you to question or examine them, you are taking a *census* rather than a sample. On the other hand, when you study the characteristics of only some of the people, situations, or items within the group, you are taking a *sample*. Sampling has been used to provide some of the major findings that we read about in newspapers and magazines, such as the results of voting polls, most surveys, and experimental results of various sorts.

The words 'population', 'universe', 'census', and 'sample' can be confusing, because they have popular as well as statistical meanings. We think of populations as large and samples as small, but populations can be quite small. For example, if you want to study a single kindergarten class, all the children in it form a population even though the class might only consist of ten children. A sample, by contrast, can be large. A national sample of kindergarten children could include hundreds or thousands of children. So if there are 300 public parks around the country, and you select a sample of 25, your sample will happen to be the same size as that of the universe in our previous example about public parks. So size alone does not tell you whether a universe or a sample is being used.

Samples have a number of advantages. Studying the entire group may take too long and cost too much, both in money and in opportunity time. In an entire region, for example, by the time you asked every woman with children under five whether she would use a day care system and what kind of system, those particular children under five might be too old to use it. Also, you may not be able to compare answers given at the beginning of a long study with those given at the end. The labor market may have changed, so that fewer or more women are working outside the home than at the beginning of the study. Obviously, you want your sample results to be similar to those you would have got by studying the entire group, if the entire group is what you are interested in. You cannot ensure that it reflects the population unless you carry out an identical study of the entire group. However, you can develop a sampling plan that enables you to say that your finding will not be different from the universe figures by more than, for example, 2 per cent (this is called the margin of error) more than 99 per cent of the time (this is called the probability or confidence level). Both of these must be set before you can determine your sample size, although these are not the only factors to be taken into account (see Fowler 1988, p. 41 for further discussion).

Probability Sampling

If you want to be able to specify your study's margin of error and confidence level, that is if you want to be able to say how close your results would be to those obtained from the entire group, you must use a probability sample. This is one in which it is possible to specify for each member of the universe the probability of being selected. This probability need not necessarily be equal. It just needs to be known. Such a sample, if properly drawn and not invalidated by non-sampling errors, allows you to extend or generalize your results to a larger group without studying the entire group. Non-sampling errors are mistakes that have nothing to do with how you took your sample. Some common non-sampling errors occur when a researcher asks ill-conceived questions or records the answers wrongly, or when two researchers administer the same questionnaire in different ways. We will look at this again later. Three basic types of sampling fall into the category of probability sampling: random, stratified, and cluster.

Simple random sampling

Simple random sampling is useful when you have a homogeneous population, that is the members are similar in terms of the characteristics that interest you, such as level of education. In this kind of sample, each member of the universe has an equal chance of being selected. For example, 200 people are participating in a new speed-reading program and you want to study the performance of 50 of them. You can put the 200 names on individual slips of paper, mix them up in a big bowl or box, then draw out 50. However, a more common approach these days is to give each of the 200 people a number. Then get a table of random numbers, which can be found in many statistics textbooks or which can be computer-generated, and which will look like Table 6–1. Believe it or not, the numbers in Table 6–1 are not real random numbers. We just made them up for this chapter. Strange as it may seem, you cannot make up your own random numbers. You must use a proper table constructed by people who make their living at this sort of thing. This has nothing to do with union rules. If you make up your own numbers, they will reflect your unconscious preferences for certain numbers and your dislike of others.

Table 6–1 Example of part of a table of random numbers

	1					2					3 (etc.)
	41	85	63	17	06	19	22	93	15	09	⇨
	68	01	19	18	89	30	72	99	13	17	
1	18	33	57	04	11	13	68	14	23	27	
	59	72	66	29	35	58	93	46	99	36	
	02	64	09	25	80	06	13	37	13	02	
	63	00	96	15	49	12	08	93	48	25	
	04	54	88	56	42	05	19	33	58	66	
2	70	18	06	99	87	95	43	12	73	22	
	14	51	38	23	02	28	61	15	18	43	
	16	98	45	19	44	74	55	95	41	67	

3
⇩
(etc.)

(Chart continues across for a total of ten blocks, and down for a total of ten blocks.)

To use a table of random numbers, find a point of entry into the chart using two numbers, say the first two numbers on a piece of paper money or the last two numbers of the first listing from a telephone directory opened at random, or the first or last two numbers from an automobile registration number. Let us say the numbers are one and two. Flip a coin to see which will be your first number. Let us say that it is two. Go to the second block across, in the first row (block 2, row 1).

Take the first three digits in the first line of block 2.1. (Three because your universe number has three digits. If you only took two, people whose numbers were above 99 would have no chance of being picked for your sample.) If your universe was 10,000, you would take the first five digits. The first three digits are 192, so select the person who is numbered 192 on your list. The number below is 307, but you do not have a slip numbered 307 as yours only go up to 200, so you move on to the first three digits of the next number, 136. In the fourth line you have no number 589, so skip it and move on to the next line for number 061. If you should come across the same number twice, skip it after you have selected the slip the first time. When you get fifty slips, stop. There will be fifty numbers in a column. If you run out, continue upward from your starting block. Then move to the next column if you need more.

What we are doing is called *sampling without replacement*, which is the most common method used when doing a survey. When we began drawing from our sampling frame of 200 people, people had a 1 in 200 chance of being selected. However, after we have drawn out 25 names, people have a 1 in 175 chance of being selected. (The only way around that is to put the names which have already been selected back in, and continue drawing, ignoring any that appear a second time or more. This is *sampling with replacement*. This is not used in simple random sampling.)

It is obvious from all this that statisticians who specialize in sampling mean business if they are this fussy before you even begin. It is also obvious that you have to get a list of people taking the speed-reading program before you can number them. This list is called a sampling frame. In many instances, no such frame exists — for example, you are unlikely to find a list of all people who are trading drugs illegally, or all men who wear their shirts tucked into their undershorts. In cases such as these, this method cannot be used. Notice that this whole procedure is somewhat different from what most people think of as a random sample. Two friends of your mother, a few women from the credit union, and a group of civil servants waiting for a bus do not constitute a random sample, or if they do it would be difficult to say of what.

Notice also that taking a probability sample does not mean that your group is necessarily representative, or that the people in it are independent of one another. For example, let us say that you are taking a random sample of people from Hope And Glory. You draw number 048, which is Randy Anderson, and number 334, which is chief of police, Leland DeWitt. One might say they are independent, certainly, although, as it happens, both of them have the same father, Bert Whump, a fact which none of them knows. But representative? It doesn't matter — the only claim which a probability sample makes is that each eligible person had a known chance of being selected.

A variation of a simple random sample is a systematic random sample in which you decide your sample size, say 120 in a population of 600. Divide 600 by 120 to get 5, choose any number between 1 and 5 to get the first number in your sample, then choose every fifth number after that until you have selected 120. Systematic random samples involve less work than simple random samples, but problems can arise if the sampling frame is patterned in a way which will affect your results. Let us say the sampling frame is a church seating list for a particular Sunday. The ushers sit at the beginning of each pew, and each pew is full and holds ten people. By taking the first person and every tenth person thereafter, you could end up with a sample consisting entirely of ushers. In a cinema survey of filmgoers' views on the film being shown, you could take every twentieth person going toward the back and end up with a sample of couples who may have missed the film entirely.

Nevertheless, a systematic random sample is very useful when you don't have a sampling frame. Let's say you want to talk to people walking along Route 123 in Hope And Glory: you may recall that almost no one, except the chief of police, is actually driving on it anymore. You want to get their views on how their lives have changed since the new speed limits have come in. There is no sampling frame for users of Route 123, but you can take a systematic sample as long as you can assume that people will appear in a random manner, and that enough of them will keep coming along for you to get your required number. You might not if the chief closes the highway after getting wind of your survey. But consider the advantages over a random sample: for that, you would first have to list all the people who appeared on the highway, then take a sample, then go and find them again.

Stratified random sampling

If your population varies — let us say some have a primary education, some have been to middle school, and some have attended secondary school — and you want to be sure people from each group appear in your sample, we would divide them into the three groups first. Then, numbering the members of each group separately, choose a random sample of each before combining them again to study them. This way, all three groups will be certain to be in the study. This works if the groups are of roughly equal size. What if they are not of equal size? Suppose you want to find out about attitudes toward higher education for women among 1,000 people in an urban area. Perhaps you suspect that attitudes vary by ethnicity and you want to be sure to have people from each group in your sample. You are drawing a sample of 200, and there are only 60 Nigerians and 40 West Indians among the 1,000 people. Your simple random sample might not contain people from all the ethnic groups in the area — for example, it might contain no Nigerians or West Indians at all.

To prevent this from happening, take a stratified random sample. Divide your sampling frame into ethnic categories — Nigerians, West Indians, and all your other groups and then take a sample of each. *Proportionate stratified random sampling* adds one more dimension: work out the percentage of the total that each ethnic group forms (6 per cent are Nigerians, 4 per cent are West Indians), and draw a random sample from each category that reflects its proportion in the population. So your sample of 200 will include 6 per cent, or twelve, Nigerians (6 per cent ∞ 200) and 10 per cent, or eight West Indians. Stratified sampling can reduce the costs of sampling considerably. If you wanted to ensure that a simple random sample contained two West Indians (or perhaps a disproportionate number, to make a meaningful comparison), you would have to increase the sample size substantially, and would end up with many more people than you wished to have in the other categories just to obtain the desired number of West Indians (see Fowler, 1988, pp. 24–26, for more discussion of this).

You can stratify on more than one characteristic — for example, you could add gender to the ethnicity variable, and have male Nigerians, female Nigerians, male West Indians, female West Indians, etc., drawing samples from each.

Cluster or area sampling

Even if you had all the money and time in the world, you might not be able to take a probability sample, either because a sampling frame does not exist or it is flawed. Imagine using the telephone directory for your city or town as a sampling frame. Who would have no chance to be included in your study? Who would be there, but underrepresented? Who could appear more than once in the list? Sometimes, no list of any kind is available: all good teachers, all people of mixed-ethnicity parentage, all teenage girls with children.

A third kind of random sampling, which helps to deal with this problem, is cluster or area sampling, which is the least expensive type of sampling for large studies but also tends to be less precise. It is useful when you are attempting to study something for which no sampling frame is available at the highest level from which you wish to sample. For example, perhaps you are studying long-term unemployed people who are retraining in various technical programs in a region and there is no list of their names. In such a case, proceed as follows:

1. Divide the region into parts such as counties, towns, or whatever kind of unit is appropriate. Number the counties and take a random sample of them.
2. Subdivide the selected counties into, for example, educational districts. Number them and take a random sample of these districts.
3. Find the technical courses or institutions relevant to your study within the selected districts. If there are many, number them and take a random sample. Go to those that have been selected and study the entire institution, or get the enrolment lists and draw a random sample from them. You may have more or fewer stages than this, but the advantage is that you now have a random sample without ever having had a list of all unemployed people taking technical courses in the region. The disadvantage is that the selected clusters are usually more homogeneous and less representative of their fellow clusters than one might wish.

Notice that you are not taking samples of *people* from the region or county. From the region, you are taking samples of counties; from the county, samples of educational districts, and so on. You only select people for your study when you get to the institution. Notice also that while you are saving time and money, you are also having to take a series of samples, which increases the possibility of errors

Non-probability Sampling

When you use non-probability sampling, some people will have a higher chance than others of being included in your study. For example, you decide to talk to a sample of local schoolboys at the end of a school day to find out how many of them walk six miles to school through the snow, carrying only a cold potato for lunch as you often did yourself and are quite fond of telling others. You put some questions to every tenth boy who comes out the front door. This seems very 'scientific' and impartial. Think, however, of all the boys who will have no chance to be included, for example, boys who left early because they have to walk through six miles of snow; boys who were kept behind as a punishment because they laughed at boys eating cold potatoes for lunch, etc. With a non-probability sample such as this, you have no way to predict whether your results are similar to those you would have obtained if you had used the entire population.

Purposeful sampling

Non-probability samples — such as quota, purposeful, snowball, and convenience samples (explained later in the chapter) — are taken when you cannot meet the requirements of probability sampling or are satisfied, for whatever reason, that the group you have chosen meets special requirements that do not involve generalizing your results to the larger group. Patton (1990) calls this purposeful sampling: getting 'information rich' material from special groups. He lists fifteen different types of purposeful sampling for evaluation studies.

For example, you may want to understand the difficulties that sight-impaired people face in finding employment, in order to make a film that will educate potential employers. An intensive study of a small number of the sight-impaired might lead you to a fuller understanding of their lives and problems than a broad survey of much larger numbers.

Sometimes you might want to select a community or group because it represents some dimension that interests you. For example, you have prepared a brochure on the importance of voting. You can afford to prepare only one, so you want to be certain that it will motivate a variety of target groups. You may first try it on typical groups — say communities where people have always had typical voting patterns. Does it meet their concerns, answer their questions, and make them want to vote? If it doesn't, you will be missing a big segment of the population. Then you will also need to look at groups which reflect an extreme; for example, groups which almost always vote. If they are not moved by your brochure, it's unlikely that the 'harder cases' will be. Finally, you may want to try your brochure on the 'harder cases' — people who never vote. If it works on them, you might conclude that it will work on anyone. Purposeful sampling is also used to select focus groups — for example, if you want to find out about the technical performance of the new sound system you have invented, you will convene a specially chosen group of audio engineers or a group of musicians to discuss it rather than the general public. Similarly, women who have had a mastectomy will be more helpful in a discussion of various prostheses, rather than women randomly drawn from the general public.

Quota sampling

One common type of non-probability sample is the quota sample. This is very similar to proportionate stratified random sampling — the population is broken into groups, and each group is represented in the sample in the same proportion that it represents in the larger population. However, the members are not selected randomly.

You may want to do case studies to see how nurses' careers are structured, rather than gather extensive survey information to see exactly how many nurses do what or hold an attitude about something. In such a case, identify the types of nurses from whom you need information, and then find people who represent each of the types. For example, if you are looking at trained nurses, you might decide that operating theatre nurses, pediatric nurses, and psychiatric nurses are important to your study. Choose people who fall into each of the types rather than spend time on elaborate sampling procedures. If your numbers are very small, and you have several variables, there's a danger that some of your variables will be missed out. A way of getting around this is *dimensional sampling*. You want both male and female nurses and you are worried that there won't be enough male nurses in some of the categories. Make six categories: theatre, pediatric, and psychiatric nurses, male and female, and draw the appropriate numbers from each category.

Other types of non-probability sampling

Both purposeful and quota sampling are non-probability, that is, not everyone has a known chance of being included in the study. Other types of non-probability samples include convenience sampling, in which you just take the handiest people, and snowball sampling, in which one person sends you on to another. Guba and Lincoln (1989) use a snowball sample by asking each interviewee to name someone who would hold very different opinions from those of the interviewee until they have a picture of the concerns, issues, and interests in relation to the groups involved in an evaluation. It is possible to take snowball samples on a probability basis, as well. Start with a group of people, interview or survey them, ask them to provide new names, and draw a random sample. Keep doing this as you move through each successive stage or wave of people.

You are not restricted to using only one form of sampling. A sampling design often involves a combination of methods. For example, if you wanted to study businesses located in the main shopping streets in a number of small communities across the country, you could divide the country into appropriate units and use cluster sampling to select some. You could then break those selected units into smaller units again, and then into streets, which could also be sampled. Finally, the businesses could be chosen by systematic sampling, perhaps every tenth entrepreneur on a street. However, some enterprises can suffer in this selection method, for instance, tattooing salons could be left out entirely because they occur infrequently.

They could, of course, be identified and added to the sample, if it were important to include them. Purveyors of pornographic videos might also be overlooked — they might be 'hidden' in alleys, etc., so you might use a snowball method, in which one pornographer sent the interviewer along to another, and so on. In our earlier example (p. 100) about the attitudes of various ethnic groups to higher education for women, you could combine stratified and cluster sampling by stratifying first so that all ethnic groups are covered, and then use cluster sampling to identify the people. Once you have taken a survey of your chosen sample, you might want to pick out some people who might help you to understand the issue better — for example, women who are opposed to higher education for women even though they are highly educated themselves.

Sample Size

Most social science research texts do not give you a formula for computing sample size, and this book is no exception. The reason for this is that in the case of probability sampling, choice of sample size is dependent upon having a knowledge of statistics and being able to relate your particular piece of research to the types of statistical tests and procedures that are appropriate to it. This requires an extensive knowledge of all the alternatives, and is particularly important if you are trying to test a hypothesis. Most people, including many researchers, do not have this kind of background. The simplest thing to do, therefore, if you are doing research in which you will eventually have to decide whether to accept or reject a hypothesis, is to be very clear in your mind about what you need to know. Then, before you begin to do any research, consult a statistician for advice on the appropriate sample size. (Statisticians tend to get quite annoyed if they are consulted when it's too late.)

Non-probability sampling

You will probably be pleased to know that the warning in the previous paragraph does not apply to non-probability sampling. Statisticians have no interest in non-probability samples, and no rules are laid down for selecting sampling size. Why? If you cannot take a probability sample, you cannot use the statistical tests that allow you to make claims about the representativeness and significance of your findings, so the statistical rules for computing sample size are irrelevant.

Perhaps, however, the issue is not whether you can or cannot take a probability sample. You may feel that you do not need to. Let us say that you are trying to understand cultural patterns, much as an anthropologist would. Because some ideas and patterns are culturally shared, you can reach the point of diminishing returns, in terms of information, fairly quickly: 10 people may be able to tell you what 10,000 would. Most people, men and women, young and old, in Eyesore-on-Thames, will tell you that middle-aged male senior civil servants do not paint their fingernails. That is a cultural pattern or 'rule'. Asking a carefully selected sample of 250 people would probably not enlighten you much more than asking 20. You can check your information by using other methods, such as observation. You will probably see some exceptions. Ask people why. Maybe a subset of rules is involved. Perhaps male nail-painting is OK for costume parties. Or it is acceptable for men to have paint on their nails if it is a sign of honest work such as house painting and isn't applied deliberately.

Probability sampling

Here is where the statistics police will have something to say. The larger your sample, the smaller the difference between the results you will get from the sample and the results you would have got had you studied the entire group or population. This difference is called the sampling error. Obviously, the larger the sample, the smaller the sampling error, providing the population is relatively heterogenous, which it often is not: if you took a 99.9 per cent sample you could be fairly certain that your sampling error would be very small. But if you are taking a sample, there is little point in taking one that constitutes 99.9 per cent of the entire group. However, you would still like to get a level of precision that makes your findings useful. They will not be perfect, but they will be close enough for what you want. So what is a good figure? Fifty per cent? Thirty-five per cent?

We have asked the wrong question. Many people are not aware that it is not the percentage or proportion of the entire group or population that matters. In one of those maddening features of statistical logic that appears to fly in the face of common sense, increasing the sample size proportionate to the entire group does not reduce the sampling error in the way you would expect. Instead, the relationship is based on the square root. This means that to reduce the sampling error by 10 per cent you would have to increase the sample size by 100 per cent, which in many cases is not worth the extra trouble. Sampling error depends on several things, but not on the proportion that the sample forms of the entire group or population. Instead, it depends on the size of the sample itself. This is a not a particularly difficult concept to grasp once you have a basic understanding of statistics. Most of the books listed at the end of this chapter explain simple statistics, or a statistician can help you.

Even when you have your sample size, you need to calculate how many people you need to start out with in order to get the required number in your final results. For example, if you need 200 usable questionnaires, and assume that 80 per cent of your people can be reached, 70 per cent of those will respond, and only 95 per cent of these will complete the forms correctly (5 per cent will muck them up in some way by not answering some questions, writing illegibly, etc.), your formula is 200 divided by 0.8 divided by 0.7 divided by 0.95 = 376, which is the number of people you will have to start with. Sobering, particularly if you don't have that many people in the group to begin with.

Sampling and Non-sampling Errors

Sampling error, as we saw earlier, refers to the difference between the results you got from taking a sample and those you would have obtained if you had studied the entire group or population. For example, perhaps 18 per cent of a community of 100 can read, but the results from your sample show that 45 per cent can read. This is a serious difference and something is wrong. A difference of 10 per cent or more is bad here, and the size of the acceptable difference gets even smaller the larger the sample you use (see Mitton, 1982, Chapter 11 and Appendixes 1 and 2, for clear, step-by-step explanations of these matters for non-statisticians who need to know more about statistics). Maybe you used an inappropriate sampling design or sample size, both of which are sampling errors. But another possibility exists: non-sampling error. If you used other interviewers to help you, maybe they did not follow your instructions. Perhaps they talked only to the younger people who have had a chance to go to school, and they ignored the elderly, or perhaps people who could not read refused to be interviewed, or maybe the answers were recorded incorrectly.

These kinds of sampling errors can and do occur unless you monitor the research closely. But sometimes research in non-Western countries presents additional possibilities for both kinds of errors. In terms of sampling error, you may have problems getting an accurate sampling frame or people may be inaccessible, but the possibilities of non-sampling error are even greater, partly because many research techniques are based on assumptions and experiences drawn from Western societies, so that the information you are getting is flawed. Here are some assumptions to watch for:

- That the instrument, such as a survey or test, the language, the concepts, and the circumstances of the research are meaningful and acceptable to the person who is responding.
- That people are accustomed to making individual assessments or judgements. Among people in some ethnic groups, doing this as a

family or other group may be more common. Sometimes people are baffled at the notion that assessments can, or should be, made. 'Are you satisfied with your life?' in some ethnic groups may be like asking most Westerners, 'Are you comfortable with the notion of gravity?'

• That people's answers reflect something meaningful in their lives, and that this corresponds to what the researcher is seeking.

Other problematic issues of this sort are discussed in Chapters 9 and 10. But there's a lot more... Statisticians would not have such a fearsome reputation if this were all there was to the subject of sampling, nor would they be writing books called *Statistics Without Tears* (Rowntree, 1991). For further guidance, consult Rowntree or the books listed at the end of the chapter. Once you have the basics, you might find a statistician to advise you on how to apply them to your particular project.

References and further readings

Casley, Dennis J. and Krishna Kumar. 1988. *The Collection, Analysis and Use of Monitoring and Evaluation Data*, Chapter 6. Baltimore: The Johns Hopkins University Press.

Casley, Dennis J. and Denis A. Lury. 1982. *Monitoring and Evaluation of Agriculture and Rural Development Projects*. Baltimore, Maryland, and London: The Johns Hopkins University Press.

Fowler, Floyd J., Jr. 1988. *Survey Research Methods*. Newbury Park, California: Sage.

Gonick, Larry and Woollcott Smith. 1993. *The Cartoon Guide to Statistics*. New York: HarperPerennial.

Guba, Egon G. and Yvonna S. Lincoln. 1989. *Fourth Generation Evaluation*. Newbury Park, California: Sage.

Kraemer, Helena Chmura and Sue Thiemann. 1987. *How Many Subjects? Statistical Power Analysis in Research*. Newbury Park, California: Sage.

Freedman, David, Robert Pisani, and Roger Purves. 1991. *Statistics*. New York: W.W. Norton.

Mitton, Roger. 1982. *Practical Research in Distance Teaching*. London: International Extension College.

Patton, Michael Quinn. 1990. *Qualitative Evaluation and Research Methods*, 2nd ed. Newbury Park, California: Sage.

Pyrczak, Fred. 1989. *Statistics with a Sense of Humor*. Los Angeles: Fred Pyrczak.

Rowntree, Derek. 1991. *Statistics Without Tears*. London: Penguin.

Salant, Priscilla A. and Don A. Dillman. 1994. *How to Conduct Your Own Survey*. New York: John Wiley and Sons.

Slonim, Morris James. 1960. *Sampling*. New York: Simon and Schuster.

Wilson, Ken. 1993. 'Thinking About the Ethics of Fieldwork.' In Stephen Devereux and John Hoddinott, eds., *Fieldwork in Developing Countries*. Boulder, Colorado: Lynne Rienner Publishers.

PART III

TECHNIQUES AND STRATEGIES: THE BASIC TOOLS

The Hope and Glory Vindicator

Volume 182 Issue 14 August 4, 2001

Jail shock: 50% increase in prisoners

De Witt seeks more jail funds

A 50% increase in the number of prisoners in the Hope And Glory jail has led Police Chief Leland De Witt to seek an increased appropriation from the City Council. De Witt told the council that not only were the numbers increasing, but the prisoners were now drawn from all sectors of society, high and low, local and non-local folks, putting a great strain on the jail's resources.

In the first sign of accord between the chief and the mayor in years, Mayor Randy Anderson agreed that there was a 25% increase in prisoners, and that the situation was appalling.

Mayor gets writ of habeas corpus

Mayor Randy Anderson, in a special sitting of the court last night, asked Judge Dick Quinn for a writ of habeas corpus for four researchers including Ms. Sharon Darwin, Mr. Pius Gallagher and Mr. Jean-Luc Peillon, who are currently detained in the Hope And Glory jail. Mayor Anderson said he had invited the team to do some research on the eight prisoners in the jail, in order to keep them occupied while Chief of Police Leland De Witt was away in Gstaad, Switzerland, at the Hope And Glory Local Police Association Conference. 'He just took off with basically no-one left to mind the store,' said the mayor. 'When he come back and saw so many people in the jail, he high-tailed it off to the City Council, claiming a 50% increase in his numbers, and looking for more money. Truth is, it's a 33$\frac{1}{3}$% increase. Now he won't let them go because he'll look even dumber than usual.'

Deputy Mayor Mrs. Laurinda McCardle pointed out that it could be 50% or 331/3%, depending on how you figured it. 'Four is half of eight, or 50%, but it's 331/3% if you take four out of twelve. Depends on what you're trying to prove.'

Judge Quinn called a recess to do some figuring. 'All these gozintas got me confused,' he said. 'Four gozinta eight, four gozinta twelve — I gotta clear my head.'

Rev. McCardle ordained

Mrs. Laurinda Wilcox McCardle, who goes by her maiden name, was ordained yesterday as a minister of the House of Peace Temple. Rev. McCardle said she was attracted to the temple's ministry because of its gender equality. The temple has strict requirements for joining its ministry: all applicants must have a clean driving license and be clean shaven. The Rev. McCardle completed her studies by email through the House of Peace's CyberSpace Seminary.

Wedding Plans Announced

Mr. and Mrs. Leland De Witt announce the engagement of their daughter, Sylene, to Darren 'Skip' Anderson, son of Randy Anderson and the late Mrs. Cheryl Anderson. The wedding is set for next June, when the bride graduates from Harvard Law School. The groom has just assumed a position as assistant professor of creative writing at Princeton.

INSIDE THIS ISSUE

7 CHOOSING YOUR TECHNIQUES AND STRATEGIES

Summary

The problem or issue you are studying should determine the research technique you use, not the other way around. Each research technique is a specific tool; there is no 'all-purpose' technique that is good for every situation.

The information you get will be 'stronger' if you use *triangulation*, that is, as many techniques, researchers, sources of information, methods, and possible explanations as you can.

Perfecting your technical research skills is important, but some common practical problems in getting information can seriously interfere with the validity or soundness of your research.

The aim is to do research with people, not on people.

This chapter provides more help with making decisions about information gathering techniques.

Your Research Strategy

Many people unthinkingly choose their technique before they plan their research. They say: 'What we need is a survey on why ice cream can cause an ice-pick-like pain in the head sometimes' or 'I'm going to do an experiment to see whether it is true that people tend to look like their cars.' (Each of these would be a poor choice of method for the topic, unless you were simply interested in what people thought about these issues.) Often people choose a technique simply because they don't know any others. Most people, for example, have been on the receiving end of a survey but don't know much about other ways of getting information. Even professional academics tend to fall back on the techniques most commonly associated with their own fields — for example, participant observation in anthropology, testing and measurement in psychology and education, surveys in sociology, or documentary analysis in history — without considering whether the technique actually gets at what they want to know. Some people even choose a technique on the grounds of comfort — they like it, or more likely, they do not like another technique: for example, someone who decides to do a study which will only involve studying some documents in the library because he would cut his legs off rather than go door to door with a survey.

However, picture detectives investigating a murder. Will they be satisfied simply to look up old records and see if any of the suspects had committed a crime before? Or to ask the suspects if they had done it, and leave it at that? In real life, detectives might invite everyone in the neighbourhood to fill out a questionnaire asking where they were at the time of the murder, if they had seen anything suspicious, and so on. Then they might interview some suspects personally. They would probably watch their movements as well and look up old records to see if any of them had committed crimes before. And, of course, they would examine the crime scene carefully to see if it told them anything.

Asking, watching, and looking up are all research techniques, each of which gives you a different angle on the situation. Each research technique is designed to get certain kinds of information and does not get others. For example, questionnaires tell you what people say they think and do, but participant observation can help you to see what people actually do (but only if they are prepared to let you watch). Using as many approaches as possible is part of a process that many researchers call triangulation: that is, getting the data through a variety of different strategies so as to strengthen and verify the research findings (Webb and others, 1966, p. 174). You can triangulate in a variety of ways.

Methodological triangulation

Methodological triangulation is when you use more than one technique to get the same information. Interviewing, administering a questionnaire, observing, and examining documents on the same phenomenon provide 'stronger' information than using a single technique. Each technique addresses a different aspect of the phenomenon. The use of complementary methods also reveals discrepancies that a single technique might not. For example, you are doing a study of work practices. Management tell you that women are paid less in a factory because they don't do heavy lifting. You see two women wrestling a quarter-ton tea trolley up some stairs. Another is holding up a large trap door with her head while a fellow hammers a few nails into the frame. You are told (a) the first women are ladies who are 'making tea', and (b) the second woman is 'just helping out'. Here you are interviewing and observing, and getting different results from each method.

Think of a situation in your life where good information would be important to you. Suppose you have a niggling idea that your spouse is intending to sell the house and use the proceeds to run off with someone. Perhaps the real estate agent or the local builder? Or the handyman? Who? You ask your beloved and she says certainly not. For many people, this would be enough, but you, as a researcher, know that science demands more of you. Besides, you know this spouse as of old, and nothing would surprise you. The bloom has gone off the relationship. You suspect she is fooling around. But with whom? You have interviewed your spouse and now you might want to interview the local real estate agent, because you notice a few strangers poking around your bathroom from time to time and making impertinent comments about the wallpaper in the bedroom. The estate agent seems to be out each time you phone. You scan the newspaper ads and find a house listed as 'in serious need of decoration and repair', with your builder's telephone number. Could this be your house? Hardly, although you have been a bit remiss lately, what with all the sleuthing. You've noticed that the builder seems to be avoiding you. You also observe a heavily be-wigged and mustachioed man on the drainpipe under your bedroom window when you arrive home early — an interview with him might put your mind at ease. Under interview, he says he is cleaning the gutters. Late that night, you observe a man's wallet under your side of the bed. You open it, and it belongs to…

But enough of this. These lurid details are not of interest to us scientists. What is important is the fact that you used a variety of research techniques: interviews, observation, looking at documents. Some of them gave conflicting information; others reinforced information you had got from other means. Figure 7–1 shows how these research techniques complement and support one another. No single technique duplicates exactly the function of the rest. Each technique yields information that only it can obtain, but also reinforces the other techniques.

Figure 7–1 How different research techniques complement one another

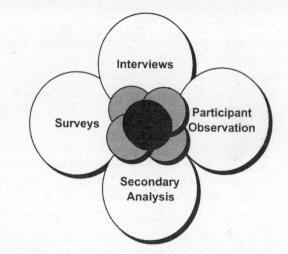

Each of the petals in the figure is a research technique. At the center they all overlap, and on the sides each overlaps with its neighbors. The clear areas represent the material that this technique particularly addresses; the shaded sections are research areas that can be studied using either, or preferably both, techniques; and the center is that part of the research that yields information through use of all the methods. If you had to stake your life on which of these three areas is likely to represent the most accurate, complete research information, you would choose the center, in which you got the information through interviews and questionnaires, reinforced it by observation, and checked it through documentary analysis. In the center section you are getting not only what people say they do and what you see them doing, but also what they are recorded as doing. The second strongest areas of information are the joint sections, where two research techniques can both address the same topic. Finally, in the clear areas you are relying on only one technique, often the only one available for the kind of information you need, but you are getting no verification from any of the other techniques.

Incidentally, it was the real estate agent.

Data triangulation

Data triangulation occurs when you:

- Examine the influence of different times, past and present, on whatever you are studying.
- Examine the influence of space, that is, compare the data with that from other places (other villages, other schools, and so on).

- Examine the person at different levels: the individual level, the group level, the collective (entire group) level. A young woman may say she would prefer to elope rather than have her parents pay for a big wedding, but her parents hold different views, as does the groom, who wants a huge bash, and she can see their point as well. Does she decide at the individual level or the group level in the end?
- Examine the situation from different angles: a school from the point of view of the head, the teachers, the students, the observer.

Researcher triangulation

Researcher triangulation is when you use more than one person to collect the same information. This allows us to examine the influence of the researcher, and if the researchers can draw on a variety of perspectives, to get stronger information. Different kinds of researchers offer different insights — in the right circumstances older and younger people, men and women, insiders and outsiders, people of different disciplines can all bring valuable perspectives. If you are studying a band of cat burglars, for example, you may find that your 'outsider' status gives you a broader perspective, allowing you to question things which the burglars themselves take for granted, such as how they know someone is a good mark. On the other hand, 'insiders' (i.e., some cat burglar research assistants whom you have enlisted) will have special knowledge and insights which will help you to ask more relevant questions and to understand the meaning of what you find. Because insiders are familiar with the situation, they can read nuances and often be more aware of what people are *not* saying or doing. They may be trusted more by the participants, and people may feel that because they probably know a lot already, they might as well tell them things they would not tell outsiders. Finally, if your team includes people from different disciplines, they will be able to look at different aspects of cat burglary — the economics, the legal aspects, the psychology, the sociological structure of the group, etc.

Theory triangulation

Theory triangulation is when you use different, or competing, theories to try to explain what is happening. Let us say that teachers in a mixed-sex school are treating the girls as though they were pretty little things who are less able to do math than boys are, and indeed, the girls are doing poorly on their mathematics examinations. You might consider two theories: one that argues that the teachers' behavior has no effect (in which case you will look for another explanation), and one that argues that it does. The first theory is called 'relative deprivation' theory. People are thought to estimate their well-being and satisfaction by comparing themselves to particular peer groups (here, the other girls), and not necessarily to people whom they see as being different (the boys). The girls, therefore, do not mind this treatment. They would only mind it if some of the girls were treated as geniuses and others as brainless twits. You could also look at a theory developed by Robert Park (1928) which, put simply, argues that people behave the way they are treated. In this case, the girls are being treated as if they were stupid and are performing accordingly. Notice in this example that you are waiting to get your results before looking for a theoretical explanation. This is an inductive approach. However, you can also start out with a theory or theories, and set up situations in which you can test them. This is a deductive approach (see Chapter 2).

Your Research Techniques

This section gives you a summary of the techniques discussed in this book, to help you choose those which are best for what you want to do.

Secondary materials and document analysis

Secondary methods use materials collected for other purposes: censuses, surveys done for other projects, school records, departmental figures, even reference books. The advantage of such materials is that it is almost always quicker and cheaper to use them than to collect primary data. The disadvantage is that because they have probably been collected for another purpose, they may have a different focus, or even have gaps or hidden flaws. For example, almost everyone in Hope And Glory has neglected to pay taxes since around 1940 but they haven't been caught, so you won't find a record anywhere. Another disadvantage is that people tend to place too much trust in recorded material, simply because it is on paper. Once immersed in secondary materials, people also tend to lose sight of their aims, gather too much, and become too comfortable at the desk to do any necessary primary data collection.

Statistics are another kind of secondary material. They have the advantages and disadvantages mentioned above, plus some of their own. They may be poorly collected, out of date, incommensurate (for example, the categories could change from one year to the next), or inadequately disaggregated (lumping rural and urban together, or males and females). Sometimes, because the units of study differ (postal districts, school districts, political divisions, official population units, etc.), the numbers may not reconcile.

Of course, in addition to using material recorded by others, you can also commission your own materials — such as school essays or records kept of hours worked, etc.

When would you use secondary materials?

Once you are satisfied about their validity and relevance, use them whenever possible:

- to develop a research idea;
- to identify gaps in information which will have to be collected through other methods;
- to get background information;
- to establish baselines and indicators if you want to monitor and evaluate changes.

Surveys

A survey can take the form of a questionnaire, in which the respondent fills out a form, or an interview schedule, where the researcher asks the questions directly. Both of these are commonly referred to as 'questionnaires', but the professional literature makes this technical distinction. Questionnaires require more care than interview schedules, since the researcher isn't interacting with the respondent; they usually require respondent literacy, although recently researchers using participatory learning approaches (PLA) have devised ways of using symbols which allow non-literate people to fill out some kinds of forms.

A survey can tell you *what is happening*: what people say they do, think, or feel, if you ask the right questions, if they understand what you are asking, and if they are able and prepared to give you the answers. In addition to being descriptive, surveys can also be analytical, that is, they can test hypotheses. For a good example of the latter see Stephen Cole's elegant example in *The Sociological Method* (1980). But if you want other dimensions of reality, such as 'how?' and 'why?', you have to use other techniques as well, such as case studies, focus groups, unstructured interviews, and observation. Finally, surveys will provide information on selected variables, but not much on their context, and the replies, when added up, will not provide a whole picture but a set of responses to specific questions.

If you want to know broad cultural patterns (the proper way to behave at a British funeral; appropriate clothing for common events), you don't always need a survey. But in rapidly changing situations, the pattern and the actual practice may differ (mothers of very young children are thought of as working mainly in the home — do the facts support this?). Also, when views vary, are they associated with particular sub-groups, such as the young or the more educated? In these cases, a survey is very useful. A useful alternative to the large traditional survey is the mini-survey: these contain between 15 and 30 questions, are given to a sample of 25–70 people, have 'closed' questions (the possible answers are provided) and can be analyzed by hand. A good knowledge of the group is important in choosing the sample and framing the answer choices, but the mini-survey provides a quick way of getting information.

Advantages

The advantages are obvious: a standard instrument can be given to large numbers of people to get a broad set of representative (assuming correct sampling) responses to questions about attitudes, perceptions, behavior. Computerized processing and analysis can bring speed and rigor which has to be obtained in more cumbersome ways using some other methods.

Disadvantages

People are often more comfortable with surveys than other techniques, such as interviews or observation, for several reasons: they produce numbers, which allow measurement and ranking; you feel you are relying more on an objective 'instrument' than on fallible people; the same instrument can be used on many people, and the analysis process seems straightforward.

Surveys are often thought to be quick and easy ways to get information, but by the time a good survey of 2,000 people is designed, administered, and processed, at least a year may have passed. And one sure axiom is that one's IQ seems automatically to drop 40 points when designing and administering a survey. It's an unforgiving process in which mistakes are usually discovered only after 1,800 questionnaires have been filled in and returned.

If you plan to work with immigrant groups or cultural minorities, or if you will be working in a non-Western society, there are even more serious problems. First is that while no other research technique has been the subject of more manuals or textbooks, almost all of the assumptions on which it is based are Western. The ordering of questions (general to particular, for example) is based on Western ideas of information flow; the circumstances in which the survey is administered (to individuals); the one-way movement of information (informant to researcher); the idea that one *can* have an opinion on some things (such as satisfaction with one's spouse) or that it is possible to speculate on hypothetical situations ('If you had enough money to send your children to secondary school, would you…?') are all ideas which are acceptable to Westerners. Knowing how to write culturally meaningful questions requires considerable knowledge of the culture. There are no universal all-purpose questions. This presents an additional problem: if you want to do comparative studies between different cultural groups, how can you write questions which are meaningful to each and still be able to compare the responses?

And in the end, the issue of precision arises again: the rigor of modern statistical analysis cannot compensate for poor design, confusing language, cultural bias, irrelevant questions, and telling the interviewer anything to get rid of him or her. The solution to all of this is to be certain that a survey is what you need, complement it with other techniques (this is also the case with all the succeeding techniques discussed below) and get a skilled survey specialist who is familiar with the culture or prepared to work with people who are.

When would you use surveys?

You should use surveys when you need broad-based data, a high level of precision, or when statistical background data are needed and lacking. You should also use them when you are testing alternatives, since you will need statistically accurate information. Surveys are good in situations where complex, detailed information is needed in exactly the same form from many people. They are also good for discovering variations on patterns which you have discovered through other methods, such as observation, case studies, or focus groups. But don't use a survey because you can't think of anything else, or because you are looking for 'objective' information. Once you've decided that you need survey information, see if a survey has already been done which might save you the trouble (you may have to check its credentials; find out the details of sampling, design, administration).

Surveys can be used:

- early in a project to get a general picture, or to decide how to focus your research;
- to look at an issue, or a small number of issues, as the main focus of your research, or to reinforce other methods;
- to get baseline information, so you can tell later on what changes have occurred. This is particularly important if your task is to monitor or evaluate a project. Again, at the end, you might then use a survey to compare the 'before' and 'after'; in other words, to evaluate.

Measures

Measures, which include scales and indexes, are particularly popular with psychologists and educators, although there are many sociological measures, as well. Measures are standardized instruments which examine everything from alienation to modernity to intelligence. As is the case with surveys, they allow you to compare responses.

Advantages
Measures have the same advantages as surveys, but since one of their purposes is standardized use in many settings, they have usually been subjected to more testing and analysis.

Disadvantages
As is the case with surveys, people may be likely to use measures because they are handy, easily administered instruments. When considering a measure, the first question to ask of a particular instrument is: 'Is it valid?' There is a lot of debate over whether something measures what it purports to measure. Witness the debate on IQ tests, and the conclusion of some experts that 'it measures something, all right, but what?' This problem is compounded when the measure is used in a non-Western society or with a minority cultural group in Western society: not only may it not measure what it claims to, but even if it does, it may not address dimensions which people in that society consider important.

Most measures are culturally biased, not simply in content, but in underlying assumptions (the idea that someone will 'project' an aspect of personality in response to seeing an inkblot, for example). Even measures which consist only of pictures can be culturally biased: the Thematic Apperception Test consists of nine picture cards with items such as violins and Western domestic settings and clothing. If these are not adapted, people are likely to read them according to their own cultural perceptions or be distracted by irrelevant items, such as background household details in the pictures. If they are adapted, the responses can't be compared with those obtained from another version. A good discussion of these problems is found in Brislin (1990).

When would you use measures?
- At any time in the research when comparing two or more populations (girls and boys, for example) on relative performance, aptitude, etc.
- As with surveys, in monitoring and evaluation.

Interviews
Structured interviews, mentioned earlier, are one kind of interview, but here the term will be used to refer only to semi-structured and unstructured interviews. Unstructured interviews are usually used at the

beginning of a piece of research, to get a broad picture. They are particularly good when you know little or nothing about a situation. They usually have the appearance of informal conversations, following the social rules of the society concerned. The skill of doing unstructured interviews rests on having a general agenda of questions, but being flexible enough to drop them, change course, follow new lines, etc., as needed. Key informant interviews are one type. These can occur early in the research, but a good key informant can also help to put information into context and interpret information obtained through other methods. Where do you get questions for interviews? Chapter 4 will help you, and the Appendix shows another way: it is a grid for assessing a problem or situation on thirteen dimensions, for a total of 169 questions, each of which can be adapted more specifically to your situation.

But you don't necessarily need questions. One special type of unstructured interview is the emic interview, based on a concept discussed in Chapter 2. The emic interview is based on a special perspective: rather than 'What do I see these people doing?', as in surveys, when the researcher chooses the issues and questions, the emic approach asks: 'What do these people see themselves doing?' The researcher creates only the first large question ('What happens in this school all day?'; 'What kinds of people are staffing the Ministry?'). Each subsequent question is based on categories which the respondent has identified.

The same kind of information can be obtained by writing items on cards (names of people in the community, for example) and asking people to sort them into categories (people who are 'old residents' who make their life in the community, versus people who regard the community as a dormitory suburb) then exploring what makes the people in each pile similar, and how they differ from those in the other pile.

When would you use unstructured interviews?

- When you want the broadest possible picture.
- To get insights from people with special knowledge or experience.
- When you are working in unfamiliar circumstances.

Semi-structured interviews have a clear pre-determined focus, but flexibility in how the questions are put and allowance for open-ended discussion of the answers. They can be held with individuals, but also with groups, such as focus groups. Community interviews involve putting a small number of carefully selected questions to a group, on the theory that the responses of 30 individuals to a survey question do not necessarily add up to the same kind of information one gets from putting the same question to 30 people in a group. In focus groups, six to twelve members work through a small number of questions or a problem. They are chosen for a particular insight which they may bring to the discussion (not necessarily an 'expert' insight).

These are not quick and cheap ways of saving time on individual interviews and careful sampling. They require a lot of preparation if they are to be useful, and you have to know why you are choosing to involve the people concerned.

When would you use semi-structured interviews?
- When you want to explore something in some depth with a group or a number of individuals.
- When you need to get a better understanding of information gathered through other means.
- In evaluating and monitoring projects.

Participant observation

Usually, when people say, 'I did participant observation', they didn't. Participant observation should not be confused with frequent visits, staying in a place while administering a survey, or generally just 'being there' and mixing with the local people. Participant observation is a standard, rigorous anthropological strategy. It is a 'strategy' because it is not a single technique but a combination, involving interviewing, observation, using key informants, doing case studies, and gathering secondary data, as appropriate. Participant observation requires prolonged contact, either by living in a community or participating regularly in activities, as in a school study (see, for example, Wolcott's study, *The Man in the Principal's Office* (1984).

Advantages
A combination of long exposure, triangulation, and first-hand empirical data allows you to get insights and meaning not easily available through other methods.

Disadvantages
Participant observation can take a long time, perhaps a year or more, requires considerable experience to adapt the techniques as the situation evolves, and calls for a resilient personality. Because the aim is a holistic picture, it is done in a small setting (community, group), and, unless the setting was deliberately chosen to be representative, the results may not be useful beyond that setting.

When would you use participant observation?

Generally, when you need to understand the whole context of a complex situation, as in the case of pilot projects, projects which have gone wrong, etc. It is also useful when trust and rapport must be established over a period of time before people will cooperate. It is invaluable in periods of rapid change, when there is a considerable gap between what people say (the ideal) and what they do (the real).

Case studies

Case studies are also strategies in that they use interviews, observation, and documentary materials to provide insights into how and why something works or doesn't work in real life, over time. Case studies are made over time, in natural settings, and can focus on individuals (girls who have become pregnant and managed to stay in school); on programs (the kinds of program which enables them to do so); on organizations and institutions (why a school has such a good record of preparing girls for secondary school); or on processes (how decisions are made in a family or a department).

Advantages

Case studies give 'in-depth' information, showing how processes work, patterns are lived out, the ideal is converted to the real, change occurs, and many other important areas which 'fall through' when using surveys and other techniques.

Disadvantages

They are more time-consuming than most people expect and require a mix of research skills. They will not give a 'representative' picture but rather a detailed understanding of a situation, institution, family, individual, etc., insights from which will complement information obtained through broader methods, such as surveys.

When would you use a case study?

You can use case studies to illustrate patterns which have been identified using other methods. For example, interviews or surveys identify children who have succeeded in remaining in school despite all the odds — how? They can also be used to show variations on a pattern; why something works in one situation and not another. Finally, they are helpful in understanding the difference between the ideal and the real: how things play out in reality as opposed to the way they are supposed to.

Rapid low-cost methods and participatory learning approaches

Rapid low-cost methods (often called Rapid Rural Appraisal or RRA) grew out of agricultural research, anthropology, and action research in the 1970s to meet the need for cost-effective, timely, valid research. Field research takes from four to ten days and usually involves a small team composed of people from different disciplines (education, sociology, economics, for example) both sexes, locals and outsiders, and any other bases which are important for understanding the situation. Preliminary planning and post-fieldwork analysis can bring the total time to as much as three or four months. The brevity of research is compensated for by:

- *careful attempts to reduce bias* (talking to the less powerful, the poor, the less accessible, women);
- *triangulation* (there is a 'basket' of over thirty techniques, and multiple researchers are used);
- *deliberately seeking diversity and variation*;
- *valuing local insights and perspectives*, which are as essential as any other 'expert' contribution;
- *reversing learning* (local people are the teachers, and researchers the learners).

Researchers use a combination of techniques, as appropriate: semi-structured interviews, mapping, ranking, using matrices, observation, key informants, small surveys based on (non-random) purposeful sampling, and many others. A more recent (late 1980s) strategy is Participatory Rural Appraisal, or PRA. It involves most of the same techniques as rapid assessment. However, while the rapid assessment perspective is *extractive* (researchers take information from local people), PRA is participatory, that is, local people, facilitated, if necessary, by outsiders, determine the agenda, collect the information and analyze it, assess options, and mobilize for action. PRA need not be 'rapid'. It also supports local capacity-building: once a group or community learns the procedures, they can apply them to new problems. The entire family of participatory approaches, which includes many others, is referred to as Participatory Learning and Action, or PLA.

Advantages

Information has validity, is cost-effective, and, in the case of rapid assessment, quick. It compares favorably with material collected through conventional methods in similar situations. It capitalizes on local knowledge, and allows local priorities and solutions to emerge. It builds local research capacity.

Disadvantages
Since these strategies are designed to gain understanding of specific communities and situations, comparing results from one place to another is difficult, although not impossible. They are not particularly useful when you are looking at issues whose causes or remedies lie at national or regional level and have to be addressed at that level, rather than by local people. For example, if the public library system is under-funded, or a national examination system is outdated, local action isn't the most effective place to start; nor is it useful if a solution involves legal changes, or national coordination.

When can rapid assessment and PLA be used?
- when identifying needs and issues in a holistic context;
- when identifying local constraints and opportunities;
- when assessing strategies for action;
- when developing projects where participation is crucial to sustainability;
- when identifying appropriate resources;
- when implementing projects;
- when refining planned/existing projects;
- when evaluating projects.

They also have some uses beyond the local level:

- to improve decision-making and policy-making through local feedback;
- to assess capabilities of organizations to meet clients' needs;
- to 'tailor' projects better to meet local needs.

Experiments

Establishing cause and effect can, theoretically, be done in one of two ways: performing an experiment, or using statistical controls. Usually, when people say, 'I performed an experiment', they didn't. To perform a true experiment, you need a treatment group and a control group, with individuals randomly assigned to each. The groups are measured (the pre-test) on one or more dependent variables (performance in reading, desire to send daughters to school, etc.). An intervention is introduced to the treatment group, and the dependent variable is measured again (the post-test) for both groups. In the social sciences, true experiments are usually conducted by psychologists. Even in a true experiment, a lot of hitches (called 'confounds') can affect the validity of your results. For example, you compare people who drink alcoholic beverages with a control group of people who don't to see if drinking could be a cause of heart attacks. To your amazement, the non-drinkers have more. Is drinking good for you, or could it be that the 'non-drinkers' include a lot of physical wrecks who have been forbidden on health grounds to drink? That is a confound, and there are a number of others. Being exposed to your test can affect children in a classroom — for example, perhaps they do better on the post-test just because they learned something from doing the pre-test. Or what you are trying with one group can 'leak' to the group which wasn't supposed to be experiencing it. Or children may change in the course of your experiment simply because they matured, not because of your intervention.

There are a number of different experimental designs which are specifically intended to get around these and other confounds. In general, some type of true experiment has a better chance of doing so.

Much more common in the social sciences are quasi-experiments, which educators, sociologists, and social psychologists often perform; and natural experiments, which are what anthropologists commonly do. Quasi-experiments usually take place in field or natural settings. The researcher introduces an intervention, but the members of the treatment and control groups are not assigned randomly. For example, parents in one village get a sensitization program, and parents in another don't. Both are measured on their attitudes to girls' education before and after.

Natural experiments just happen: the researcher makes no intervention or assignment of people to groups. For example, in one community, people are avid supporters of the local credit union; in another, they aren't. The researcher works backward to try to find out what the 'intervention' was.

If you are doing a study to see whether a new computer program for teaching students French works better in your local school than the efforts of Miss Knosewhistle, who taught you thirty years ago, it is possible that you can perform a true experiment, that is, you may be able to assign students randomly, and control for many confounds because you are working in a situation over which you have some control. However, it's much more likely that the very best you will be able to do is perform a quasi-experiment. Even then, you'll have some problems. For example, you may not be able to get a valid control group that 'matches' your treatment group, and that hasn't been and won't be affected by factors that differ from those which also apply to your treatment group. Another approach for assessing impacts is statistical: collecting information on the relevant variables over several time periods, and analyzing them through a variety of statistical procedures such as factor analysis, multivariate analysis, and multiple regression. Chapter 5 looks at these and other issues in more detail.

Advantages

The advantages of an experiment are obvious — rigor, leaving less to chance, having more confidence in your results. (One 'advantage' which many people assume experiments to have actually doesn't exist — experiments don't prove, they just rule out alternative hypotheses, in the same way that winning the boxing championship of the world doesn't 'prove' you are the best, it just rules out from title contention the others who were entered.)

Disadvantages

The difficulty of meeting the requirements of experiments, the cost, the time.

Other approaches

If you read the professional literature in a social science discipline, you will come across many research approaches, such as project measurement systems, constructivism, and others. The reason they are not disclosed here is that they are strategies, rather than techniques. Strategies are combinations of traditional techniques, tailored for a special purpose or directed at a special audience. The techniques themselves are not new. Participant observation, for example, is a long-established strategy. It includes more than simple observation: it involves interviewing, learning from participating, using secondary analysis, and so on, to cross-check the results obtained from one technique and get greater depth of understanding. Another strategy which we will look at is participatory learning and action, or PLA (Chapter 14). The aim of PLA is to work with local people to set the research agenda, collect the information, analyze it, and create their own action programs. It uses most of the qualitative techniques described later in this book, often expressed through visual devices, such as matrices and diagramming. These enable local people, including non-literate people, to describe and analyze their situation and to work out options.

When you come across an approach that sounds like something entirely new, such as constructivism (see Guba and Lincoln, 1989), remember that the traditional techniques — asking, listening, watching, reading — have not changed. It is how they are combined and for what purpose that makes the strategy new. Before casting your lot in with a new strategy, take care to find out what its purpose is and whether it meets your needs. No strategy meets every need.

Style

The ideal, when possible, is to get information the way local people do. See if you can adapt any of their methods to the more structured needs and time constraints of your research. People spend a great part of every day gathering enough information about themselves, other people, and their environment to run their lives. Picture people sitting at the lunch counter in Winkle's Party Pak and Live Bait, in Hope And Glory. They are most comfortable with the information-getting methods they use themselves: conversations (interviews) and keeping an eye out (observation). One of the reasons, for example, that most people are not particularly happy with questionnaires is that this is not one of the usual ways people anywhere in the world get or give information, whereas interviewing (conversations) and observation are. We still use questionnaires, however, because they have advantages in terms of efficiency, standardization, and cost.

Words and numbers

Some of the techniques in the following chapters are more likely to produce qualitative data (information in words) while others are more likely to produce quantitative data (information in numbers). As should now be clear, no form of information is more scientific than another. The chief of police in Hope And Glory claims a 25 per cent increase in his prisoners, and he's right — he had eight and then there were twelve. Does using the words or the numbers make more sense here? As you will see in Chapter 16, almost all material in words can be converted to material in numbers. It might make it easier to handle, but it does not make it any better. In the Hope And Glory example, it is deceptive.

The instrument

The techniques for collecting information (Part III of this book) and the methods for analyzing the information (Part IV) involve different tools. For example, in informal interviews, the main instrument is the researcher, who develops his or her skill, personality, ability to see patterns, draw conclusions, and so on. With other techniques, such as questionnaires, tests, and measures, the main instrument is the device itself. Both involve human judgment in developing the instrument, knowing how and when to use it, and determining what procedures are best for analyzing the results. Neither is intrinsically more 'objective' or 'scientific'.

The paradigms

In our discussion of the debate in the social sciences today (Chapter 2), we looked at several paradigms, or philosophical approaches to viewing the world and collecting information about it. Most techniques do not fall neatly into one philosophical approach or another. For example, a questionnaire, often thought of as the plaything of positivistically-oriented social scientists, can use questions or issues that you have discovered through a phenomenological approach. In contrast, interviews and participant observation, which may seem to allow much more scope for the individual's perspectives or actions to emerge, may simply be cunningly constructed around the researcher's predetermined categories.

Validity, reliability, accuracy, and precision

In your research, you need validity (is it sound?), reliability (would you get the same answers if the research were done again?), and, to a somewhat lesser extent, accuracy and precision. Think of your watch. It is a valid measure of time, not of height or temperature. It is reliable if it tells you the same time if you look at it exactly twenty-four hours later. It is accurate if the time is right, not 11.30 when it is really 9.45. It is precise if it tells you the exact time down to the smallest fraction of a second. The notion of less accuracy and precision can be upsetting to some people who believe that only absolute precision, down to a decimal point, is scientific. In Chapter 14 we look at an idea that might frighten such people: recognizing the principle of 'appropriate imprecision', that is, not being more accurate or precise than necessary, for as Chambers (1981, p. 95) has pointed out many times, it is better to be vaguely right than precisely wrong. You probably prefer to be quite right but you do not necessarily need great precision. For example, finding out how much money, to the penny, people would be prepared to spend on new computers for the school; or, to the last household, the exact number of people who haven't a clue how to program their video recorder. General pictures, patterns, and trends and their relationships are likely to be more important in much research.

Most researchers tend to look for great precision in their own field but may use fairly rough indicators when dealing with material from another field, or when dealing with material that is somewhat marginal to their problem. For example, someone might use great precision to measure reading skills, but pay little attention to the fact that the measures may contain material that is culturally meaningless to some of the children who are being measured.

Selection biases

Problems of validity, reliability, accuracy and precision can be aggravated by some common biases in research. To whom do you talk? Even if you are doing probability sampling, there will probably be many occasions when you want background information, help with questions that have arisen in your research, and insights into interpretation, so you will need to choose people to help you. If you are not using a probability sample, the issue is even more important. Chambers (1981, 1983, 1991, 1992, 1994a, 1994b, 1994c) has done more than almost anyone recently to make us aware of how easily we can bias our results by an almost unconscious selection process, so that we end up with certain kinds of people and totally overlook others. His work is mainly in developing countries, but the points he makes are valid anywhere. For example, some researchers might be unconsciously tempted to:

- stay close to familiar surroundings;
- go to more easily accessible places;
- talk to people they are more comfortable with — usually people like themselves;
- avoid the embarrassment of intruding on the disadvantaged, such as poorer people, older people, the homeless, etc. It's easier to ask people in authority over them — social workers, for example;
- look at the visible or the easily enumerated (such as records and figures) rather than the 'invisible' (such as people's attitudes toward sex among the severely mentally handicapped);
- look at the immediate rather than the longer-term trend;
- find out what people say as opposed to what they do;
- play the important person or expert and intimidate people into cooperating with you.

The following sections look more closely at some biases. Note that many other kinds of biases are involved in research in addition to those mentioned here. Chapters 9 and 11 discuss biases on the part of interviewees, and Chapter 16 discusses biases that can affect your analysis.

Network biases

Most social research is targeted at people who are less privileged, of lower status, and poorer than the researcher. Social researchers usually get to those less privileged through people who have some authority over them, such as employers, school principals, community leaders, union officials, prison wardens, or project directors — in other words, through their own social and professional peers. These people are easy for you as a researcher to get to and are often more comfortable to talk to. You have a lot in common: profession, social standing, a common social and professional language. If you are faced with a large, confusing mass of target people and a brief amount of time, letting your peers 'translate' the people's condition, needs, and wishes, and using their networks is easier. This may give you quicker entry but you may be narrowing your options in terms of getting representative information because what you are really doing is taking a purposive sample (see Chapter 6) without knowing what the selection basis is. Placing too much trust in people similar to yourself is easy, because they speak your language. Unfortunately, they will probably also reinforce your own prejudices and conceptions, accurate or not. You must talk to your peers for many obvious reasons, but their version of reality is not necessarily more accurate than that of the target population. It is just easier to get.

At this point you might wonder about the towns we've picked to study: Hope And Glory, and later on, Hancock Towers. Are we studying 'down'? You might be, but some of the other researchers are definitely studying 'up'.

Bottom-up biases

The bottom-up bias is the reverse of the network bias. It is usually found among people who take a critical theory approach (see Chapter 2 for more on critical theory); they do not want to talk to elites at all: they only want to talk to 'the people'. They want to work from the bottom up, from the grassroots, rather than the top down. This is entirely reasonable, but is often said with a certain amount of irritating sanctimoniousness, implying that you yourself are doing all your research from the back seat of a Rolls Royce Silver Cloud. Actually, there is little chance of doing true top-down or bottom-up research in a society of any size. Most researchers are middle-class people, and the people at the absolute bottom of the place you are studying are nearly invisible except to the group immediately above them, who are knowledgeable about them because they are desperate not to fall down into this group themselves. You are also unlikely to work from the top down either. True elites are nearly invisible as well except, once again, to the people immediately below them, who are trying to join them and wouldn't dream of asking them awkward questions, even if they had the chance. You will, however, be able to talk to people who are in social classes somewhat above you, because your work may be useful to them, because they want a hand in shaping it, or because they cannot quite identify your lowly role in the general scheme of things, particularly if you are well-educated or an outsider.

Another reason for not working exclusively from the bottom up is that most groups and societies are hierarchical, and their members either respect the hierarchy or fear it. In either case, by bypassing it you are insulting the system, showing that you do not know, or do not care, how things work, thereby increasing the possibility of your research being sabotaged, reducing the possibility of it ever leading to anything practical and possibly endangering the people who are participating in your study. Going out to work with a group of Third World women and deliberately bypassing their community leaders, or even their husbands, may present a danger to the women, who may take the brunt of your high principles and/or arrogance later. On the other hand, by going through husbands first, you may reinforce a patriarchy which the women themselves are resisting. The best approach will involve learning enough about the situation in advance to understand the consequences.

The 'one-of-the-people' delusion

The one-of-the-people bias is not a selection bias, but a rather pathetic self-deception on the part of some researchers, who believe that in the course of their work they have become part of the group they are studying. It is worth stating here that you will never become one of the people, whoever they are, unless you already are. The exceptions, throughout history, are almost too few to mention. Right now, researcher Tiffani Shapiro is working with the Mescoito Indians in Hope And Glory? Will she be able to become a Mescoito? Stay tuned…

Some researchers also believe that no one understands 'their' particular group of people the way they do. Such researchers then begin to think they are spokespersons for the people they have studied and become fanged tigers if any one else ventures into 'their' territory. And you will find yourself in an awkward position if 'one of the people' themselves becomes a researcher and obviously has more street credibility than you do. The Irish have a saying about outsiders: 'He's more Irish than the Irish themselves.' This is not a compliment. Taking this stance affects your ability to be useful to anyone. Your value comes from doing good humble research.

Working With 'Insiders' and Learning From Their Knowledge

'Insiders' are those who are involved in a situation, not simply 'officials' or 'experts', but rather those who are actually participating, or not participating in some cases. For example, if you want to understand why gangs and cliques are so prominent in the local school, educational psychologists and administrators are fine, but only the students understand some aspects of the situation. There is another advantage to using insider knowledge. Everywhere in the world, people will usually give you information geared toward your level of understanding, and, if you are new to a situation and have the knowledge of a four-year-old, they will start from there. Thus, working with 'insiders' from the beginning to determine what is important to study, or what questions to ask, can provide more sophisticated information in a shorter time. They can help you to refine or even change your focus entirely.

Sometimes, researchers require full-time or part-time assistance in carrying out the work, particularly people who are doing surveys, or those who are working through an unfamiliar language. Involving people who are similar to your study group (for example, ex-prisoners, if you are studying prisoners, or newly literate — and sometimes even non-literate — people if you are studying the problems of non-literate adults) can bring a lot of benefits — not just because they speak the same 'language', but because they can bring an informed perspective to the direction your research is taking, to the questions, and to the interpretation of results. (Of course, if you are doing participatory research, the group you are studying will also be doing the research alongside you — see Chapter 14.) To achieve anything useful, you have to choose assistants wisely. University students or graduates are not necessarily the best bet. They are often tied up in demonstrating technical expertise, such as doing surveys. What you require is someone who is intelligent, astute, and non-threatening who fits in well with the people you are studying. Whoever you choose, it is an advantage if your assistants understand the larger goal of your research, not just the bit they are doing.

Ethics

Since one is often studying people more vulnerable and less fortunate and powerful than oneself, a single paragraph on the ethics of your research is inadequate except to guide you to more detailed discussions. The problem is that there is no universal set of ethical principles, or even a core hierarchy of values, that can guide us. Most professional associations have statements of research ethics which are often debated among their members and often are not applicable somewhere, or are not workable in real life. Vexing questions arise. To whom, or what, are you responsible? The organization for which you work? The sponsors of the research? Your profession or discipline? The people who help you in your research? The answer is all of them, but problems crop up when any one of these comes in conflict with another. Every circumstance differs. The most vulnerable are probably the participants in your research, and the repercussions of your research on them must always be the first consideration. One cardinal rule is that merely by doing your research, you will often raise people's hopes and expectations — less advantaged people may hope for some improvement in their situation, people in a troublesome situation may hope for a resolution, people who have no particular problems may hope to see some findings, a report, or something on paper. Never promise anything you cannot deliver. Make it clear from the beginning what you are doing and don't make promises just to get cooperation. When you are finished, never leave people wondering what happened to you and your study. Share the results, at the very least, in a form that is accessible and understandable to the audience you worked with.

Wilson (1993) provides a thoughtful view on ethics from the outsider researcher's point of view. Here is the view of an 'insider' who has obviously been on the receiving end of a lot of research:

> The kind of behavior researchers have towards locals tells us that really they just want to exploit them and take from them their ideas and information. It also tells us that they really don't care at all. Not all researchers are exploiters but most are, and I think it is time up for this now.
>
> (Florence Shumba, in Wilson, 1993, p. 199)

Have you ever been on the receiving end of research? What have you learned as a result? Try to apply the lessons as you begin your own research career. For a discussion of these issues and more see works such as Deyhle, Hess, and LeCompte (1992); Kimmel (1988); or Miles and Huberman (1994).

References and further readings

Brislin, Richard W., ed. 1990. *Applied Cross-Cultural Psychology*. Newbury Park, California: Sage.

Casley, Dennis J. and Denis A. Lury. 1982. *Monitoring and Evaluation of Agriculture and Rural Development Projects*. Baltimore, Maryland, and London: The Johns Hopkins University Press.

Chambers, Robert. 1981. 'Rapid Rural Appraisal: Rationale and Repertoire.' *Public Administration and Development* 1:95–106.

——. 1983. *Rural Development: Putting the Last First*. London: Longman.

——. 1991. 'Shortcut and Participatory Methods for Gaining Social Information for Projects.' In Michael M. Cernea, ed., *Putting People*

First, 2nd ed. New York: Oxford University Press.

——. 1992. *Rural Appraisal: Rapid, Relaxed and Participatory*. Discussion Paper No. 311. Brighton, U.K.: University of Sussex, Institute of Development Studies.

——. 1994(a). 'The Origins and Practice of Participatory Rural Appraisal.' *World Development* 22(7):953–969.

——. 1994(b). 'Participatory Rural Appraisal (PRA): Analysis of Experience.' *World Development* 22(9): 1253–1268.

——. 1994(c). 'Participatory Rural Appraisal: Challenges, Potentials and Paradigm.' *World Development* 22(10):1437–1454.

Cole, Stephen. 1980. *The Sociological Method: An Introduction to the Science of Sociology*, 3rd ed. Chicago: Rand McNally.

Deyhle, Donna L., G. Alfred Hess, Jr., and Margaret D. LeCompte. 1992. 'Approaching Ethical Issues for Qualitative Researchers in Education.' Margaret D. LeCompte, Wendy Millroy, and Judith Preissle, eds, in *The Handbook of Qualitative Research in Education*, pp. 597–641. San Diego, California; London; Tokyo: Academic Press.

Guba, Egon G. and Yvonna S. Lincoln. 1989. *Fourth Generation Evaluation*. Newbury Park, California: Sage.

Kimmel, Allan J. 1988. *Ethics and Values in Applied Social Research*. Newbury Park, California: Sage.

Lonner, W.J. 1990. 'An Overview of Cross-Cultural Testing and Assessment.' In Richard W. Brislin, ed., *Applied Cross-Cultural Psychology*. Newbury Park, California: Sage.

Park, Robert. 1928. 'The Bases for Race Prejudice.' *The Annals* 140:11–20.

Miles, Matthew B. and A. Michael Huberman. 1994. *Qualitative Data Analysis*, 2nd ed. Thousand Oaks, California: Sage.

Webb, E.J., D.T. Campbell, R.D. Schwartz, and L. Sechrest. 1966. *Unobtrusive Measures: Nonreactive Research in the Social Sciences*. Chicago: Rand McNally.

Wilson, Ken. 1993. 'Thinking About the Ethics of Fieldwork.' In Stephen Devereaux and John Hoddinott, eds. *Fieldwork in Developing Countries*. Boulder, Colorado: Lynne Rienner Publishers.

Wolcott, Harry F. 1973. *The Man in the Principal's Office: An Ethnography*. New York: Holt, Rinehart and Winston.

The Hope and Glory Vindicator

Volume 182 Issue 17   August 25, 2001

Mescoitos come out in favor of new church

The local Mescoito Indians have thrown their support behind the proposed House of Peace Temple on Route 123. Chief Myron Grey-Wolf III, in an interview with visiting researcher Tiffani Shapiro, com-plained that the Mescoitos were treated as pariahs in Hope And Glory, despite the fact that they had been settled in the area behind the boiler factory for the past eight years. They had hoped for many years to be invited to local barbecues and other nice social events but this had not happened. 'You offer your hand to these people and they crap in it,' said Chief Grey-Wolf III. On the other hand, the House of Peace Temple officers had reached out to them, sharing their pain. The Chief has agreed to handle their first gala, a finger-food buffet, featuring his speciality, spaghetti with all the trimmings.

Mr. Stephen Barker, president of the House of Peace congregation, said they welcomed their Indian breth-ren. He said in his opinion, Tonto had always been twice the man the Lone Ranger was.

***

In a separate development, Mrs. Juanetta Wilcox reveal-ed to the Vindicator that she had sold the Precious Lambs Daycare Center to two Mescoito ladies, Mrs. Myron Grey-Wolf III-Whump (Bert's girl DeeDee), who goes by her maiden name, and Mrs. Ralph Hardspritt. The ladies intend to manage the Center themselves. Mrs. Wilcox said it had all got too much for her, and she was going to be glad to be off her feet.

Three researchers to return home

Three of the five visiting re-searchers, Mr. Pius Gallagher, Dublin, Ireland, Mr. Jean-Paul Peillon, Paris, France and Ms. Tiffani Shapiro, New York, New York have finished with their research in Hope And Glory, and are returning to their homes. Their research, to be published in the Journal of Abnormal Psychology, is described as 'riveting' by the journal's editor, who is planning to print an extra 10,000 copies to be sold in airport bookshops and adult bookstores.

On behalf of the three, Mr. Gallagher thanked the mayor and all those townspeople who had petitioned the governor of Ohio for their release from jail. He also thanked those who had gone on hunger strike in sympathy, and the organizers of the candlelight vigils.

Court Notes

Mrs. Laurinda McCardle vs. Septus McCardle: divorce granted on grounds of irreconcilable differences. Plaintiff will resume her maiden name. Defendant to have all carpets de-haired and shampooed.

INSIDE THIS ISSUE

8 GETTING HELP FROM THE LIBRARY AND THE INTERNET[1]

Summary

In the first half of this chapter, we look at how you find *secondary materials* through the library, the Internet, and other sources. Later we will explore some issues you need to think about when you are using these kinds of materials.

Secondary materials are materials that have been prepared by someone else, while data that you collect first-hand, such as your interviews with people or your observation of situations, are *primary material*. Secondary materials include books, journal articles, records, and many other kinds of written, visual, and audio sources.

Even when you are doing primary research, you can use secondary materials to:
- become familiar with what has been done on the topic;
- get the facts and figures you need to provide a background picture of your topic, or to support points you want to make.

[1]We would like to thank Eliza McLeod, Barbara Rodes, and Louise Vimmerstedt for the important contributions that they each made to this chapter.

You can do this in a library. You can also do it on the Internet, which also allows you to:
- join a professional-interest network;
- find and communicate with other researchers;
- get software to help you organize and analyze your material;
- publish your work;
- participate in other people's research.

This book is about doing your own research — collecting new material or creating primary data, as you do when you interview young people at risk to see what they think their major problems are and what they think might help to solve them. Their replies will form the major part of your research. You will not draw as much on *secondary data* — articles, books, and records written by other people. Of course, some research is based almost entirely on secondary materials — for example, it is possible to study changes in the roles of women by seeing how they are portrayed in magazine pictures and stories over time. You can even do correlations — a case could be made, for example, that improvements in football teams' scores are related to changes in management, simply by reading the newspapers. Historical research, critical essays, topical reports, and some term papers draw heavily or entirely on secondary materials, as well.

But even when you are doing primary research, which is the focus of this book, you will still need to consult other people's work, i.e. secondary materials.

There are many kinds of secondary data that the researcher can draw upon, both published and unpublished, public and private: books, journal articles, newspapers, magazines, records, diaries, autobiographies, film, videos, and work prepared especially for your study. For example, you might ask teachers to keep a log of what they did all day to see how much time is actually spent on the curriculum. There's also a vast amount of material called 'gray literature', which includes in-house publications and materials prepared for organisational use that are not in general circulation. You can use all of these creatively in your research — we will give some examples after we show you how to get at the materials. For many secondary materials, this means going to the library, or going on to the Internet. By doing this you can:

- See what has already been done on the topic — who else has studied youths at risk recently in communities such as yours? What problems emerged? Is it worth exploring those issues with your own group? Can you use some of the same questions so that you can compare your group with the one in the study? Did the author have any problems doing the research? Are there any tips that might be helpful to you?

- Get routine facts and figures — how many youths are thought to be at risk, nationally? What kind of risk — drugs, sexually transmitted diseases, pregnancy? What kinds of services and facilities are available for them? What has been tried in other communities? What non-profit organisations work with youths at risk?

Both of these tasks can be carried out in a library. However, both can also be done on the Internet, which will also allow you to take advantage of some opportunities that aren't available in a conventional library. On the Internet, you can:

- Become part of a 'professional interest' network and get news of recent findings, textbooks, course offerings, workshops, and conferences dealing with youths at risk.
- Join discussion groups and networks so you can talk to other researchers and to academics working on similar problems, ask questions, and offer some answers from your own experience. You can also communicate directly with other researchers through email.
- Download interactive software to help you to do your research, such as software for analyzing qualitative data (which is what your interviews will probably produce), and get tools and tutorials on specific research topics, such as sampling and experimental design. For example, you can get a set of instructions for social workers on how to carry out a telephone survey on youths, complete with the questions to ask at **www.inetwork.org**.
- Publish your work, and get feedback.
- Finally, you can also help other researchers by participating in their studies — for example, in 1999, researchers at the University of Nevada ran a Dating Practices Survey in which people were invited to fill out a well-designed anonymous questionnaire on 'breaking up'. If you were interested but worried about becoming involved, you could actually email the professor who was supervising it (**www.greatbasin.net/~michael**).

It is impossible to overestimate the impact that these last five facilities can have on your research when you are just starting out and may have no professional or institutional connections. No longer are you isolated — one click can connect you with more people than you would meet in person at an academic convention.

Before we begin, we have to face the fact that some people are intimidated by the library, or the Internet, or both. In the case of the library, bear in mind that the librarian who used to terrify you has probably retired by now, and a more welcoming spirit prevails. Most libraries today are open, cheerful places staffed by people who not only love books, but also want to share them with you, unlike old Miss Ziegler in Hope And Glory, whose joy in life comes from imposing fines on people whom she suspects are reading their library books in the bath. It is also easier to find what you are looking for in libraries today because the card catalogue is likely to be computerized, and the new breed of librarian will actually help you to use it.

In the case of the Internet, some people are afraid that they will be taken prisoner in a pornographic chat room or find that they have bought a lifetime supply of bicycle pumps when they thought they were reading a nice piece about the Arizona desert. Even worse, they fear that they may become addicted to the Internet, lose all human contact, and forego bathing.

All of these fears are quite reasonable: on a day in September, 1999, for example, 25 million visitors to popular Web pages were deliberately re-routed to, and trapped in, pornography sites. Some were delighted about this page-jacking, but most weren't, and, in the end, their only way out was to shut down their computers and start over again. And from our own experience as researchers with a special interest in girls' education, we have entered the search words 'girls' and 'education' and been directed to sites on spanking and bondage. Some pornographers include seemingly innocuous words and phrases in the keywords that describe their sites. For example, 'Mandy has a bust measurement the size of the federal budget deficit', so when you search for 'federal budget deficit' or 'Himalayan Mountains' you can find yourself viewing Mandy, and wondering what on earth her parents must think. But the thing to remember is that over 200 million people use the Internet (that was in October 1999 — the figure is still rising), and most of them get what they are looking for. It is an invaluable resource for researchers, and although it has become popular to tell Internet horror stories, the benefits far outweigh the disadvantages.

Let's begin with the traditional way of getting access to secondary materials, libraries.

The Library

Up until a few months ago, Laurinda avoided the Hope And Glory library because Miss Ziegler, the whiskery librarian, took no prisoners. She regarded all library patrons as would-be thieves, perverts, and page-benders. But Laurinda is now deep into her studies on beards as secondary sex characteristics, and the only book she has on the subject is her old high school biology book, which seems to be fixated on the life cycle of the newt. So she braves the library, to find Miss Ziegler gone and in her place a beaming young woman in a denim skirt and Birkenstocks. She is patient and unflappable, even after learning the gist of Laurinda's subject.

She explains that libraries are now able to store information in many forms — books, journals, microfilm, microfiche, and electronic databases. They can also provide patrons with Internet access to the electronically published pages of the World Wide Web, so that all the advantages of the Internet can be enjoyed in any library with Internet access. Also, Laurinda isn't restricted to what is physically available in the Hope And Glory library, which is very little; she can consult major libraries around the world through the Internet, link easily to relevant subjects, titles, and authors, and order many of the items she wants through inter-library loans.

The librarian in Hope And Glory helps Laurinda to get at the following sites for National Libraries:

Bibliotheque National de France
www.bnf.fr
British Library
www.bl.uk
Library of Congress (United States)
lcweb.loc.gov
She also tries this site, which provides links to libraries worldwide:
Libweb-Library Servers Via WWW:
sunsite.berkeley.edu/Libweb/

Of course, even in these cyberspace days, a library still has real books. Below are some *printed* reference collections that can help to do the same job:

Armstrong, C.J., R.R. Fenton. *World databases in social sciences*. 1996. London, England: Bowker-Saur.

Encyclopedia of Associations. Annual. Issued in three volumes, some subdivided into parts: vol. 1, pts 1–2: national organizations of the US; vol. 1 pt 3: name and keyword index; vol. 2: geographic and executive index; vol. 3: new associations and projects (issued as cumulative supplement to each edition). Detroit: Gale Research Co.

International Research Centers Directory. 1998. Detroit: Gale Research Co. [formerly Government Research Centers Directory].

Government Research Directory. 1998. Detroit: Gale Research Co.

Social Trends, Great Britain. Annual. Central Statistical Office. London: H.M.S.O.

So by the time Laurinda leaves the library, she has books, computer print-outs of titles, and summaries of content from all over the world, copies of textbook pages and magazine articles.

But she is intrigued now at how much the librarian found for her on the Internet. She still isn't ready to take the plunge herself, but she's curious to find out what's in there. Here are some books she can look through to get a listing:

Harley Hahn's Internet and Web Yellow Pages. 1999. Edition Harley Hahn. Osborne McGraw-Hill.

This gives a comprehensive list of categories and sub-categories: art, computers, movies, sports, politics, environment, philosophy, support groups, literature, personal finance, world cultures, music, and more. It includes an index and a CD-ROM with a searchable database of the sites listed in the book.

Layton, Marcia. *New Rider's Official World Wide Web Yellow Pages*. 1998. New York: New Rider Publishing.

This is organised by category and set up with an easy-to-use 'A-to-Z' tab format. This book is the definitive guide to what's on the Internet and features thousands of site listings.

The Internet

Laurinda is still more comfortable in 'meat space', i.e. the traditional world of people and dogs, and so on, than in the cyberspace world of the Internet. Otherwise, she could have gone onto the Internet herself and got a lot of the information she needed, plus buying some rather nice kitchen curtains through an Internet catalogue while she was there. But she has a problem common to many people: the whole concept of the Internet baffles her. She sees some people using it to find a spouse; others are doing their banking on it; others still are reading the newspaper. Her husband Septus is building a pond using step-by-step instructions written by a fellow in Wales who never built a pond in his life. And at this very moment, Reverend

Wayman is coming out on a gay discussion network. What *is* the Internet?

The Internet began in 1969 as a US government-financed computer network called Arpanet, and was intended for universities, government departments, and military sites. It is only in the last decade of the century that it became generally available to the public. And now that we are becoming used to the Internet, a new version, Internet2, has been developed and is being used by universities and a few corporations to create new hi-tech applications, such as advanced forms of virtual reality, where people look and even feel real. Applications such as this will eventually filter down to the ordinary Internet, and by then you will know enough about the Internet to decide whether you want to be looked at and felt.

But don't worry if you still don't know anything about the Internet — you are probably the kind of person who doesn't like to jump onto faddish bandwagons until you know whether they are really going to catch on or not. Over the centuries, people have agonized about whether or not they should throw caution to the winds and join the Palaeolithic or the Industrial Revolution. In your own case, perhaps this natural reticence has helped you to avoid many nuisance fads, such as the pet rock craze or navel piercing. But now it's safe to turn your attention to the Internet, because it isn't going to go away. In this section, therefore, we will take you through a set of steps to help you get online and find helpful research information and services.

How Do You Get Online?

Equipment

What do you need in order to get at the Internet? If you have a computer, you will need a monitor, a modem, a mouse, a phone line, and an Internet service provider (ISP). Some Internet providers are now giving away computers free if you commit yourself to their service for several years. But if you don't have a computer, you can use one in your local library, school or community centre. Even better for the computer-shy are special devices that allow you to connect to the Internet through a television set — you don't need to go near a computer at all. Some types of pagers and cell phones use the Wireless Application Protocol (WAP) to provide Internet access. The technology is more advanced in Europe and Asia than elsewhere, but the range of sites is still too limited to be useful to the researcher. So too is 'Invisible' Internet, which is now being developed: a program called Voyager, for example, will allow you speak into your phone, and through a voice recognition system link you to audible sites. But in a few years these, and others not yet even thought of, will lead to new research applications.

If you are using the 'traditional' computer, you will need to choose an online service or service provider. This will allow you to have a Web browser to search for Web sites. Two common ones are Netscape Navigator and Internet Explorer. Before you choose a provider, ask other Internet subscribers about the service they are using, their ability to get online easily, and the back-up support they get when things go wrong.

How does the Internet work? Don't ask. We haven't a clue. We also don't know the firing order of the spark plugs in a 1987 Yugo, but we could drive one if we had to. You don't need to know anything about computers, except how to turn them on and use a mouse, and you don't need to know how the Internet works to get any of the benefits we've been talking about.

Getting started

A portion of the Internet is called the World Wide Web, and this is where you will be doing most of your research. Connect to the Internet, and launch the Web browser provided by your service provider. This has a 'search' or 'find' facility. You can also use a global *search engine* to find things. There are two types of search engines; *directories* or *guides* such as Yahoo!, and *indexes* such as AltaVista and Hotbot. There are also *subject gateways*, which are more specific than global search engines: for example, the Social Science Information Gateway, Socioweb or Sociosite will direct you to reliable sociological sites, so that you are not searching the entire Web. Subject gateways exist for most areas of interest to social science researchers.

Directories or guides

A directory is like a table of contents, while an index is more like the index you would find at the back of a book. Picture it this way: when an author writes a book, he or she decides what chapters it will contain, names them, and decides what to put in them. A machine cannot do that. On the other hand, these days a machine can create an index once it is told what words to look for. It can list the words and tell you what pages they appear on.

Internet directories contain subject categories created by human editors, and material is grouped under these categories. For example, Yahoo! (Yet Another Hierarchical Officious Oracle) has fourteen major categories. To get to Yahoo! enter the address

(UK) **www.yahoo.co.uk**

(USA) **www.yahoo.com**

or just type 'yahoo'.

Simply click on one of the categories, such as 'social science', or one of the sub-directories, such as 'anthropology'. You can also search the directories by entering a keyword or words in the search box — for example 'glue sniffing' — and Yahoo! will search among its titles and subtitles to find material on the subject. You can search the entire collection of directories (in which case, you might end up with material from the 'health' category on the medical dangers of glue sniffing), or just the category 'social science', where you are likely to find material on the culture of glue sniffing as a youth phenomenon. Yahoo! does not search within the contents of documents for the occurrence of the words, just among its directory titles and subtitles. Because it is searching titles, which tend to be broader than their contents, it is better to use broader search words than you would if you were searching an index. Otherwise, you might miss your topic altogether. Also, it is a good idea to use lower case letters — if you use upper case letters, the search will only yield items that are listed in upper case, but lower case will get both upper and lower case words.

Learn how to narrow your searches. If you enter

British public libraries

you will get a number of items that contain not only the phrase 'British public libraries' but also 'British' or 'public' or 'libraries' — for example, *public libraries* in the Cariboo region of *British* Columbia. However, if you use quotation marks or inverted commas around the phrase 'British public libraries' you will get only results in which all three of those words appear together. You can also click on 'an exact phrase match' to get only results on 'British public libraries'.

Use asterisks when you don't want the search tool to be too literal-minded — for example,

'sample★'

should yield not only 'sample' but also 'samples' and 'sampling'. If you are not sure how to spell a word, or make a typographical error, as we did when looking for an 'online English grammar' text, you should still end up with a useful result. We entered '*one*line English grammar' and were surprised to get no results, but the addition of the asterisk would have saved us. If a word has both a British and an American spelling, 'theatre★' will get both. You can also use + and − signs to make your research more specific: putting a + in front of a word means that the word must appear in every result; putting a − in front of a word means it must not appear. Thus,

'social science + sampling★'

will give you only results dealing with sampling and samples in the social sciences, rather than sampling in medicine, the laboratory sciences, etc. If you had simply listed

social science sampling

you would have had references to social, science, and sampling (but not samples, because you did not use an asterisk after 'sampling.') If you had listed 'sampling* – medicine'

you would get references to various kinds of sampling, but sampling in medicine would not be among them. Thus, 'Dan Quayle – potatoe' will yield references on the former US Vice President other than those on the spelling gaffe that seems to have doomed his career. And you can string a list together, such as

'social science + experiments – students'

if you want to read about experiments done on people other than students, who are a common source of subjects for psychology professors. If you want to restrict a search to government sites or academic sites you can type

'gun control + host: gov.uk'

to get government sites in Britain, or 'creationism + host: edu' to get at information on creationism on US educational institution sites. (US sites normally do not have a place name, but sites in other countries do.) If you would like to learn more about searching, click on 'Advanced Search Syntax' in Yahoo!

Once you get pointed in the right direction, you will probably find that you are getting much too much information. Stay focused on your topic — otherwise you will find that several hours have elapsed, you are reading about aboriginal folk songs rather than glue sniffing, and you have no circulation in your legs.

In addition to Yahoo! there are a number of other Web directories available to you. You may not need search engine addresses — your server may list these names and you just click on one of them:

Infoseek (www.infoseek.com)
Lycos (www.lycos.com)
Excite (www.excite.com)
Galaxy (www.galaxy.tradewave.com)

There are many others, and each has its own special strengths. You can go to Yahoo! (Computers and Internet: Internet: World Wide Web: Searching the Web: Web directories) and find a more specialized one if you need it.

Indexes

Unlike directories, which are assembled by people, indexes are produced by automated tools — if a piece of text on the Web contains special words, the tool will take note of them, and when you search for the words, you will be directed to the Web page containing them. This is done daily, covering millions of Web pages. Some of the search engine companies, such as Lycos and Infoseek, combine indexes and directories at the same site, and Yahoo! will send you to an index, Alta Vista, if it can't find what you asked for.

Here are the Web site addresses for some of the most popular indexes:

Hotbot (**www.hotbot.com**): A large Web index with advanced search capabilities including filtering features to help you focus.

AltaVista (**www.altavista.com**): The advanced searching feature improves simple search queries and provides strong returns.

EuroFerret (**www.euroferret.com**): Index of over 30 million Web pages. You can search by keyword and limit search to a specific country. English, French, Spanish, German, Italian, and Swedish.

There are also a number of speciality search engines such as:

AskJeeves (**www.askJeeves.com**): This is a site where you can ask questions using natural language: 'Where can I learn about sampling?' or 'What is the population of Manchester, England?'

SearchEngineColossus (**www.searchenginecolossus.com/uk**): This site has links to a large number of United Kingdom navigation tools.

MetaCrawler (**www.metacrawler.com**): Searches *across* Web indexes and directories such as AltaVista, Excite, Infoseek, Lycos, Yahoo!, WebCrawler, Thunderstone, and InfoSpace's Ultimate Directory. You can make a customised search page and keep preferences for future searches. It integrates returns and gives useful quality rankings.

Tips

It's important to spell your search words correctly, or you may get a 'no results found' message. Be particularly aware of differences between British and American spellings, such as colour and color. Some databases make allowances, but most are quite literal and unforgiving. You can try to get around this by adding an asterisk to the word, as we explained earlier, but of course if you don't know you are misspelling a word, you may not think this is necessary.

When in doubt, click on the 'help' button to find out why a search isn't working. It could be that the system is case sensitive or you may need to use quotation marks around the phrases.

If you are having difficulty finding the author or source for a particular document, it could be because it is actually a *subdocument*. You might want to try re-entering the Web address minus the directory portion. This might

Some of the terms associated with the Web

Browser: Software that allows you to view the Web. The two most popular are Netscape Navigator and Internet Explorer.

Search engine: A type of software that creates indexes of databases of Internet sites.

MetaCrawler: A search engine that has no database of its own. It searches across the major Web indexes and directories to compile information.

URL (Uniform Resource Locator): A Web address. Each address has three parts: the *protocol*, the *domain*, and the *directory*. To illustrate these, we have just created the following fake Web address, which, if it actually worked, would enable you to find out how the Queen Mother celebrated her last birthday, or possibly where she buys those lovely hats:

http://www.queenmum.uk/royalty

The protocol that you will find most often is http:// (Hypertext Transfer Protocol) as seen at the beginning of our address. It tells you that it is a Web item. Some other protocol prefixes that you might see are Gopher (an older one) (gopher://) and File Transfer Protocol (ftp://). FTP is a vast collection of computer files that is separate from the World Wide Web.

The second part is the domain, which, in this case, is www.queenmum.uk/. This shows you exactly where the computer is located, in other words, the host computer. In Web addresses you will find abbreviations such as gov (governmental), co [UK] or com [US] (commercial or corporate), org (non-profit organisations) and edu or ac (educational or academic). They indicate the type of source that is providing the information. Except in the United States, most Web addresses include, at the end, an indication of country: for example, .uk for the United Kingdom, .ie for Ireland.

The third part is the directory. It indicates the file where the resource is located.

Web pages: Individual computer files that compose Web sites.

Portal: A newer phenomenon, created since the Web has become more commercial. 'Portal' is usually used as a term to describe a Web site that is, or is intended to be, the first place people see when using the Web. Typically, a portal site has a catalogue of Web sites, a search engine, or both. It may also offer email and other services to entice people to use that site as their main 'point of entry' (hence 'portal') to the Web.

Bookmark (or *Favourite*): A tool that enables you to 'flag' a particular Web page so that you can retrieve it without having to re-enter the Web address.

Hypertext: While reading a document, you might come across a word that is highlighted. When you click on it, you will be linked to another document or picture that can provide related information.

Hypertext mark-up language: This is the language in which all Web documents are written. At the end of the directory portion of the web address, you might find '.htm' or '.html'. If you are curious to see what hypertext mark-up language looks like, try using the VIEW SOURCE option on your browser.

Annotated hypertext: Simply means that someone with knowledge on the subject has provided critical comments or explanations regarding the information.

FAQs: Frequently asked questions. Some Web sites anticipate your questions and provide this information in advance.

allow you to back up a bit and gain access to the original document. For example, you might wonder whether you should pay people who participate in your research, and by searching for 'paying survey respondents' you could find the University of Surrey's Social Update Page at **www.soc.surrey.ac.uk/sru/SRU 14**, which presents a discussion of this issue. You might like to read what else the Social Update Web page offers, so omit the last part of the address, and you will be 'back' at **www.soc.surrey.ac.uk/sru**, where you will find a lot of other helpful information about doing research.

How can you use the Internet for your research?

The Internet can be a treasure trove for the researcher — library catalogues, online books and articles, databases, discussion groups, bulletin boards, and the ability to send files by email have made the researcher's life much easier.

Let's say that after reading Chapter 16, you are interested in doing some qualitative research. You can search the Internet for 'qualitative research' and related words. This will connect you to associations, articles, books, universities, individuals, courses, tutorials, mailing lists and discussion groups, and email conferences.

By joining or subscribing to a mailing list, you can keep abreast of forthcoming training programs, workshops, conferences, and issues. You can find entire books on qualitative research free on the Internet — for example, *The Knowledge Base*, an online hypertext textbook in applied social research methods, available at **www.trochim.human.cornell.edu/kb/index**.

You can find out who is doing qualitative research in the inner city classroom, or on street children. You can post questions — you might search for the discussion group DRUGABUS and find out if anyone used qualitative research with glue sniffers, and what they found? Of course, you can also search for 'social science and glue sniffing' to see if there are any references, but perhaps someone did some work that was never published, and you may find him or her through your discussion group.

Perhaps you want to buy a software program for analyzing your qualitative data. Given the kind of data you have, which is the best one? The University of Surrey has a Web page on social research at **www.soc.surrey.ac.uk/SRU/sru**, which explains the common programs: Ethnograph, NUDIST, HyperQual, and many others. It also directs you to a short course, or to a discussion group or mailing list, so that you can keep up with the issues involved in using these programs. Some software programs allow you to download a 'sample' so you can try them out before making your final selection. Of course, you can also use the Web to download free software — you may have done this already when updating your computer's software — but you can get useful research software from sites such as the Virtual Software Library, the Shareware Web site, and the Higher Educational National Software Archive, among others.

Or perhaps you have an ethical problem — for example, should you change the name of the town you are studying to protect people's identities? Should other people be allowed access to your raw data? People who have faced these kinds of problems will respond, often giving completely conflicting advice. And of course you can also communicate by email with people who have done qualitative research on your subject, and often maintain contact throughout your project.

Finally, when your study is finished, you can create a Web page and publish the results, or a summary of the results. But there are many other ways to use the Internet to get your findings into circulation, as you will see later in this chapter.

And by the time you read this, the Internet will have moved on, becoming easier to access and offering even greater resources for researchers.

Getting at Internet research help

So here is how to start getting access to some of these resources yourself. If you want to try this on the Internet, you might go to a library site such as the one at Old Dominion University, at **www.lib.odu.edu/research/tutorials**. This will explain the various kinds of literature available in a library and how to get them.

Finding academic literature

You can go to a site such as Libweb US, and get academic libraries on the Internet, or library catalogues, which have British and international library links. And there are many virtual reference libraries. For example, two university-based virtual reference libraries are those at Princeton (**opr.princeton.edu/resources**), and at the Massachusetts Institute of Technology (MIT), (**libraries.mit.edu/services/virtualref**).

At the MIT site, the reference collection includes links to:

Acronyms	Jobs and Employment
Associations and Societies	Law
Colleges and Universities	Libraries
Companies	News
Consumer Information	People
Conversion Factors	Politics
Dictionaries and Thesauri	Publishing
Directories	Quotations
Diversions	Sciences
Encyclopedias and Yearbooks	Statistics
Geography	Style Manuals
Government Information	Taxes
Grants	Time/Date
Health	Travel
Internet	

For a specialised US social sciences virtual library, see:
www.clas.ufl.edu/users/gthursby/socsci/index
and a good social science directory, compiled in the United Kingdom, can be found at:
sosig.esrc.bris.ac.uk/
An International Data Base (IDB) containing statistical tables of demographic and socio-economic data for 227 countries and areas of the world is:
www.census.gov/ipc/www/idbnew
For links to survey research and methodology as well as public opinion centres, explore this rich site:
www.ukans.edu/cwis/units/coms2/po/index
You might also find electronic journals on the Internet to help you stay abreast of trends in your field. For a list of academic and reviewed journals, see:
www.edoc.com/academic
or a site from the Digital Librarian at:
www.servtech.com/mvail/magazines
If all of the sources listed above have provided you with no information on your topic, go to Northern Light:
www.northernlight.com

At the time of writing (September 15, 1999 at 3.10pm — the Web develops quickly) Northern Light was unique on the Web. For a researcher without access to a major university who has exhausted all avenues for retrieving professional literature, this could be a lifesaver. If a publisher has made articles available free, they are mounted on this site, in full text. However, if a journal article is under copyright, you can actually buy the article, using a credit card. The article will be faxed to you. Using this service might be money well spent.

Finding people: directory services and email discussion groups

Once you know the names of some of the people who are relevant in your field of research, there are many services that will help you to find them and their institutions or businesses — you use these services to track down phone numbers, email addresses, and corporate or personal Web pages. To find a person, you might try to pose a question to **AskJeeves**. Another possibility would be **Peoplesearch** at:

www.w3com.com/psearch

There are international address finders available as well. For Europe, try:

www.worldmail.com/wedemail.com/wede4e

or

www.iaft.net

You can also join academic discussion lists and email discussion groups. Some of the most useful information on the Internet can be found inside academic discussion lists, which are usually housed on university campus host servers. Most Internet experts consider academic discussion groups and the associated email lists to be the most civilised type of online community, because this format generally lends itself to calm, thoughtful, literate, and mature discussion. These groups are excellent sources for locating peers or experts in a field. (You can also acquire information by subscribing to lists related to your topic and you can pose questions for experts to respond to.) But up until recently, these lists haven't been easily available to the average Internet user. Now, there are several ways to identify these discussion groups: you can search the Directory of Scholarly and Professional E-Conferences at:

www.n2h2.com/KOVACS

or search the Liszt database at:

www.liszt.com

Finding records: national, regional, state, and municipal

Governments, under statutory provisions, must maintain records. If information from any of these records will be helpful to you in your

research, you might find that a library with a collection of government reference materials and directories and a knowledgeable librarian will make your search easier. A Web-based online yellow page directory might help as well. For listings of US state and local government on the Web, see:
www.piperinfo.com/state/states
For the Public Records Office in the United Kingdom, see:
www.pro.gov.uk
Local newspapers are additional sources of records on deaths, births, marriages, and divorces, as well as news articles. The site below lists digital local US newspapers. For an example of a listing of the local/regional newspapers for eight mid-Atlantic states, see:
www.erols.com/erols/search/newspapers

Finding research help

Would you like to learn more about doing research with young people? Or using email as a research tool? **www.soc.surrey.ac.uk** will help you. If you have a question about how to analyze a sample that you have taken, you can click on **www.trochim.cornell.edu/selstat/sstart** and by answering a few simple questions, you will be directed toward the appropriate statistical test. Or you can learn how to use SPSS (Statistical Package for the Social Sciences) by clicking on www.spss.org, where you can subscribe to SPSS for Beginners, oriented toward people from a non-math background.

There are many social science sites that contain helpful information on these and other issues, and some even provide tutorials. Look at QualPage at **www.ualberta.ca/~jrnorris/qual**, or Bill Trochim's Center for Social Research Methods at **www.trochim.cornell.edu.** These, in turn, will direct you to other sites. You can also go to **www.QUALRS-L@uga.cc.uga.edu** to reach Qualitative Research E-Mail Resources, or find qualitative methods listservs at: **www.chre.vt.edu/nespor/qual.**

Doing research on the web

You can use the Internet to carry out many of the techniques described in this book — surveys, interviews, inviting people to prepare accounts such as time logs, etc. But there are problems that you should be aware of. For example, if you want to do an electronic survey, your respondents are limited to people who have access to email. This plays havoc with sampling, since it is still a rather unrepresentative group — the majority of people online are in the United States, and a large number of those are young male university students (Kenway, 1996). Also, respondents' identities cannot be protected, since their names or their email addresses are part of their reply.

The advantage of electronic surveys is that they are cheaper to send than postal surveys; they can be returned more quickly; and some research suggests that the response rate is as good or better than with postal surveys (Anderson and Gansneder, 1995; Mehta and Sivadas, 1995).

Interviewing online also has advantages and disadvantages. For example, distance is no object — you can communicate immediately with people anywhere, providing they have access to email. Writing up the interview is not a problem — it is already written up, and can even be analyzed using one of the software programs mentioned earlier in this chapter. The researcher won't have the same kind of impact, good or bad, on the respondent because he or she cannot be seen or heard. The disadvantages include not being able to see the respondent's non-verbal communications in the course of the interview — signs of confusion or reluctance, for example, as well as the problems of getting at people who are not on email, and the sampling difficulties mentioned earlier.

Writing up your results and citing references

The Internet and the library also have resources to help you to write your study. What is good grammar? What is acceptable usage? What are the rules about ending a sentence in a preposition? Do you know the difference between 'affect' and 'effect'? Between 'it's' and 'its'? If not, try *The Elements of Style*, an American university mainstay, by William Strunk, Jr. and E.B. White, 3rd ed., which you can find at **www.cc.columbia.edu/acis/bartleby/strunk**. You can also get access to an Online English Grammar at **www.edunet.com**.

At some time or another, we have all forgotten to record a source of information in the frenzy of research. On a recent trip to the Hope And Glory library, Laurinda found an article that she thought would prove her point, once and for all, that for reasons of modesty men should wear their beards in bags. She'll read it the next time she's there — she doesn't bother to write down the title or author because she has a great memory, and besides, who could forget the author and title of such a useful work? But she steps into something nasty right outside the library, and now the reference has gone right out of her head. All she can remember was that the book had a sort of brownish cover — not really brown, maybe, sort of taupe. Or a lightish olive drab.

Keep meticulous records of material you take from books, articles, or electronic references. You'll have regrets and possibly nightmares if you fail to record the title and author of some material that you now want to use in your research paper. If you use the material without citing it properly, you can be accused of plagiarism, so you have to trek back to the library or try once again to find the Internet Web site. Valuable time is wasted. If this does happen, you can go to an online library, as discussed in this chapter, or you can try one of the major online booksellers, where you may find the reference.

We look at the issue of citation again in Chapter 18, but unless a specific format is requested, sources from the Internet should be cited in the same format as the sources from print publications, with the addition of the Web site address and the 'date viewed' in parentheses. These are two books that will provide further guidelines as to how to cite information that you find on the Web or in a database:

Walker, Janice R. *The Columbia Guide to Online Style*. 1998. New York: Columbia University Press.

Xia Li and Nancy B. *Electronic Styles: a Handbook for Citing Electronic Information* 2nd ed. 1996. Medford, N.J: Information Today.

Publishing your research

It is difficult for a novice researcher to get research findings published — even new researchers working in universities find it hard to get work accepted by professional journals. There are some exceptions: one is *PLA Notes*, published by the International Institute for Environment and Development at:

iiedagri@gn.apc.org

which welcomes articles on participatory research by all comers, as long as they have some insights to share. But there are other ways you can publish the results of your study: in community newsletters, local, student and employee newspapers, and specialist publications put out by organizations for their members, employees, or an interested audience. But closer to the subject of this chapter, you can create your own Web page and post your results, update them, invite comments, etc. There are a number of software programs to help you do this — some word-processing programs even give you the option to save your document in HTML form — or you can get help on the Internet itself. We asked AskJeeves 'How do I make a Web page' and got a page that takes you through the process. We also asked AltaVistaUK 'How do I build a Web page' and got 20 pages of links to sites on creating your own Web page.

Or you can go to the Social Science Paper Publisher at **www.ssoo.net**, an informal electronic journal where you can submit papers for publication and get feedback. This is open to professionals and students alike — nearly half of the papers are submitted by students, nearly half by graduate students and faculty, and 16 per cent by others, into which category you may fall. QualPage at the University of Alberta will help you with information on how to present your paper in an academically acceptable form **(www.ualberta.ca/~jrnorris/qual)**. Most professional journals have their own style requirements — look for their Web pages and see what they tell you. Some book publishers will also allow you to submit a proposal for a book — for example, look at the Web page for Sage, a major publisher of social science methods and other books of interest to social scientists, at **www.sagepub.com**.

Of course, this ease of publication is a two-edged sword. Until now, it was almost impossible for people who were the subject of a study to respond to the findings. Even people who have been furious, such as the townspeople of Ithaca, New York, subject of Vidich and Bensman's *Small Town in Mass Society* (1960) had no way to circulate their views in the same venue in which the book appeared. Instead, they held a parade in which the authors were depicted peering into a manure spreader. Today, you can save people the trouble by inviting them to respond to your study and post their comments. Of course, there is nothing to stop really disgruntled people from banding together and creating their own Web page as an antidote to your study.

Hope And Glory surfs the Net

If you've been following the activities of the people in Hope And Glory in our newspapers, you've noticed that they have pretty diverse research interests — dog training, beards as sexual characteristics, and Native Americans, among others. Hope And Glory is a small isolated place — 'inbred' is the word visitors often use — and the library is only open on Tuesdays, so the Internet is a godsend to people like Septus McCardle, who has been trying to teach old dogs new tricks. He's found that some breeds are hopeless for the purpose — old or young, they're too stupid. He's found some Web sites on canines and canine intelligence, so he is now able to eliminate breeds with IQs in the red numbers: **www.petrix.com** lists breeds from most intelligent to least intelligent. He can also access **www.publicaffairs.ubc.ca** to get a canine IQ test, which will be very useful in his pre-tests and post-tests. Until now, Septus made up the tests and tried them out on himself first. Sometimes some dogs, Airedales in particular, outscored him.

At the same time, Mescoito Indian Chief Myron Grey Wolf III is participating in a discussion group called Native-L at **tamvm1.tamu.edu**, about and for indigenous peoples. But one of our researchers, Tiffani Shapiro, has been taking a hard look at Chief Grey Wolf. She's gone into

AskJeeves to ask 'Who are the Mescoito Indians?' and drawn a blank. The *Menominee* are the closest thing.

Randy Anderson, still smarting from the comments people are making about his poems, has joined the Kalliope Online Poetry Workshop at **poetry.tgu.com/arts/books/poetry**, where he can do some exercises in poetry and get critiques. He's also corresponding with Americans United for Separation of Church and State at **www.au.org** to find out if there's some legal precedent he can call on to stop the House of Worship from destroying his property values.

And over at Winkle's Party Pak, Sylene, the police chief's daughter, and Skip, Mayor Anderson's son, are eating meatloaf with loveable old Bert Whump. Sylene and Skip have just announced their engagement and are gazing into each other's eyes — Sylene's, blue with golden flecks, and Skip's, blue with golden flecks — and… Wait a minute, heck, Bert's eyes are blue with golden flecks as well! Sylene looks at Skip and Bert. Those sticky-out ears… Skip looks at Sylene and Bert. That nose… Hmmm.

Maybe they have more in common than they thought. They could look at many sites — for example, the WorldGenWeb Project at **www.worldgenweb.org**, which covers more than half the world's countries, or the USGenWeb Project at **www.usgenweb.net**, or even, since they have some British connections, the UKGenWeb Project at **www.rootsweb.com/~ukwgw**.

Of course, what they really need is not a family tree, but some genetic testing. They can learn about the science behind it by looking at the Natural History of Genes at **raven.umnh.utah.edu**. And if they ever find out that Bert is their grandfather, since he's the unofficial sire of both the mayor and the police chief, they can then explore the genetic consequence of marrying by looking at BioWeb, the online life sciences magazine at **www/saunderscollege.com**.

But right now, the police chief has other things to think about than his ancestry. His speed restrictions are bringing a bit of unwelcome notoriety to Hope And Glory, and Mayor Randy Anderson now complains that it's the worst speed trap in the US. Is it? Chief De Witt goes to:
www.speedtrap.com
and sees that although the site is packed with details, Hope And Glory doesn't even merit a mention.

Final warnings about the Web

The World Wide Web is growing by roughly a million pages every day. No one really knows how many pages it contains now, but it is estimated that over 80 per cent of the sites contain commercial content, *while only about six per cent contain scientific/educational content.* Learn how to use tools such as search engines to get to the sites that represent that six per cent.

Don't trust everything that you read. Nowhere is it more important than on the Internet. Why? A lot of information is simply dumped onto the Internet because someone thinks it is useful or accurate, and it may be neither. Think of the most obnoxious opinionated bore in your local pub — the one who believes that eating lettuce is fattening, because you have only to look at the elephant, which lives on salad. There is nothing to stop him assembling bits and pieces of crank literature and creating a Web site. One precaution is to check the credibility of information by seeing if the URL is a government site or an educational site (.gov, .edu, .ac). For example, if you are tempted to respond to a survey on sexual practices, **www.harvard.edu** is a better bet than **www.whoopee.com**. You can also check to see if there is a person responsible for the site whom you can email. Even at 'respectable' sites, the material can be dated or incomplete. Be careful about sites that might be biased, such as ones set up by special interest groups. Also, people can hack into Web sites and change information. Finally, use common sense. Never divulge information about yourself beyond what you are comfortable providing. Don't give your password to anyone, and think twice before clicking on 'Accepting a Cookie' or anything similar. 'Cookie' refers to a Web browser's capability to keep track of your Web site visits by establishing a file (cookie) on your hard drive from which it can access information about your browsing habits and then use that information in many ways, including the possibility of 'custom tailoring' future information that is presented to you, and possibly accumulating data that might at a later date be used for marketing purposes. If you don't want this, your Web browser can be set up to warn you that this is happening, or instruct you how to remove a cookie file.

Now that you've found some secondary material, you need to think about other issues, such as the actual content of what you have found.

What do you have and what does it mean?

When you are working with academic books and journal articles, you may have a certain degree of confidence in them because they usually have gone through a process of 'peer review' or scrutiny by others in the scholarly community before being published. And in many cases they may be the subject of ongoing reviews, debates, and challenges that you can also read. This is not to say, of course, that you can place blind faith in academic research: it can be faked or biased, and it can be a reflection of what topics are popular with funders, and what topics are thought to be more impressive when promotion is sought. For example, some years ago a prominent woman anthropologist used to advise her female students not to make gender the focus of their research, or they would become marginalized in the discipline. In those days, one could have assumed from scanning the anthropological literature that women's perspectives and issues affecting women weren't important.

In addition to books and journals, there are other kinds of secondary materials — records, diaries, accounts, laws, religious texts, literary works, and many others. People tend to take one of two views of these kinds of secondary materials. For some, they are 'impressionistic' and therefore of little value to the researcher. The positivistic tradition that we discussed in Chapter 2 has a lot to answer for here: positivists would argue that works — such as diaries, old letters, etc. — obviously present individual 'subjective' accounts, when the aim of science is to establish 'objective truth' and get at absolute reality and facts. On the other hand, others give some secondary materials, particularly records such as censuses, account books, etc., more credence than they may deserve, simply because they are written records and therefore 'objective'. Thus, a person's notation of his or her day may be thought to be of less value than the record of the same day as written down by someone doing a study of time use.

Both are simply points of view, and judgments about the value of a document are influenced by many other factors.

When we talk about secondary materials, we usually think of written documents, but photographs, videos, and films can also be important sources of information. And valuable social information is recorded in ways other than writing, as any archaeologist will tell you. For example, Webb et al, in their classic work *Nonreactive Measures in the Social Sciences* (1981) distinguish between records that arise because of deposits on objects — 'accretion measures' — and records that arise because an object has been worn away — 'erosion measures'. Thus, you could tell which exhibits in a museum were most interesting to children by the fingerprints, or accretions, on the glass cases housing the exhibits. On the other hand, you could also tell by the wear and tear, or erosion, on the floor in front of each of the exhibits. Dust on some machines and not others, wear and tear on books, car settings on radios left in for service, all reveal something.

In the case of written materials, there are many kinds, public and private — for example, works prepared especially for a study, such as a diary or an account of one's school day, versus works recorded for a different purpose, such as school records kept in accordance with departmental or ministry requirements. A teacher could keep a daily record for you of who came to school that day, and who was absent and why; on the other hand, you could come across an official school register that recorded attendance and absenteeism. People sometimes mistakenly assume that these are the same, and treat the latter kind of record almost as if it were designed for their study. For example, in some school records in Ireland in the last century, a child's name was recorded when he or she entered school, but also when re-entering school after a long absence. Since many children left school to work on the harvest and for other reasons, their names might appear two or three times a year in the record. Added to this was the fact that in many rural communities, there were only two or three surnames and a small pool of given names, so that 'Sean McCormack' might appear as an entrant many times over. A researcher who happened on such a record might think that a simple count of the names would reveal how many children were in school, and, since boys left more often than girls and were therefore re-entered more often, might conclude that a disproportionate number of boys were in school. In fact, the reverse might be the case. This is only one pitfall of working with records, which can be biased in any number of ways.

Another issue is what the document represents. First, what kind of resource is it? Is it something to be studied: a topic of research? Or is it something to draw upon: a resource *for* research? (May, 1993:140). Second, no document is an independent record of reality. We use our own cultural understandings both to produce documents and to interpret them. Readers engage with the meanings of a document in different ways. We can ask: 'What is the intended purpose of this document?' 'How was it produced?' 'Who produced it?' 'What circumstances — political, practical, economic, historical, or cultural — have influenced it?' 'What were the intentions of the author?' 'What assumptions is it based on?' 'What is left out?' 'Why has the document survived?'

Documents should be evaluated using the same questions that you would ask of other sources: is it authentic (not a fake)? Is it valid, dealing with what you want to use it for (the old Irish school records we mentioned were not valid for studying enrolment numbers)? Is it accurate, that is, free from bias and error? Is it representative? If you are drawing conclusions about something, does this document properly reflect the 'something' or is it atypical? Of course, atypical documents can be very useful for research: the diary of a 1950s female executive; the writings of a free black in the early 19th century US; the experiences of a Pakistani family in a small English town in the 90s are all instructive.

These are some of the issues that face the researcher who is using secondary materials. But look at it this way: when your own study is finished and published in some form, it will provide secondary material for *other* people, who then have to find it in the library or on the Internet and evaluate it in terms of the issues raised here.

References and further readings

Anderson, S.E. and B.M. Gansneder. 1995. 'Using Electronic Mail Surveys and Computer Monitored Data for Studying Computer Mediated Communication Systems.' *Social Science Computer Review* 13, No. 1.

Burke, John. 1996. *Learning the Net.* New York: Neal-Schuman Publishers.

Coomber, R. 1997. 'Using the Internet for Survey Research.' *Sociological Research Online* 2. http://www.socresonline.org.uk. Kenway, J. 1996. 'The Information Superhighway and Post-Modernity: the Social Promise and the Social Price'. *Comparative Education* 32, No. 2:217–231.

May, Tim. 1993. *Social Research: Issues, Methods and Process.* Buckingham, England: Open University Press.

Mehta, R. and E. Sivadas. 1995. 'Comparing Response Rates and Response Content in Mail Versus Electronic Mail Surveys.' *Journal of the Market Research Society* 37, No. 4:429–439.

Owen, Trevor and Ron Owston. 1998. *The Learning Highway.* Toronto: Key Porter Books Limited.

Pondiscio, Robert. 1999. *Get on the Net.* New York: Avon Books

Proctor, M. 1993. 'Analysing Other Researchers' Data' in N. Gilbert, ed., *Researching Social Life.* London: Sage.

Schmidt, W. 1997. 'World-Wide Web Survey Research Made Easy with WWW Survey Assistant.' *Behaviour Research Methods, Instruments and Computers* 29:303–304.

——. 1997. 'World-Wide Web Survey Research: Benefits, Potential Problems and Solutions.' *Behaviour Research Methods, Instruments and Computers* 29:274–279.

Thach, E. 1995. 'Using Electronic Mail to Conduct Survey Research.' *Educational Technology*, March/April:27–31.

Thorne, S. 1990. 'Secondary Analysis in Qualitative Research: Issues and Implications' in J.M. Morse, ed., *Critical Issues in Qualitative Research Methods.* London: Sage.

Vidich, Arthur J. and Joseph Bensman. 1960. *Small Town in Mass Society.* Garden City, New York: Doubleday.

Webb, Eugene, et al. 1981. *Nonreactive Measures in the Social Sciences.* Boston: Houghton Mifflin.

The Hope and Glory Vindicator

Volume 182 Issue 18   September 1, 2001

Mescoito shock stuns community

Researcher Tiffani Shapiro, who spent some time in Hope And Glory, has written a report showing that the group located behind the boiler factory are not Mescoito Indians. 'They're not any kind of a Indian at all,' said Ms. Shapiro to this reporter. 'They're not even related to each other. When I discovered this during my research, I was, like, "Hey!" '

The group, which consists of several famous ex-Mafia figures, some Mormon women who have reported on their bishops, and a government whistleblower, are part of the Federal Government's Witness Protection Program. They were given new identities and relocated to Hope And Glory eight years ago after testifying in various high-level cases.

Chief Myron Grey Wolf III, a.k.a. Tony Anzvino, said last night that he was relieved that the ghastly charade was over. This was the Federal Witness Protection Program's first attempt to settle a group of witnesses as a community, he said, and as far as he was concerned, it had not been thought out properly. 'Most of us are from New York City or Washington DC — we can't even understand what they're saying around here. The Mormon ladies had to translate for us until I married Bert Whump's daughter. I was a securities trader, and they make me an Indian chief working as a chimney sweep. No-one in the entire town has a fireplace.'

Had he ever been close to being discovered before? 'One time the local Boy Scouts invited me over to a pow-wow and I seen them looking at me funny — I don't whoop too good. We never got any kind of in-service training.'

When asked by a Vindicator reporter whether he would now be fearful for his safety, Mr. Anzivino said he had joined the House of Peace and was nestled in the bosom of the Lord.

When contacted late yesterday, agents for the Federal Witness Protection Program refused to confirm or deny the allegations.

Sign culprit caught

Rev. Dwight Wayman admitted yesterday that he had written the signs that have recently appeared in town. He said he was only trying to help Mayor Randy Anderson, who had been sentenced by Judge Dick Quinn to write anti-speed slogans. Rev. Wayman said that Mr. Anderson had developed 'writer's cramp or stage fright or whatever they call it, and it was pitiful to see an artist in that state, so as a Christian I stepped in.' He said he wasn't an educated man, but he did his best.

No charges are planned.

Social Notes

In a quiet ceremony on Saturday evening, August 11, Mayor Randy Anderson and Mrs. Laurinda McCardle were married. Mrs. McCardle, who will keep her maiden name, performed the ceremony herself, assisted by the Rev. Dwight Wayman of the House of Peace Temple.

INSIDE THIS ISSUE

9 GIVING A SURVEY

Summary

Surveys are useful when you want responses to the same questions from a number of people.

Surveys take two forms: *structured interviews* such as face-to-face surveys and telephone surveys, which the researcher administers; and *questionnaires,* such as postal surveys, which respondents fill in themselves.

Mini surveys (small number of questions, small number of respondents) are useful for short projects and can be analyzed easily without a computer.

Work out the information you need by consulting your research outline or using a similar procedure.

Decide to whom the survey will be given and whether you will ask everyone in the group or a sample.

Design the survey, and assemble the instrument:
- create a statement explaining the research to the respondent (*a face sheet*), or, in the case of postal surveys, a cover letter;
- plan the order of your questions and use *filter questions* to guide people through the interview;
- check for poor questions and poor answer choices, including

inappropriate questions and answers, two-in-one questions, loaded
questions and answers, vague words, overly broad questions, and
questions requiring second-hand information;

- decide if the answers will be *open-ended* (blank spaces provided) or *forced-choice* (answer choices provided). A survey may contain a combination of both;
- decide how to prepare answers for counting.

Pre-test the survey.

Select and train the interviewers if you are not working alone.

Administer the survey.

Process the data: count the answers and do any cross-tabulations you need
by relating a person's answer to one question to their answer to another.
You can do this yourself or use a computer.

Surveys and Questionnaires

One of the best ways to learn about using surveys is to be on the giving or
receiving end of a bad one. Figure 9–1 is an example of a bad survey
designed to help the Swamp Broadcasting Company to assess reactions to
its programming. Following the survey you will see how it is made worse
by a poor interviewer who carries it out in Hope And Glory.

Figure 9–1 Example of a bad survey

Greeting and Brief Introduction _____

Surname and Christian Name?

Age? (Circle One)

15-20 20-25 25-30 30-35 35-40 40-45 45-50 50-55

Sex? (Circle One)

MALE FEMALE

Do you have a radio and a television?

YES NO

How many radios? _____

How many televisions? _____

Do you listen to 'Acrobatics for the Elderly' on the radio?

YES NO

What do you find not unattractive about that program?

THE POSITIONS

THE COSTUMES

THE CASUALTIES

THE LIGHTING

THE DIRECTION

OTHER

Do you watch *Father Bob Reads the Bible* on television?

YES NO

Do you think this program is too racy and should be cancelled or is Father Bob's criminal record none of the public's business?

YES NO

Here's the interviewer (I) and a respondent (R), Wendy, from Hope And Glory, Ohio

I. Good morning. I am here from the advertising division of Swamp Broadcasting to ask you some important questions. Surname?

R. Hiya.

I. Surname?

R. What are them questions about?

I. The management wants to know more about why people have stopped listening to their programs.

R. Well, but I never listened to your programs. I watch MTV — my favorite group is The Flaming Pimples. Anyhow, how come you're asking me?

I. Because this is a random sample.

R. Can't you ask the people next door? They got an opinion on everything, especially me. Anyhow, as I said, I don't know squat about these programs and right now I'm trying to smother a little fire in the kitchen — my Mama is fixing to put up some tomatoes and she left me to mind the pot, and...

I. This will only take a moment. And anyone is intelligent enough to answer these simple questions. Name?

R. Will my name go to the school principal? They were kinda expecting me in school today.

I. No. Surname?

R. Then why do you want my name?

I. Because it says 'Surname_____' here on the form.

R. Well, my name is Goldberg.

I. What is your Christian name?

R. But I'm not a Christian. We're the only Jews in three counties here. I often asked my Mama how come we…

I. What is your first name then?

R. Wendy.

I. Age?

R. Fifteen.

I. Wait a minute. Where do I put that? It says here 10–15 and 15–20. Which is it?

R. Well, I don't really know. Let me see that paper. I did good in accounting. Failed cooking over my French toast, though. Which reminds me — my Mama's tomatoes…

I. Sex?

R. Not yet. I'm only fifteen. Mama'd kill me. But thanks for askin'. You single?

I. I mean WHAT IS your sex? It asks it here on the form.

R. What do you mean what is my sex? What do I look like? Robert de Niro?

I. Do you have a radio and a television?

R. I have a television but no radio — Mama's boyfriend threw up in it one time after a party and we ain't got it fixed. Mama says we're gonna buy new, it's cheaper.

I. It says 'YES' or 'NO'.

R. That can't be right. Let me see that paper. You ain't reading those right, honey.

I. It says it right here on the form. We got an eminent professor from the university to draw this up for us. YES or NO?

R. Oh, sheesh, I don't know. I suppose 'yes'.

I. Do you listen to 'Acrobatics for the Elderly' on the radio?

R. I been trying to tell you, I don't have a radio. Is that smoke or is it getting dark?

I. Nonsense, it isn't noon yet. What do you particularly like about that program?

THE POSITIONS

THE COSTUMES
THE CASUALTIES
OTHER

R. I told you. Oh, well, I suppose the casualties. I hope to be a surgeon some day. I love those outfits, and the little paper shoes they wear in surgery.

I. Do you watch *Father Bob Reads the Bible* on television?

R. No. I don't watch *nothin'* but MTV. Nada. Zip.

I. Do you think this program is too racy and should be cancelled or is Father Bob's past criminal record none of the public's business? Could I have your attention here, Wendy?

R. That is smoke.

I. Yes or No.

R. Yeah, yeah, yeah, the program should be cancelled and Father Bob should be forgiven. Your coat is smoldering.

Some of the problems in the interviewing technique and the survey form may be obvious to you already. By the end of this chapter, you should be able to identify other weaknesses in both. Remember that in addition to those described here, many other mistakes are possible, some of which you will probably invent on your own. This happens to most researchers when designing a survey, so don't be disheartened if things go a bit wrong. People — not only the general public, but some researchers, too — often believe that the survey is the best, most scientific way of getting objective information. They think that doing a survey is a simple and quick process and that the survey is a standard, universally useful tool that can be used anywhere for almost any information-getting need. As a result, they believe that whatever methods you use, it is best to begin with a survey to get a general picture; that if you can use only one technique, it should be the survey; and that you should verify the results you get from other 'softer' methods by a doing a survey. In effect, they are saying use a survey at the beginning, at the end, or alone, but use one. In reality, the survey requires a good deal of expertise and a considerable investment of time and money. Like every other research technique, it has a specific function: it tells you what people say they do, think, or feel if you ask the right questions, if they understand what you are asking, and if they are able and prepared to give you answers. If you want other dimensions of reality, you have to use other techniques as well.

And as we saw in Chapter 2, just because the responses to a survey can be converted into numbers and percentages, it does not make them more valid or accurate. The survey will provide information on selected variables, but not their meaning or context, and the replies, when added up, will not provide a holistic picture — they are just a set of responses to specific questions, and a snapshot at one point in time. So a survey is a specific tool that when used for the right reasons does the job better than anything else and, when used for the wrong reasons, is a waste of everyone's time, effort, money, and hopes.

Some of the right reasons for using a survey are:

- You need a broadly based response to a specific set of questions or items. You may be using the survey as your main technique, or you want to plan the next stage of your research, and getting a broad picture will help you to focus the issues, the target group, and the techniques more carefully.
- You want to compare the results from one group with that of another. Using the same survey for both groups lets you do that.
- You want to cross-check the results which you obtained using another technique, such as observation.

Some of the wrong reasons for using a survey are:

- It seems the most 'scientific' way to get information.
- It seems quicker and easier.
- You don't know any other way to get the information.
- You think no one will believe your results unless you use a survey and produce some numbers and percentages.

We have been using the word *survey* to refer to a standardized set of questions put to a number of respondents. But surveys can take two forms: a *questionnaire*, or something that the respondent fills in, or a *structured interview*, whether face-to-face or over the telephone, in which the researcher fills in the answers. There are also other kinds of interviews that are more individually tailored to each respondent or situation, such as semi-structured, focus group, and informal interviews. See Chapter 11 for a discussion of these.

In practice, questionnaires and structured interviews take one of three forms:

- the postal interview
- the telephone interview
- the face-to-face interview

In this chapter we will look at some issues common to the first and the last, and explain why we are skipping the middle one. We will also be suggesting that, whenever possible, you carry out a 'mini survey' rather than a longer one. Longer surveys, which are large in terms of numbers of respondents, numbers of questions, or both, are labor intensive to design, administer, and process. If you must take on a task like this, you should try to get help from a specialist in survey design, sampling, coding, and analysis to avoid some of the pitfalls that can and do happen, even to experts. Several good sources on surveys and questionnaires are listed at the end of this chapter. An excellent one for beginners is *How to Conduct Your Own Survey* by Priscilla A. Salant and Don A. Dillman, 1994 (New York: John Wiley).

Mini Surveys

You should seriously consider using a *mini survey*. Mini surveys are carefully focused on a specific topic; contain only fifteen to thirty questions; are given to a small sample of twenty-five to one hundred; and usually use more closed than open-ended questions, that is, they use questions that force the respondent to choose from a small set of alternative answers, rather than inviting a freely expanded reply. A mini survey can be completed in three to seven weeks, whereas many large surveys can take a year and often much longer for the whole process to be completed and the results analyzed. Technically, mini surveys are usually structured interviews rather than questionnaires.

A mini survey has some disadvantages. The main one arises from the size. Perhaps your entire group is 100 or less, in which case a mini survey is ideal. But if your 25–100 people represent a sample, and you want to claim that your results can be applied to a much larger population, you may have problems. Some statistical tests do not work with the small numbers you will find in your study. Also, 100 may not be a sufficiently large sample size for your population. But also note that a sample of less than 100 can be appropriate for a population of 100 million, under certain circumstances.

For the best results follow the nine points explained in the following sections.

1 Clarify your objectives

As you would in any piece of research, ask yourself: 'What do I want to find out?' 'Why?' 'Is this technique the way to get this kind of information?' 'When I get the answers to these questions, will they meet my needs?'

2 Find out what else has been done

Someone may already have done a survey that is good enough for your purposes, that will provide you with some useful questions, or that will allow you to build on existing work and go a step further. However, don't automatically use someone else's questions for your own survey unless you are convinced they will work for you. If you want to compare your results with those obtained by someone else in an earlier survey, you will have to use the same questions as the other researcher did. In the process, you may sacrifice local meaningfulness for comparability: some of the questions may not mean the same thing to the people you are studying as they did to the other researcher's study group. However, if you do adapt the questions for the group you are studying, then your respondents are answering different questions, so you can't compare the results. Researchers have been pondering this conundrum for many years. If you think of a solution, telephone us, but not before you read the note on telephone surveys at the end of this chapter.

Another possibility is that a standard scale or measure has been developed for your topic (see Chapter 10). These can present the same problems as described in the last paragraph.

3 Choose the respondents

First, you must decide whether you are going to ask your questions of the entire group, whatever it might be (for example, all the bald men in the country, or just some of them). The first is a population or universe. The second is a sample. If you are using a sample, you must choose the type of sample. Reviewing Chapter 6 will help you decide.

4 Develop the questions and answers

a. Develop the questions

There are no universal, all-purpose questions. You cannot even assume that you should start by asking respondents their name, age, and sex, because you may not need to know those things. So where do you get your questions? If you are using a research outline approach (see Chapter 4), look at the points in the outline to see which of them might be studied through a survey. Look at these points, taken from the outline we developed in Chapter 4. Which of these could be studied through a survey?

Hope And Glory

1. General characteristics
   A. Location
      1) geographic
      2) economic (in relation to suppliers, markets, etc.)

```
B.    Size
     1) area
     2) population
        a) by age
        b) by sex
```

Women entrepreneurs

```
1. General characteristics
   A. Age
   B. Area of residence
   C. Marital status
   D. Domestic responsibilities
2. Work-related characteristics
   A. Occupation
   B. Other employment
   C. Training — occupational
      1) type
         a) formal
         b) non-formal
      2) institution attended
      3) accreditation received
```

You could get individual responses to the second group of points, but a survey would not be useful for the first. There are studies in which you would want people's estimates of sizes, but in this one you do not want individuals' opinions of the size of the district; you want to know its actual size. When you have selected the points for study, write each one on its own card or piece of paper and on the back write the question that you will use for the point. Then you can rearrange the cards to put them in the best order (we will return to this later).

If you do not have a research outline, think about the topic you need to study. Let us say you want to develop a course for homeless people on how to get back into housing and find suitable jobs. Consider what you need to know. To help yourself ask 'who?', 'what?', 'where?', 'when?', 'why?', and 'how?' and you will begin to get your questions.

First the people...

Who are they (age and sex)? Where are they? What led to their being homeless? Have they left school? When? Why? How are they making their living now?

Then the course...

Who would attend courses, if offered? What courses do they want? Where could they attend them? When would they be free to attend? Why do they want particular courses?

And so on...

For each of these points, you can ask more detailed questions using the same method. For 'When would they be free to attend?' you might want to know 'How often?' For 'Where could they attend them?' you might want to know 'How would they get there?' Of course, the approaches mentioned so far will lead to questions that you think are important. However, you will almost certainly have overlooked important areas in your planning or emphasized certain issues more than the situation warrants. Open-ended investigation will help you here. Use some of the approaches discussed in Chapters 11–14 to get people to talk about their concerns and perspectives. For example, you can also use focus groups to develop questions, particularly when you aren't very familiar with the issues. You could convene a group of women entrepreneurs to explore the issues which concern them. Of course, this in itself may be enough for the purposes of your study, but you can also use what you learn in the session to create areas of questioning for a survey. These approaches will make the focus of your survey, the questions, answer choices, and language more relevant. Further questions will occur to you when you think of the possible answers people can give you.

Plan the direction your survey will take by making a flow chart. If you ask 'Did you complete primary school?' you will want to plan what to ask next depending on the possible responses (Figure 9–2). You can use the flow chart to decide how many of the lines of inquiry are worth pursuing.

Framing the questions

As you are planning the questions, try to picture the people who will be answering them and their circumstances. For example, some of the people will be long-term unemployed; some will never have finished primary school; some will be voluntarily homeless some will have children with them. Knowing these facts will help you to include other important questions. Will the person need child-care facilities in order to attend? If someone has taken a course like this in the past and dropped out, why? You learn to write good questions by thinking things through, knowing about

Figure 9–2 An example of a flow chart

Did you complete secondary school?

⇩   ⇩

No		Yes
Did you attend primary school?		Do you intend to go on to third level education?

⇩   ⇩   ⇩   ⇩

No	Yes	No	Yes
⇩	⇩	⇩	⇩
Why not?	For how long?	Why not?	What kind?
	⇩	⇩	⇩
	Why did you stop?	What will you do?	Where?
	⇩		
	Would you attend secondary school now if you had the chance?		

⇩

No	Yes
⇩	⇩
Why not?	What would you need to help you?

the people who will answer them, and making mistakes. You will usually discover these after the survey is over and you will be astonished at how stupid they are. Nonetheless, you can learn in advance from other people's stupid mistakes. Here are some:

Asking inappropriate questions

Wording can be equally meaningful to both parties without the meaning being shared. Several years ago I asked eleven-year-old children in schools in Eritrea, Africa, the following questions:

When you grow up, would you like to marry?
When you grow up, would you like to have children?

These questions had been used in a survey in various developing countries, and the answers had provided useful information (Brock and Camish, 1991).

Here are the Eritrean replies, summing up the results from 21 communities:

When I grow up, I would like to get married
Boys 90%
Girls 41%
When I grow up, I would like to have children
Boys 92%
Girls 44%

The more traditional the community, the bigger the difference between boys' and girls' replies. Were 'traditional' girls rebelling and planning single, childless lives?

In fact, the questions, even ones as straight-forward and simple as these, meant different things to boys and girls. The girls, at eleven, were of marriageable age and they felt they were being asked if they wanted to marry *now*. The boys would not be able to marry until they were in their twenties, at least, and they were answering in relation to the future.

Asking two questions in one

Sometimes one question is actually two. *'As part of the new affirmative action plan, the government is hiring more women than men in civil service positions. What do you think about this plan?'* is two questions: *'What do you think about the affirmative action plan?'* and *'What do you think about the fact that more women than men are being taken on?'* If someone says, 'I disagree', is it with the plan, the extra numbers of women, or both? Instead, try: *'The government has a new affirmative action plan. One of its requirements is that more women than men be hired as lumberjacks. Do you favour this requirement?'*

Asking loaded questions (questions that bias the answer)

The very fact that you ask a question in the first place tells the respondent that you attach some importance to the subject. If a major part of your survey is on services for the aged or on the need for childproof medicine containers, your respondents realize that an 'educated' or 'official' person sees this as an issue worth bothering about. No one likes to admit that they never thought about childproof containers, or even worse, that they have to get a child to open such containers because no one else can. Their replies may be affected, even though the subject may not be important to them. So questions are already loaded, but you can take care to reduce other kinds of biases. If you begin a question with *'Don't you think…?'* or *'Wouldn't you say that…?'* you are setting up the respondent to agree. If you invoke authorities or use emotive or pejorative words (*'The parish priest welcomes the bishop's call to the faithful to reject Godless holiday cards and put Christ back into Christmas. What do you think?'*) don't expect much disagreement. Calling tattooing and ear-piercing 'bodily mutilation' is going to get you off on the wrong foot with many teenagers.

Often, loaded questions presuppose something that may not be true: *'Why do you like this company?'* *'Why do you think it is important for mothers with young children to stay at home?'* *'How do you think we should expand the after-school programs?'* For the last, try: *'Should the after-school program be expanded?'* instead.

Sometimes, researchers deliberately construct a question that appears to presuppose something. If you are trying to find out what people do not like about your program or project and feel that they may be reluctant to say, you can ask: *'What do you like about the project?'* and then: *'What don't you like about it?'* and people may feel easier about making criticisms.

Asking a question that appears to have a 'right' answer is pointless: *'Teenage pregnancies appear to be increasing at a very alarming rate. Is this a cause for concern?'* Or *'Did you enjoy the free gourmet coffee we provided with your dinner?'*

Answer choices can also bias the replies, for example, consider the following question:

If someone witnesses a car accident, he or she should first
A. PHONE THE POLICE   1
B. TRY TO HELP THE VICTIM   2
C. ACT LIKE A RESPONSIBLE CITIZEN   3

Most people will choose 'C'. Some will think it is the same as 'A' and others will think it is the same as 'B'. A third group will think it is something else entirely — what, you won't know.

Using ambiguous or vague words or phrases

One of the major assumptions of a survey is that all respondents are answering the same questions. However, if the questions mean different things to different people, this is no longer the case. Ambiguous or vague words and phrases are one cause. 'Frequently' can mean daily to one person and annually to another. Thus, 'Do you bathe frequently?' can truthfully be answered 'yes' by two people, but you might find that you prefer not to share a seat on the bus with one of them. *'Do you think bilingual people are more successful?' 'Do you revise your lessons often?' 'All things considered, would you like to live nearer to town?' 'Do you attend the parent-teacher meetings regularly?'* are all open to interpretation. Can you see which words are causing the problems? Using undefined concepts presents problems, as well. Words like 'income', 'household', or 'employment' can mean something entirely different from one place to another. When you ask what employment a person has had in the past five years, what do you really want to know? Ask that instead.

Sometimes, vague wording will confuse you, rather than the respondent: You might ask: *'How much time did you spend watering the garden last week?'* By the time all your interviews have been completed, many weeks will have passed. In some weeks, droughts may have occurred; in other floods. Which week was each respondent talking about?

Finally, nervous novice researchers often feel that using pretentious language (*'Do you regard unilateral school board interventions in curriculum assessment as being productive?'*) will make their respondents more respectful and cooperative, but all it will do is annoy and confuse them. However, if you are dealing with people who use a specialized language, such as technical words, you need to use them or the respondents will assume that they are wasting their time on an amateurish effort. Asking equestrians about the top and bottom of a horse will create the suspicion that you are not entirely familiar with the geography of the animal, and are not to be taken seriously.

Asking questions that are too broad

When you are planning your survey, you might ask people some broad questions such as: *'What do you think of the job the police are doing in this community?'* to see what dimensions of the situation are most important to them. Their answers will help you to focus the questions you ask on the final version of your survey and to omit issues that appear to be irrelevant. Asking such a broad question on the survey itself, however, is not very useful. Some people will complain that the police are more interested in responding to the burglar alarms of the rich than preventing decent citizens from being mugged. Some will say that police brutality worries them, and others will say that when they were young and the world was run properly, the police were sizable white men, whereas now one has to know Samoan to ask a slip of an officerette the time of day.

Start over. Decide instead what aspect of the police system you want people to comment on and phrase the question more precisely: *'Do you favour the new plan to arm the police with bows and arrows?'*

Asking for information people do not have or will not be able to remember accurately

Even if people do not have the information you seek, or cannot recall it well, they will often give you an answer anyway, and you have no way of judging its accuracy. Researcher Benjamin White (1984, p. 20), looking at the ability of people in rural Java to recall hours of income-producing work, found that asking people twenty-four hours after finishing the work produced one set of figures; thirty days later they recalled only about two-thirds of the hours; and one year later, between 43 and 60 per cent of the hours. Most of us would have the same problem. The following question not only asks people to remember, but to do some mathematics, as well: *'What percentage of your time is spent on personal hygiene?'*

Try this:

About how many minutes did you spend on the following activities yesterday?
A. BATHING AND SHAMPOOING
B. CLEANING TEETH

Asking for second-hand information or opinions when you need direct information or facts

'Why don't your neighbors participate in the recycling program?' should be asked of the neighbors themselves. *'What percentage of parents would send their children to religious instruction if it were provided?'* will tell you people's opinion about the percentage, not what it is. On the other hand, in sensitive situations, a very similar kind of question might be used to get the respondent's own views; to someone jailed for murdering a spouse, for example, one might put the question *'Why do you think people poison their husbands?'*

Question checks

Sometimes intentionally, and sometimes because of poor questions, people will answer questions incorrectly. If people are intent on deceiving you, it is pretty difficult to catch, but you can insert question checks for some items: you can ask husbands, for example, *'Do you do any of the cooking at home?'* Let us say that 75 per cent of the respondents say 'yes'. Later in the survey you can ask *'Where is the kitchen in your home?'* If only 23 per cent of respondents know the answer, you know something is probably wrong.

b. Develop the answers

Once you have the questions, you have to think about the answers. It is often said that good lawyers, when cross-examining a witness in court, never ask a question unless they already know the answer. In a survey, you do not have to know the answer but you have to know the possible answers so that you can decide how to handle them.

Open-ended or forced-choice questions

Your questions will either be open-ended (in which blank spaces are left for answers), or forced-choice or closed (in which you provide the answer categories and people choose). Open-ended questions allow more freedom for the person replying but are more difficult for you to process when the survey is over. You have to read all the answers, decide what categories they include, go back and sort the answers into the categories and then count them. If you ask 'What is your age?' you can get answers from about 2 to 100+. If you provide a set of forced-choice answers (1–10, 11–20, 21–30 and so on), the grouping is already done. Open-ended questions are useful when you are doing exploratory research and want to see the range of possible answers, or when the material is intimidating or sensitive (research in Western societies shows that people will report socially unacceptable behavior more readily when asked in an open-ended question).

Forced-choice questions require that you know enough about the situation to give relevant choices. This takes a lot of preliminary work, but once the survey is administered you can process forced-choice answers quickly simply by counting the answers in each category, either manually or with a computer. Make sure your answers are exhaustive (cover all the possibilities) and exclusive (do not overlap). For example:

Sex of police officer
A. FEMALE   1
B. MALE   2

'Female' and 'male' are examples of exhaustive and mutually exclusive answers. There are no more possibilities, and everyone will fall into one or the other. In a face-to-face interview, you do not ask this question, of course, you figure it out for yourself.

An example of not being inclusive enough would be:

What do you look for when you are buying a car?
A. DESIGN   1
B. COLOUR   2
C. FAST ACCELERATION   3
D. LOW FUEL CONSUMPTION   4

Features such as comfort, size, running costs other than fuel, reliability, resale value, anti-lock braking, and storage capacity, among others, have been left out. You can put in a category called 'other' but you would not be able to tell what it included. Once you are satisfied that you really have offered the likely categories, you could add

E. OTHER   5   *Please explain* _____

Some questions can have as a final category: 'Don't know' or 'Anything else?' Be sure you are not using these categories just to save time when designing the survey, because they will add time when analyzing the results.

A very common mistake of not being exclusive enough is overlapping number categories:

When do you think sexual passion begins to fade? (This is, of course, a good example of a loaded question.)
A. 60–70   1
B. 70–80   2
C. 80–90   3

Let's say you think the correct answer is eighty. Which one do you circle?

Forced-choice questions can include sliding scales, such as the one given to our researchers when they were guests of the State of Ohio a while ago:

How would you rate the food here in jail?
A. VERY POOR   1
B. POOR   2
C. FAIR   3
D. GOOD   4
E. VERY GOOD   5

You can use words like 'always', 'most of the time', 'sometimes', 'very rarely', 'never' as categories to describe the frequency of something. Another common set of categories is various stages of agreement: 'strongly agree', 'agree', 'disagree', 'strongly disagree'.

However, be careful about the way you divide the scale:

A recent survey shows that women with children under two years old have about half an hour to themselves each day. Do you think this is:
A. FAR TOO LITTLE
B. TOO LITTLE
C. SLIGHTLY TOO LITTLE

D. ABOUT RIGHT

E. TOO MUCH

This is biased toward the 'little' end, and even if the question were useful the answers won't be.

Another way of showing degrees of response is to use an adaptation of the Semantic Differential developed by Osgood, Suci, and Tannenbaum (1957). (The original purpose of this scale is more sophisticated than the one described here.) Concepts, presented in polar opposite terms, are placed at the left and right of a seven-point scale, and the respondent is asked to rate people, objects, places, and so on along the scale for each concept (Figure 9–3). The center is neutral. For example:

Figure 9–3 Example of a semantic differential-type scale

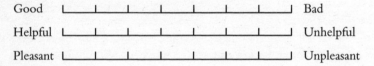

The police in Hope and Glory, Ohio

Good ⌊__⌊__⌊__⌊__⌊__⌊__⌊__⌋ Bad

Helpful ⌊__⌊__⌊__⌊__⌊__⌊__⌊__⌋ Unhelpful

Pleasant ⌊__⌊__⌊__⌊__⌊__⌊__⌊__⌋ Unpleasant

Other pairs of choices are presented on the same page, with the scale redrawn for each pair. You might use the same pairs for other categories of public servants — firefighters, traffic wardens, ambulance drivers, etc. The order of answers can also have an effect on responses. Salant and Dillman (1994, pp. 86–87) present an interesting finding: in telephone and face-to-face interviews, people are more likely to choose the last answer or among the last few answers in a list; in a postal survey, the first, or among the first few. Two possible solutions are to keep your answer categories short, and to vary the order of the list from one respondent to the next. If it is essential to present people with a long list in face-to-face interviews, you can hand people a card and ask them to choose their response from it.

Categorizing the answers

When thinking about the answers, you should also think about making the completed forms easier to deal with. If you use open-ended questions, they might look like this:

*What level did you complete in school?*_____

A forced-choice question might look like this:

What level did you complete in school?

NONE	[ ]
PRIMARY	[ ]
SECONDARY	[ ]
THIRD LEVEL	[ ]

But you can make counting the answers easier if you give each choice a number. If you are going to use a computer to analyze the results, you will have to do this but, even if you are not, it will help.

NONE	1
PRIMARY	2
SECONDARY	3
THIRD LEVEL	4

If you are going to use a computer to count your answers, you should number them, starting with '1'. If your answer choices will exceed nine, you should insert a zero before each number: '01', '02', etc. Remember to allow for 'no reply' when you are counting the possible answers. 'CIRCLE ONE' is written in upper case letters as an easily visible instruction to the interviewer.

Writing the questions

Now write out your questions in such a way that when the researcher reads them out they sound natural, like spoken rather than written language. This, for example, is written English in many countries: 'I wish to address a number of questions to you. However, I shall be pleased to answer any queries you might have first.' Spoken colloquial English would be more like: 'I'd like to ask you some questions. Is there anything you'd like to ask me first?' Read your questions aloud to see how they sound.

The following guidelines for writing questions were adapted from work by cross-cultural research experts Brislin, Lonner, and Thorndike (1973), who created them to help in translating questions from one language to another. But they are useful even when you do not have to translate.

- Use short, simple sentences of less than sixteen words. However, sensitive questions may require a softener: 'Some women find that for one reason or another, they need to take birth control measures without consulting their partners. Have you ever found yourself doing this?')
- Use the active rather than the passive voice: 'Should the teachers discipline the students?' rather than 'Should discipline be carried out by the teachers?'

- Repeat nouns instead of using pronouns: 'When the managers met with the workers, they were nervous.' Who was nervous?
- Avoid the subjective mode, such as verbs with 'could' and 'would': 'If the transit system could improve its security, would more people travel after dark?'
- Avoid vague words such as 'nearer,' 'often,' and 'frequent': 'Would you like to live nearer to work?'
- Avoid possessive forms where possible: 'The mayor's spokesman has taken his request to his nominating committee.' Whose request? Whose committee?
- Use specific rather than general terms: the council chair, the managing director, rather than 'the authorities'; the soccer club, the debating team, rather than 'extracurricular activities'.
- Avoid sentences with two different verbs if the verbs suggest two different actions: 'Should parents attend and challenge the teachers at the parent-teacher meetings?'

Many more could be added to this: for example, don't write in double negatives: 'Would you find it impossible to believe that your partner wasn't practicing safe sex?' A vast literature on writing questions is available, much of it very helpful because it is based on question variations that have been tried on large numbers of people. Since most of these surveys have been carried out in the Western world, we offer a few pointers for surveys in non-Western societies at the end of this chapter. Finally, you can use a guide like the following to get some perspective on the value of each question to your research (adapted from Leedy, 1989).

Outline Point	Question	Answer form (forced-choice, open)	What will the answer tell me?	How does this relate to my research?	Do I need to use a question check?	What is the question?	How does this provide a check?

When you pre-test the questions (discussed later in the chapter) you will learn more about how potential respondents evaluate your questions.

Planning filter questions

Sometimes your study will contain people who have very different characteristics or experiences, and not all your questions should be answered by each person. You may have to use filter questions to guide people. For example:

1. *Did you ever attend secondary school?*
   YES   ⇨   Question 2
   NO   ⇨   Question 8
2. *Did you complete secondary school?*
   YES   ⇨   Question 4
   NO   ⇨   Question 3
3. *Would you like to complete secondary school?*
   YES
   NO

This keeps people who did not go to secondary school from going on to tell you they completed it, and people who completed it from being asked whether they would like to complete it. If this format is not clear enough for your interviewers, try other methods. For example, after question 1, you can write: 'If respondent never attended secondary school, go to question 8'.

If you do not plan your filter questions properly, you may be sure that at least one man will answer questions on his pregnancies, or one teenager will say she is still in school and in the next question will give you the reason why she left. Even worse, your respondents may simply give up. If you know that the groups you are interviewing are so different in their experiences that you will have to include large numbers of filter questions, making the survey difficult to administer, you might consider developing a separate survey for each group.

Ordering the questions

Order your questions. On the principle that once people invest some time in a survey they are less likely to balk at unattractive questions, ask general, open-ended, easier, more interesting, less personal, and less sensitive questions first. Sensitive questions differ from one cultural group to the next: many Westerners are used to the idea of giving details of age, sex, number of children, and so on while bristling at questions about income, but people in a study in Ghana (Devereaux, 1989), for example, were prepared to discuss income and assets, but not numbers of children (apparently fearing a tax). There is not a lot of point in trying to get around this by assuring people that the information they give is confidential. You must assure them, but often they do not believe you and think you are amazingly naive for believing it yourself, or else they start having second thoughts about the wisdom of discussing the matter if you, an 'expert', think it is such a confidential matter. Of course, it still must be kept confidential, whatever people believe.

You may have taken points in your research outline, converted them into questions, and written each on a card as we suggested earlier in the chapter. One way to order them now is to write them all on cards and move them around until you find an arrangement that seems to work. Keep questions on related items together, and when you change the subject, use a bridge: 'Now I'd like to talk to you about something else', or 'Now I'd like to ask you a little about the recent elections'.

Writing instructions for the interviewers on the survey form

Since an interviewer other than you may read your questions to the respondent, you need to write some instructions on the form itself, in addition to training the researchers and preparing a manual for them, as discussed later. These instructions take several forms and should be typed in different formats, so that the interviewer can easily see what to do. You can choose the format, but be consistent. For example, instructions intended only for the researcher which should not be read out can be underlined:

<u>Ask of male respondents only</u>
Have you ever had prostate cancer?
YES
NO
DON'T KNOW

Each time the interviewer sees underlined text, he or she knows that these are interviewer instructions only, and should not be read out. Examples of other items which are not read out are instructions such as '<u>Skip to question 6</u>' and forced choices such as '<u>Don't know</u>' and '<u>Not applicable</u>', even though they are marked off, if they apply. In other cases, it is necessary for the interviewer to read out instructions: *Now I am going to show you a set of numbered cards. Each card contains the name of a form of punishment that parents have used on their children. I would like you to look at each card and read out its number if it is a punishment that you have used.*

Each time the interviewer sees italicized letters, he or she knows to read out the text.

A third kind of instruction is one which is sometimes read out: for example, if a respondent can't give an answer to a particular question about income, the interviewer is told to ask: *If you are not sure, could you give an estimate?* The researcher knows that these words in bold italics are to be asked only if needed.

5 Assemble the instrument

Now that you have the survey ready, it needs a face sheet and a closing.

The face sheet

Begin by making a face sheet. This will contain the following kinds of information, adapted to meet your circumstances.

Title of Survey   Respondent's Identification Number
Interviewer's Name
Date
Reason for no interview [if no interview can be obtained]

Introduction:
My name is (name). I work for the Children's Association, which provides courses for young people who would like to work as baby-sitters. We would like to make our courses more useful to people.

(Name of authorizing person, if appropriate) has given us permission to come to your school and ask young people what courses they need. I would like to get your opinions. I do not need your name and I will not discuss your answers with anyone else. Is there anything you would like to ask me before we begin?

Keep your introduction short.

The serial number helps you to keep track of the respondent's survey form. If 75 people are being interviewed, the first person will be numbered '01'. You can keep the respondents' names on a master sheet, along with their numbers, in case you need to follow up the interview. You can also enter it into the computer if you use one to analyze the results. You will need the master sheet, which should be kept in confidence, if you want to follow people up later. For example, after a postal questionnaire you might write to thank people who replied and remind people who have not that you still need their replies. Even with face-to-face interviews, you may want to compare survey results with other materials from the same respondent and giving the same number to all the materials for an individual will be helpful.

Closing the survey

On this final page, close your survey by asking once again if the respondent has any questions to ask or anything to add. Thank the respondent. If there is going to be an occasion when people can hear the general results of your study, such as at a community meeting, tell the person when and where you will do this. Or if you are going to prepare a summary page of your results, you can ask if the person would like to receive it.

6 Pre-test the survey

Pre-test the survey on people who will not be taking the final version. One way is to ask five to ten people to sit down with you, answer the questions and then give you comments about each question. A pre-test should help you to find out whether the survey:

- flows properly, is arranged in a workable way for the interviewer (boxes in the right places, enough space for answers, manageable filter questions) and asks the questions in an order that seems reasonable to the interviewee;
- sounds good when read aloud;
- does not take too long. For standard surveys, research in Western societies indicates that people are prepared to be interviewed for anything up to an hour, but mini surveys will require much less time;
- is interesting to the respondent. If the questions are all 'yes–no', or all involve ranking on a scale from one to seven, people will probably find even the mini survey a bit dull, but the biggest cause of uninterest will be if the questions have little or no bearing on the respondent's life. Sometimes you have to ask things that are not central to the respondent's interests and, in those cases, you need to make the survey itself lively by wording the questions in a conversational way, varying the tasks the person is asked to do, and so on.

After the pre-test you need to discover the following:

- Were the questions clear to everyone?
- Did they mean the same thing to each person?
- Were people able/willing to answer them?
- Were the answer choices suitable?
- Did the questions/answers give you the information you need?
- How long did the interview take? Did people get tired or bored?
- Can you code the answers if you need to?
- If you are planning to use assistants, did the people who assisted you on the pre-test find that your instructions to them worked? Have they any suggestions for improvement?

- When you look at the results, is there any information you will need that is missing?

7 Work with the interviewers

The following sections cover the things you need to remember if you are using other people to help you. The discussion here presupposes that you are employing interviewers, but many people will either work alone, or will have a volunteer group assisting them, such as members of the community association. Except for the issue of payment, all the points apply to volunteers as well as interviewers whom you employ.

Choosing interviewers

When choosing interviewers, their personal characteristics — personality, intelligence, honesty, and ability to work with people — are far more important than their formal educational qualifications. A young woman who has completed secondary school, or perhaps an older person who never completed primary school may prove to be a better interviewer than someone with a sociology degree. Relate your selection of interviewers to the group you are trying to study and to the subject: many teenage girls are not going to discuss the virtues of various sanitary products with a male interviewer, and people using street drugs are going to be reluctant to talk to someone who looks as if he or she is fresh from the police academy. By the same token, try not to use people who are very involved with, or are seen to be associated with, the topic. If you send known teachers out to ask about the value of education, people will hardly 'insult' them by saying that they have more important priorities. The teachers themselves may have a stake in the findings as well — for example, recording more people as wanting a new school may lead to getting one.

How many interviewers do you need? Depending on the distances between interviewees, interviewers can usually carry out between two and five interviews a day. If you need 100 interviews and are using one interviewer, you will need somewhere between 20 to 50 working days, or up to two and a half months. You will have to calculate the number of interviewers you will use by weighing the cost of employing more interviewers and the length of time you have available.

Training interviewers

You can help your interviewers by pre-testing your survey, writing out the questions exactly as they are to be presented, and writing all instructions throughout the survey very clearly. You should also prepare an interviewers' manual that contains a sheet on various topics: how to explain the purpose of the study, how to handle refusals, how to return the forms, etc. Prepare for all the circumstances you can anticipate. If you are doing random sampling, tell the interviewers exactly what procedure to follow. When things don't work out properly, make sure they do not simply substitute one household for another. Box 9–1 presents interviewer instructions for carrying out a systematic random sample, when the interviewers had no names and addresses.

Box 9–1 Example of an instruction to interviewers

Take the first house that you come to as you approach the village. Toss the coin. If it is heads, take that as your first house. When you have visited your first house, decide which two houses are nearest to that house. Choose the further of the two. When you have visited that house, decide which two houses are nearest to it, not counting any of the houses you have considered already. Choose the further of the two. Carry on like this.

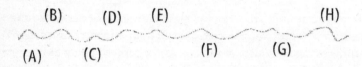

Example. (A) is the first house you come to. You toss a coin. It's tails, so you take B as your first house to visit. (C) and (D) are the nearest houses to (B), so you take the further one—(D). The nearest to (D), not counting (A), (B), or (C) are (E) and (F). You take the further one—(F). The nearest to (F), not counting (E), are (G) and (H). You take (H).

Source: Mitton (1982, p. 69).

Plan the human elements of your survey as well. Work with the interviewers on the best way to dress, how to approach 'gatekeepers' (people who can give you access to the people you want to talk to, or refuse it, such as school principals if you want to talk to students; chiefs of African villages; governors of prisons, etc.), the courtesies expected, how to explain the work, how not to raise expectations that cannot be met, what to do if asked for payment, and how to handle refusals.

Interviewers should be aware that:

- questions must be read slowly, clearly, and word-for-word;
- standard responses should be given after the respondent replies: 'I see', 'Thank you', etc. These should be planned and used by everyone;
- standard probes should be used, for example:
  ⇨ Repeat the question.

⇨ Allow an expectant pause.

⇨ Repeat the person's reply so far.

⇨ Offer neutral comments, such as, 'Why do you feel that way?' or 'Anything else?' 'Can you tell me more about that?'

⇨ Ask for clarification: 'I'm not quite sure what you meant when you said that "The best place for dogs is in the stewing pot." Can you tell me a little more?'

Once again, these are planned and used by all.

• questions should not be skipped, even if the interviewer is certain of the answer because it has already arisen in another context. Instead, say something like: 'I know we discussed this before but I need to ask every question,' and then continue with the question.

• questions should be clarified, if necessary, in the same way.

To help plan these, you can practice by using role-play. Take the role of the respondent and ask the interviewer to administer the survey to you, then reverse the roles. Both you and the interviewers can also create some bad interviews and identify the mistakes. Create a difficult interview, one which is interrupted frequently, a household where no one is at home. If you are not familiar with the area, and the interviewers are, this kind of role-playing may help you to deal with things you had not thought of.

Interviewers should understand that their job is to make the respondent feel respected and comfortable. The interviewers should accept all answers neutrally, without displays of disapproval or shock. Lecturing the respondent is unacceptable. This is a survey, not an educational campaign.

Practice recording the answers. Pay particular attention to recording open-ended answers. The interviewer should record the answer verbatim, not in summary form. No two interviewers will summarize in the same way, and two answers summarized as 'No' may be very different. For example: 'The community association is intending to offer marriage counseling and reconciliation services for a small fee. Would you be interested in attending?'

Answer 1: 'No, because even if the fee is small, I still don't have the money.'

Answer 2: 'No. If people can't solve their own problems, they should just pack it in. We have too many do-gooders giving advice as it is.'

Making sure the conditions of work are clear

Your interviewers must understand the study, exactly what is expected of them, how to administer the survey in a variety of circumstances, how to follow your sampling procedure, how to record the results, how to get them to you, the ethical requirements of their work, the need for treating the results confidentially. However, there are other practical issues as well: do you pay by the hour, the day, or the interview? What about fringe benefits and insurance? What about arrangements for accommodation and transport? Will the team work together in one place and move on together or work separately? What happens in an emergency? How can they reach you? Your interviewers need to know the answers to such questions before starting work.

8 Prepare a code book

Now you should plan a code book. This is needed for all but the smallest surveys with no open-ended questions. A code book lists each question by number, and the codes for its answers. These will be used by a coder to enter your data on paper or in a computer as each answer comes up. The codes will be used to process your open-ended answers as well. Understanding what a code book does becomes a little clearer if you think about what has to be done when you ask an open-ended question:

- Go back through all the survey forms and read the answers to a particular question.
- Create a set of categories that you feel will cover all the answers to that question.
- Give each category a number and record its name and number in the code book, along with the question number.
- Go back through the survey forms and assign the appropriate category number to each response to the question.
- Add up the various responses, or enter them into the computer.

Let's say we have done a survey of people's needs in relation to drug education. We wanted information such as where they live, what they think the problems facing children today are, whether they have attended any classes on the subject, etc. Here is one question we asked:

Question 7: What do you think are the biggest problems facing children today?

Imagine that one respondent says 'drugs'. Another says 'alcohol'. Another says 'divorce'. Another says 'sniffing glue'. Depending on your study, you may want to group the first two and the last replies together under the category 'prohibited substances'. And give it a code: '5' for the sake of this example. Whenever a respondent gives any one of these three answers, it is coded as '5'.

Among your forced-choice questions, you asked 'Sex', 'Where do you live?', 'Did you attend the evening class on drug education in the

community hall?' and 'Did you attend the advanced evening class program?'
On the survey form, you gave each answer a code, like this:

Did you attend the evening class on drug education in the Community Hall?
A. YES   1
B. NO   2
C. DON'T KNOW   8

The same codes are now entered into your code book. For example:

Question 1: Sex
A. FEMALE   1
B. MALE   2

Question 2: Residence
A. MILLTOWN   1
B. SANDYFORD   2
C. PORTNEW   3

Question 3: Attended evening class in the community hall
A. YES   1
B. NO   2
C. DON'T KNOW   8

Question 4: Participated in the advanced evening class program
A. YES   1
B. NO   2
C. DON'T KNOW   8

You must also plan what to do if people don't answer the question, or if the
question does not apply. For example, anyone who did not attend evening
class cannot have participated in the advanced evening class program, so she
is directed elsewhere after question 3. Here are some standard codes for
these situations (just as '08' is often used for 'Don't know'):

INCOMPLETE   9
NOT APPLICABLE   0

9 Send out an advance letter

If you are working with names and addresses, try to send out a letter to the
respondents before the survey begins. But you don't always need names: for
example, in a large building, if you are working on a systematic random
sample without names, you can put letters in letter boxes or under doors,
once you choose your respondents. The letter will explain the purpose of
the study and the sponsorship, and contain an appeal for cooperation.

10 Administer the survey

Conduct the interviews at times that are convenient for respondents. Interviews should wear a name-tag and introduce themselves using the material on the face sheet. Sometimes it is useful to carry an original letter of introduction from the survey director or the sponsor of the research, such as the president of the community association. If people have questions, try to reassure them and put them at ease.

Check the completed survey forms periodically to catch problems. Are the interviewers filling them out correctly? Are one interviewer's survey results very different from those of others? Why? You can begin coding the survey forms now, if necessary.

11 Record and process the data

You have several choices in relation to recording and processing your data. Counting forced-choice answers straight from the forms need not require coding. Everything else does, whether you are simply recording the results on large sheets or computerizing the results. The approach you choose will depend on how much data you have, what you want to do with it, and whether you have access to and are comfortable with a computer. The best rule is 'simplest is best'. Use the least complicated method that still produces what you want. If you have done something as small as a mini survey, you should be able to record on paper and count directly. For larger surveys, or large numbers of people, you can enter the codes into a computer program.

In our survey of evening classes for drug education, here are the responses once again from the first two people in our pile of survey forms. Let us say the first respondent (serial number 01) is a male; for question 1 the code book tells us to give him a '2'. If he lives in Milltown, he will get a '1' on question 2. He doesn't attend evening class, so gets a '2' on question 3. When we get as far as question 9, he will get a '5' because he said 'drugs'.

The recording form will look like Table 9–1.

Table 9–1 Counting answers for a mini survey

Respondent number	Question number		
	1 (sex)	2 (residence)	3 (evening class)
Respondent 01	2	1	2
Respondent 02	1	2	1

Now you want to count your results. But before you do, figure out what information you want. You almost certainly want the total figures and percentages for each of your questions. These are called frequency counts.

Frequency counts

Because all approaches evolved from the practice of doing your own counting, we will look at that first. Here are two questions from our evening class survey:

5. Did you ever go to school?
YES ⇨ Question 6
NO ⇨ Question 7

6. What is the highest level of education you have attended?
PRIMARY   1
SECONDARY   2
THIRD LEVEL   3

You can sort the forms into three + piles and count the answers. Or you can keep the forms in one pile and record the answers on forms (see Table 9–2).

Table 9–2

	Primary	IIIII IIIII II
	Secondary	IIIII IIIII I
Question 6	Third level	IIIII IIIII
	Don't know	I
	Not applicable	IIII
	Incomplete	I

Twelve people completed primary school, eleven completed secondary, and so on. Four people have not answered the question because they never went to school, and the filter at Question 5 has directed that they skip Question 6 and go to 7. They are counted as 'not applicable'. For others (one in this case) the respondent skipped the question, or something else happened that prevents you from reading the reply. This is 'incomplete'.

What do you do if people can choose more than one answer? For example:

Which of the following company services have you used in the past six months?
(Circle as many as appropriate)

CANTEEN	01
TEA SERVICE	02
CRÈCHE	03
FITNESS CENTER	04
ESCORT SERVICE TO PARKING AREA AT NIGHT	05
EVENING CLASSES	06
ACCOMMODATION ADVICE	07
HEALTH CENTER	08
TAX ADVICE	09
INVESTMENT AND RETIREMENT PLANNING	10

For such questions count the answers. When you give your totals in a chart, you will have numbers that are higher than the number of people in your study. Put a note at the bottom of the chart: 'Respondents could choose more than one answer'. Notice that, in this example, double numbers are used for answers, because 'investment and retirement planning' takes us up to a two-digit number, 10. If you are counting by hand, this does not matter, but if you are using a computer, your answer category numbers all have to have the same number of digits.

If you ask people to rank their answers, you need to show which ones were considered more important. For example:

Here are some reasons why people don't use the local shopping center. In your opinion, which are the most serious? Please rank them from 1 to 5, giving a '1' to the most serious and a '5' to the least serious.

Range of shops too limited	[ ]
Prices higher than in larger shopping centers	[ ]
Not enough parking	[ ]
Dangerous entrances and exits	[ ]
Not well-lighted at night	[ ]

You can add up the scores for each answer. In this case, the answer with the lowest score is considered the most important. You cannot read a long list to people and expect them to remember. Even for a relatively short one, you may be better off giving people cards with words or pictures on them and asking them to arrange them in order. When you have finished, you can record the answers on a blank survey form. If you have a large number of survey forms, a large number of questions, or want to do extremely complex analysis, you should use a computer. It will do the work very quickly once you have the material in proper form. However, putting the material in proper form is time consuming, and for small surveys may take more time than simply doing all the processing yourself.

Cross-tabulations

So far, we have only talked about counting the answers to one question at a time. Now we might like to know what is the relationship between the answers to two questions. In our evening class study, we asked people their sex, place of residence, whether they attended evening class, and whether they participated in the advanced program. Now we might want to look at the relationship between sex and attendance at evening class. How many of those who are female attended evening class? This is called a 'cross-tabulation', or 'cross-tab' for short.

Before you start cross-tabulating, think of your report and try to work out the tables you will need. Make up some blank forms or 'dummy tables' as discussed on page 259. Will this table be useful? This way you will not be counting things that you do not need. This is especially likely to happen if you are using a computer program, since you can cross-tabulate every question by every other, and end up with hundreds if not thousands of tables, most of which will be meaningless.

To get the information for this table, we could separate our survey forms into 'female' and 'male', and count them. We could then take the 'female' pile and sort them again into two piles, those who attended evening class and those who didn't. We could repeat the process for the males. As you can imagine, for a large survey or a large number of cross-tabulations, you could be knee-deep in survey forms for quite a while.

But if you have coded your questionnaires, you can do such a count more easily. Here is the beginning of the recording form again, see Table 9–3 below.

Table 9–3

Respondent number	Question number		
	1 (sex)	2 (residence)	3 (evening class)
Respondent 01	2	1	2
Respondent 02	1	2	1

Look at each female (anyone who answered '1' in question 1) and see what she said on question 3, attendance at evening class. Do the same for each male. Table 9–4 shows the codings for thirty respondents, fifteen women and fifteen men, for the cross-tab of questions 1 and 3. As you can see, some people didn't know if they attended or not, and some didn't answer.

Table 9–4 Cross-tabulation of two questions by hand

		Question 3 (evening class)			
		Code 1 (yes)	Code 2 (no)	Code 3 (don't know)	Code 4 (incomplete)
Question 1 (sex)	Code 1 (female)	IIIII III	IIII	I	II
	Code 2 (male)	IIIII III	III	II	II

Doing this on a large sheet is feasible if you do not want more than thirty cross-tabs. Beyond that, a computer is a better choice. You can also do cross-tabs for three or more questions: of the females (question 1) who attended evening class (question 3), how many had children (question 6)?

If you use a computer, cross-tabulations take very little work. You can enter the data using a program such as dBase. Once the codes and instructions are in the computer you can use a program such as SPSS, SPSS-X or SYSTAT to analyze the material. These programs will do the calculations discussed in Chapter 17. Unfortunately, they also make it all too easy to cross-tabulate everything by everything else, and apply statistical procedures that are irrelevant to what you are doing. If you are not careful, you can end up with a lot of meaningless stuff — for example, of men who do not know whether they attended the advanced program (question 3), how many have four children? Who cares? So choosing what to cross-tabulate is important, or you will end up with kilos of computer paper, and everything on it will look very 'scientific' and worth putting in your report, but it won't be.

An appropriate computer program will not only count and cross-tabulate, it will perform statistical tests of significance, association, and others (see Chapter 17) on your material, even when the tests do not apply to what you have collected. Putting all that in the report is also very tempting.

If you intend to use a computer program, you should get help before and during the survey design process, so that the answers will be in a form that is easy to enter. You might consult someone who has used the program, or read a manual or guide.

Postal Surveys and Drop-off Surveys

Until now, we have been talking about face-to-face interviews. Much of what has been said about question construction and coding applies to postal questionnaires, as well. However, since a questionnaire is a form which the respondent fills out, the procedures for preparing one are more demanding, because you will not be there to work with each respondent, clarify questions, make sure that the answers are in the right places, and encourage the person to complete it. Everything has to be there on the paper in clear, relevant, and attractive form. How many questionnaires have you ignored because they lacked these characteristics?

The advantages of a postal questionnaire are:

- Lower costs: while a face-to-face interview can cost between 10–20 British pounds or 15–30 US dollars, or more, excluding the costs of sampling and data analysis, a postal survey, even with all the letters, postage, follow-ups, etc., costs considerably less. You do not need a team of interviewers.
- Less time: you can survey your group all at one time, and even if it takes several weeks to get all your answers back, it is quicker than using interviewers to talk to people one-by-one.
- Convenience and a sense of anonymity for the interviewee.
- Removal of interviewer-related issues, such as training, supervision, and introduction of interviewer-error into the results.

The disadvantages include:

- A possible lower response rate, although some studies suggest that this may no longer be the case. Postal questionnaires usually have a response rate of below 50 per cent (but are usually 50–60 per cent when the three mailings described later in this chapter are used, and it is even possible for the rate to rise to over 90 per cent). Those figures assume, among other things, that you are working with people who stay in the same place and that their post reaches them. Student populations, transient workers, or the homeless, for example, are going to be harder to reach. When people don't reply, is it because they don't want to, or the survey never reached them? Another problem is that those who do not respond may be different in some important way from those who do.
- Little control over the respondent. People may invite others to help them; they may pass the form on to someone else; they may skip around on the form and omit some questions. You may have to simplify your survey so that everyone can understand it and, even then, you are less certain that people have understood than you would be by talking to them face-to-face.

What is involved in a postal survey?

Much research has been done on the mechanics of postal questionnaires: the days of the week that are best for mailing; what kind of incentives might be offered to get people to cooperate; the appearance of the questionnaire; its length; how much you can increase the rate of response by sending 'waves' of follow-up letters asking people to return the forms; and so on. Until recently, studies of these issues were done on a one-off basis and often tended to contradict one another; one study, for example, showing that color of pages made a difference, and another not. Moreover, a lot of these studies are quite old. In the 1980s and 1990s, however, researchers began doing 'meta-analyses', using statistical techniques to synthesize the results of a number of studies. Some of their findings — on color of survey paper, for example — are reported in this section. You should also keep in mind that most of what we know about making questionnaires accessible and motivating people to return them comes from the Western world, so if you are working with cultural groups whose ideas are different, some of these points may not be relevant.

Having said all this, there are some basic steps that have proven to be sensible and effective in the West, at this time. These are shown in the box below. Three mailings are shown here, but the number can vary. We will discuss the items in bold.

Steps in a postal survey

- select the respondents
- design the questionnaires
- **prepare a cover letter**
- **create an attractive cover**
- **print the questionnaires and assemble**
- **preliminary mailing: advance invitation**
- **first mailing packet: send out**
  the cover letter
  the questionnaire
  a return stamped, self-addressed envelope
- **second mailing packet: send out**
  a cover letter asking for cooperation
- **third mailing packet: send out**
  a plea for cooperation, a new questionnaire,
  and a return stamped self-addressed envelope

(Adapted from Salant and Dillman, 1994)

Prepare a cover letter

This summary shows the items which a cover letter should contain. They should be simple and clear.

⇨ who is sponsoring the study
⇨ the purpose of the research
⇨ how the respondent was selected
⇨ an assurance of confidentiality
⇨ an appeal for cooperation
⇨ contact number and address

> 'The functions committee of the community association would like to get your views on the proposed function room in order to help us plan the facilities. Your name was chosen randomly from a list of community association members and your reply will be held in complete confidence. We would appreciate your taking the time to complete the questionnaire so that the thinking of community association members is reflected. If you have any questions, please write or telephone me.

While the cover letter is not the place for giving instructions on completing the questionnaire (these should be placed later in the questionnaire with the specific question) it might, if it seems helpful, reassure people that there are no right or wrong answers, and that their views are valuable.

Create an attractive cover and questionnaire format

The front cover should show the title of the study — straightforward and clear; the sponsor of the research (community association, company, or perhaps your own name if you are a student with no affiliation); and the address to which people should return the questionnaire. A simple, relevant graphic may make the cover more attractive. On the back cover you should invite the respondent to write any comments he or she might have, and to mark a box in order to receive a summary of the findings. (Do this, of course, only if you are able to get such a summary to them.) The back cover is also the place to thank people for their cooperation.

Salant and Dillman (1994) suggest that the questionnaire be printed in brochure form, on both sides of the inside pages, using legal-size paper. With recent advances in computer software, this is easy to do; you can then simply get good quality photocopies and arrange for the document to be covered and bound. Postal surveys should be welcoming and easy to follow. Running up a few questions on an old typewriter with the 'e' missing and sending it out on newsprint will not work anymore. Questionnaires that are crowded, have misaligned answer categories, and that include filter questions that seem to lead nowhere are all likely to discourage the respondent. Length also makes a difference: Yammarino, Skinner, and Childers (1991) found in a meta-analysis that surveys longer than four pages can lead to lower response rates.

Researchers often use different colors for different parts of a survey. For example, if you are directing respondents to a major sub-section of the survey by using a filter question, that sub-section might be printed on a different color. For the color of the survey generally, Fox, Crask, and Jonghoon (1988) found, in a review of ten studies, that the response rate for green forms was higher than for white. Whatever else, however, choose a color which does not reduce readability.

Preliminary mailing: advance invitation

This and all successive mailings should be dated, personally-signed, and stamped with first-class postage. All of these have been found to improve response rate (for meta-analyses of such issues, see Fox et al (1988), Armstrong and Kusk (1987) and Yammarino et al (1991). Not every researcher sends a preliminary mailing. In many cases, the mailing sequence starts with the questionnaire itself. However, a preliminary mailing explaining that you will be sending a questionnaire, telling what it is about, and saying that you welcome participation may create greater interest, and people may be less likely to throw your survey out when it arrives.

First mailing packet

This contains the cover letter, the questionnaire, a return stamped, self-addressed envelope, all in a business-sized envelope.

Second mailing packet

This is a letter or postcard, sent about a week after the questionnaire was mailed, and sent to the same people. It reminds them that a questionnaire was sent, says how valuable their cooperation is, thanks them if they have returned it and asks, if they haven't, to do so now. People are invited to telephone for another copy of the questionnaire if they have lost it.

Third mailing packet

You have been checking off identification numbers on your master list as each completed questionnaire comes in, and the people who have not replied are sent this mailing, about three weeks after the second mailing (the reminder letter). You send people a new cover letter, explaining why their cooperation is important and how much you appreciate it. People may have lost the questionnaire, so enclose a new one, plus a return, stamped, self-addressed envelope.

Postal questionnaires are not the only type of self-administered questionnaire. You can also administer questionnaires to 'captive' groups, such as schoolchildren or teachers attending a seminar. The likelihood that these will be returned to you is good and the potential for confusion lower if you are present to go through the questions with the group. But sending them to a school, for example, and allowing individual teachers to administer them is not a good idea. Each will have a different idea of how to do it, some will think the good name of the school depends on the children giving the 'right' answers and so on. A major disadvantage of this approach is that although you might have large numbers, they cannot be said to represent anything except that group. If that is all you want, however, this can be a good method.

Telephone Surveys

We do not cover telephone surveys in this book for two reasons: firstly, they are a specialization unto themselves with different procedures for sampling, interacting with respondents, etc.; and secondly, we, like many people, have been over-telephoned by people making 'courtesy calls' (jargon for selling and begging calls) and are now devoting our time to creating an invention which will trap unsolicited callers in a permanent holding pattern over Reykjavik. Therefore, although our advice about how to get at hard chaws like ourselves would be invaluable, it seems a bit inconsistent to provide a section on how to do telephone interviews on others. Nevertheless, we realize that they do have their place (in national political polls, for example), and one good source for learning more is Priscilla A. Salant and Don A. Dillman's *How to Conduct Your Own Survey* (John Wiley and Sons, 1994). They are nicer people than we are and will help you.

Special Considerations for Non-Western Cultural Groups

Lack of familiarity with the situation, the particular group, or the even the culture, can lead to asking the wrong questions, giving poor answer choices, or constructing an awkward survey form. You can guard against the first two by doing your homework, but the last is more subtle. Many of the pieces of advice given in this chapter are inappropriate somewhere in the world, or with some cultural group. In some places, talking about the future is presumptuous, because the future is in God's hands. In other places, hypothetical questions ('If you were to start over, would you send your child to boarding school?') are meaningless.

Sometimes, you may find yourself working with speakers of another language: perhaps part of your community consists of recent immigrants or people who, for one reason or another, are not comfortable in your language. You will need to have your survey translated by a bilingual person whose first language is the one in which you will finally present the questions to your respondents. Then, as a check, try to have the questions translated back to the original by a bilingual person whose first language is the one in which the questions were first drafted. If the 'back translation' says what you want, use the first translation as your survey. Of course, it may not be easy to find people with the linguistic skills you need. In that case, work closely with the person who is translating from your language into his or her own so that your ideas and intentions are clear.

Surprising things can happen in the translation process. Researcher Roger Mitton (1982, p. 64) wanted to ask people in Lesotho: 'What do you do on Sundays that is different from other days?' meaning 'What do you do on Sundays that is different from what you do on other days?' This was translated as 'What do you do on Sunday, which is the Lord's day?' A lot of people said they went to church. This may have seemed to be the 'right' answer. A substantial body of literature is available on back-translation (see, for example, Brislin, Lonner, and Thorndike 1973 for good advice). For an excellent manual on basic research in a developing country context, look at Roger Mitton's *Practical Research in Distance Teaching* (London, International Extension College, 1982) which, despite its title, is applicable to most social research topics.

Looking Back at Our Interview

Now that you have read this chapter, look back at the interview at the beginning of the chapter. Can you identify all the problems with it?

References and further readings

Armstrong, J. Scott and Edward J. Kusk. 1987. 'Return Postage in Mail Surveys: A Meta-analysis.' *Public Opinion Quarterly* 52:223–230.

Brislin, Richard W., Walter J. Lonner, and Robert M. Thorndike. 1973. *Cross-Cultural Research Methods*. New York: John Wiley.

Brock, C. and N.K. Cammish. 1991. *Factors Affecting Female Participation in Six Developing Countries*. Hull, U.K.: University of Hull.

Bulmer, M. and D.P. Warwick. 1983. *Social Research in Developing Countries*. New York and London: John Wiley and Sons.

Devereux, Stephen. 1989. '"Observers Are Worried": Learning the Language and Counting the People in Northeast Ghana.' In Stephen Devereux and John Hoddinott, eds., *Fieldwork in Developing Countries*.

Boulder, Colorado: Lynne Rienner Publishers.

Finsterbusch, Kurt. 1976. 'Mini-Surveys: An Underemployed Research Tool.' *Social Science Research* 5(1): 81–93.

Fox, Richard J., Melvin R. Crask, and Jonghoon Kim. 1988. 'Mail Survey Response Rate: A Metanalysis of Selected Techniques for Inducing Response.' *Public Opinion Quarterly* 52:467–491.

Kumar, Krishna. 1990. *Conducting Mini Surveys in Developing Countries.* A.I.D. Program Design and Evaluation Methodology Report No. 15. Washington DC: US Agency for International Development.

Leedy, Paul D. 1989. *Practical Research: Planning and Design*, 4th ed. London: Collier Macmillan.

Mitton, Roger. 1982. *Practical Research in Distance Teaching.* London: International Extension College.

Osgood, C.E., C.J. Suci, and P.H. Tannenbaum. 1957. *The Measurement of Meaning.* Urbana, Illinois: University of Illinois Press.

Salant, Priscilla A. and Don A. Dillman. 1994. *How to Conduct Your Own Survey.* New York: John Wiley and Sons.

White, Benjamin. 1984. 'Measuring Time Allocation, Decision-Making and Agrarian Changes Affecting Rural Women: Examples from Recent Research in Indonesia.' *IDS Bulletin* 15(1):18–32.

Yammarino, Francis J., Steven J. Skinner, and Terry L. Childers. 1991. 'Understanding Mail Survey Response Behavior: A Meta-analysis.' *Public Opinion Quarterly* 55:613–639./

The Hope and Glory Vindicator

Volume 182 Issue 23 · October 6, 2001

McCardle, Anzivino to England

Mayor Randy Anderson announced today that he is funding airfares for two local men, Septus McCardle and Tony Anzivino, to travel to London, England for six months on October 10. Mr. and Mrs. Meryl 'Bob' Matthews, 125 Garfield St., visited London last year, but Mrs. Meryl Bob didn't care for it that much.

The mayor had originally intended to go himself, but his wife Laurinda's current indictment for forcibly shaving visiting author Alexander Solzenitsyn prevented him. The mayor hoped to twin Hope And Glory with the quaint English community Hancock Towers, which contains a castle.

Mr. McCardle will also carry out some social science research while there. He became interested in doing research after he and one of the visiting researchers performed some groundbreaking experiments, which are to be published shortly in the American Kennel Club journal, Dog's Life.

Mr. McCardle and Mr. Anzivino will be staying with the family of researcher Sharon Darwin. Ms. Darwin said Mr. McCardle was an excellent researcher and caught on very quickly for an elderly bloke. Mr. Anzivino has not done research before but finds it convenient to be out of the country at the moment.

4,000 sit down to spaghetti dinner

Folks traveled from far and wide last Wednesday to attend the first gala function at the House of Peace on Route 123. The lights from the event, a combination spaghetti dinner, dog show, craft fair, and youth festival, could be seen as far as the state line, and were commented on by several airline pilots who thought it was Pittsburgh. Two hundred extra motorcycle police were brought in from neighboring towns, and four tons of litter are now being removed.

Police Chief Leland De Witt said it was a great day for the community. Many had contributed generously. The Fin 'n' Fur Kennels and Bible Classes, for example, had donated its entire inventory, and ladies from the Precious Lambs Daycare Center looked after 400 children, featuring a fun fair and rifle practice. By the end of the day, at least 1,500 cars had passed through, many of them, he regretted to say, above the new speed limit of 12 miles per hour.

Busy Bee Club marks farewell

At a lovely social, which featured umbrellas and bowler hats as party favors, Mrs. Meryl 'Bob' Matthews of the Busy Bees presented locals Mr. Septus McCardle and Mr. Tony Anzivino with a six months' supply of paper toilet seat covers for their trip to England.

Court Notes:
Upcoming cases:
De Witt vs. Anderson, Oct. 8, 10.30
Anderson vs. De Witt, Oct. 8, 11.30
Solzhenitsyn vs. Mrs. McCardle-Anderson, Oct. 8, 1.30
His Honor Judge Quinn vs. Anderson Oct. 8, 2.30
Whump vs. McCardle, Oct. 8, 3.30

Chimney sweeping. Closed.

Grand Opening! Hair Today, Gone Tomorrow Waxing Salon (formerly Fin 'n' Fur Kennels and Bible Classes). Call Laurinda at 965-CHIN.

INSIDE THIS ISSUE

10 USING MEASURES, SCALES AND INDICES

Summary

Scales and *indices* are quantitative measures.

Many standardized scales and indices are available to the researcher, particularly in the fields of psychology, sociology, and education.

If they meet your information requirements and are relevant and valid, scales and measures can be very useful if administered properly.

Some possible problems arise because many standardized scales and indices are culturally biased in their assumptions, concepts, language, and form.

A common scale used in the social sciences is a *Likert* scale.

Scales can be *nominal* (the items are named differences, like red or green); *ordinal* (the items are ordered, for example, cool, warm, hot); *interval* (the differences between items can be given in numbers, say, ten degrees, twenty degrees); or *ratio* (the numbers are based on something that has a true zero, for instance, ten years, twenty years).

Perhaps you have an idea that some people's reluctance to support the local gay men's choir is related to their conservatism, perhaps even more than to their dislike of choir music or their tone deafness. You feel that, if this is true, you might be better able to address people's worries by launching a public education campaign, rather than making musical changes. But how can you find out if the people who object to the choir are more 'conservative' than those who do not? Will you just ask them? Or will you put a set of questions to them, the answers to which, when assembled, might tell you?

You may also be wondering if those people in Hope And Glory who are hostile toward the people behind the boiler factory score higher on measures of prejudice than those who are more· amicable toward them. Social researchers often use scales and indices as measures or tests to show degrees of difference among people in relation to an attribute or characteristic, such as attitudes, behavior, mental abilities, or psychological characteristics. A scale or index is standardized, that is, given in the same form to everyone and is intended to be objective, that is, not dependent on the researcher's biases or personal opinions.

Using Scales and Indices

Thousands of standard scales and indices have been designed to assess people on characteristics such as intelligence, achievement, aptitudes, prejudice, authoritarianism, modernity/ conservatism, social competence, leadership, alienation, and many others. Perhaps you or your children have been given a scale or measure, such as an IQ, an aptitude, or a personality test. Such tests may be part of the testing and assessment procedures used in your education system. They are being discussed in this chapter because they are commonly used in the social sciences, and in the fields of educational research and testing, so readers may be familiar with them and want to use them, especially because they are ready-made. One advantage is that none of the preparatory work involved in a survey is necessary: experts have already designed the questions or items and worked out the systems for scoring them.

Beginning researchers are often tempted to use standardized tests and measures because they can give the novice a sense of confidence and professionalism — after all, many of the tests have been constructed by experts. Some of them even come in a handy kit, complete with scoring systems, so the beginner assumes that the whole process must not only be quick and easy, but scientific as well. And, once one gets the hang of it, why not create a few tests and measures, oneself? Is there a test for eccentricity? If not, why not draw up one of your own and use it on Septus? This chapter is really no more than a set of cautionary notes about some of the pitfalls of using tests and measures without proper consideration of their functions, validity, and applicability.

Even though they may seem simple, tests and measures that use scales and indices are complex instruments based upon sophisticated theoretical assumptions. Simply applying them in a 'cookbook' approach — asking the questions and scoring the answers from a book — is not enough. There's a second consideration as well: in their standard forms they may be culturally biased and inappropriate, except in the societies for which they were designed. Some of them were even designed with middle-class Western males in mind. If you are working with minority groups, as you sometimes will be later on in the book when we go to Hancock Towers in London, you may find that the items on the measure are irrelevant or meaningless to them. However, it's useful to know more about tests and measures, if only to be able to complain when you take a personality test in a magazine and come out as a Grade II ogre. First, let us distinguish between an *index* and a *scale*. An index is a self-contained measure: 'How would you rate your school? Very good, good, fair, poor, very poor'. You might assemble a number of such questions. When the questions are interrelated in such a way that the answers form a pattern, you have a scale. A scale might show, for example, that people who say 'Yes' to the question 'Would you support a woman candidate for prime minister?' are also likely to say 'Yes' to 'Do you think women should be allowed to vote?' or 'Should girls be allowed to attend school?' If you have devised a valid scale, people who say 'No' to the last question are probably going to say 'No' to the other two. Those who say 'Yes' to the last but 'No' to the second are likely to say 'No' to the first as well. One type of pattern — the Guttman scale — is discussed later. Indices and scales can be used in two ways: you can ask a person to make a judgment about her own characteristics, or about those of others, see Figure 10–1 below.

Figure 10–1

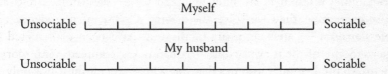

A second possibility is to give a set of multiple items, for example, a number of questions, each of which looks at some aspect of the characteristic, as in Dawson's (1967) Traditional–Modern scale. When all the questions on a scale have been answered, each response is given a value, and the values are added up to produce a score. In the first example above you are relying on the person's judgment. In the second, you are assuming that your items are valid measures of whatever you are studying, such as 'intolerance'. If you create the items yourself, you have no guarantee of that. What you think of as intolerance and what someone else thinks may be very different. If you simply want to compare your own respondents, one against another, this does not matter too much, as you are giving them the same scale, whatever it measures. You just cannot prove that it measures what you say it does and you cannot compare your results with those obtained by using someone else's scale. A distinction should be made between measures which assess performance and those which attempt to 'get at' personality characteristics. The former make fewer claims for themselves, are less complex, and do not rely upon as many Western cultural assumptions as the latter. Nonetheless, all the reservations mentioned below should be considered when choosing any kind of measure.

Some Warnings

Even if you use a standardized index or scale, you can still have problems. There is no absolute guarantee that a standardized form measures what it says it does. What does the Raven Matrices or the Wechsler intelligence test measure, for example? Some experts have argued that intelligence is a universal, measurable characteristic. Others have argued that it is culturally relative, that is, what is a crucial feature of intelligence in one society may not be valued or recognized in another. Newer theories of intelligence have emerged (see, for example, Gardner, 1983; Sternberg, 1985), but in the meantime, we are left with the existing tests, which measure something, but what? The same question applies to personality tests. One of the tests most commonly used around the world, the Minnesota Multiphasic Personality Inventory (MMPI) and its successor, MMPI-2, contain Western cultural biases in the assumptions about mental illness, in the items presented, in what constitutes 'normal', and in how the results are interpreted.

Defenders of standardized tests point to years of testing. They can show that people who score a particular way on one kind of personality test, for example, tend to score the same way on some other personality tests (in other words, the test is highly correlated), so something is being consistently measured. It is almost certainly being measured in a better way than something you put together yourself. But you still face a major question: is the scale valid for the people you are working with, that is, does it measure what you want it to measure? Many standardized tests are culturally biased in several ways. They may draw upon cultural knowledge or assumptions or concepts which a particular group may not share. You don't have to go to another country to encounter cultural variation: New York City, or our next research site, Hancock Towers in London, contains people who think 14 is a good age for marriage, that planning the future is an insult to God, that one's mother-in-law has all the answers, that toad-in-the-hole is a tasty dish, or that a nice cup of tea will see you right. It takes all types, and most tests and measures don't cater for all types.

For example, in the Western world people commonly think of the very intelligent as impractical or unworldly: the mad scientist, the absent-minded professor. They almost consider it surprising when a genius carries out ordinary tasks, like remembering to get a haircut or planning a party. In many societies, such practical sense is a fundamental attribute of intelligence, along with many others that are not measured on standard IQ tests. An instrument called the Myers-Briggs Type Indicator, or MBTI for short (Myers and Meyers, 1980), is particularly popular in the United States. It measures individual personality type on four dimensions:

(E)   Extroversion/Introversion(I)
(S)   Sensing/Intuition (N)
(T)   Thinking/Feeling (F)
(J)   Judgment/Perception (P)

Thus, of the sixteen possible combinations, a person might be classified as 'INTJ': taking an introverted, intuitive, thoughtful, and perceptive stance in relation to situations. Even if the MBTI is a valid indicator, what it is measuring may not be important in another society, or not as important as other dimensions that are not measured. Suppose that the pre-eminent distinction in a society is between those who are optimistic and pessimistic or competitive and non-competitive, no matter how else they approach life. That will not show up on the indicator, which was not designed to accommodate dimensions other than those mentioned. Or suppose that a society recognizes something more sophisticated than these bi-polar concepts, something that combines aspects of both. The danger is that because the standardized indicator exists and has been widely used, you might be tempted to use it, even if it does not tap the distinctions that are meaningful in the group you are working with.

Even the interpretation of drawings and pictures can be affected: an old woman dressed in a black shawl can be a witch in one society, a respected grandmother in another, or a member of a religious order, a widow, or any number of other interpretations in other societies. That means that sometimes psychological tests that are based on pictures, such as the Thematic Apperception Test (a psychological test) have to be redrawn to be meaningful in other environments. Once they are redrawn, of course, the results cannot be compared with those obtained from people who took the original test. Finally, ideas about who is actually taking the test differ: in some cultural groups, teamwork is valued over individual effort, and people may want to consult others while working on the test. In Western society, this is 'cheating'. Among some other cultural groups, however, it is the sensible thing to do.

Trimble, Lonner, and Boucher (1983), experts in using measures cross-culturally, say that three assumptions underlie measurement:

- First, that people can order or rank the ideas or items you present to them along a single line. For example, people may be asked to rate the school system on a scale of one to seven, one being very good and seven being very bad. However, there is no evidence that people in all cultures think this way.
- Second, that the items in the test reflect all people's real-life way of thinking: 'Which two of these three items are more alike, and which is different?' This may be alien to some cultures.
- Third, that people are able and prepared to be self-reflective, and to share their thoughts with the researcher. For example, 'How satisfied are you with your spouse?' may be too personal for some people, but it can be simply baffling to others. 'Satisfied' may not be a concept to be applied to spouses, or it may be irrelevant. One can do nothing about one's spouse, so what is the point of thinking about whether one is satisfied or not?

These are some of the simpler obstacles to cross-cultural use of some standard tests. For others, consult sources such as Lonner (1990).

Types of Scales

Scales in the social sciences, whether standardized or not, tend to fall into one of three main types: Likert scales, Guttman scales, and Thurstone scales. In this chapter, we will look at the first two, which are the ones you are most likely to consider.

Each scale is based upon a different set of assumptions about the way people respond to things. For example, in the hypothetical Guttman scale shown in Table 10–1, you have asked people who have home offices what equipment they possess — a computer, a fax, a scanner, a copier. You have recorded the answers, and as you can see, they form a pattern.

In a perfect Guttman scale, anyone who has a copier has all the other items. Anyone who does not have a copier but has a scanner has a fax and computer. Anyone who lacks a copier and a scanner but has a fax has a computer, as well. If you were targeting people for sales, you would try to sell faxes to people who had only computers, but if someone had a fax, you would try to sell them a scanner. Notice that our scale is almost perfect: only respondent Number 1 breaks the expected pattern. You could try this in relation to attitudes, as well: do people who allow their children to stay out all night also permit them to miss school, wear what they like, and skip wiping their feet before coming in? Do people who support one community activity also support a predictable set of other activities?

Table 10–1 Example of a Guttman scale

Respondent	Copier	Scanner	Fax	Computer
7	+	+	+	+
5	+	+	+	+
8	-	+	+	+
4	-	+	+	+
6	-	-	+	+
2	-	-	+	+
1	+	-	+	+
3	-	-	-	+

Likert and Likert-like scales are the most commonly used today for a variety of theoretical reasons (see Judd, Smith, and Kidder, 1991 for a discussion of this). In a Likert scale, people are invited to respond to a set of items. Let's say you want to look at people's liberalism or some other meaningful concept and you have tried to work out all the dimensions of this concept as they apply to liver transplants for older people. Now you ask people whether they strongly agree, agree, don't know, disagree, or strongly disagree with these statements (Figure 10–2).

Figure 10–2 Example of a Likert-like scale

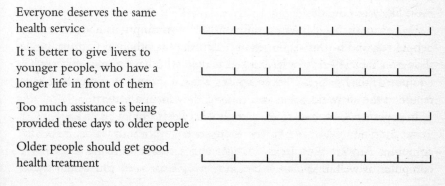

Everyone deserves the same
health service

It is better to give livers to
younger people, who have a
longer life in front of them

Too much assistance is being
provided these days to older people

Older people should get good
health treatment

The assumption is that people with a strongly favorable view toward something (liver transplants for older people, for example) will agree with 'favorable' items and disagree with 'unfavorable' ones, while people opposed to them will do the reverse, and people who are neutral, or undecided, will fall somewhere in the middle. The person's score is obtained by subtracting the numbers of responses to items that are considered negative from those that are considered positive. On a standardized Likert scale, the positive and negative items have already been chosen, so the scoring instructions are clear.

Many researchers put some Likert-like questions in their survey. These may be taken from one of the many standardized scales or created by the researcher, as we did in Chapter 9. Let us say you show six pictures of men — at one end is a well-groomed man in conventional dress with a conventional haircut and at the other is a ragged unkempt man. In between are pictures of men ranging between the two extremes, each one representing one level of difference from the previous. You ask people to rate them on trustworthiness, responsibility, honesty, willingness to help others and so on. You use a word scale like very good, good, and so on, or a drawn scale with good on the left, bad on the right, and five or seven spaces to choose from in between. Perhaps you have a good idea, as a result, that many people think that unkempt men fall on the 'bad' end. This is a modest effort: you are simply using the scale as a form of forced-choice question. You may even find that the answers form a pattern, as on a Guttman scale. However, experts warn against assuming that you can easily create an acceptable scale yourself: research expert Delbert C. Miller calls it 'an activity of last resort' when you cannot find a scale that suits your needs, or the scale you want to use is poorly constructed. But, as he points out, 'putting some items together and assigning arbitrary weights to them' is not the answer (Miller, 1991, p. 579). Good measures are tested extensively and their results compared with those of instruments that are already thought to be valid and good predictors (you may have noticed a leap of faith there, but that is how it's done). So if you are satisfied about a test's validity and relevance to your project, it is better to use it than to design one yourself.

For example, look back at Figure 10–2. How do we know that people who agree with the statement 'Older people should get good health treatment' are liberal? They may be highly conservative gerontocrats. Or maybe they mean 'good, but short of heroic measures'. If we change it to 'Older people should be treated exactly the same as other people', is this necessarily a liberal idea? Items that do not 'work' should be discarded. This is usually done by asking an independent panel to rank items for liberalism/conservatism. Items with high agreement among the panel are more likely to be useful. The final results of the scale are then compared with other results and tests: for example, on your scale, are the people who scored as liberal the same ones who on their organ donor cards stipulated that their organs should not go to gays, the elderly, or members of the Liberal Party?

The measures and scales discussed in this chapter are almost always etic: you, the researcher, decide the categories, the mode of ranking, and so on. In Chapter 14, we will look at participatory measures and scales, which are usually emic. They enable people who are participating in the research to develop and rank concepts, problems, and solutions as they see fit. The participants decide what constitute the important dimensions of a situation and what weights to assign them. As a result, each scale or measure is unique to the group concerned.

Whatever the scale, it can take four different forms:

- *Nominal*: one object is different from another: men or women, red or green. White (1984, p. 27) used a nominal scale to classify whether husbands, wives, or both participated in decision-making (see Chapter 16 for the scale itself).
- *Ordinal*: One object is bigger, or better, or more of something: never, sometimes, frequently; primary, secondary, third level education.
- *Interval*: one object is so many known units more than another, and there is no true zero: ten degrees Fahrenheit, twenty degrees Fahrenheit; an IQ of 75 and one of 150.
- *Ratio*: one object is so many times more, in multiples, and a true zero exists: ten inches, twenty inches. Note the difference between interval and ratio: twenty degrees is not twice as hot as ten degrees, but twenty inches is twice as long as ten; a thermometer has an artificial zero, a physical object measured by a yardstick has a true zero.

The scales most commonly used in the social sciences are ordinal and interval. Table 10–2 shows these and the statistics that can be used with them. For some of these statistics, see Chapter 17.

If you decide that a scale is what you need and you are choosing a standardized scale, try to get as much information as possible on these questions:

- Is the scale valid: does it measure what it says it measures? What is the evidence? For example, are its results consistent with those of other, similar measures?
- Is it reliable: does it produce the same results each time if the circumstances are the same?
- Does the scale fit your problem?

- Will the scale be relatively easy to administer and score?
- Do you understand the statistics that are used to interpret the scale?

How do you find scales and measures? You might start with a work such as Miller (1991) for an extensive list and a discussion of the issues.

Note: Laurinda is still looking for that reference. Now she thinks she may have written it on a scrap of paper that fell between the seats in her car. She has the front seats out on the lawn now.

Table 10–2 A Summary of measurement scales, their characteristics, and their statistical implications

Measurement Scale		Characteristics of the scale	Statistical possibilities of the scale
Non-interval	*Nominal scale*	A scale that measures in terms of names or designations of discrete units or categories.	Can be used for in determining the mode, the percentage values, or the chi square.
	Ordinal scale	A scale that measures in terms of such values as more or less, larger or smaller, but without specifying the size of intervals.	Can be used for determining the mode, percentage, chi-square, median, percentile rank, or rank correlation.
Interval scales	*Interval scale*	A scale that measures in terms of equal intervals or degrees of difference but whose zero point or point of beginning is arbitrarily established.	Can be used for determining the mode, the mean, the standard deviation, the t-test, the F-test, and the product moment correlation.
	Ratio scale	A scale that measures in terms of equal intervals and an absolute zero point.	Can be used for determining the geometric mean, the harmonic mean, the percent variation, and all other statistical determinations.

Source: Leedy (1989, p. 26). Reprinted by permission of Prentice-Hall, Upper Saddle River, New Jersey

References and further readings

Dawson, J.L.M. 1967. 'Traditional versus Western Attitudes in West Africa: The Construction, Validation and Application of a Measuring Device.' *The British Journal of Social and Clinical Psychology* 6(2):81–96.

Gardner, Howard. 1983. *Frames of Mind: Theories of Multiple Intelligences.* New York: Basic Books.

Hall, Budd, Arthur Gillette, and Rajesh Tandon, eds. 1982. *Creating Knowledge: A Monopoly? Participatory Research in Development.* New Delhi: Society for Participatory Research in Asia (45 Sainik Farm, Khanpur).

Judd, Charles M., Eliot R. Smith, and Louise H. Kidder. 1991. *Research Methods in Social Relations*, 6th ed. Fort Worth, Texas; London: Holt, Rinehart and Winston.

Leedy, Paul D. 1985. *Practical Research: Planning and Design*, 2nd ed. New York: Prentice-Hall.

Lonner, W.J. 1990. 'An Overview of Cross-Cultural Testing and Assessment.' In Richard W. Brislin, ed., *Applied Cross-Cultural Psychology.* Newbury Park, California: Sage.

Miller, Delbert C. 1991. *Handbook of Research Design and Social Measurement*, 5th ed. Newbury Park, California: Sage.

Myers, Isabel Briggs and Peter Myers. 1980, 1990. *Gifts Differing.* Palo Alto, CA: Consulting Psychologists Press.

Slim, Hugo and John Mitchell. 1992. 'The Application of RAP and PRA Techniques in Emergency Relief Programs.' In N.S. Scrimshaw and G.R. Gleason, eds., *Qualitative Methodologies for Planning and Evaluation of Health-Related Programs.* Boston, Massachusetts: International Foundation for Developing Countries.

Trimble, J.E., W.J. Lonner, and J. Boucher. 1983. 'Stalking the Wily Emic: Alternatives to Cross-Cultural Measurement.' In S. Irvine and J.W. Berry, eds., *Human Assessment and Cultural Factors.* New York: Plenum.

Sternberg, R.J. 1985. *Beyond IQ: A Triarchic Theory of Intelligence.* New York: Cambridge University Press.

White, Benjamin. 1984. 'Measuring Time Allocation, Decision-Making and Agrarian Changes Affecting Rural Women: Examples from Recent Research in Indonesia.' *IDS Bulletin* 15(1):1–5.

HANCOCK TOWERS, LONDON

In the early morning, gentle freshets of fetid air drift through the tower block, smoothing the cheeks of the sleeping here, whispering half-dreams there, drying up the bronchials something awful. Soft old sheets caress their bodies as they slumber on, sighing, knowing, for a few moments, the innocence of Eden.

That's in the early morning. Later in the day, up, washed, and wary, they will be suing London County Council over the fetid freshets, sabotaging each other's music systems, sending anonymous notes about whose husband is doing what, getting mugged, trying to grow African violets in the noxious grit which passes for local air. And, believe it or not, they will be doing some social science research, because one of their own, researcher Sharon Darwin, has arrived back from Hope And Glory, Ohio, with Septus and Tony in tow. Shar would just like to doss for a bit — the spell in jail in Ohio gave her a nasty turn — but Septus is on a high after his dog experiments and wants to share his enthusiasm with the locals. So far, participation has been restricted to two German Shepherds who bit Tony. In their sleep the people of Hancock Towers are gentle, mild, kind, genial, tender, and considerate. Awake, they are leery, guarded, and fearful, and no wonder.

We — you, Shar, Septus, and Tony — will be working as a research team here in Hancock Towers for the next while, using what we learn in this book to find out more about the place and its people. They, of course, will be doing the same; there isn't a tower block in any city in the world where people don't observe their neighbours, question them, and read their police records — if they can get their hands on them.

Mavis Darwin: 14-A, Hancock Towers

Funny you should mention police records, luv — I'd be happy to chat with you, only I'm getting ready for visiting day for our Kev. Got himself locked up in Glasheen Prison in Dublin, didn't he — nicked some electronic goods, he did. I said to him, 'How is it you couldn't get locked up closer to home and make it easier on your old Mum?' but oh, no, Dublin's the trendiest place in Europe, he says. Anyone who's anyone is there. Centre of the computer revolution. Nothing's too good for our Kev.

Glasheen is a nasty place but the governor, Mr. Lonergan, is ever so nice. He even lets the prisoners put on plays. Brings in a real director and all. Our Ken was Tinker Bell the other week — he loves poncin' about. I asked Mr. Lonergan wasn't he worried some of the prisoners would scarper — sorry, luv, 'escape' in the Queen's English — what with all the hubbub, but he says, 'Not at all, pet, there's plenty more where they came from.' Thinks the world of our Kev, does Mr. Lonergan. Makes a real pet of him.

Anyhow, I got my ticket and I'm off on the boat today. Two days' traveling for an hour visit — half-hour, if Kev's been acting up. Bloody hell. And now our Sharon has turned up from the States with two Yanks. One of them, Septic, can't talk about nothing but dogs. He's divorced. From what I can tell, his ex-wife had a beard or something. Poor bastard. The other fellow, Tony, goes out in a different wig and sunglasses every day.

Our Sharon's a researcher. She got her brains from my late husband Harold's side. He was on the buses for 30 years, but he was a very intelligent man and there's a story in his family that his great-great-great grandfather was a famous genius. Worked with monkeys, I think. I once said to Harold, 'Was your ancestor black, too?' and he says, 'What do you mean?' and I says, 'It stands to reason, don't it, you being black. ' Anyway, Harold said no, it was his granny on his mum's side was from Trinidad, like mine. He didn't know much about his dad's side. Anyhow, I keep telling our Sharon to look up the Darwin relatives as it was her dad's dream to find them and see what the story really was. Our Sharon says they're not black, and that Darwin wasn't, neither. Pity.

Dermot O'Connor: Kensington Park

My dear, I don't live in Hancock Towers — I live in a quite exquisite bijou residence just down the road from them, a very desirable address, actually, but the noise, my dear, from some of the local restaurants and clubs late at night — appalling! Hooray Henries singing on the pavements at 3 am, motorcar doors banging — too tiresome. Last night, for example, I was in and out of my hall door like a cuckoo, remonstrating with the revelers. Actually, I met a quite sweet girl, Sharon Darwin, sitting in the road outside

Stringvests. She said to me, 'Wot's yer problem, Granddad?' and I said, 'Dear heart, my nerves are absolutely frazzled,' and we got to talking. A darling girl, my dear, but what an accent. And it turns out she's a researcher, of all things, and said to me, 'Why don't you toffs and the restaurant owners do some research — maybe focus groups — and make an action plan?' My dear, young people today, so bright, so *comme il faut* — so Shar is coming round to tea and we're going to plan something. I have a Jamaican char, and Shar seems to be of Caribbean persuasion, so they should get on.

I forgot to say, I'm a tribunal psychiatrist — I decide whether criminals are insane or not. Shar's brother, for example, is in prison in Dublin and I'm tempted to have an unofficial word with my old friend the governor there, because Kev must be barking mad — before fleeing with the goods he acted out Ophelia's final scene from Hamlet for the security camera. I mean, I ask you — was that a good choice? A very weak role, I always thought.

Jennie Richards: 15-C, Hancock Towers

I'm the president of the Residents' Association. Your mayor wrote to me — bit of a nutter, is he? He seemed to think this was a castle. Hancock Towers is public housing. No, being president is not an honour, no one else wanted it, and I missed the meeting, didn't I, working the night shift, so I got landed with it. I might have done it anyway — after I broke a wrist on a kiddie's skateboard going down a flight of stairs, I said, 'Hang on, someone's got to take charge — muck everywhere, lifts broken, little kids selling crack, pimps with complete stables of fourteen-year-olds—not nice.' So I said fair enough, I'd give it a shot.

What are our problems? Are you blind? Or deaf? OK — noisy neighbours, for a start. People are reluctant — sometimes terrified — to complain, but the Environmental Health Service officers can prosecute, if people call them. Or we can get an injunction. Another problem is graffiti — although not as bad as it used to be. Dogs fouling the pavements, men urinating in lifts, drug dealing, youths causing a nuisance. On the other hand, we have a lot of community activities — bingo, dominoes, an Arabic after-school class, a day care facility, a community alarm service for people living alone, and so on. We have twelve nationalities here — 60 per cent of the people here speak English as their second language. We have Moroccans, our biggest group, and Spanish, Portuguese, Brazilians, West Indians, Kenyans, Nigerians, Ethiopians, Eritreans, Sudanese, Iranians, and I know I'm missing some out.

I have to give this up in a few months, though. I'm doing a Ph.D in comparative international company law, and working all night, and I'm wrecked. I'll keep on for one more year, and after that, I'm nominating someone else.

Rose Darwin 14-A, Hancock Towers

I a days' worker fi Dr. O'Connor.

Me husband, Colin, he carry me from Jamaica to London in 1997. I never know a ting bout England. But a whole heap a people going to England inna dem time deh. Ay! Was like going to annoder world. I fraid to walk pon deh street even a day time. Di men deh whistle and di cars — oh! di noise and di bangarang get pon toppa me nerves.

And me husband no good, him hardly give me notten. Him hardly ever home. Pay no rent, no bill. Deh landmissus stop pon di premises and she say, 'Gimme me money! Me no waan hear no explanation.' And Colin, he love to lick me. One day I find out me pregnant and he give me bad lick. I did tired of it and I say, 'You hit a bellywoman? No more.' After dat, he lef we and go a Manchester go work inna factory, but still him don't give me nottten.

So I meet Kev. Him nah lick me. Him never even tell me a bad word. But him is a genius where tiefing and gambling is concerned. Him in Approve School by time him twelve years old. Last year him go tief a computer in Dublin. Him shouldn't did do it — his madda and me mus go a long trip every month go see him.

So I a walk go out pon di street, go see if I get a work. I go dis restaurant and no get notten, but Dr. O'Connor him siddung in deh restaurant and he say he want someone fi work as days' worker. So I lef my two-year-old boy Marcus pon my neighbour and go work fi deh doctor. Deh doctor he say he a New Man and he try to help wid di cooking but I get vex and tell him go inna sitting room. But he a good man — he call me Dear Heart. He say, 'You are absolutely exquisite Rose, a true original.' I say, 'Gwan, Doctor', but he OK.

Den I met Jenny, deh president of deh place and she tell me carry Colin go a court fi get money fi deh two-year-old lickle boy. She tell me go a school, learn something. We became good friends. Until den, I know no odder woman fi talk to. Now I work wid her in deh Residents' Association. Di women dem need courses learn how fi protect demself and how get a work. And di men always get more wages than we. But don't is women as good as deh? Di bosses dem tek more advantage when yuh is a woman. I waan fi find out what courses deh need and then help set dem up. Deh women dem never going fi live in ignorancy again.

Ay! One thing fi sure. No man hit me again. Anyday him lick me, I cut off him teapot.

Kevin Darwin: # 426130, L Wing, Glasheen Prison

Dear Tony,

Thanks a million for your letter. Of course I'll help you with your prison study. Odd thing to be interested in, but it takes all kinds. Ever do any time yourself, ha ha? Anyhow, what do you want to know? Why not come over next time my mum and Rosie come?

This is a rum place. The Guv is great but some of the wankers in here would put years on you. And I don't even come across some of the real tough cases — like in the Muppet Wing — all the head cases and loopers are over there — or take the M Wing — those old lags have been in so long they eat with their hands. They'll have to learn to use a knife and fork all over again if they ever get out. And the HIVs over at the Base. One thing — I'm not walking out of here with HIV. My wife Rosie would have my balls. I'm in the L wing — short-term, knock on wood, and I'm a trusty — I dole out the grub in the staff dining room. But I see myself swanning about in a chef's hat some day. Fancy myself a bit of a genius with the old spaghetti bolognaise. Ever do any cooking, Tony?

My old Mum told you I played Tinker Bell? It was Mary Bell, the child murderess. I'm kinda slight, and I can do a girl's voice in an English accent, see? You want to catch my Ophelia sometime. It was on TV.

So that's it. End of story. All she wrote. See you soon, Tony, old son.

Your friend,

Kev Darwin

Graf: 18-B, Hancock Towers

So you're working with Shar. I went to school with her brother Kev — a right dozy bastard. Always bragging he had some famous ancestor. And always had something off the back of a lorry.

I'm a graff — a graffiti artist. I've been doing some of my best work over in Cooper Towers. Nah, this stuff on the walkways in Hancock isn't mine — thing is, mine's a lot better, and anyway, us graffs usually don't tag our own buildings. I get a mate to do it, and I do his — professional courtesy, like. I did my own building once about a year ago, and never again. Never.

Anyhow, I'm thinking of setting up legit — a little graphic design business. Why should these wankers just out of some hole-in-the-wall art college get all the money?

A few of us 'bombed' Cooper last night — painted some brilliant stuff. Funny, I thought when the doorbell went that you might be from the Council — the Grimebuster Squad is looking for a couple of us in a serious way. The Council come in and clean the walls down with power hoses — all that talent just down the drains. No collected works for me. Anyhow, they're really pissed about it, and they got this squad of effing bollockses that wouldn't know Warhol from Etch-a-Sketch nosing around now.

I know what you're doing—sanctimonious bleeding hearts with your notebooks, going to write some drivel about the alienation of the urban underclass for some professor who thinks getting on the Tube is anthropological research. Publish it later in some seedy journal to further your squalid little career and then we have a couple hundred more of you lot turning up over the years, leeching on the lives of the poor fuckers who live here. Do you live here? Pull the other one. Shar does — I might talk to her, I dunno, but not about my life. Anyhow, why don't you lot study something useful? There's a girl here—her parents made her marry at 15 to a total stranger, when she really loved somebody else. It's happening a lot here with girls who have immigrant parents. How come you don't study that and put a stop to it? Nah, you're all useless.

Avril Matthews: 20-B, Hancock Towers

No, dearie, I'm afraid I don't need no research. Funny line of business for a grown man like you. But maybe you'd give me a hand here — it gets harder and harder for an old woman like me to get my shopping into the lift. Ta. Well, if you're getting in the lift with me, don't breath too deep. Some of the weekend rum drinkers in the building think this is a public toilet — my eyes aren't half streaming by the time I reach the 20th floor. The Residents' Association put cameras in the lifts to stop it, but the blokes used it as a beauty parade. I don't know what they think they have to show off about — I read in the paper the other week that 60 per cent of sperm donors in London are turned down. I think it said there's only one good donor in Manchester. He must have his hands full. I doubt very much he waves his willy at the cameras in his lift — I'm sure he was brought up proper. It stands to you, in the end. I hope you don't mind me speaking my mind like this — you being a Yank, I suppose sex is nothing new to you. Certainly wasn't to the last Yank I talked to, back in 1942.

Here we are, right as rain — sorry I can't invite you in, but I, ah, well, I — the place is a sight — yes, that's it — a bit of a shambles because I've got a good few dogs — ten — in there just now — on the quiet, like, of course — the Residents' Association don't allow it.

Where did they come from? Well, ah, let's see, how it started was — well, my neighbour rescues greyhounds when they're too old for the track, and I said I'd take a few, if he was stuck. Lovely fellow — a Chinese Jew for Jesus. Gay, too, I think. Did some time a while back for peddling crack and cocaine, but lovely to his mother. Anyhow, I've got about eight dogs now in there, and they bite. Did I say they were Airedales? Well yes, that's what they are.

How do I feed them? Well, let's see. Yeshua —Yeshua Chong's his name, like — he brings me the tins — I couldn't be popping out to the shops for twenty tins a day, not with my feet. Here — I'll show you my feet —

shocking bad, you never saw nothing like them — I said to Dr. Boudafcha the other day, Doctor, I says to him sign me up for the first foot transplants — black, white, big, hairy — can't say fairer than that, can you, although I always did have dainty feet — but with the National Health, by the time I get another appointment, they'll be fitting me for wings, not feet.

Yes, you would think that a dozen dogs would make more noise. I daresay they're asleep. Ever have a dog yourself, Septus? Well, ta-ta, luv.

Mengeh Joof: 20-A, Hancock Towers

I live next to Mrs. Matthews. What dogs? Isn't she a lovely lady? She's a martyr to her feet, though. God give her strength.

Well, I will tell you my story. I was a headmistress in a school in Africa until I came here to do a Ph.D I just stayed here, teaching, and later brought my son and his wife. They live in 18-B. They have two girls now.

I feel great sadness for my son — he's never been happy here. He says there's no respect for the black man, and it's true, I think it is harder for the men. He's a senior engineer for the Council but last week he turned up at a site and someone told him to start cleaning the loos. Just because he's black. The Asians and Arabs — they're doing much better.

Anyhow, Modu was always strict with his girls. He wouldn't allow them to attend mixed-sex schools. 'Would you put a hyena and a goat in the same field?' he asked. Last year he discovered that his oldest girl — my granddaughter Haddy — well, someone had painted her name on the walkway, with hearts and teddy bears around it. He thought she was friendly with a boy in the next flat. Immediately, he arranged a marriage with a young man from our country, and brought him over. She was only fifteen, and she wanted to study medicine, but that's all finished now. My son says all he has is his religion and his culture, and his daughters will abide by those. I say nowhere does it say his religion requires his daughter to marry at that age. He also made her undergo initiation ceremonies. You don't know about those? Female genital mutilation is the correct term. Yes, it was done to me many years ago, but I swore if I had a daughter, never! And now my granddaughter!

His second daughter, Isatou, was told she would be initiated soon, so she ran away. People think I am hiding her, but I am not. But I support her right to resist. They are sick with worry, Modu and his wife. No daughters at all now — Isatou gone, and Haddy's new husband won't let her out of the flat, not even to visit her parents.

What sadness.

Hancock Towers Newsletter

October 26, 2001

Lord says Towers are 'architectural masterpieces'

What will they come up with next? Arts Minister Ken Maxwell announced last week that the two twenty-storey Hancock Towers buildings are to be given listed status, putting them in the same league with the Globe Theatre and Kensing-ton Palace. Sir Evelyn Pettigrew, chairman of the British Heritage Council, made the rec-ommendation. 'They are a magnificent pair,' said Sir E., 'part of England's historical heritage.' Sir Evelyn is a frequent visitor to the Towers and takes a keen interest in affairs here.

Having listed status means no changes can be made to the building without the approval of the Heritage Council. Also, all changes must be in keeping with the architectural period.

You live here. What do you think? Our next issue will include your letters.

Researchers to study Hancock Towers

Maybe Sir E. should have consulted Sharon Darwin of #14-A, who intends to carry out a study of the Towers. Shar spent the last six months in a little place in Ohio studying the natives and is back now with two blokes, Sep and Tone (way to go, Shar!). The three could come knocking at your door any day now asking about the old sex life. (Seriously, they will study problems among teenagers in the Towers, an issue that worries all of us.)

Association members sent on course

Mr. Hamid Hussein and Mrs. Sheila Braithwaite have returned from courses in Brighton which were sub-sidized by the Residents' Association. Both said they intended to put their new-found training to immediate use for the good of the Towers. Both will be offer-ing courses shortly.

Recipe for spaghetti bolognaise

Kev Darwin, who, accord-ing to his mother, is currently touring Italy with a theatre group, has sent us the recipe for spaghetti bolognaise on Page 3. The novel add-ition of capers and the garnish of crumbled Weetabix adds that con-tinental touch to this quintessential British dish. Try it!

11 INTERVIEWING PEOPLE

Summary

This chapter and the next two look at qualitative techniques, or techniques that produce material in words rather than in numbers. When you are using qualitative techniques, your main instrument is yourself. Your personal qualities will really come into play now.

Many of the underlying principles of structured interviews also apply to *semi-structured* and *unstructured interviews*. This chapter explores a particular type of unstructured interview, the *emic approach*, using *interviews*, *card sorts*, and *triads*. A checklist is also provided for semi-structured interviews.

You can carry out interviews with individuals, such as *key informants,* or with groups. Some special types of group interviews are *community interviews* and *focus groups*.

The techniques in this and the next two chapters are often called *qualitative*: they produce material in words rather than in numbers, although it can later be converted to numbers, if appropriate.

Introduction to Qualitative Techniques

Qualitative techniques usually, but not always, resemble the everyday methods that people use for getting information and take place in the same kinds of settings: in people's houses, in enterprise centers, in the office — that is, the places where what you are interested in actually happens.

Because of this, you get the context in which the action, behavior, or process occurs, which gives you a more holistic picture, as you can see the background in which your material is embedded.

Qualitative research can be used for:

- Getting a preliminary picture so that you have enough information to refine your strategies and questions.
- Interpreting the meaning of material collected through quantitative techniques.
- Illustrating and fleshing out findings from quantitative research.
- Ruling out hypotheses.

In some cases, qualitative research is the best way of getting certain kinds of information. In quantitative techniques the instrument is the questionnaire, test, or measure. In qualitative methods, the instrument is the researcher. Part of the reason why rules for qualitative research have never been set forth as clearly as those for surveys is probably because a lot more depends on the researcher's good sense, experience, and personality. Used properly, qualitative techniques can give you a richness and depth that you are not likely to get through other methods. Used carelessly, they produce material with no more value than a tourist's snatched impressions. As always, using a variety of methods to strengthen your information is a good idea. Some of the techniques in this section are time-honored methods and others are less common. You should adapt all of them to your own cultural situation and requirements.

Unstructured or Informal Interviewing

Unstructured or informal interviewing is often used at the beginning of a piece of research to get a broad picture, or because you don't know what is important to ask. 'Tell me about…' is a good way to start. Another, which can produce useful information, but has to be used in a way that shows you are trying to learn rather than being frivolous, is: 'What questions should I be asking you about this?' Of course, people may then wonder why you are the researcher and they are the interviewees, but being humbled is not the worst thing that can happen to a researcher. You can also use informal interviewing to crosscheck pieces of information, to fill in details, to explore new areas as they arise, and to take advantage of unexpected opportunities. Informal interviews have the appearance of conversations, and follow the social rules appropriate to the people you are working with. The difference is that if it seems acceptable and practical, you will be taking notes (if not, you have to take them later). When analyzing and presenting what people tell you, you must, of course, be careful about their integrity and uphold the trust they placed in you.

Emic techniques for interviewing

In Chapter 3 we discussed etic and emic research. In etic research you determine the agenda and the categories in which people give information back to you. In emic research you try to see from within, to discover perspectives, interests, and problems as seen by the insider. In emic research the respondents, rather than you, decide what information is important and they create the categories for the interview. This is particularly important in relation to women's concerns, such as labor force activities, or disabled people's concerns, such as provision of services, because many established categories of information — certain census categories, for example — were created for male activities, while others were created with an unconscious bias toward able-bodied people.

Some applications of emic research require considerable sophistication and are quite time-consuming. The following discussion presents a more general way of using the approach to complement other techniques as a rather unusual type of unstructured interviewing. Nevertheless, however unstructured the technique may appear to the observer, its purpose is to discover the structures, categories, and groupings that the people you are working with use to organize the way they see things.

Emic interviews

Chapter 4 has already provided an example of emic questioning using the grand tour approach developed by anthropologist James Spradley (1979). Here is another example. Remember, the aim is to learn how people categorize things, ideas, concepts, processes and so on. The only question that you create is the first one. The rest arise from what the respondent tells you. You may recall that Kev, formerly of Hancock Towers, is now doing a stint in Glasheen Prison in Dublin. Tony, who has been doing some research in Hancock Towers, is now working on a study of prison life.

Q.1 Kev, great to see you… I came over on the ferry with your mom and Rosie to do this interview. I know it'll use up a bit of your precious visiting time, but we got an extra half-hour from the Governor, so let's make the most of it, okay? You know I'm interested in prisons and the like…well, prisoners, really.

A.1 Yeah, Tony, well, you don't look a bit like what I imagined — those shades are cool, man. So, you want to talk about prisoners, well, I can tell you a thing or two, believe me. This place is full o' them, ha!

Q.2 Okay, Kev, fill me in then…I've never been to Dublin before, never inside this prison… Glasheen, right? So, you're the expert! Why don't we start with you telling me what kinds of prisoners there are in here?

A.2 Well, there's the Muppets and the Jockeys, then, eh, the Lifers, and the ones like me, ODCs!

Q.3 Tell me about the Muppets?

A.3 Ah, well, they're the loopers, the crazies, you know, locked up there in J Wing. Pretty much segregated from us normal chaps. No-one goes there. They're a bunch of weirdos, just like I said in my letter.

Q.4 So, the Muppets are loopers and crazies, and they're over on J Wing…

A.4 Yeah, you know, they're a bit psychotic, the loopers do weird stuff at night, howl and stuff…of course, some of them are 'alcos', alcoholics, real psychotics, they don't say much. The rest are just crazy. But there's great business in here brewing beer for the alcos, only I wouldn't get involved in that, jeopardize my chances of getting out quick. I like what I am, just a plain old ODC.

Q.5 So, you're an ODC — tell me a little about that?

A.5 Ordinary Decent Criminal — that's me. Respectable in here, that is. See, ODCs are just the ordinary run of the mill blokes, wouldn't harm a hair on your head, us lot, but show us your latest computer hardware, and we're off — can't resist a nice bit of hardware, us lot. Or whatever else happens to fall off the back of a lorry — jewelry, silk underwear, the odd video library, you know what I mean…but we don't harm nobody, no guns, no violence, we're above that. We grab, we scarper. Get caught, do some time. That's the story.

Q.6 So ODCs are respectable — you don't harm anyone, no violence, just do your time and…?

A.6 Yeah, then move on…get back with your wife and mum an' all, get back with your mates down the pub Saturday nights, flash them the story…this'll be a rum one, Glasheen an' all, how I got to be a trusty here… I'm trusted, see? I dole out the grub in the officer's mess, feed all the screws and screwesses, don't I? Started cookin' there recently, and what with me recipe for spaghetti bolognaise, I'm virtually famous here. See, I figured out you had to impress the right ones, the 2-bars and 3-bars, or you could end up like the Lifers or even them bloody Jockeys, stuck here. Not me, I'm on me way out. Them blokes, they're stuck, never going nowhere.

Q.7 Kev, what's the difference between ODCs like you, and Lifers?

A.7 That's easy, mate. Lifers are in here for life, murderers and the like, nasty buggers some of them. I told you in the letter — they end up eating with their hands, they forget what it is to eat normal, like, with a knife and fork. Rosie'd kill me if I did that — she's very particular. You don't want to get mixed up with that lot, I tell you. Nor the Jockeys. They're as bad, if not worse.

Q.8 Hey, Kev, slow down, slow down…who are the '2-bars' and '3-bars'?

A.8 Ah, they're the toffs in the prison, the chiefs. See, the head chief is a 3-bar, three bars on the uniform, the chief only has 2 bars, him being a lesser mortal altogether. And the assistant only has one bar.

Q.9 Okay, so who are the Jockeys, then?

A.9 You don't want to think about them. They're the ones who committed sex crimes. No one wants to know about them. Weirdos. But the sky pilot — he talks to 'em, but then, that's his job.

Q.10 The sky pilot…fill me in a bit here, Kev, okay?

A.10 Well, the sky pilot's the religious bloke, the chaplain, what's known as 'the priest' or 'Father' depending on who you're trying to impress, see? And the air hostesses, they're all right, nuns, like, not doing nobody no harm. Mind you, the Muppets are forever having a go at them, callin' 'em Druids and Devil-chasers. Weirdos, those Muppets. Them sky pilots are alright, I suppose, gave me a good write-up before I went before the wind-ups. Made a difference, that did.

Q.11 So, who are the wind-ups?

A.11 The welfare and probation lot. Got your life in their hands, they have. I gave mine my famous spaghetti bolognaise recipe. Shoulda seen her licking her lips, ha! I tell you, Tone, I'll be out of here before you can say 'bucket of stew'…that's our word for the screws…hey, Tone, not meaning to be personal, like, but is that a wig you're wearing?

And so on. When your understanding is complete, you could construct a diagram — taxonomy or a tree — showing types of prisoners and characteristics as seen from the insider's point of view (Table 11–1 and Figure 11–1).

Table 11–1 Types of prisoners and characteristics in Glasheen Prison presented in tabular format

Long-term stay			Short-term stay
Muppets	Jockeys	Lifers	ODCs
Loopers or crazies			
Alcos			

or

Figure 11–1 Types of prisoners in tree form

Long-term stay ⇩			Short-term stay ⇩
Muppets ⇩	Jockeys	Lifers	OCDs

Loopers Alcos or crazies

This is what we learned about them:

Table 11–2 Categorization of prisoners by other prisoners in Glasheen Prison

Category of prisoner	Subtypes	Length of stay	Characteristics
Psychotics (Muppets)	Alcos	Long term	'real psychotics' 'don't say much'
	Loopers or crazies	Long term	'just crazy' 'do weird stuff (howl)'
Sex offenders (Jockeys)	Weirdos	Long term	'stuck in jail' 'segregated from normal chaps'
Lifers (Lifers)	Lifers	Long term	'eat with hands' 'not normal' 'stuck in jail'
'Remands' (ODCs)	Trustys	Short term	'respectable' 'run of the mill blokes' 'no guns – no violence'

You might then move on to try to discover the characteristics of groups of prisoners you have identified by looking for similarities and differences among them. You will ask the prisoners, of course. In fact, Kev's interview has already given you some details. You can also ask prison officers what kinds of prisoners are in their care. You could then try to discover what distinguishes them in the officers' minds, and might come up with a chart like that in Table 11–3.

Table 11–3 is actually an example of a *componential analysis*, which we look at as a method of analysis in Chapter 16.

Table 11–3 Categorization of prisoners by prison officers in Glasheen Prison

Type of Prisoner	Wing Identity	Types of crime	Education
Psychotics (Muppets)	J wing	Various	Mainly second level
Sex offenders (Jockeys)	K + L wing	Sex offences	Second & third level
Lifers (Lifers)	K wing	Violent crime, murder	Mainly second level
'Remands' (ODCs)	M wing	Minor offences, fraud	Mainly primary
HIV	'The Base'	Various	Primary & second level
Political prisoners	L wing	Terrorist activities	Mainly second level

Card sorts or pile sorts

We saw examples of card sorts in Chapter 4 and will come across them again in Chapter 15. In this procedure you ask people to sort cards, photographs, drawings, or objects into categories of their own choosing. For example, give people a set of cards with the names of local community organizations (e.g. the local library, women's shelter, cab service, enterprise center), the types of services provided, or activities they engage in and ask them to sort them into groups. Then ask what the categories are, what their characteristics are, what makes the organizations in one pile more similar to each other than they are to the organizations in another pile. Keep repeating the process. Since you are looking for shared cultural knowledge, not purely personal views, you need to ask a number of people. You will know when to stop when the categories become repetitive. Everyone's categories will not necessarily be identical; see if you can find the common ones. You can then check the categories by doing the process the other way around: give someone the pack of cards, list the categories, and ask that person to sort the cards into the categories. If the sorter has some organizations left over, or can't fit the cards into the categories, they may not be meaningful, and you might have to start over. You might give someone a pack of cards with names of local organizations and ask her to sort them into those that are user-friendly and those that are not. Then ask why. If you are working with non-literate people you could read out the names of the organizations one by one and have people assign them to the 'user-friendly' pile or 'not user-friendly' pile.

Or you could refine this process, and begin at the other end — ask people to name characteristics: 'What makes for a user-friendly local organization?' Write the answers on cards (of a specific color). Then ask:

'What's the opposite of user-friendly?' and add these cards to the pile. Take the whole pile, shuffle it, and ask the person to choose several that go together, make one pile, then ask what others don't fit there but need a separate pile? You might end up with several piles, reflecting the fact that there are usually areas of gray in between the extremes of 'user-friendly' and 'not user-friendly' you started out with. If you end up with several piles, the person has made quite fine distinctions and has produced piles that are, in themselves, categories. But they are not yet overtly named from the person's perspective. She has created categories using some internal meaningful system, and now you might want her to name those 'hidden' categories: 'Taking all the cards in this pile, what would you call organizations that share these characteristics?' And so on for each pile.

Imagine she says the first pile of characteristics is shared by 'very user-friendly organizations', the second are 'OK organizations', the third 'put people off', and the fourth pile are 'totally intimidating'. You can now take the pile of cards with the organizations' names and ask her to lay them (make sure they are a different color card from the characteristics) on, or next to, the pile where they belong. Now you have a double set of distinctions — local organizations that are considered very user-friendly, OK, put people off, or are totally intimidating and you have the content of those categories. For example, 'very user-friendly' organizations might include a set of characteristics such as 'easy to get an appointment', 'clean toilets', 'no-smoking area', 'provides toys for children', 'provides magazines', 'returns your calls promptly', and so on. When working with a group and attempting to achieve consensus, starting with the characteristics and then matching the organizations to them has one great advantage. Once the group has identified the characteristics, established and piled them, the meaningful content is out there, in front of everyone and is not up for further negotiation. Well, not too much negotiation...be prepared still to move some characteristics around.

Triads

To get more refinement on the card sort method, you can present people with groups of three cards or items and say, 'Choose the one that doesn't fit' or 'Choose the two that seem to go together' and then ask 'Why?' Regroup the items within other sets of three cards and repeat. This allows you to understand the grounds on which some things share characteristics — for example, 'Which two are more alike in this group: library, local enterprise center, women's shelter?' If the first two are grouped together it might reveal that they are places where anyone in the community can readily go without attracting undue attention, while the women's shelter might have a different status, even a kind of stigma, and be considered a 'women-only space'. You can also use triads as a major research technique using large numbers of people and many items. These are still presented to people in groups of three in all possible combinations. Then you need to work out how often each possible pair is selected. See Bernard (1994, pp. 231–234) for a discussion of how to work with the combinations that arise when using large numbers of respondents.

You cannot read anything other than cultural information into your sortings when using either cards or triads. For example, in the Western world some experts think that categorizations based on perception (color, size, shape, number) reflect a simpler level of analysis than sortings made by function (things that are used together or have a similar purpose). Sortings based on taxonomies are thought to be the most sophisticated of all (putting certain plants or animals together because they belong to the same species or family). Although schooling can create a tendency to classify by taxonomy, people are more influenced by their culture when grouping things together. This is useful to know, because what you are trying to get is cultural information, not individual intellectual or personality assessments.

Semi-structured interviews

In semi-structured interviews you don't have a standard interview form. You have an agenda that you use as a reminder to ensure that you eventually cover the basic points, but your questions are tailored to the individual or category of person and to the circumstances. For example, you may want to know what kinds of skills training programs should be developed for young women in the local community. Some of the people you may be approaching could include government officials, non-governmental organization heads, employers, old people in a community, and young women, each requiring a different approach to the interview, including different wording, order and length. The issue is not simply a matter of people not understanding your questions if you don't adapt them. If you fail to use appropriately professional language to experts, they may feel you don't know enough to warrant their expenditure of energy on you; if you use professional or official sounding language on people who are wary of officials, they may not cooperate; if your language is not sufficiently respectful to the elderly or sufficiently sensitized for strongly committed people, you may get a lecture rather than your answer.

Good books on actual interviewing rather than on how to approach people are difficult to find, because sense, style, empathy, on-the-spot thinking, and responsiveness are more important than sets of guidelines. However, some general pointers follow. Some of these are also useful for participant observation (see the discussion later in this chapter) because observation usually involves asking questions as well.

Before the interview:

- Develop a brief list of points, perhaps ten at most, or a mental map of what you want to know but be prepared to be flexible. Because these kinds of interviews are ideal for getting more 'in-depth' information, you will lose this advantage by asking too many questions.
- Choose interviewers or decide whether you yourself can do a particular interview, remembering that all else being equal, people are usually more comfortable with people like themselves in terms of age, ethnic group, gender, social standing, and so on, although sometimes they see an 'expert' as more broad-minded, unshockable, or impartial.
- Choose the people you are going to interview. You can select them on a probability sampling basis, but you are more likely to have some other basis on which to choose them: some people have specialized knowledge, some people have undergone an experience that you need to understand, some people represent a good example of a pattern you have found, some people fly in the face of everything you thought would be the case.

During the interview:

- Behavior is important. Observe local courtesies — for example, not sitting on a higher seat than a senior person is important in some cultures, or not pointing a finger at anything in others. Try to use local conversational patterns and colloquial language. Introduce yourself, explain briefly the purpose of your study, tell how the person was selected, say about how long the interview will take, and ask if it is convenient for the person to talk to you now. Fit your interviews in with people's timetables. Offer to help people with what they are doing, if appropriate. For example, if you are studying a residents' association and they are bundling paper for recycling, you might lend a hand. Don't lecture people and don't show surprise or shock or distaste. When you ask a question, let people talk. Don't interrupt them or finish their sentences for them. Listen to what they actually say, not what you expect them to say.
- Choose the questions. Where do you get your questions? If you are using the research outline approach (Chapter 4), 'interviews' will be listed beside some of your points:

Outline	Technique	Source
Prison officer's attitudes toward —prisoner taking degree courses	Interviews	Prison officers in 'K' wing in Glasheen Prison

Convert the outline point into a question or questions. If you are using an emic approach (Chapter 4), you have a grand tour question: 'Tell me about prisoners' training interests?' and perhaps a card sort or a triad: 'Of these three (things, people, processes) which two are more alike and why?' 'Why is the other one different?' These will lead you to more questions for clarification. If you are using the grid approach shown in the Appendix, you can use the questions in the boldly outlined boxes to give you a basic picture, and any others that may be relevant.

- Ask the questions. In organizing your questions, try to ask for neutral facts first, eventually moving on to the interviewee's opinions and to any sensitive issues. Take the trouble to find out from someone who is sympathetic to your research what the sensitive issues might be, such as current prisoners' rights disputes, or recent media stories about a prisoner who demanded the right to enroll on a degree course and then escaped while attending it. Don't try to discuss them until the interviewee is comfortable with you. This may take several visits. People may not discuss some topics at all. If you really need the information, see if you can get it in other ways, for example, can you use a *proxy indicator*? If you wanted to work out which types of prisoners take adult education courses while inside, you might check the prison library records. Who borrows the books on the course outlines? While not foolproof (Kev might not take the cookery course but he might still borrow the books) it is an indication you might be able to crosscheck later.

Sometimes you can deal with sensitive issues by showing that you already know something about the subject: 'As I understand it, some people think prisoners don't deserve to enroll on degree courses. Others feel it's a basic human right. What is your own feeling?' If you simply asked: 'Should prisoners be denied places on degree courses?' a prison officer might say: 'I don't know. We don't have that issue here.'

An interview can give greater depth than a questionnaire, because you can probe — encourage people to expand on their answers — and crosscheck information. Chapter 9 mentioned some probing strategies that are also appropriate for interviews.
⇨ Ask questions that allow people to develop their answers, not questions that can simply be answered by 'yes' or 'no'.
⇨ Pursue useful information further by asking questions that will tell you 'Who?', 'What?', 'Where?', 'When?', 'Why?', and 'How?', as appropriate.

⇨ Encourage people to expand on an answer by pausing after the reply, and perhaps giving some sign of encouragement, and using phrases like: 'Can you tell me more about that?' 'Can you give me an example?'

⇨ Encourage people to clarify their answers: 'Let me see if I understand this correctly. You say 50 per cent of prisoners are currently taking degree courses?'

⇨ Crosscheck the answers by phrasing the question slightly differently — for example, to someone who wants to see prisoners take courses but acknowledges that many do not: 'What are the main reasons why prisoners don't take courses?' and later: 'What would help prisoners to take courses?'

• Observe: people communicate both verbally and non-verbally (through actions). The better you know a group or a culture, the better you will be able to 'read' its members. Noticing interviewees' gestures, body movements, hesitations, pauses, tones, and other signs may help to give you a better understanding of what they are saying. But don't jump to conclusions. In your notes record both what they said and what they did, rather than your interpretation.

After the interview:

• Thank the interviewee. If you are not going to see this person again, tell her or him what to expect next. Are you eventually going to return with a report showing your findings? Is a report going to come back to the governor? Will a research team come to the prison? Will there be government involvement and policy meetings on the issue? Will the media be involved? Although you can use what you learned to develop new questions and, in subsequent interviews, you can test the ideas you gained, never carry information from one interviewee to another.

• Evaluate the answers. For many researchers this seems to be a more important issue in informal and semi-structured interviews than it is in surveys. However, the problem is the same, no matter what the technique, and no foolproof way exists to ensure that what someone tells you corresponds to what the person actually thinks or experiences, no matter how many crosschecks you insert. However, this is a good opportunity to make a few points that people often forget:

⇨ Often you are not really interested in the truthfulness of individuals. You are studying social and cultural factors, and, unless an entire group is deliberately deceiving you by every means available to them, this is not an important issue. The more important issue is your own ability as a researcher, which is a far more common source of major error.

⇨ If you are using triangulation (multiple methods, researchers, sources, and so on as discussed in Chapter 7), serious errors based on deception should emerge. You will find discrepancies between what people say, do, and may be recorded as having done. Also, experience and theory in your own field may tell you that something cannot be the case. For example, an anthropologist who is told that a group of people who are herders trace their descent through women and observe the practice of giving a bride price when a girl is married to her mother's sister's son would hear a warning bell go off. Anthropologists know that these customs don't go together anywhere, and the combination does not make sense. Your own field or area of expertise probably has 'bells' like this.

⇨ What people say and what happens are often two different things. When a culture is changing, for example, people often fail to notice that the ideal and the practice no longer correspond. You may be studying a neighbourhood and people tell you: 'Couples move into a place of their own when they marry,' and yet perhaps you discover that most young couples are living with one set of parents, perhaps because jobs have become scarcer or house prices have soared. However, people still hold to the ideal.

⇨ When people say one thing and do something else, you can often learn much more about what is going on than when everything matches. Of course, first you have to know enough to know that things don't match. This can be difficult when the subject is sensitive and not easily checked. Wolf Bleek (1987), who studied subjects such as family quarrels, suspicions of witchcraft, sexual relationships, and birth control practices, including induced abortions, in a Ghanaian town, provides one of the most striking examples. He lived with and studied a large family group that included nineteen women of childbearing age. He concluded after some time that induced abortion was common among the women. However, at the time of his research, he notes that 'statistical data enjoyed higher esteem than at present,' and therefore he arranged for 179 women (from many different families) to be interviewed during their visits to a child welfare clinic. The women reported few induced abortions and little use of birth control. The nurse–interviewers believed that many of the women were lying. Only 4 per cent of the 179 women admitted to an induced abortion, while more than half of the 19 women in Bleek's earlier study of the family group had. Only 14 per cent admitted to ever practicing birth control, while 63 per cent of the women in the earlier study had.

  In retrospect, Bleek concludes that the women had reason to lie to the survey researchers, because abortion was not only very private, but also a criminal act. He also realized that his 'detective-like' approach with the nineteen women, while revealing hidden facts, prevented him from recognizing their serious social and psychological importance.

Remember as well that people's beliefs and perceptions are as important as what they may actually be doing at the moment, even though what they are doing seems to conflict with what they say. What they say may be the general pattern, all other things being equal; what they are doing at the moment represents an attempt to accommodate the pattern to the circumstances. Both are important. Beliefs are facts just as much as activities are. Don't fall into the trap of thinking that beliefs are subjective, and what people do is objective. Both are, or neither is, depending on your philosophical approach (see Chapter 2).

Because many cultural patterns are shared, don't discount anyone on the grounds that he or she couldn't know anything useful. Everyone has a sufficient command of his or her own cultural repertoire to be able to function. Some people are better at communicating this than others; predicting who is difficult. Don't persist with people who can't or won't participate. You don't have the time.

- Write up your notes immediately. Record:
  ⇨ The circumstances in which the interview took place.
  ⇨ What you were told, in direct quotes where possible.
  ⇨ What you saw.
  ⇨ Any judgements of your own that you think might be useful ('I think Mr. Okoro was more at ease before his wife joined us'), and record them separately.

See Chapter 15 for advice on recording techniques.

Cultural Bias

If you are planning to work with people from a cultural tradition other than your own, you may have to re-think some of your assumptions about the interviewing process. You might assume that because conversing is a natural process everywhere in the world, the interview would be less liable to cultural bias than, say, questionnaires and measures. Certainly, the interview can appear more natural, particularly when you observe proper local protocol. Still, even an informal interview is not the same as a conversation, because the expectations of both the interviewer and the interviewee are different.

Two researchers, Slim and Mitchell, have discussed some other problems. One is the researcher's expectation that people have an answer to, or an opinion on, every question. The second is 'nutshelling', the Western notion that people should give a brief, to-the-point summation of their experience or knowledge in response to a question, whereas in many cultures talking through and considering all angles is the most judicious way of presenting one's ideas. In many cultural traditions, people feel that 'one cannot know everything, and that the little one knows cannot be uttered in a moment' (Slim and Mitchell, 1992, p. 69). A third problem, which applies to surveys as well, is that most people prefer a two-way exchange, or even more. People may want to know what you think, how many children you have, and may even want to call in a few neighbors or family members to ponder some questions in a more companionable way. Often, this does not matter. You are trying to understand what is happening, how, and why, so if this helps you, fine. If it interferes with your learning what you need to know, you will have to develop strategies to withhold your own opinions without seeming rude, and figure out how to talk to people privately. Other useful books on this topic are McCracken (1988) and Spradley (1979).

Key informants

A special kind of interviewee is the *key informant*. Key informants may be people with a particular specialization, such as childcare providers, or they may represent a particular viewpoint or experience. People want a crèche facility in their area. How can it meet the needs of various groups? Someone with a disabled child, someone who works shift hours and needs part-time crèche facilities, lone parents who can tell you the problems they have in getting suitable crèche facilities, can each tell you something about the needs that may have to be taken into account.

There is another kind of key informant who is much more difficult to find: the unusually insightful person who can provide analytical information, context, or insights in relation to what you are studying. The ability to make valid generalizations beyond one's own immediate situation and experience is in part a function of personal sagacity and in part an exposure to a range of experiences. You may be fortunate enough to find such a person. You still must use all the other techniques at your disposal, of course. No one person can provide a total picture. The reliance of some anthropologists in the past on a few male key informants alone has led to very peculiar interpretations of some societies.

Key informants can help to explain a technical process, put parts of a pattern together for you, or show how facts and experience come together. You can also use their services in a more organized way. For instance, you have identified four categories of parents using childcare services in Hancock Towers: 'well-off parents' who send all their pre-school children to the crèche, 'disabled parents' who send some of their pre-school children, 'male-focused parents' who send only male children, and 'poor parents' who send none. You have learned something about these families through other methods, a short survey, for example, or a card sort. Now you want to know more about their circumstances and attitudes. You could interview based on a probability sample but you could also choose some people deliberately for their ability to provide valid insights beyond their own experience, that is, key informants.

Selecting key informants is a form of purposeful sampling (see Chapter 6). You may choose them because they are typical, in that they represent a pattern or attitude or have experienced something that you have identified as common, or you may choose them because they are unusual, that is, they hold a different view, their experience has been different, they have more expertise. Key informants are not necessarily representative or 'important' or 'official' people. They can be childcare experts or crèche inspectors, but they can also be long-time users of the crèche service, astute observers of the local situation vis-à-vis the history of the crèche, or a parent who has helped in the crèche for many years. Sometimes 'marginal' people are good key informants. These are people who, for whatever reason, have been forced to watch the situation at a slight remove, or have had to study and accommodate to the ways of others in order to function, such as members of minority groups. Whoever you choose, you must understand the advantages and limitations of their viewpoints.

Sometimes, of course, people see others as key, not because they are able to give a broader picture, but because they or their positions are due respect, or because they have a vested interest, or because they can influence events and decisions. You may be wise to consult them, while recognizing that they are pivotal people rather than key informants. Interviewing key informants requires careful preparation. Each probably requires a specially designed set of questions. Once again, flexibility is important. For further information, see Johnson (1990); for work in non-Western societies, see Kumar (1989).

Group interviews

So far, we have been discussing interviews with individuals, or perhaps with several people who are sharing a household or working together, but you can also use semi-structured interviews with larger groups. Two common types are community interviews and focus group interviews. These are not cheap substitutes for surveys or individual interviews: they give people the opportunity to put aside individual considerations and discuss something in the larger community context. As researcher Budd Hall (1981, p.16) has pointed out: 'Responses to problems offered by groups of people are not necessarily the same as the sum of individual responses of people speaking alone.' Group interviews are useful for getting a general picture of a place and its needs or possibilities; developing tentative hypotheses; getting a better understanding of material you have collected; or finding out what people think about the current situation, a planned project, or a completed project. You put a small number of carefully selected questions or topics to the group — for example, to parents in Hancock Towers who are worried about children's security in the local crèche: What are the most worrisome situations? Which children are most vulnerable? What is being done about the problems now? What might be done? What would this involve? What would it accomplish?

Community interviews

In community interviews you are seeking information from a 'natural' group, one that comes together at other times for a common purpose, such as a community meeting or an organizational discussion. Many people may be present, although groups larger than thirty are probably too big and may have to be broken up. Individual views are not sought. The aim is to put a small number of questions to the group for general discussion: 'How can the security of children be ensured at the local crèche?' 'Would a barter system for lone parents help with the problem of crèche costs?' Sometimes a research project is based almost entirely on community interviews — for example, certain categories of beneficiaries of a project may need to be consulted in depth. If you are using community interviews for this purpose, you have to consider how you are going to select the communities. You are most likely to use some form of purposeful sampling (see Chapter 6).

One problem with community interviews is that you don't necessarily know what, if anything, the group represents. Who didn't come? Why? You can't automatically take the results of a community interview as 'the voice of the people'. Also, even though you are working with a group, you may still be getting individual views. Certain categories of people — men, the dominant ethnic group, the wealthier, the people already involved, a faction, people who agree or disagree with what they think your position might be — may dominate the meeting. If you anticipate these kinds of problems, you can consult members of the various groups in advance and at the meeting, say: 'I've already discussed this with the [men, crèche owners, staff of non-governmental organizations] and would like to hear what others here think.'

Others may not be accustomed to putting their views forward or may fear repercussions, such as community ridicule, loss of business, or a host of other possible dangers. For people likely to be left out, you could say: 'The women who are providing voluntary services to the crèche may have some concerns about this. For example, is _____ a problem?' You must use this approach carefully. If people are still afraid to speak, it may sound to others as if they have no problems. If you are not really familiar with their problems, your example may direct the discussion away from their real concerns, and if you reveal something they thought they were saying in confidence, they will probably never trust you again.

Focus groups

Focus groups differ from community discussions in a major way: in community discussions the major interaction is between the researcher and the group, whereas in focus groups the interaction is among the members, who work through an idea, issue, or problem that the researcher has selected. Focus groups consist of people you have specially selected for their experience in relation to whatever you are studying. Usually, the group consists of six to twelve people of similar background in terms of age, sex, class, and so on who are brought together to discuss a small number of questions or issues — no more than ten — for about an hour or two. For some purposes meetings are longer and may occur over a period of days. Sometimes a more complex strategy is used: a researcher starts out very generally with one group, allowing it to map out the discussion and later, using what was learned from the first group, creates new types of focus groups to explore points identified in the first session. In focus groups, the group interaction, rather than answers to questions, produces the insights. People may argue points, correct one another, give exceptions, and support their points with examples from their own experiences. An approach like this can save time if planned properly.

Let us say you are trying to find out how to meet the needs of lone parents who have primary school children and who have said they would like to attend adult education classes in the mornings. You have discovered that the classes start at 9.30am, and the primary school starts at 9am, making it impossible for parents to get from the school to the class on time, given the distances involved. What ideas do people have about how this problem might be managed so lone parents can take adult education courses? This is a kind of brainstorming. Parents who are in this position know their own problems best. Feedback from them will help you to assess your ideas. Or perhaps you have worked out some ideas for providing transport direct from the primary school to the adult education classes, or you have suggested that the adult education classes be moved to a venue right beside the primary school. Will these work? What else are parents doing that might not have been identified? What else do they need to be able to take the classes? You will probably need other focus groups as well. Perhaps various community or non-governmental organizations have tried some of these ideas before. Their representatives may be able to tell you what happened and how you should amend your plans. Another possibility is that your scheme has already been implemented and does not work. Lone parents are still not taking adult education classes. Why? A focus group may help here too.

For some topics you might use a number of separate groups. For example, if adult education classes are being planned for women in a community, you might hold a series of discussions with groups with different viewpoints: women with children, women without children, women with no formal education, women with special needs, women who work outside their homes and require evening classes, women with literacy needs, and so on.

Holding a group interview

Controlling a community interview or a focus group can be difficult for a novice researcher. Feelings may be high, some people may overwhelm the meeting, or someone may hijack the meeting for another purpose. Kumar (1987) has outlined some techniques for preventing this. These include: giving non-verbal cues to the respondent to stop, such as looking in another direction, showing a lack of interest, and stopping note-taking; politely intervening, saying that you have somehow missed the point and would like to summarize what the respondent was saying, then refocus the discussions; taking advantage of a pause to say that the issues raised are of vital significance and should be discussed in a separate session.

You probably called a community interview meeting or a focus group to get more information faster. The temptation is to speed up the process even further by drawing hasty conclusions from your sessions, hearing what you want to hear, and accepting the ideas of the 'more important' people, the more articulate, the more potentially troublesome, the people most like yourself. Try to ensure that people with other views are heard. Did anyone have a different experience? Does someone think an idea won't work? Is it true for the women? Is it true for people who live in different parts of the area? Drawing conclusions that rely mainly on community interviews or focus groups requires considerable experience and skill. Beginning researchers should use a variety of techniques. A group interview approach may help you to complement information you obtained by interviewing people on their own, by observing, or by looking at records and documents.

References and further readings

Bernard, Russell. 1994. *Research Methods in Cultural Anthropology.* Newbury Park, California: Sage.

Bleek, Wolf. 1987. 'Lying Informants: A Fieldwork Experience from Ghana.' *Population and Development Review* 13(2):314–322.

Dobbert, Marion Lundy. 1984. *Ethnographic Research: Theory and Application for Modern Schools and Societies.* New York: Praeger.

Grandstaff, Somluckrat B. and Terry B. Grandstaff. 1987. 'Semi-Structured Interviewing by Multidisciplinary Teams in RRA.' *Proceedings of the 1985 International Conference on Rapid Rural Appraisal.* Khon Kaen, Thailand: University of Khon Kaen.

Hall, Budd, Arthur Gillette, and Rajesh Tandon, eds. 1982. *Creating Knowledge: A Monopoly?: Participatory Research in Development.* New Delhi: Society for Participatory Research in Asia (45 Sainik Farm, Khanpur).

Johnson, Jeffrey C. 1990. *Selecting Ethnographic Informants.* Newbury Park, California: Sage.

Kreuger, Richard A. 1988. *Focus Group Interviews: A Practical Guide for Applied Research.* Newbury Park, California; London; New Delhi: Sage.

Kumar, Krishna. 1987. *Conducting Group Interviews in Developing Countries.* Washington DC: U.S. Agency for International Development.

———. 1989. *Conducting Key Informant Interviews in Developing Countries.* Washington DC: U.S. Agency for International Development.

LeCompte, Margaret L., Wendy L. Millroy, and Judith Preissle, eds. 1992. *The Handbook of Qualitative Research in Education.* New York: Academic Press.

Liberty, Margot with Barry Head. 1995. *Working Cowboy: Recollections of Ray Holmes.* University of Oklahoma Press, Norman, Oklahoma.

McCracken, Grant. 1988. *The Long Interview.* Newbury Park, California: Sage.

Morgan, David L. 1988. *Focus Groups as Qualitative Research.* Newbury Park, California: Sage.

Slim, Hugo and John Mitchell. 1992. 'The Application of RAP and PRA Techniques in Emergency Relief Programs.' In N.S. Scrimshaw and G.R. Gleason, eds., *Qualitative Methodologies for Planning and Evaluation of Health-Related Programs.* Boston, Massachusetts: International Foundation for Developing Countries.

Spradley, James P. 1979. *The Ethnographic Interview.* New York: Holt, Rinehart and Winston.

Wolcott, Harry F. 1994. *Transforming Qualitative Data.* Thousand Oaks, California: Sage.

Hancock Towers Newsletter

Women complain of harrassment

The Grannies Club has registered a complaint with the Residents' Association ('Always at Your Service') against Mr. Hamid Hussein, who disrupted a recent meeting by flinging Mrs. Avril Matthews to the floor.

'Well, I never,' said Mrs. Matthews to this reporter. 'My nerves have been at me ever since.' Mrs. Parveen Rashid also complained, saying she had been invited by Mr. Hussein to take her best shot at his stomach. In the process, she lost her lower plate. Mr. Hussein said he was simply trying to run his course. 'Course, shmorse,' said Mrs. Rashid. 'I may sue.'

Mrs. Hamid Hussein said she was mortified. 'I have always performed my obligement, whenever he required it, often even when I didn't feel like it. Why is he molesting these elderly ladies? When I run my course, I don't behave in this scandalous manner.'

Mrs. Hussein's course, 'Making the Earth Move for You and Your Man', is very popular with ladies in the building.

Your Association ('Always at Your Service') is looking into the situation.

Tower of babel no more!

Children were entranced recently at their Beginning Arabic course when Mrs. Sheila Braithwaite sang the 'Postman Pat' song in Arabic, followed by 'Jerusalem'. The course meets every afternoon at four o'clock and is open, of course, to children of both Arabic and non-Arabic speaking families.

Note from the Editor:

Some people took exception to the tone of the first Residents' Assoc-iation newsletter. Sister Concepta Maria of the Little Sisters of the Holy Scribe, a teaching order devoted to training news anchors and reporters for tabloids, said that she may have misjudged her audience when she volunteered for the job. Several of the Little Sisters live in the Towers, where they have been teaching Spelling for Graffiti.

'We attract them any way we can' said Sr. Con.

12 USING CASE STUDIES AND PARTICIPANT OBSERVATION

Summary

Case studies and *participant observation* are not usually grouped together. Here they are, because both are strategies, that is, combinations of techniques, rather than single ones.

Case studies allow you to collect and present information in a way that provides more context. They are good for showing how something happens or works in a real life situation.

Participant observation is a strategy for interviewing, observing, and sometimes participating. It can be used to get preliminary information, to check other information, and to understand something in its larger context.

You may remember that in Chapter 7 we emphasized the importance of triangulation of techniques, that is, using several techniques to get the same information. Both case studies and participation have built-in triangulation: each involves using a variety of approaches to get a better understanding of what you are studying.

Case Studies

Case studies provide insights into how and why something works in real life. Consider this. If you added up all the answers to 1,000 questionnaires on participants' evaluation of the 'user-friendliness' of a new literacy program, you could assemble them to produce a picture of what helped and hindered people in terms of being attracted to, and participating in, the program. In a case study, you examine attitudes, behaviors, and the environment all together, in a natural setting, to give you a better understanding of how things work. You can do case studies of individuals (people who have never taken a literacy class but chose to try this one); of programs (the kinds of literacy programs that attract first-time students); of aspects of organizations and institutions (why a particular literacy program is over-subscribed); and of processes (how staff of a particular program make decisions).

You can use case studies at the beginning of an investigation to obtain enough understanding to create appropriate questions and choose appropriate techniques; to illustrate patterns you have identified using other methods; to show variations on a pattern that you have identified, that is, how it manifests itself in different ways; to show exceptions; and to show the difference between the ideal and the real (what people say they would like to do and what they really do in various circumstances). Experienced researchers can also use case studies as the main form of research in a study (see Yin, 1989, for a discussion of this approach).

As a first-time researcher, you could probably make the best use of case studies to get some initial insights into a situation or to illustrate patterns you have discovered. Suppose you have found that, while most young women taking literacy classes remain in the same kinds of jobs they held previously, others continue with second-chance education, take degrees, and get much better-paying jobs. What made the difference in these young women's lives? Case studies use almost all the research techniques in the social scientist's tool kit. Let us say you did a survey of these women and found certain patterns emerging: they had a dynamic literacy teacher, a supportive parent, high attendance rates, took a particular approach toward life, and so on. One factor is unlikely to be the cause. This is what a case study is good for: showing how factors and circumstances come together over time.

You can select your case studies from among women who seem to illustrate the pattern and build a picture of them. Interview the women, their families, their teachers, and anyone else who seems relevant. Look at documentation relating to early schooling, any other courses they may have attended, and attendance records for their literacy classes. Not only can these documents and interviews give you information, they can tell you whether the timing was important. Was a particular kind of support present at a particular stage in their schooling? Do they have some very positive memories of early schooling that may have contributed to a positive approach to later literacy classes? Observe how the women behave, their attitudes, how they go about things now. Do these give you any insights into the qualities that have helped them? Using material from all these techniques and sources, you try to show how these factors worked in real life.

Of course, you need to do more than one case study, particularly if several patterns are evident or if you are using this as one of your most important techniques. Look for cases that contradict your pattern as well. What can you learn from them? Why did the factors you have identified not work in this particular case? Or why did someone who experienced none or only a few of these factors succeed? You can create a much more sophisticated understanding this way.

A special kind of case study is the life history, in which the patterns you are seeking to identify or understand are manifested in the context of someone's life story. This is a particularly good approach if what you are studying needs to be understood over time. You can construct life histories from several sources, including interviews and written materials such as records and diaries, if they are available. Robert Burgess, an anthropologist, used teachers' life histories along with many other techniques in his 1983 study of a British comprehensive school. Liberty and Head combined the life history of a retired cowboy with detailed descriptions of the tasks in a cowboy's life in *Working Cowboy* (1995), to show the changes in ranching during the course of this century.

Another way of using case studies is to create small panels, such as families or work groups, and monitor them over time. Using this approach you can see time differences, how events impinge on strategies, how the group's composition affects the division of labor. In other words, you are looking at the dynamics of change. Longhurst (1981, p. 24) argues that such case analysis is more useful in rapid research than is extensive sampling: 'Even where quantitative data is necessary in an academic study, the careful observation of a few case-study families, albeit at a sacrifice of part of a large sample size, can provide insights that survey techniques completely ignore.'

Participant Observation

In its most narrow definition, participant observation provides information about what people let you see them doing, as opposed to the survey, which gives you information on what people say they are doing, what they say other people do, or what they say should be done. However, participant observation, as practiced by anthropologists, who have been its main users, is a strategy rather than a single technique.

Participant observation usually involves:

• Participating on a long-term basis in a natural setting: a tower block, an adult education classroom, a government department, and so on.

- Using a flexible, open-ended approach based on induction (allowing the data to unfold and lead you to conclusions, and perhaps to hypotheses).
- Drawing on whatever research techniques are useful, not only watching and doing, but listening, asking, and looking at records.

Participant observation can include:

- Direct observation: looking at classroom interaction in a multi-ethnic environment; looking at how a tower block's physical condition relates to users' needs.
- Observation with some participation: attending a wedding and asking about the ceremony, the gifts, and the participants.
- Full participation for the purpose of learning how to do something or learning more about what is involved in a situation — for example, working with a group of women to plan a sale-of-work to raise funds for the local adult education center, exploring the problems they face, the time they must spend on it, the supports they need.

Participant observation can be short term, which is what you will probably be doing, or long term, which is what many anthropologists do. At its simplest level, the aim of participant observation is to describe a setting (the adult education center); a process (how participants are motivated); behaviors (what women from specific ethnic groups do during the group introductions); or interactions (whom the tutor calls on, how often, who speaks up, who remains silent). At its most complex, the researcher tries to understand the ideas that shape people's behavior and what this means for the issues and problems that face them. What are the roles of women in the various ethnic groups represented at the adult education center? What expectations do they have about learning new skills, speaking out, and gathering in mixed-ethnicity groups? Do these beliefs differ between men and women, older and younger people, educated and those not educated, rural and urban dwellers? How? And how do these beliefs and activities reveal themselves in various aspects of life: decision-making, employment, taking adult education courses, social interaction? Participant observation helps you to get a better understanding of complex behaviors, processes, relationships, and interactions, and it is particularly good for understanding something in the larger context.

Uses

You can use participant observation as a preliminary technique to get enough information to plan a study or to create useful questions, or you can use it as a strategy in itself. You can also use it as a check on other techniques — for example, tutors say that women from each ethnic group in Hancock Towers attend the literacy program, so why are the Brazilian women missing? It is valuable when you need to understand something in its natural setting: what actually happens during the course of a literacy program, as opposed to what the advertised plan says will happen? You can use it for *negative case analysis*, that is, disproving something: tutors say that they call upon women and men in equal numbers, but a simple count of observations shows they don't. It can help you to make sense of information you get through other techniques by providing context: a project to set up cookery classes in Hancock Towers failed, yet women still travel quite a distance each week to cookery classes in the next neighbourhood. By observing their activities, you might find that their attendance at the class has a lot of other functions besides using the service. They might be getting a sense of another neighbourhood, seeing or making friends, having an evening out, bringing home some news.

Participant observation has been used quite extensively in educational research, from long-term studies of schools, classrooms, or staff, such as Wolcott's (1973) study, to Obura's (1991) studies of classroom interaction in Kenya.

Many years ago, Whiting and Edwards (1973) did a classic observation study in six countries around the world. They examined common stereotypes about boys' and girls' behavior, including the idea that girls are more passive and more nurturing, and boys are more aggressive and more dominant. They observed 67 girls and 67 boys between the ages of three and eleven in a total of 3,000 observations. Each term was carefully defined in observable ways. Dominance, for example, was defined as one child interrupting the ongoing behavior of another child to get that child to do what the first child wished. A number of interesting findings came out of this study, most of which the investigators could not have obtained using any other research method. For example, contrary to expectations, they found that girls dominated as much as boys, but simply used different modes. While boys dominated 'egotistically' ('I want you to do this because I want it'), girls dominated by 'invoking authority' ('Mother won't like it if you...' or 'God says...'). They also found that everyone felt free to issue more 'mands' (commands, interruptions, and so on) to girls than to boys.

Participant observation isn't useful for things people won't let you see — for example, spouse abuse isn't a likely subject for observation, participant or otherwise. It isn't useful for making generalizations to other settings unless you have done careful sampling to select the situations you are observing. It can't be used to establish causal relationships, although as we saw earlier, it can be used to disprove. It also is not useful for studying a large mixed situation, for example, one involving many different economic, social, and ethnic groups, but you could focus on a more limited aspect of the situation, such as interactions between Arabic and non-Arabic children attending Mrs. Braithwaite's 'Beginning Arabic' course in Hancock Towers.

Doing participant observation

Everyone looks at the world through spectacles colored by his or her culture, experiences, class, age, sex, training, and so on. Participant observation requires that we shed our spectacles as much as we can. If we want to understand the life of travelling people, looking at them through the eyes of 'settled' people is not going to give us a good understanding of their way of life — it is only going to highlight the ways in which they differ from settled people. People tend to notice the exceptions, the unusual, the strange. A white student who rarely sees black people may describe a crowd this way: 'There was a big crowd at the bus stop. A black man was playing a fiddle.' We have no idea if the other people were black from this description, but probably not. To the student, white was not worth mentioning. Sometimes, however, it is the usual that you want, the ordinary things that normally go unnoticed or unanalyzed: the daily routine in the adult education center, in the community, or in the office, not what happens on holidays, or days when an official comes to visit.

Doing participant observation seems easy. After all, everyone is a participant in life, and everyone observes. Because of this, participant observation also seems the most natural of research techniques. In daily life, everywhere in the world, most of us get our information this way, whereas few of us manage our affairs by giving people questionnaires. But observations in daily life and observation for research purposes are different. Participant observation is more 'primitive' or 'naive', as we will see.

Try this observation exercise. Choose a small setting (not a crowd or a busy event) and observe for a few minutes. You might look at what people do while they are standing in a lift, or a girl trying to study at home when other people are around, or some fellows from Hope And Glory planning their annual fishing trip. Write down what you saw, in as much detail as you can remember. Pretend you are going to send this to someone in a very different country, who will only have your account of the event. Remember to try to shed your spectacles: it won't help this person to see the scene only through male eyes or urban eyes. Now answer these questions:

The setting
    1. Where was the observation?
    2. What was the time?

3. What season was it?
4. What was the weather?
5. What was the setting?
6. What objects were in the setting (on the floors, walls, ceilings, if inside)?
7. What were the sizes, materials, colors, textures, shapes?

The people
1. Who was there?
2. What were they wearing (colors, textures, designs, and hair styles)?
3. What were their approximate ages, heights, weights?
4. What were they each doing?
5. What were the other people doing while people spoke or carried out actions?
6. What did each person say?
7. What gestures and body movements did they use?
8. How did others respond?
9. Where were the people in relation to each other? Did this change?

You
1. Where were you? What were you doing: sitting, standing, participating? Did you seem to be noticed? Did this change?
2. Were you part of the event before you began to observe? Did you let people know what you were doing? Once you began, did anything change? Did their behavior appear to change, toward you or toward the others? How?
3. How did you feel doing this exercise? If people didn't know you were observing in this way, what would they have thought if they knew? How would they feel if they read your notes? How would you feel?

If you gave the person in another country some actors and a stage, would she or he be able to recreate the scene, send a film of it back to you, and present a good account of what you saw? The answer is probably not. First-time observations are usually poor. What did you overlook? What were you good at? Describing people? Dimensions of objects? Conversation? Did you process or summarize the information by putting judgmental nouns ('dive', 'rags', 'louts'), adjectives ('handsome', 'nervous', 'short', 'old'), and adverbs ('nastily', 'frequently', 'rudely') in your notes, rather than describing what you saw that made you draw those conclusions? Because we observe every day, and sometimes save our lives through good observation in places like busy roads, why are we so bad at it in exercises like this? Daily observation involves getting just enough information to draw a conclusion based on past observation and experience. For example, you're walking along a road and you see a yellow creature approaching. You don't pause to say 'Here's something interesting: a mammal approximately eight feet long and four feet high, with a mane six inches long, a tail over two feet long with a tuft at the end, and incisors approximately three and a half inches long.' You probably shout 'A lion!' and run. Our ancestors probably did the same, which is why we are here today. You are not observing in the research sense. You know what a lion looks like and, in a flash, you related some basic features to your accumulated knowledge. This kind of observation — the ability to relate the general configuration to experience — is what has enabled all of us to survive. We process the information and draw conclusions in the most economical way we can. Our culture also helps by telling us how to read what we see; what it means. Sometimes, of course, our processing is wrong, and dangerous — we say 'Ah! A dog,' when perhaps we should be saying 'Ah! A wolf!'

Working with people who are different from ourselves — rural if we are urban, Irish if we are Brazilian, women if we are men — can lead us to read a situation through our own eyes and process incorrectly. We say 'Ah! women helping on the farm,' when we should be saying 'Women doing the farming.' To do basic observation that is useful for research, you need to take one step back — before the processing, before the conclusions — and be able, consciously, to record what you actually see, not what you read in the situation. Later, when you have more information from using a variety of different methods and a variety of sources, you can begin to think about what it means. If you don't know much about a situation, a people, or a culture, this approach is essential to keep you from imposing your experience on things that you cannot interpret properly through your own background. And if you do know a lot about a situation, you should also use this approach to bring a fresh eye to it, to avoid making snap judgements, and to allow for the possibility of drawing other conclusions and making other interpretations.

Most of the famous anthropologists who have used participant observation were never trained in its use, they were thrown in head first. The experience of working with an old hand is probably the best training you can get, because participant observation requires other skills in addition to observing: the ability to relate to other people, to 'mix in', to hold your judgement while at the same time being able to separate the relevant from the irrelevant.

Your own observations are likely to be much shorter than those of anthropologists, who may spend a year or more living in a community and who are bringing an extensive social science training to their analysis. You are also unlikely ever to do an observation like the one in our exercise, the purpose of which was to test your abilities. It was a 'free' observation: you were to observe everything. In a real project your observation will be more focused. If you are observing whether Mrs. Braithwaite interacts equally with her Arabic and non-Arabic students, you are hardly going to be noting the number of electrical outlets or the graffiti on the walls, although for some projects these could be important.

What do you look at?

When you first embark on participant observation, you can start by finding standardized sets of observational categories. One such set is Bales' Interaction Process Analysis for studying group interaction (Bales, 1952, 1970), which many social scientists think is cross-culturally valid. Another is Flanders' (1970) system for classifying classroom behavior. The researcher codes ongoing behavior into one of Flanders' ten categories every three seconds. If you are not using standardized categories, where do you get your instructions on what you should observe? Look at your research outline, if you have made one. What points in it are best obtained through observation or would benefit by combining observation with other techniques? Where will you observe them?

For an event, you might simply want to know:

- Who is here? What is each person supposed to do? Why?
- What does each actually do? Why?
- How often does it happen?
- Is the event typical?
- How is it like other events of this sort?
- How is it different?
- What do the differences mean?

Or perhaps you have taken an emic approach and discovered patterns: people tell you that there is paid work and unpaid work and list the tasks under each category. It may seem that unpaid workers don't do much. Then you observe for a few days and see that unpaid work involves a lot more than you were told. Some of the tasks do not have names — they involve attending to others, being responsive to requests, making the preparations and arrangements so that others can carry out their 'paid work' activities, doing a lot of the filling in, and performing the services that keep the whole system going. Because they don't have names, they are 'invisible' tasks, and were not originally listed. Yet unpaid workers are busy doing them. A final way of getting questions involves the grid approach discussed in Chapter 4. Work out the subject of your observation — for instance, a woman's unpaid workday, women's participation in community meetings, or decision-making meetings in Hancock Towers. Then use the boxes in bold lines in the grid to get a basic description of whatever you are looking at. The questions in the other boxes won't all be relevant; scan them and circle those you think might be useful to watch for. Of course, you won't get all your information simply by observing. The grid approach also helps you to develop questions about the event, activity, or process.

Recording your observations

How do you record participant observation? One way is by using the note-taking method described later in Chapter 15. You must take notes of your observations, at the scene if possible, and then write them out more fully some time later the same day. You will think you will remember, but you should take a note of the following fact, if nothing else: you won't. As new information piles up in your brain each day, you will lose what you learned in previous days except for the strange, the unusual, and things that have already begun to form an expected, and perhaps incorrect, pattern in your mind.

However, you may be observing something that lends itself to a quick-recording device. Let us say that you have been observing many instances of adults in a literacy class while they are planning end-of-year projects. You have noticed that women and men participate in different ways and you want to characterize their behavior. Your observations show nine major types of interaction:

- Giving orders (O)
- Accepting orders (C)
- Refusing orders (R)
- Agreeing (A)
- Disagreeing (D)
- Not participating (N)
- Giving information (I)
- Asking for information (F)
- Peacemaking (P)

You record what is happening on a regular basis, depending on what you are observing. Table 12–1 shows the interaction of five adults:

You can see that Rose gives an order to Ahmed, disagrees with Joseph, gives information to Polly, and accepts an order from Emmanuel. Ahmed asks Joseph for information, gives information to Polly, and engages in

Table 12–1

Rose				
O	Ahmed			
D	F	Joseph		
I	I	I	Polly	
C	P	C	C	Emmanuel

peacekeeping with Emmanuel. Polly accepts an order from Emmanuel. However, this shows only one-way interaction. A slight modification of the grid allows you to show the other person's response. By using upper case letters for what happens first and lower case for the response, you can show which of the two interactions occurred first (see Table 12–2).

Table 12–2

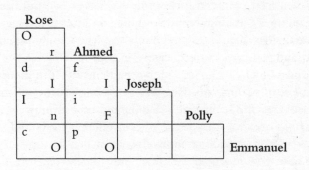

So while Rose gives an order to Ahmed, Ahmed refuses it; she disagrees with Joseph, who has given her information; she gives information to Polly, who is not participating; and she accepts an order from Emmanuel, who has given her one. Ahmed asks a question of Joseph, who has given him information; he gives information to Polly, who has asked him a question; he engages in peacekeeping with Emmanuel, who has given him an order. And so on. To record behavior over a period of time, you would need to have a number of these recording forms prepared in advance. In using a form such as this, you are hoping to see a pattern emerge, if one exists. Perhaps you discover that while women give orders, they are accepted by other women but not by men; or that women ask for information more than they give information; or that men engage in more peacekeeping with other men than with women.

Do you remember Mrs. Braithwaite? She's teaching the Beginning Arabic course to children in Hancock Towers. Suppose you want to find out how she interacts with the Arabic and non-Arabic children in the class. Does she simply acknowledge a correct answer or does she respond with praise? Does she pass over an incorrect answer, help the child, or ignore her/him? If you decide to observe, should you tell Mrs. Braithwaite and the children what you are doing? Will they change their behavior as a result of your presence? You are observing all the time, and cannot request permission from everyone who passes your line of sight, but if observation is a primary part of your research, and people would not participate if they knew what you were doing, you should explain in general terms what you are trying to do — you want to see an Arabic class in operation — and seek permission. Then you have to ensure that the people you observe don't suffer as a result of what you write or report about your observation.

As you can imagine, extended observation notes in written form contain information on people and contexts that makes them readily identifiable. If others read these notes, including those being observed, they won't understand why you have recorded such mundane things. You must think something is wrong or something different is going on: ordinary things are not worth recording. Mrs. Braithwaite might want to know why you chose them, what is so strange or interesting about what they were doing, and are you trying to ridicule them by writing down such 'private' things. (Even when they are performed in public, we tend to think that others don't notice when we are glancing at the clock or rolling our eyes when a boring person begins a long speech.) They won't always understand that you are studying patterns and processes, not individuals, and may be fearful that your study will have consequences for them individually. (As it will, of course, in a small world like Hancock Towers if you write in your study that 'Mrs. Braithwaite seems to have a fairly limited repertoire of Arabic, and she never called on any of the Arabic children.') This problem is also serious in academic research, where the results will be published in books and journals that have a wide circulation, and that provide little opportunity for those studied to respond.

In all research, you must protect the confidentiality of the information you receive. This is even more important in participant observation for two reasons: first, people will not necessarily have agreed to participate, and observation often includes what people think of as invisible behavior, no matter how public the setting; and second, if the notes are to be of any use, the amount of detail you record makes people easily identifiable. You have a responsibility to ensure that no-one reads and uses your notes to the detriment of the people you are working with. For participant observation notes, a good rule of thumb is that no matter whom you are working for, your notes belong to you and you have sole responsibility for their security.

Observer teams have to work out ways of sharing information and still protect the people in the notes.

What do these 'dangerous' notes look like? Let us look at three examples, one poor and two better sets of notes. The more detailed notes can be more offensive to people, because they will assume that there is something wrong with the behavior you have recorded. Otherwise, why bother to write it down?

The students were disorderly in the classroom, but in the end the men cooperated in reaching a decision.

could be:

A man of about fifty came into the classroom and said, 'Hi everyone, I'm sure happy to be here. I'm your substitute teacher for the evenin'.' A pile of papers, three books, his hat, and a paper package fell out of his arms onto the floor. A dog biscuit fell out of the package. Two of the ten female students left their desks and picked up the things from the floor. When they returned to the desks, they sat in different seats. One in the back near me said, 'Who is this guy? He's got no coordination.' 'I saw him before,' said another. 'He's American — got a weird name, Septic or something.' 'Where are y'all beginnin' tonight, then? Your teacher said you have just finished alphabet character recognition,' the substitute said. The guy next to me said, 'He hasn't a clue — who sent him here?' The woman on my right began to hum a Bob Marley song. The four men in the class caught a dog that had come in, and tried to put it outside the door but the tutor said, 'Aw, he won't harm nobody, he's just a pup.' After some discussion, the men let the dog stay.

or it could be:

The teacher said to the children in Class 2B, 'We're going to stop class a little early today to practice the puppet show for the holiday concert. Who would like to help?'
Mark said, 'I would.'
The four other boys in the class laughed. Marianne, who was sitting behind Mark, poked him in the ribs. 'Boys don't do puppets,' she said. 'They do the sets.'
'Puppets are girl things,' said Robert, who is about a year older than the others.
'Who said so?' asked Mark, who had tears in his eyes.
'God said so,' said Robert.
'God did not say that,' said Leila. 'My father is a puppeteer.'
The teacher, who had been watching all this, handed a glove puppet to Robert.

Robert put it on his desk. The teacher looked at him. He picked up the glove puppet and put it over his right hand and arm.
'When I grow up,' said Robert, 'I'm not going to do girl stuff like this!' He waved the glove puppet at Leila.
'Yes,' said the four other boys.

So far, we've been discussing direct observation, which is sometimes called obtrusive. You, as the observer, are part of the situation and have an effect on it, whether you like it or not. Unobtrusive observation, first made popular by Webb and his associates in 1966, involves looking at something after the fact, either at what people have left behind (accretion studies) or what they have taken away (erosion studies). In both cases, you have no effect on people's behavior, because they are not there. For example, you can figure out what books in the library are used most by the wear and tear on them (erosion), or which museum displays are most popular by the number of hand prints that the staff have to wash off every day (accretion). These may be considered *proxy indicators* — something that can be used to give an estimate of something else — for example, here handprints are taken to indicate popularity. As with all proxy indicators, you have to be sure the indicator reflects what you think it does. If the floor in front of the museum display is uneven or the light in the display is poor, handprints may indicate something else.

Analysis of observations

Analysis of participant observation notes is guided by the question you are asking or the hypothesis you have formed. Suppose you suspect that tutors call upon women in literacy classes only when one or more conditions prevail: more women than men have indicated they want to respond and/or no men are making eye contact with the tutor. You can disprove the hypothesis if you find negative cases, that is, tutors sometimes call upon women irrespective of these conditions. You may also be able to show that one or more conditions must be present before a tutor calls on a woman. Analyzing the kind of data that participant observation produces is discussed in more detail in Chapter 17.

References and further readings

Bales, R.F. 1952. 'Some Uniformities of Behavior in Small Social Systems.' In G. Swanson and others, eds., *Readings in Social Psychology*, 2nd ed. New York: Henry Holt.

——. 1970. *Personality and Interpersonal Behavior*. New York: Holt, Rinehart and Winston.

Bales, R.F. and S.P. Cohen. 1979. *SYMLOG: A System for the Multiple Level Observation of Groups.* New York: Free Press.

Burgess, Robert G. 1983. *Experiencing Comprehensive Education: A Study of Bishop McGregor School.* London: Methuen.

Chambers, Robert. 1991. 'Shortcut and Participatory Methods for Gaining Social Information for Projects.' In Michael M. Cernea, ed., *Putting People First,* 2nd ed. New York: Oxford University Press.

Fine, Gary Alan and Kent L. Sandstrom. 1988. *Knowing Children: Participant Observation with Minors.* Newbury Park, California: Sage.

Flanders, N.A. 1970. *Analyzing Teaching Behavior.* Reading, Massachusetts: Addison-Wesley.

Jorgensen, Danny L. 1989. *Participant Observation: A Methodology for Human Studies.* Newbury Park, California: Sage.

Longhurst, Richard. 1981. 'Research Methodology and Rural Economy in Northern Nigeria.' *IDS Bulletin* 12(4):23–31.

Obura, A.P. 1991. *Changing Images: Portrayals of Girls and Women in Kenyan Textbooks.* Nairobi, Kenya: ACTS (African Center for Technology Issues) Press.

Salmen, Lawrence F. 1987. *Listen to the People: Participant Observer Evaluation of Development Projects.* New York: Oxford University Press.

Spradley, James P. 1980. *Participant Observation.* New York: Holt, Rinehart and Winston.

Whiting, Beatrice and Carolyn P. Edwards. 1973. 'A Cross-Cultural Analysis of Sex Differences in the Behavior of Children Aged Three through Eleven.' *Journal of Social Psychology* 91(2):171–188.

Wolcott, Harry F. 1973. *The Man in the Principal's Office: An Ethnography.* New York: Holt, Rinehart and Winston.

Yin, Robert K. 1989. *Case Study Research: Design and Methods.* Newbury Park, California: Sage.

Death of young wife

Police are investigating the death of Haddy Joof Bah, wife of Ousman Bah, daughter of Mr. and Mrs. Modu Joof and granddaughter of Mrs. Mengeh Joof. Mrs. Bah's body was discovered late Monday evening by her husband when he returned from his university classes. It is thought that she took her own life.

Mrs. Bah was born on October 30, 1984 and had been married one year. Until her marriage, she had been a very popular student at Marwood Girls' School. Friends say that she had not been seen outside her flat since her marriage.

Police are also investigating the disappearance of her sister, Isatou, who has been missing for three months.

The Association extends its deepest sympathy to her family and to her many friends.

Graffiti returns

Walkways throughout the Towers were covered in graffiti on Tuesday night. From the style of hearts and teddy bears, it appears to be the work of one person. Police are looking into the matter.

Notice

Mrs. Sheila Braithwaite has asked us to say that she will not be teaching the Beginning Arabic courses in future. The only Arabic she knows is the 'Postman Pat' song, and 'Jerusalem', which she learned on her course at the Wellbeing and Empowerment Institute in Brighton. 'I was way behind the rest of the class. I think I missed something the first morning, when I had to go to the loo. I never caught up.'

Research course offered

What problems do you see around you? Would you like to study them and work out what action might improve the situation? Ground Work, an organization which teaches local people how to do their own research, is offering a course on participatory research in the Community Room each afternoon for one week, starting next Wednesday. Anyone interested is welcome to attend.

Memorial service will be held by her friends for Haddy Joof Bah in the Community Room tomorrow.

Your Horoscope by 'Graf' *has been discontinued.*

13 TRYING SOME OTHER QUALITATIVE APPROACHES

Summary

This chapter looks at some less conventional methods, which might give you ideas for developing new techniques yourself. Here we look at *story completion*; using *pictures, games*, and *traditional stories*; *content analysis*; *role-play*, and *drawings*. Although some of these techniques are adapted from psychology, they do not give you insights into people's personalities, they simply provide you with other ways to encourage people to talk about themselves and their experiences.

While some of the approaches in this chapter are borrowed from fields such as psychology, they are not used to draw inferences about people's personalities, but to get them to help you identify cultural patterns. Some fall into a category that anthropologists call 'analysis of cultural productions', that is, looking at literature, songs, pictures, and films produced by people of a particular culture, which tells you something about people's values and interests. Some of these approaches can be time consuming, and are not appropriate in all cultures.

Story Completion or Sentence Completion Devices

Story completion devices are simply another way of asking an open-ended question, but ideally they place it in a more realistic context, or they shift the focus from the person herself to a hypothetical situation or person. For example:

Lucy lives in a flat and the people who live next door are very noisy. She complained to them a few times and now, whenever she leaves her flat, they shout at her and make threats. She has informed the Residents' Association and they say that she will have to file a complaint. But Lucy is afraid that she will then have to go to court, and be a witness. What can Lucy do? Are there other actions she can take? What do you think will happen?

or

Isatou is a young woman very much like you, about fourteen, who wants to study and have a career. She also hopes to marry later on. Now her father says she must undergo an initiation ceremony, or female circumcision. This was a common custom in her father's country of birth. He believes it is part of his culture and religion. She loves her father but believes the custom is dangerous, and that she will be forced to marry soon after. Is there any answer to this problem? What should Isatou do? What might happen then?

or

Therese has three children. The oldest girl, Sarah, is 13. She got involved in drugs and now has a £200-a-week habit. She steals from the local supermarket to pay for her drugs, and hardly ever goes to school anymore. Her mother thinks she can be helped by the new community drugs rehabilitation program, 'Get a Life'. Her father says she is a lost cause. What are Sarah's main problems now? What do you think she might do? Who could help her? Who else should help? In what way? What might Therese, the mother, do? How will she do it? What will that achieve? What problems will she face?

or

The residents in a tower block have noticed a lot of graffiti on the walkways. Some think it is very artistic and should be retained as 'community art-in-progress'. Others think it lowers the tone of the neighbourhood and regularly call the local Grimebuster Squad to remove it. Tempers have been rising. What do you think the residents might do to resolve this? What will that accomplish? What problems might they have?

You can also offer sentences for people to complete, such as:

Many women fail to achieve their goals in life because…
Men seem to take most of the decisions in the family because…
If parents haven't enough money to send all their pre-school children to a crèche,

they should…
Once a woman takes up self-defense classes, she…

You may have been on the receiving end of devices like this as part of psychological testing. The examples here do not test psychological or personality characteristics, they are simply stimuli for a guided discussion. Sometimes they can be quite useful in group discussions, because you get a greater variety of comments, and people will challenge or supplement other people's solutions. Bear in mind that people will not necessarily tell you what really happens, but what they think should happen. You might then ask, 'Did that ever happen to you or someone you know? What happened?'

Pictures

You can ask people to tell you what is happening in a picture or drawing. Decide what pictures might be used to get people to talk about the subject you are studying. For example, in an HIV-AIDS project, you might show a picture of a group of young women and ask what are they talking about. What are young men in a similar picture talking about? Or, for a study of household decision-making, show a picture of a husband and wife who seem to be arguing. About what? How does it end? A child looks tired. What has caused this? Use simple pictures that can be interpreted in many ways. You are not trying to look into people's personalities. You are trying to get people to talk about common themes and patterns in their society.

Do remember that all pictures are culture-bound. Every society has different ways of representing and 'reading' three dimensions in two-dimensional form. Westerners show distant objects by drawing them smaller, but people from a different culture may assume that a distant elephant is a house fly. Pictures can also contain culturally unfamiliar objects or show representations that are culturally unacceptable — for example, in some Arab societies the human figure should not be represented in a drawing. People in some societies read from right to left — not only text, but a series of pictures. A three-frame drawing which shows an impoverished person in the first frame, the same person getting a university degree in the second, and holding a wonderful executive position in the third will give a very different message if it is read right to left: 'Education makes you poor.'

A number of standardized picture tests have been used in psychology and psychological anthropology, such as the Thematic Apperception Test or the Rorschach Test (commonly known as the 'inkblot test'). Psychologists use them for their original purpose: to look at personality. Anthropologists have used them to see if people produce common responses that might be typical of their culture. Using these outside the cultures for which they were designed can cause serious problems, and these problems are compounded if you are not experienced in the theory and practice of these tests. Do not try to use them.

Games

Every society has games, stories, riddles, proverbs, and songs. Can they be used to make the research process more familiar or more pleasant? Can they be adapted to get at issues more readily? The oldest game in the world, which anthropologists call Mancala, is found in more than 200 versions in Africa, the Middle East, and southeast Asia. (Similar games are found in almost every society.) Whatever its local name, you may recognize it from the diagram below, a wooden board with rows of holes. The number of holes and rows varies from one place to another.

Figure 13–1 Mancala board

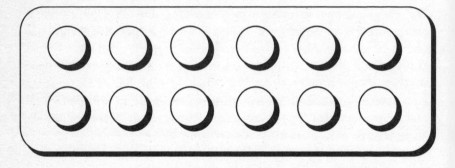

You can use the Mancala board and some stones or markers as a Likert scale (see Chapter 9), in which people rate items (people, processes, plans, and so on) on a scale of six, with minus three being most negative and plus three being the most positive, or from one to six. You can also use it as in the Semantic Differential (see Chapter 9 again) — for example, the left side of the board can represent good, the right bad, and concepts such as state education can be ranked along the scale.

Obviously, as the board above has two rows, two concepts can be ranked or scaled. You can create your own Mancala board by chalking one onto the pavement, scooping holes in sand, or drawing the board on a sheet of paper. You can make as many rows as you like: if you plan to rank seven concepts, make seven rows.

You can create games yourself. For example, at a women's self-defense conference you want to find out what women from different regions of the country think are the biggest obstacles and the most promising interventions in relation to getting more women trained in self-defense. If they are familiar with board games, you can create one.

1. Invite the participants to assemble in teams by region or any other useful grouping. Ask them to list promising interventions for maximizing self-defense training in their area, then rank and number them. Assign the highest number to the most promising and the lowest to the least promising.
2. Do the same for obstacles, except give the biggest obstacle the highest *negative* number, and the smallest obstacle the lowest negative number. Write each intervention and each obstacle on its own card, with its number, and paste one in each space on the board game.
3. The game can then be played like any board game, using dice or any other system that allows players to move markers toward a final winning destination, such as 'More women enrolled in self-defense classes'. As players' markers land on obstacles, they must move backwards on the board spaces by the number shown in the obstacle. A serious obstacle might send a player back eight spaces.

The research value of this, of course, is not playing the game, but doing the first part of the exercise — getting people to prioritize interventions and obstacles, and seeing how they differ from one team to another. It is important at the end of the exercise to discuss the reasons why each group chose and ranked their priorities as they did. This kind of game can be used by children as well as adults, in any place where the conventions of such play are familiar and are culturally acceptable.

Traditional Stories

The analysis of folklore crosses several disciplines, and researchers use it for a number of purposes, some quite sophisticated, such as attempts to study themes in folk stories as clues to the personality of a society (see, for example, Barnouw, 1985). Here its purpose is much simpler: a device to get people to talk by asking 'What if…?' What if the sex of the main character is changed? What if a character does something that is uncharacteristic for a person of that sex? Be careful not to offend people. Do not alter sacred literature, for example.

Drawing

In many societies, drawing or modeling can be a way to get people, particularly children, to discuss their ideas. Asking children to draw rich and poor farms, rich and poor households, households in which the females are free to go to discos and others where they are not, and to explain what they have drawn, can give you insights that you have not obtained through other methods. You can say to a group of children: 'Please draw a child being called to the front of the classroom to receive a prize,' to see if the children draw boys or girls, and who draws them. By 'interviewing' their drawings, you can delve further into the way they see things.

Role-play and Figures

Sometimes you can ask people to act out scenes. You might ask them for some typical issues that arise in relation to male/female interactions and act some of these out — for instance, a strict father has just discovered that his daughter was seen talking to the young man from the next flat. Now what? Or the board of the local school has nominated the first woman principal when everyone expected a man to get the job. Or a disabled child has just been born into a family. Neighbors are gathering to hear the news. How do they react? You can use what you learn from these little scenes to create questions that you can direct to the group or use in other interviews.

You can also provide figures to people, particularly children, and ask them to enact a scene. For example, in a study of how to protect children against drug dealers, a figure of an older, smartly dressed person is holding something out to the figure of a poorly dressed child. What is the older person saying? How will the child respond? What will happen next?

Psychologists and anthropologists use many of these techniques to analyze people's behavior and to provide therapy. It is important to keep repeating that you are not interested in testing individuals, but that you are looking for cultural patterns. Do men make the decisions? Do women have covert ways of influencing decision-making processes? What kinds of things are children concealing from their parents? How do people resolve conflict? What is the 'correct' way to behave in a situation?

Content Analysis

Stories need not be traditional, of course. The anthropologist Kenneth Little analyzed the roles and situations presented in modern African novels for his book *African Women in Towns* (1973). You can do something similar with popular literature and other media, including magazines, newspaper features, children's books, films, and videos. What occupations, roles, behaviors, and activities are associated with men? With women? You can count these kinds of activities and behaviors.

Gender-proofing is another type of content analysis that can produce both quantitative and qualitative data. Extensive checklists for gender

Box 13–1 Gender sensitivity indicators: criteria for appraising gender sensitivity in textbooks and examination questions

The following checklist is not exhaustive and is open to adaptation to suit the analysis of any text.

Summary indicators
- Frequency and nature/manner of appearance of characters by gender
- Named and unnamed characters, individualized or grouped
- Work/employment images
- Sociopolitical images — ownership, buying, investing, giving, sharing, receiving, etc.
- Family roles
- Psychological traits — courageous, docile, innovative, dynamic, simpleton, authoritative, etc.

Analysis strategies
- Breakdown of characters by gender and number and count frequency of mention
- Listing of number of females mentioned by name and those nameless
- Listing of gender-indicated common nouns and classification as female/male adult, female/male child
- Order of appearance by gender in terms of page of appearance and placement on page and sentence
- Listing, categorizing, and counting roles of characters identified by gender
- Determining centrality of characters by in-depth analysis of relationships and prominent patterns of presentation
- Counting pictures of female/male adults and children
- Determining role models for females as compared with males
- Noting method of presentation of characters by gender — order of presentation, autonomy/dependency, a corollary or complement, respective female/male roles in the home, etc.
- Awareness of language and the way traditionally neutral words are used, e.g., man, people, traders, farmers, and how pronouns are used, e.g., the farmer and her cows.

Proposals for improving accuracy of gender roles (including affirmative portrayal to counter/redress current imbalances)
- Increased use of neutral pronouns
- Deliberate allocation of positive roles for women and girls and increased reference to girls and women with due regard to first appearance, order of presentation, and centrality of character
- Increase in the number of named female characters and in the use of feminine descriptions — headmistress, businesswomen, etc., as appropriate
- Deliberate care in presentation of relationships between characters —

balancing the role of dependency, authority, and autonomy by gender
- Increased portrayal of women and girls in economic and political roles
- Deliberate increase of female role models, with particular reference to female participation and achievement in science and technology, agriculture, professions, and in leadership roles
- Greater emphasis on female intellectual and professional capacities
- Depiction of males in family-related capacities and increased depiction of sharing of domestic roles

Source: Sigurdsson and Schweitzer (1994).

content analysis of textbooks are available (see, for example, Obura, 1991). Some common items to look for are found in the checklist shown in Box 13–1. All these items can also be applied to textbook animals, mythical creatures, and historical figures. All kinds of texts can be gender-proofed: manuals for health and safety in factories, school textbooks, fire regulation manuals, advertisements, campaign literature prepared by organizations, even radio programs when a written text is available. You can video a television program and invite a group to listen to its content carefully, noting gender bias in language, image, and concept.

An analysis of English and social studies texts in one country using these criteria produced information such as:[1]

Males are consistently associated with technology, teaching, medical, and political leadership, religious observance and a wide range of occupations in business/financial/community settings. They are also identified with building, repairing, inventing, and exploring. Males rescue people, heal people, tell stories, and are associated with power and magic. Males engage in energetic physical exercise and labor. They solve problems, are resourceful, clever, sly, decisive. Throughout the texts, it is men who give orders and are presented as heroes, leaders, judges, and emancipators.

Females are consistently associated with cooking, cleaning, sweeping, washing, and carrying goods and babies. Other tasks include fetching water, sewing, marketing, teaching, requiring medicine, and helping males to do various things. Females are also presented listening to males, being frightened, proving inept with regard to technology, dropping/breaking/ burning things. They are rarely shown solving problems or being resourceful. They tend to be the rescued rather than the rescuing party, are easily hoodwinked, and, with the very odd exception, have no apparently powerful roles to play in the broader social environment.

[1] The country is deliberately not mentioned here. The purpose is to show the kinds of results you can get.

References and further readings

Barnouw, Victor. 1985. *Culture and Personality*, 4th ed. Homewood, Illinois: The Dorsey Press.

Cole, M., J. Gay, J.A. Glick, and D.W. Sharp. 1971. *The Cultural Context of Learning*. London: Methuen.

Cushner, Kenneth. 1990. 'Cross-Cultural Psychology and the Formal Classroom.' In Richard W. Brislin, ed., *Applied Cross-Cultural Psychology*. Newbury Park, California: Sage.

Little, Kenneth. 1973. *African Women in Towns: An Aspect of Africa's Social Revolution*. Cambridge, U.K.: Cambridge University Press.

Lonner, Walter J. and John J. Berry. 1986. *Field Methods in Cross-Cultural Research*. Newbury Park, California: Sage.

Obura, A.P. 1991. *Changing Images: Portrayals of Girls and Women in Kenyan Textbooks*. Nairobi, Kenya: ACTS (African Center for Technology Issues) Press.

Sigurdsson, Sverrir and Eluned Schweitzer. 1994. 'The Use of Sectoral and Project Performance Indicators in Bank-Financed Education Operations: A First Edition Note.' Washington, DC: World Bank, Education and Social Policy Department.

Van Maanen, John, ed. 1983. *Qualitative Methodology*. Newbury Park, California: Sage.

Webb, E.J., D.T. Campbell, D.R. Schwartz, and L. Sechrest. 1966. *Unobtrusive Measures: Non-reactive Research in the Social Sciences*. Chicago: Rand McNally.

Hancock Towers Newsletter

November 30, 2001

Teams to study here and in West Africa

Two research teams of Towers residents are planning to study the issues of early marriage among girls, and female genital mutilation. One team, consisting of Mrs. Mengeh Joof, Mr. 'Graf' Wilkins and Ms. Sharon Darwin will go to West Africa to look at the issue in Mrs. Joof's home village. A women's group in the village have been asking her for some time to come back and help prepare an action plan.

The second team, consisting of Mrs. Rose Elliot Darwin, Mrs. Mavis Darwin, and Mr. Septus McCardle, will study the problem in London, and specifically in the Towers.

The death of Mrs. Joof's granddaughter, Haddy Joof Bah, and the disappearance of her other granddaughter, Isatou, who was due to undergo an initiation ceremony involving genital mutilation, prompted Mrs. Joof to suggest this research after the group recently took a course in participatory research in the Towers Community Room.

Mrs. Joof said the male researchers were participating in the project because they would be able to discuss the issue with fathers and husbands, and get their perspectives.

Mrs. Joof emphasized that this is not a West African problem: 100,000 women a year, in various countries, undergo genital mutilation, and the problem of little girls marrying before completing school is common throughout the world. Many parents genuinely believe that both customs are required by religion, and are simply trying to do right by their children. 'We are approaching this problem in a respectful but concerned way, and I decided to start with my own home place.'

Readers may remember that Mr. McCardle is from Hope And Glory, Ohio, the place where Shar Darwin went to carry out some research last spring. He became interested in the research process, and accompanied her back to England to study issues in Shar's home, the Towers. 'I did it for a little fun,' said Septus. 'I never thought it would get this serious. That poor little girl. Funny thing is, it's not anyone's fault. Everyone thought they were doing what was best. Awful on the family.'

When interviewed, Mr. 'Graf' Wilkins said, 'I never thought I would get involved in this research crap. I'm doing it for Haddy.'

More research!

Tony Anzivino, another pal of Shar Darwin's from Hope And Glory, is off to Dublin to do a study of Glasheen Prison. He will be assisted by Mr. Kevin Darwin, who is currently doing some sort of participatory research there in between his world travels.

14 DOING PARTICIPATORY RESEARCH

Summary

Rapid assessment approaches grew out of the urgent practical needs of development practitioners, and out of new ways of thinking about development. They have been used in agricultural, health, and natural resource management research projects, among others, but less often in other fields such as education, gender, and social policy.

Two that hold great promise for these fields are *rapid rural appraisal* (RRA) and *participatory learning and action* (PLA). They are used at the local level, but can provide useful information at all stages of policymaking, planning, and implementation.

Participatory rural appraisal strategies help to get a more holistic picture and to avoid common biases, involve the participants as partners, and tie action to research.

Decision-makers need information that is relevant, timely, accurate, and usable. In rural development, a great deal of information that is generated is, in various combinations, irrelevant, late, wrong, and/or unusable. The information is often costly to obtain and takes a long time to process, analyze, and digest (Chambers, 1981, p. 95). Robert Chambers, who is often referred to as the grandfather of rapid assessment and participatory learning techniques, calls this 'long and dirty' research.

The development of participatory techniques has arisen out of the following schools of thought, which became prevalent in the 1970s:

- Economic inputs and technology transfer alone do not produce economic and social development. A more holistic approach is necessary. The environment, the economy, politics, and 'human' factors — such as social organization and culture — are all interrelated and all have to be taken into account when working toward practical, meaningful change.
- Each of the partners in development has a unique perspective to contribute, especially local people. The views of donors, national governments, development workers, technical experts, and researchers had always been recognized, but various project failures around the world were demonstrating that the participation and perspective of local people is as essential as any other 'expert' contribution.
- Many social scientists who could help to provide a holistic dimension and give insights into the often forgotten human factors of development were still carrying out research in ways that met the requirements of universities and professional journals, rather than the immediate needs and constraints of development practitioners.

Participatory techniques were first used in farming systems research and farming systems analysis and have evolved to cover a variety of other development research needs, adding new techniques, strategies and philosophical insights in the process.

Rapid Rural Appraisal and Participatory Learning and Action

Two approaches, in particular, have attracted a number of supporters, have acquired a respected track record, and have accumulated a growing body of literature. The first, developed in the late 1970s, is *rapid rural appraisal* (RRA). The name is misleading, however, because the approach is not restricted to rural settings, its uses extend beyond project appraisal, and it is not always rapid.

The second approach is *participatory rural appraisal* (PRA), which evolved out of RRA in the mid-1980s, and has more recently been renamed *participatory learning and action* (PLA). As you will see later, both RRA and PLA are grounded in all three philosophical orientations described in Chapter 2: postpostivism, phenomenology, and critical theory.

By the early 1990s, RRA and PLA had been used in many countries, in both the northern and southern hemisphere. The Institute of Development Studies of the University of Sussex in England has been a major force in developing theory and methods.

RRA and PLA are similar in their attempts to deal with some of the problems we have mentioned, and many of the approaches and techniques are the same. A major difference is that, like most conventional research methods, RRA is *extractive*: 'we', as experts, take information from 'them'. PLA, by contrast, is more *participatory*: outsiders act as facilitators for local people, who join in determining the agenda, issues, and concerns and in collecting the material, interpreting it, and acting on it. PLA places a value not only on local knowledge, but on local analytical abilities.

You may recall that a research team from Hancock Towers has traveled to West Africa. Mengeh Joof, Graf Wilkins, and Sharon Darwin are planning to study issues of female education, early marriage, and genital mutilation among girls in Mrs. Joof's home village. They are going to use a PLA approach, so they will stay in the village, live and work alongside local people, and learn about the problems and possible solutions first hand, in the socio-cultural context in which they occur. They have begun their participatory research in exactly the right way: they have been invited by a women's group in the village to come and help prepare an action plan. The team is not planning on extracting the information — they want to become partners in learning with the local people.

RRA and PLA are based largely, but not entirely, on qualitative research techniques, such as participant observation, interviews, social and physical mapping and diagramming, case studies, and various emic techniques. They can also include brief surveys carried out using innovative sampling techniques.

RRA and PLA have several distinctive characteristics, including the following:

- Taking a *holistic, multidisciplinary approach*, that is, studying the entire context of a situation using insights from various fields.
- Applying a *'reversal of learning'*, in which researchers recognize that local people are their teachers, not their subjects. Local expertise is a valuable resource in planning projects that are sound and sustainable.
- Taking active steps to *avoid bias* by including in your study the less powerful, the invisible, the voiceless, and the socially, economically, and geographically marginal.
- Using *triangulation*, that is, employing multiple techniques, methods, researchers, and perspectives, including those of local people, to address the same issue or problem.
- Adopting an *iterative approach*, a concept borrowed from systems theory, in which a system (in this case your study) repetitively feeds information from the environment back into itself to allow you to use

the insights gained to direct or redirect your research.

- *Seeking diversity* by deliberately looking for variations, exceptions, and contradictions to the pattern you have found. For example, most families in Mengeh Joof's village send only a few of their children to school, yet one particular family sends them all. How does it do so and why?

- Recognizing the principles of *optimal ignorance*, that is, knowing what is not worth knowing, and of *proportionate accuracy* or *appropriate imprecision*, which is not being more accurate or precise than necessary (Chambers, 1992, p.14). If you do not need to know down to the last ounce how much paper the local gender-proofing campaign has used, why be so precise? As the anthropologist Clifford Geertz (1983) has said: 'It's not necessary to know everything to know something.'

- Avoiding the kinds of *anti-poverty biases* that have characterized much research done from the outsider's viewpoint, such as the 'tarmac bias' (studies done in more accessible places), the seasonal bias (studies done in the more comfortable seasons), the 'garland bias' (overwhelming people with your importance), and the elite bias discussed in Chapter 7 (Chambers, 1983, pp.13–23).

- Using a *wide range of techniques* to enable the practitioner to investigate topics, explore problems, and appraise, plan, monitor, or evaluate projects.

These techniques are adaptable to local conditions, levels of literacy, and cultural norms. They can be done outside or inside. Local people can diagram many of these techniques on sand, on the pavement, or on large sheets of paper.

How do you know if a project is taking an RRA approach or a PLA approach? Sometimes, it is quite obvious: it is RRA when a team of technical experts, composed largely of outsiders, tries to gain relatively rapid insights from local knowledge to develop a project or adapt an existing one to meet local needs. They do the research and analysis. It is PLA if local people, facilitated by insiders or outsiders experienced in PLA, determine the issues, get the information, analyze it, and act on it.

A project can contain both RRA and PLA components, however. For example, the agenda (female health) may be determined by an outside organization, while the process of identifying specific priorities and solutions may be led by local people.

Of course, simply involving some local people does not necessarily mean that an approach is participatory. Unless everyone else who is concerned with the issue participates in the research and analysis, your approach will be extractive.

Uses of RRA and PLA

RRA and PLA can be used in organizations, institutions, and a wide variety of other settings, both rural and urban. Both RRA and PLA have been used by people in local communities and by economists, agronomists, biologists, social scientists, educators, health workers, and engineers, among others, working in government departments and bureaux, national and international agencies, and research organizations. They are not always the most appropriate approaches to use, however, and it is important to recognize their strengths and limitations.

RRA and PLA are good for:
- providing basic information in situations where little is known;
- identifying and assessing problems;
- appraising, designing, implementing, monitoring, and evaluating programs and projects;
- getting a better picture of needs and organizations' ability to meet them;
- developing and transferring appropriate technologies;
- appraising emergencies;
- planning projects that are more relevant, restructuring administrations, assisting in decision-making and policy formation;
- generating hypotheses, ruling out inappropriate ones;
- providing guidelines for survey designs and assessing the applicability of their results to other places;
- fleshing-out, complementing, interpreting, or giving depth and context to information obtained through other methods.

RRA and PLA are not very useful for:
- working in situations in which the problem is not usefully addressed at the local or group level, for example, in situations where national policy change is required, or where large-scale structural reorganization is necessary (but even then, local views may help to shape the change);
- working on projects or in situations in which there is little ability to act flexibly or change direction if necessary;
- working in situations where there is little or no possibility of implementing the community's plans.

RRAs and PLAs can be categorized as exploratory (to determine problems or opportunities), topical (to investigate one aspect or problem), monitoring and evaluation (to track ongoing developments and to assess completed projects), conflict resolution (to resolve conflicts between groups), and participatory: these are the subject of much of this chapter. In this chapter you will see how the Hancock Towers research team and the women's group use the techniques to explore girls' education and related issues, such as early marriage and genital mutilation.

Comparisons with Conventional Methods

Comparisons between the results of traditional surveys and RRA/PLA have shown comparable degrees of accuracy. For example, Chambers (1991, pp. 22–24; 1994b, pp. 1257–1261) cites a number of studies in which RRA or PLA approaches were more reliable and valid or tapped an important dimension of reality that conventional methods missed (see Box 14–1). The following section shows the stages in an RRA project. Notice how in RRA you are taking a positivistic approach (see Chapter 2). You have decided that local knowledge is important, but it is you who are determining what is to be collected, how, and so on.

Stages in an RRA Project

The first thing to consider is: who initiates a project? Sometimes the local community asks a team to come in and work with them, just as the women of Mengeh Joof's village have done. Alternatively, the initiative may come from you or your office, department, or organization.

Preliminaries

A research plan is developed. Some projects begin with basic guideline questions, but others have only a general list of guiding points. Flexibility is the keynote here: no matter how carefully you prepare the plan, you will have to amend it as the situation develops. You want a general idea, but the details may be altered as you move through the research.

Table 14–1 shows part of a research plan worked out. You can see that it is similar to the research design approach we used in Chapter 4. You might use this kind of plan as a reminder of points and methods, but it's essential to keep an open mind about the topics, the tools, and the people to be involved. Otherwise, you are losing one of the advantages of these approaches, which is their flexibility.

To get the benefit of multiple insights on problems and issues, you should select an experienced multidisciplinary team of at least two people and usually less than ten, including outsiders and insiders (local people) of both sexes. Next you need to consult knowledgeable people and examine

Box 14–1 Comparison of survey and PLA results

A survey with a pre-tested structured schedule was administered by five experienced investigators in South India. Data were collected from 412 households residing in three clusters on:

- Type of house
- Caste
- Education
- Occupation of each member
- Ownership of land, trees, assets
- Number of dresses per person
- Yearly income

A composite index was calculated for each household. Households were then assigned to X (poor, score 3–5), Y (middle, score 6–7) or Z (rich, score 8–9). This was the professionals' classification, as determined by professionals with a conventional method.

A community classification was conducted in each of the three clusters separately by a group of four knowledgeable women and a group of four knowledgeable men. Some groups were instructed on the characteristics/criteria of each economic group, and others were given freedom to decide their own criteria. However, in making the ranking, all groups went beyond the original professional criteria and weighed a wider range of considerations. These included:

- Type of land ownership
- Type of livestock ownership
- Landless but with a job
- Assets, including whether just a gift from relations
- Professional job — whether permanent or temporary, and the income
- Employment
- Fixed deposits
- Money lending — large or small amount, effect of it on the family, repaying capacity
- Number of members in the house
- Bad habits — drinking, smoking, adversely affecting the household
- Rights to house — own, rented, belonging to relations, without land rights
- Children's education — capacity to give children education
- Father a coolie but son a white collar job
- Son in the military, no help from him, rest doing coolie work

Each household, represented by a card, was allocated to one of three economic groups. The groups gave reasons for their classifications of each household. The outcome was the community classification.

The professional and community classifications were compared. In the largest village cluster, discrepancies were investigated by teams in detail, visiting houses, having extended conversations with members of the family and others, and making direct observations of a sort not possible with either the questionnaire or the wealth ranking.

The research concluded that the professionals, using the questionnaire method and with their fixed indicators, were 57% accurate in identifying the economic levels of the households, whereas the community members, using wealth ranking, were 97% accurate.

The formal survey of 412 households took 680 person-hours of staff time, and the wealth ranking of 421 households took 144 person-hours.

Source: RUHSA. 1993. 'Validating the Wealth Ranking by Participatory Rural Appraisal Versus Formal Survey in Identifying the Rural Poor.' Christian Medical College and Hospital: Tamil Nadu, India.

existing studies and materials to see what is already known and what research might be most useful. Finally, the team or a member may make a preliminary visit to the study site.

Field research

Fieldwork lasts from four days to three weeks. As information is collected and fed back into the system, the direction and context of the research is changed and refined as necessary (an example of the iterative approach). The team will need to hold frequent meetings (perhaps once daily for the entire team and twice daily for sub-teams), to share material and insights, to identify major patterns and relationships, to explore variation and diversity, and to change the approach as awareness grows. To do this, each team member should take notes during each interview, if possible.

Sometimes, in a strategy called the *sondeo* approach, the team breaks up into research pairs. Their results are discussed in group sessions and the next day different pairs are formed. An educator working with an economist one day might be paired with a sociologist the next day to get the most benefit from looking at the situation from different perspectives and to reduce bias. The information is analyzed continuously (see Box 14–2, at the end of this section).

As the research comes to a close, if the purpose of the study is to recommend options, the team and local people may meet at workshops to develop the most promising alternatives or solutions to problems that have been identified. The local people might rank the options and decide how to implement them.

Table 14–1 Part of an RRA research plan

Goal: To improve understanding of the social and economic roles of women in Gaza

Topic	Sub-topics	Techniques					
		SSIs with women	SIs with key info-rmants	SSIs with groups	Direct observation	Secondary sources	Diagrams
Liveli-hood	women's work opportunities	x	x			x	
	women's activities	x			x		
	savings and assets	x			x		
	inheritance	x					
	income	x					
	household spending	x		x			
	home production	x			x		
	household duties (daily routine)	x					x
	family size and dependents	x					
	division of labour	x					

SSIs = Semi-structured interviews.
Source: Theis and Grady (1991, p. 128).

Completion of the study

Completing the study may involve return visits for follow-up, consolidation, and discussion of the materials collected. The outcome may be a plan, a project, or a publication. All participants in the process are encouraged to share information and experiences with other researchers, whether they are facilitator experts or local people in other areas.

An important feature of the RRA approach is to embrace error and learn from it. A good RRA team will welcome criticism from participants and each other, analyze limitations and failures, and pass their insights on. Scoones and McCracken's (1989) study is a good illustration of how this process is carried out.

Stages in a PLA Project

Often, a group or community initiates the process. It may be a village, a parent-teacher group in a town, residents in a tower block, or any group that shares a common interest or problem. For convenience here, we will call this group 'the community'. People who have participated in or heard about PLA may want to try it. Once they have, they can usually continue to apply the process to new problems or situations as they arise. Many organizations are now using participatory approaches, and may decide that a PLA process will be helpful.

Preliminaries

First, the focus of the project has to be clarified. The community decides what the issues are, what it needs to know, how it will find out, and from whom. Outside facilitators usually bring special expertise about the problem or interest that concerns the community, as well as experience of the PLA process. Once the community has been through the PLA process, it may feel comfortable repeating it and training others without the help of outside facilitators.

The research

Unlike RRA, the emphasis in PLA is not on 'rapid': 'relaxed' is a better approach. Because PLA is a flexible, participatory process, it takes as long as it takes. Where facilitators are involved, their task is to share their experience of PLA, rather than to run the show. This is probably the most difficult challenge facing the facilitator, but the aim is to empower local people to carry out the process so that they do the work and 'own' the results. This requires 'handing over the stick' (or the pen or chalk) so that the people concerned do the research, rather than the facilitator(s).

The community may require input from people with special expertise or control of resources. For example, in countries where girls' security at school is an issue, would the ministry of education pay a local woman to act as a chaperon for girls in classes taught by male teachers? Or how much would it cost to provide a lending library of school texts for children who can't afford to buy their own?

Completion of the process

Appropriate action plans, together with procedures for carrying them out and monitoring them, then have to be developed. The process continues for as long as necessary.

Analyzing RRA and PLA Findings

Data collected during the RRA and PLA process needs to be analyzed and organized in a clear, simple way so that it can be used by communities to develop their action plans. See Box 14–2 overleaf for some guidelines to help you analyze the information you collect.

A Sample PLA Project

Now let us see how these principles and procedures might be used in a real project. You are now joining Shar, Graf, and Mengeh, the Hancock Towers research team who have just arrived in Katama, Mengeh Joof's home village in West Africa. You may recall that the local women's group asked you to come and help them prepare an action plan to address problems associated with early marriage and female genital mutilation.

It's always a good idea to make a preliminary visit to the research site, particularly when the team is mainly composed of 'outsiders', like yourselves. Luckily, Mengeh has 'insider knowledge' of how things operate in her village, and she knows it is very important that you are perceived as trustworthy and respectful by the elders, male and female. She creates a list of Dos and Don'ts to help you.

Because a certain formality is culturally appropriate in Katama, Mengeh has also arranged for the village chief to officiate at a small ceremony. He welcomes you, introduces you to the community and invites you to explain what it is you are here to do. Shar explains the purpose of the PLA exercise and the basic approach to all the local people who have gathered and who expect to be informed — the teachers, the parents, the regional director of education, the village elders and religious leaders. You and Graf give a basic explanation of the philosophy behind the project. You've noticed some young men and women, and some schoolgirls, hovering on the edge of the crowd of 'dignitaries'. You take the opportunity to invite these young people to join in and help you role-play one or two PLA techniques, showing that everyone's participation is possible and valuable. Mengeh stresses that the success of the PLA work will depend upon everyone concerned getting involved, and she formally invites the community to participate.

Box 14–2 Guidelines for analyzing findings

- Analysis is a continuous process of reviewing information as it is collected, classifying it, formulating additional questions, verifying information, and drawing conclusions. Analysis is the process of making sense of the collected information. It should not be left until all the data have been collected.

- Prepare a list of key issues and arrange the findings according to this list. Rearrange, break up, and reassemble pieces of data. Sort and sift through information and look for patterns, differences, variations, and contradictions. Weigh the relative importance of the information. Be self-critical.

- Create a series of questions based on the research topic (including new questions that may have come up during the fieldwork) and try to answer them with the help of the collected information.

- Discuss each sub-topic in turn, summarize the results, and draw conclusions based on the information gathered during the fieldwork.

- Use diagrams, matrices, ranking methods, and other analytical tools.

- For further clarification, tabulate the information. Tabulating pulls out key information from interviews and observations, and allows comparison of differences between individuals. Tabulating also helps the team to avoid relying on general impressions rather than facts.

- Check findings and conclusions by presenting them to key informants or to a group of community members.

- Be self-critical.

- Findings have to be consistent and must not contradict each other. If the findings contradict the secondary sources or other sources you must be able to explain why. Your findings have to be believable.

Source: Theis and Grady (1991, p. 139)

You spend the next part of the day with the women's group, and you discover two important things. First, you'll have to build a lot of rapport with the community before people will talk about sensitive issues like female genital mutilation, or early marriage. Second, you realize that you can't fully understand these issues until you have first learned about the broader context of female education. In the afternoon, you help women in their gardens and carry water with young girls; as evening draws in, you talk with the regional director and local teachers. You find out that girls start school at seven years, and complete primary level at about fourteen.

If they progress to secondary level, they will learn a lot about primary health care, pre- and post-natal care, and safe sex. But many girls are taken out of school at twelve or thirteen, when they reach marriageable age. Most often, they never return to finish their education. They lose their chance to learn about basic health issues that will radically affect their lives and those of their children. So basic education is a key need in these young girls' lives.

A preliminary visit is an ideal opportunity to situate a PLA topic in its real context, and a chance to learn about the community's composition in terms of ethnic, religious, language, and economic groups; what projects are going on; what has worked and what has not worked and why; what agencies and groups were involved; and so on.

Using all this information, you revise your original plans. You plan your *fieldwork strategy*, which will have the following steps:

- Identify local basic education needs and prioritize them.
- Identify possible opportunities and options for meeting those needs.
- Get any necessary technical advice on inputs and costs of various options to meet each need.
- Select the best option or options.
- Identify possible internal and external resources.
- Help the community to assign responsibilities and tasks.
- Set target dates or estimated times for achieving aims.

You recognize that you can't run before you walk. Assessing basic education needs and encouraging community action on this topic may open the door to further levels of the project — talking about early marriage and female genital mutilation, and developing elements of the action plan to address these related issues.

Background research

Now you are clear about your research topic and strategy, what other preliminary work can you do? It may be helpful to find relevant published and unpublished material that will put the community and the problem in context, such as census data, government and donor agency project reports, school records, and information about university studies. The aim is to get a picture of the community and to avoid repeating work that others might have done, not to write a book or a thesis. Delaying other work while collecting these kinds of data is easy. You always have one more 'essential' figure to track down, but don't be tempted.

Forming a PLA team

What about the composition of the team? PLA teams are simply the facilitators who help to move the process forward. The size and composition of any PLA team depends on the skills required and the scope of the work. A team can consist entirely of local people or a mix of insiders and outsiders. It usually needs to include men and women, older and younger people, and may also require people of particular language, ethnic, or religious groups. That's why Mengeh is so central to your team — she speaks six local languages, was the headmistress of the school here in Katama for many years, is respected by the community elders, and loved by the young women and girls. Graf is important because he can spend time with younger men around his own age, drinking 'green tea', sharing information — he will answer their questions about his life, they will share their views on female education. If he can build really good rapport, he might learn something about early marriage, too.

In this culture, it is unlikely that the young women would speak to Shar about female genital mutilation and how this relates to education, so Mengeh is hoping to encourage two young women from the village to join the research team. She will show them how to run a focus group, and they can encourage other young women to talk in a safe environment, without 'outside' intervention. She has already recruited two schoolgirls — they will be able to encourage the girls of the community, who are not accustomed to being consulted, to join in the PLA techniques and discussions about basic education. In PLA, you build your team according to the needs of the situation. You expand it where necessary. Your team is now more than twice the size it was when you made your preliminary visit to the village. When you begin your work, local people will see that most of the team members are, in fact, their own people. You have begun to achieve one of the most difficult things in participatory research: 'outsiders' melting into the background as 'insiders' take ownership of the PLA. You are off to a good start, but there are a few other preliminaries you must attend to.

You know that, as part of the PLA process, local people will probably need to identify and assess various options for solving problems. They may need technical experts, either on the team or readily available, who can help analyze various ways to provide options or identify the resources required and their costs and possible sources of help. As you begin to see the 'shape' of the information local people are sharing and analyzing, you will be able to identify the technical expertise the project needs.

Choosing techniques

What about techniques? Shar is quite experienced in PLA techniques. Graf and Mengeh took the GroundWork PLA course back in Hancock Towers, but this is their first time in the field, and they know they will probably lean on Shar's expertise. You have all worked through a good training manual (like those listed at the end of this chapter), and share this information with the new 'local' members on the team. Most manuals still focus on agriculture, natural resource management, or health, so you spend several days practicing the techniques and adapting them to education. The young women and schoolgirls have also offered important insights on how to make them culturally appropriate.

During the field research, you will use what you think are the most useful research tools from the 'basket' of techniques. Ones that worked on a previous project will not necessarily work on this one, and some that you plan to use will have to be dropped or adapted during the course of the work. Because PLA is a flexible process rather than a 'cookbook' approach, the mix used has to be tailored to the situation, the aims of the research, and the local context. For this project, you will use group discussions, pie charts, matrices, mapping, card sorts, well-being rankings, interviews, observations, seasonal diagrams, Venn diagrams, questionnaires, pairwise rankings, resource access ranking, and options assessment charts. You will make some mistakes, and at least one of these techniques will turn out to be more trouble than it is worth in this particular project.

Identifying local organizations

During your preliminary visit to Katama, you heard locals refer to various village associations. Because this particular project is intended not only to identify problems, but also to address them, the community will have to find ways to implement plans and monitor projects that emerge as a result of the research. You don't want to re-invent the wheel; some of the local associations mentioned might be ideal channels through which the work of implementation can take place. If no appropriate local association is available, the community may establish a new committee to follow up the work on completion of the research. Such a committee should include both men and women.

Doing the field research

Katama is a medium-sized village of about seven hundred people. You have now returned and the whole team is assembled. Today is a good day to begin your work, because it's a holiday, and people have free time to spend with you. Tomorrow, you'll fit your research activities into the daily routine, and not interrupt people's work or important events. Led by Mengeh, you begin with a group discussion, using an historical profile, pie charts drawn on the ground, and matrices drawn on the ground. You could work indoors, too, perhaps in a classroom, but you would need large sheets of paper, things to write with and a blackboard or flip chart, all of which have disadvantages: it is not as easy for people to wander by and contribute; it may intimidate non-literate people; shy people may have to approach the front of the room unless you take great care to set up a circle; you may not have as much space; and you will probably have to bring many of the materials with you.

The outside setting has several advantages: when diagrams are required, people will draw them with a stick; when materials, such as symbols, are needed, people will pick up whatever happens to be handy, such as leaves, stones and seeds. This way, everyone sees what is being done, and people recognize that research and analysis can be done with familiar, easily available resources. Also, people who cannot read and write can participate. But there are some disadvantages: diagrams will have to be protected while being made, and must later be transferred to paper; and you and the diagrams may need some kind of shelter during wet or inclement weather.

Historical profile

The people of Katama tell you about the place, its history, achievements, and problems. Sometimes this kind of historical profile is a good way to get the conversation going, because people are expert on their own history. Often, outside researchers are surprised at the richness of oral tradition and memory, particularly among non-literate peoples. Many village histories go back several hundred years.

Pie chart

As the team proceeds with the rest of the techniques in this chapter, notice that almost all of them are visual modes for interviewing, recording, and analyzing, all in one. Basically, they are a form of interviewing, whether done by a facilitator or by people in the group.

Shar and Mengeh are working with women on pie charts (sometimes called chapati diagrams), learning about community sources of income and expenditure, and their relative proportions; they could also use pie charts to learn about ethnic and language composition, daily routine, or any other distribution they might need.

Graf will work with the men because in Katama, as in many places, men and women don't publicly discuss such things together. If women, young people, poorer people, or members of particular social or ethnic groups do not usually speak, or do not speak candidly in the presence of others, the PLA processes must be repeated with several groups.

Because an essential part of PLA is 'handing over the stick', local people draw the pie charts and other figures. Some are reluctant to start, so Mengeh draws a circle and asks how much of it should be given to each of the items people are discussing. Which item should get the biggest slice of the pie, which the smallest? Then it's easier to work out the size of the slices in between. People may not be familiar with the idea of dividing a circle or may prefer another method. On a Gambian project, villagers decided to state these proportions in percentages, which is the way information is presented to them over the radio (Kane and O'Reilly-de Brún, 1993).

Figure 14–1 Examples of pie charts

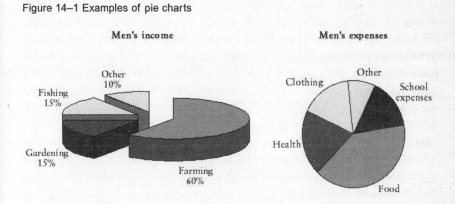

An alternative to the pie chart is a pile of seeds, sometimes called 'the hundred seeds' technique. In this, the participants divide a pile of seeds, which, if they number 100, make percentage calculations easy. It also allows people to adjust the proportions more easily, and more people can take part.

People may argue about the relative proportions within the pie chart. If the differences seem important, use other methods to check them during the course of the research, and try to find out why people have different perceptions.

Community problems
Next, people discuss the general problems in Katama. Although your focus is female education, knowing where education fits into the general range of problems is helpful. As each problem is identified and agreed, people assign a symbol to it, say a battery to represent the need for a generator, a

book for the refurbishment of the school, a match box or whatever else comes to hand for the broken milling machine. Use whatever is around, provided that using the object in this way is locally acceptable. Using symbols rather than words allows non-literate people to participate, and in any case, writing on the ground is difficult.

As the discussion proceeds, people rank the items in terms of importance to get some idea of the size of the overall problem and the relative importance of individual problems. This can be done by moving the objects around or assigning stones of different sizes to them. The biggest stone is the biggest problem, and so on. When you have a stone assigned to each problem, you can compare and contrast any two, remarking: 'This stone looks about twice (three times, four, etc.) as big as that one. Is this problem twice as big as that one? In what way? Tell me more.' It can be surprising how much additional information you can get by doing this.

Education matrix

Now it's time to move on to education. Shar and Mengeh are using a matrix to show correlation between education problems and possible solutions. What are the problems? Not enough desks and chairs in each classroom? The cost of uniforms? School fees? The need for a secondary school? Distance from a school? Symbols are assigned once again and, because resources are always limited, people rank them. This can be done in one of several ways. If there is general agreement, people just place the symbols on the ground on what will be the vertical axis of the matrix. They might use stones again to show the relative size of the problem. (They can also use pairwise ranking, discussed later in the chapter, if the order of importance is not that clear.) As the people of Katama have split up separately into men's and women's groups (in other places, people might split up into groups whose concerns are different), it is likely that the identification of problems, their rankings and possible solutions probably won't match. This is important — and we will return to it later.

Now Mengeh and Shar ask: 'What do people think are some possible solutions?' The discussion heats up. 'Self-help: make our own school furniture.' 'Improve our marketing facilities so we can pay for uniforms.' 'Set up a credit union that lends to women!' 'Ask the ministry of education to delay payment of school fees until after the harvest.' 'Approach a non-governmental organization (NGO).' 'Organize a local bus to take girls to secondary school in the town.' Shar looks puzzled. She points out to everyone that they are beginning to mix up *solutions* and *sources of help*. If not having a secondary school is the problem, a *solution* might be a local bus to take girls to the secondary school in the town, while a *source of help*

Figure 14–2 Example of an education matrix: problems and solutions

Problems			Solutions		
	Self-help: make furniture	Improve marketing facilities	Women's credit union	Delay payment	Local bus
Lack of school furniture	★★★★★ ★★★★★ ★★	★★★★	★★★★		
Costly uniforms		★★★★★ ★★★★★ ★★★★★	★★★★★		
High school fees		★★★★★	★★★	★★★★★ ★★★★★ ★★	
Lack of secondary school					★★★★★★★★★★ ★★★★★★★★★★
Distance from school					★★★★★★★★★★ ★★★★★★★★★★

might be a non-governmental organization, or a government ministry. Shar advises the group to concentrate on the problems and solutions for the moment. Later, they can deal with solutions and sources of help. She shows the women how to relate the problems and possible solutions in a matrix diagram. The problem symbols are already placed vertically on the ground. They use this as one side of the diagram. Then they put the solution symbols horizontally across the top (Figure 14–2).

The group takes a set number, say twenty, of seeds, stones, beads, or whatever is handy, for each problem. They discuss how to distribute them across the range of possible solutions that relate to that problem. If the problem is 'costly school uniforms', two solutions seem to relate: improving marketing facilities (to help women earn more from their garden produce to pay for school uniforms) and having a women's credit union (from which they can borrow to buy school uniforms). They must now decide how to distribute the stones: they put fifteen stones in the box where 'costly school uniforms' and 'improve marketing facilities' meet, and the remaining five stones go into the box where 'costly school uniforms' and 'women's credit union' meet. Figure 14–2 shows what the completed matrix looks

Figure 14–3 Example of an education matrix: solutions and sources of help

Solutions	Sources of help			
	Community	EU Micro Project	NGO	Ministry of Education
Self-help: make furniture	********** **********			
Improve marketing facilities		**** ****	**** ****	
Women's credit union	***** ***** ***	**** **		
Delay payment of school fees until harvest				********** **********
Local bus	***	***** ***** *******		

like when Mengeh transcribes it onto a big sheet of paper. She could also have written the number of stones in each box: '14', '23', and so on.

Mengeh, Shar, and Graf are creating matrices on sand, and it's easy to lay down stones or shells — they don't move. But during their GroundWork course in the Towers, they used the reverse side of old rolls of wallpaper, markers, and beans.

While Mengeh finishes drawing the matrix, the women want to go back to the issue of solutions and sources of help. Shar shows them how to take the symbols for the five solutions and draw a new matrix grid in the sand, placing the solutions along the vertical axis. Now, what sources of help might address these solutions? Symbols for these are placed on the horizontal axis. Again, twenty stones to distribute for each solution, and you can see the result in Figure 14–3.

Clarifying the difference between *solutions* and *sources of help* is crucial because the community will have to make decisions about how sustainable and feasible many of these ideas are, and they need to be clear about what they think will work, who they need to approach and why. 'Interviewing' the matrices will provide lots of additional information, which will be useful later on, when options are being assessed.

Mapping

Many PLAs that are looking at agricultural or natural resource problems begin with local people drawing a map of the community on the ground. This is an attractive idea. Most people are fascinated by maps of their own area, so it often draws many people in. It also starts local people out on the right foot: they are definitely more expert at preparing their map than anyone else, and it sets a tone for discussion and debate — people argue about such things as the scale, where things are, what has been left out. People usually feel quite a strong sense of ownership around maps. Maps are also useful for non-agricultural projects, and in your project you're going to use one to look at who is going to school and who is not. You can show educational participation by household, compound, or whatever unit makes most sense.

Why don't we just use school records? Current records may only tell who is in school, and perhaps who has left. Children who left a few years ago will have to be identified through older school records, and those who never attended at all or are in another school, such as a Koranic school (Madarassa) will not appear at all. Sometimes, of course, an exhaustive analysis of school records over the years can be helpful if everyone who recorded information has kept them properly and in the same way. For your purposes, however, the map will tell you what you want to know.

Mengeh and Graf start the map by asking one of the local elders to draw an important feature of the village — she draws a river, the main road leading into the village, and then hands over the stick to a male elder who marks out where the central gathering place lies in relation to these features. Now Mengeh asks the teachers to draw in the school and other important features like the health center, the market, and the mosque, marking them with stones, leaves, or twigs. Young girls mark out the fields on the boundaries of the village.

The map should be large. Eventually it will show information about every household or compound. If it is too small, people will have to start again, wasting everyone's time. Also, the map may attract a crowd, and people should be able to see it. Katama, with seven hundred people distributed in households grouped in compounds, is small enough for a single map. But if you work in a large community, you might need to get local advice about how to split the map into sections, with key landmarks which show where the sections overlap, so you can piece them together when you transcribe the map onto paper.

Now the major features are in. (Some may have been forgotten, which is another reason for leaving a lot of space to insert them as other people pass by and comment.) People start inserting the households by drawing squares in the sand, each representing one household and its exact position along the road, by the river, or next to the school. Wherever you work, use the locally appropriate unit: apartment, house, compound, etc. In Katama, it's household. Shar begins with one household — the chief's, recognized by everyone — and holding up a green bead to represent 'girl', she asks how many school-aged girls are in the household (the age depends on the country and the school system). How many of them are going to school? People mark them by putting down the correct number of green beads. How many are not? They are marked with blue beads. Repeat the process for boys using two new colors. If you want to show other things, such as whether the parents are literate, you will need more symbols or new color beads, one for literate father, one for literate mother, one for non-literate father, one for non-literate mother, and so on. Depending on your study, you may discover other things that are important to record (these are the variables we discussed in Chapter 4).

Mengeh and the schoolgirls are transcribing the map data onto a huge sheet of paper. Figure 14–4 shows the beginning of this process. The girls keep track of the households (they know them well) calling out the numbers of beads going down for girls in school and not, boys in school and not. Graf and his young friends, who are literate, are getting the names of household heads, and numbering them sequentially on a separate sheet. Figure 14–5 shows the beginning of this process. Graf also checks with Mengeh to make sure the correct number goes on the corresponding household square on the paper map. Towards the end of the process, people run out of beads. They don't have enough to record the remaining girls and also show whether they are going to school or not. One young woman suggests putting the green 'girl' beads just outside the household square in the sand, to show she leaves the household for school. The girls who don't go to school are placed inside the square. This solves the problem. Although it's getting dark, everyone continues until every household is on the map. It's unlikely the sand map will remain undisturbed until morning, so Mengeh and her young friends continue until the paper map is also complete.

Seeing a map like the one shown in Figure 14–4 helps everyone to think about school participation. People passing by may add information. In a study in The Gambia, a little boy wandering past said, 'But where's the girl in that house? She's not on the map?' The men making the map said, 'Of course she's not. She's fourteen and about to get married.' Because the map was very detailed and appeared to be exhaustive, this was the first warning the researchers had of the possibility of 'invisible' girls. Eventually they found that villagers in this and many other places tended to classify about

Figure 14–4 Example of a partially completed mapping exercise

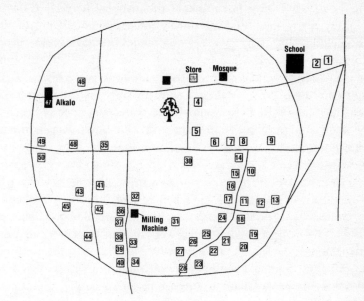

Figure 14–5 Partial record of the map on paper

Head of household	Girl attending school	Girl not attending school	Boy attending school	Boy not attending school
1. Tamsir Camara	1	3	3	0
2. Modou Samba	0	2	0	3
3. Isatou Jeng	0	2	2	0
4. Alieu Ngum	2	3	3	1
5. Mustapha Kenteh	2	2	2	0
6. Lamin Njie	1	0	2	2
7. Ebrima Ndong	2	3	3	2
8. Abdou Touray	0	1	0	2
9. Malick Jobe	0	0	1	0
10. Salhou Ceesay	0	2	0	0

25 per cent of their girls as not being of school age because they were married, about to be married, or had never attended school (Kane and O'Reilly-de Brún, 1993).

Besides serving as a kind of education census, the map has other functions. You can use it as the starting point for other research activities, and it can be checked — and used as a check itself — against information gathered in other ways. For example, the map can be used as the basis of the next two activities: card sorts and interviews.

Card sorts

You may remember that in Chapter 4 we discussed two approaches: the etic approach ('What do I see these people doing?') and the emic approach ('What do these people see themselves doing?'). We discussed card sorts as one way of getting emic information. Your team has spent some time looking over the data gathered so far, and, with the help of local experts, you've worked out your next step. A card sort to identify people's well-being in the village, which you plan to compare to the paper map data to see what choices people with high well-being tend to make about sending girls and boys to school. Do people with comfortable lives send more girl children? Do poorer people send fewer children in general, or just fewer girls, or none?

Graf and his friends take the list of household heads they made when the map was being copied. They write each name on a separate piece of paper or a card. Mengeh makes an identical set of cards. She'll work with some women, while Graf works with men, perhaps six or seven at most. They begin by asking: 'What does being well-off, comfortable, and secure in this community mean? What would be the opposite? What would be somewhere in the middle?' When everyone seems clear about these general categories, people begin to sort the cards by well-being. Some of the women in Mengeh's group don't read, so she shows each card and reads out the name to them. She asks: 'When you think about the categories we've been talking about, where would this person (or household) go?' and people put the card in the appropriate pile.

When all the cards are piled, Mengeh takes the first lot and reads them all out. Do they still belong together? Is there any card that should move sideways into a different pile? As people make finer distinctions and confront real cases, they may have to make more piles. (Researchers often use well-being instead of wealth for several reasons — for example, wealth may be a more limited concept, relating only to money and/or livestock, and people may be more reluctant to discuss wealth, whether their own or that of others. However, people may also be reluctant to discuss well-being in a group. You may have to work with one person at a time, or perhaps you may not be able to do this part of the research at all.)

Now Mengeh wants to know: what are the characteristics that make for high well-being? Taking the first pile, she asks: 'What makes these people similar to each other?' 'What makes them different from the people in the next pile?' She does this with all the piles and writes down the answers. Your research strategy involves relating participation in education to well-being, so when the bases for the sortings are clear, begin again with the first pile, and ask: 'Tell us about their school-aged children. Do the girls go to school? Do the boys go to school?' Table 14–2 shows how the results of the card sort might look.

Table 14–2 Well-being ranking: categories and characteristics

Well-being level	Characteristics	Children's schooling
Richest	May have more than one compound Ready cash on hand Reserves of food Help others Have relatives or grown children who send money Lots of cattle More than enough plough animals and domestic animals More than enough farm implements Many helpers; big family May hire other villagers Some villages: cement buildings	All go to school unless something is wrong with the child.
Rich	Cattle Enough food Help others Plough animals and domestic livestock Farm implements Some have relatives outside Some may have a few helpers; family relatively big Some are skilled workers Some villages: a few cement buildings	Almost all in school; maybe one or two not (would be girls), priority given to boys.
In-between	Just enough food; some may seek help in hungry season Few or no farm implements Little livestock Few or no plough animals Many depend entirely on farming Often small, young family No helpers Some villages: corrugated iron buildings	Very few go to school; may send one boy; girls don't go.

Poor	Not enough food	Few children; cultural
	Rely on others in village	beliefs would prevent
	Generally very few in compound	them from sending
	Usually no livestock	children to school.
	Few or no farm implements	
	No children in some households	
	Some villages: grass roofs	

Notice in the chart the references to cement buildings. These may be proxy indicators, that is, perhaps they can be useful as substitutes for other kinds of information that may be difficult or time consuming to get. If a cement building or a corrugated iron roof is a good indication of wealth or well-being, you can get a good idea of a family's standing or the relative well-being of a village without asking sensitive economic questions. However, proxy indicators are only good if they can really be used as a substitute for what you are interested in.

People in a group may not always agree. If you encounter much disagreement, you might carry out the process separately and privately with individuals and combine their answers. Also, well-being ranking can be sensitive, which is another reason for working with individuals. Do not dwell on the relative ranking of families within the piles. You are looking for patterns, not taking a detailed census.

Triangulation

In Chapter 7 we mentioned triangulation — the use of more than one researcher, more than one method, more than one possible explanation to crosscheck your information. Shar and two local women now look back to the map to see if people's card sorts of school participation by well-being of household match the figures recorded on the map. For example, households 2 and 3 fell into the 'poor' group. In the card sort, people said that cultural beliefs prevent people in this group sending their children to school, boys or girls. Shar looks at the list made from the map to see if the map information agrees. If it does, fine. If it does not, perhaps people have a set of ideas about rich people and poor people that are based more on stereotypes than on fact. Maybe people are prejudiced, or maybe times are changing and people just have not noticed that poor people are now sending more children to school. When Shar looks at the card sort information she sees that the information on household 2 corresponds to the map, but that for household 3 does not. The team needs more information on household 3 to see which is right (Box 14–3, below).

Box 14–3

Head of household	Girl attending school	Girl not attending school	Boy attending school	Boy not attending school
2. Modou Samba	0	2	0	3
3. Isatou Jeng	0	2	2	0

Of course, perhaps it is the map that is wrong, and Shar can check this through some of the methods we will now be discussing, but it is not as likely. Many people have participated in making the map and correcting it. In one village where this method was used, a man announced that he had five children, all in school. There was a silence, until someone started laughing and said, 'What do you mean? You have eleven children and five are in school.' The man good-naturedly agreed. You might not be lucky enough to have this correction made so easily, but the public nature of the map does encourage people to cooperate. (For this reason, it is important not to use any public information-gathering device of this sort to gather information that could embarrass, diminish, or endanger people, particularly because not everyone on the map will have had a chance to agree or to refuse to participate.)

The map can lead to another technique, interviews, and you can then check the information on the map against information derived from them.

How are the interviewees chosen? If you recall our discussion of sampling, we said that the entire group constitutes a universe, while a selection from the group constitutes a sample. The map is supposedly a universe, and we can use it to take either a probability or a non-probability sample to select households or people for interviewing. Mengeh could put the cards from the card sort in a box or a basket, mix them up, and draw them out one by one until she reaches the desired sample size. (Note we said 'supposedly a universe'. Maybe some households were missed. Also remember our 25 per cent of invisible girls.)

Another way to use the map is for purposive sampling, which is a non-probability type of sampling. Here you have a purpose in selecting particular people or households. You may want to pick:

- Extreme cases: houses in which no school-aged children go to school, all go to school, all boys and no girls go to school, all girls and no boys go to school.
- Typical cases: households whose characteristics reflect what appears to

be the usual situation.

- Information-rich cases: households where you think you can learn a lot about something — for example, poor households that have managed to send all their children to school. How did the family accomplish this?

In your study, you use the map to do some of each kind of sampling. You also deliberately do convenience sampling, that is, you work with school-aged children you come across in the village. Are they on the map? Does the information they give about their situation correspond to the map's information? You also talk to people other than children. Perhaps entire households have been omitted. If so, try to figure out why. Perhaps they are migrants or refugees or are not considered part of the community. Maybe they were simply overlooked.

Researchers often refer to the 'six helpers' for talking to people: 'who?', 'what?', 'where?', 'when?', 'why?', and 'how?' will help to cover the main aspects of an issue when you do not have or do not want a prepared set of questions.

Case studies
The mapping and interviews help the team to identify people for case studies. How did a 'successful' woman accomplish what she did? What is daily life like in a family that needs its daughters' labor to survive? How do some families cope with the loss of a daughter's work while she is in school? Fleshed-out accounts of these supplement the more basic information you get from semi-structured interviews.

Daily activities
In your study, you might find that knowing something about the daily activities of people is useful. Certainly you want an account of the daily activities of both girls and boys, but looking at those of adult men and women might also be helpful, because children's work often frees adults to do other work. You can interview girls and boys, women and men, and you can observe what they do as well. Observation not only enhances your understanding, but also gives you a chance to participate in some of the girls' chores to see what they involve.

Seasonal diagrams
A seasonal diagram is a good complement to the previous activity. People can draw a framework, either on the ground or on a large piece of paper, showing various activities, trends, and processes, by month or season. They can fill in, item by item, the relative proportions using seeds. The same number of seeds should be used for each row going across. You can see in

the village seasonal diagram shown in Figure 14–6 that community income is lowest when school expenses are highest, and that girls' workloads are biggest at the most demanding time of the school year.

Once again, different groups may give different accounts. Women's incomes and expenditures will probably not be the same as those of men. The team knows this already from the pie charts on income and expenditure. Girls' accounts of their most demanding school times can be compared with those given by teachers and parents. They may be very different.

The team needs to supplement this information. Women's income may be high when school fees are due, so what is the problem? Some key informant interviews show that men pay school fees while women are responsible for paying all other expenses. But perhaps fees are only paid at the secondary level. If men pay the fees, are they the ones who decide who goes? If that is the case, finding out what men think about second-level education for girls is important. As you can see, this is like a puzzle, and the team is trying to understand it by using a variety of techniques.

Figure 14–6 Example of a seasonal diagram

	Jan.	Feb.	Mar.	Apr.	May	June	July	Aug.	Sept.	Oct.	Nov.	Dec.
Income in general												
Expenditure in general												
Men's income												
Men's expenditure												
Women's income												
Women's expenditure												
School expenses												
Girls' work												
Boys' work												

Venn diagrams

Every community has highly visible organizations such as religious, financial, or business groups, as well as informal associations or groups that are busy planning, acting, and introducing change. It is important to learn about local institutions, their relative importance, how they interact, how successful they have been in the past, and so on. You also need to know which individuals in the community have access to resources and are key people when it comes to making decisions. Graf and his young friends make cut-out paper circles of various sizes. They focus on a single issue, 'subsidizing school expenses' and ask people to name groups and individuals involved in decision-making around that.

People will use larger circles for those whose role is more important. They arrange the circles so they show, by overlapping, the amount of cooperation among the groups: no overlap means no cooperation; if circles merely touch, they simply exchange information; if they overlap, they cooperate in decision-making (Figure 14–8). People can add to these kinds of diagrams by using arrows to show which way information goes, the sequence of the decision-making process (school to teacher's union to department of education, for example).

Ideally, people rearrange the circles until everyone agrees that the desired picture is achieved, and then the drawing is transferred to paper. But there's a problem. People seem confused. 'Everybody belongs to practically everything,' they say, 'so how are we supposed to show degrees of overlap? When dealing with a problem, a person might be "Red Cross" at one moment and "Parent Teacher's Association" at another. That makes us want to put these circles inside one another, because the overlap is total.' People are getting frustrated and eventually make one single pile of the circles. Now all the circles are sitting inside one another. Graf recognizes a challenge: how can people express these relationships in a way that is meaningful to them? Either this technique does not meet the complexity of this particular situation, or, culturally, people in Katama do not conceive of things in this way.

Innovations regularly occur in PLA. They often arise in response to a limitation or problem people have with a technique, prompting them to 'stretch' it to do something more, or something more effective. For example, during a PLA on disease perception in New Delhi, India, participants were struggling with the 2–D limitations of Venn diagrams. They could show the perceived danger of the disease by circle size, and the prevalence of the disease by putting circles close to or distant from a symbol depicting the village. But they also wanted to show the relative costs of treating the disease. Someone had the bright idea of stacking coins on top of the 'disease' circle to show the cost — a low pile indicates low cost, a big pile indicates high cost. Now Venn diagrams can be 3-D.

Surveys

Robert Chambers, who helped to develop many RRA and PLA methods, says that surveys, if given at all, should be 'late, tight and light' and tied to *dummy tables*, which are tables whose categories you have already planned and drawn up. The only thing missing is the figures, which are filled in when the survey results come in.

Work the dummy tables out first, then you will know what questions you need to ask on your survey.

It is possible to get broad-based information using techniques other than surveys. Recently, for example, villagers in a thirty-household Sri Lankan community made a thirty-by-eleven matrix on the ground and filled in all the items very quickly (Chambers, personal communication, 1995).

Using information obtained from many of the techniques we have already discussed, you should be able to construct a simple survey that addresses meaningful issues. Don't ask for anything more than you need. It is tempting to try to discover all you ever wanted to know about everything, but your survey will be unworkable and exasperating for everyone concerned. Follow the steps for survey construction, administration, and analysis in Chapter 9.

Analyzing What We Have So Far

Mengeh, Shar, Graf, and the other team members spend three days gathering and sharing information. During the day and each evening, they take time to analyze the data, sometimes with the help of local people. (How much data you gather and analyze depends upon how much time people can contribute.) They compare, review, and analyze information as it emerges from the various techniques, the various researchers, and the various subgroups who participated. If you recall, Mengeh and Shar made pie charts with women, Graf with men. Are the views of the two groups very different? They try to figure out what they have learned so far, what is missing, what contradictions have to be clarified. Learning from the data helps the team to plan the next stage of the research. What mistakes did you make? What went right? How can you use this information to strengthen your approach?

Identifying priorities and strategies for action

In preparing matrices, participants have already shared their ideas on the various causes of — and solutions to — their problems; if all the other research simply supports what people have already said, the community can begin to think about how to address them. A more likely scenario, however, is that during the research you will have gathered additional information using various methods, and different groups of people, that perhaps reveals more problems and other possible solutions. Asking groups in the community to comment on the findings is a good idea. This is what happens in Katama.

Mengeh suggests asking four separate groups to comment on the range of problems and solutions (older men, younger men and teenage boys, older women, younger women and teenage girls). Graf, who, as we know, is an artist, creates four sets of twelve cartoons to symbolize each problem that has surfaced. Each group carefully considers the cartoons, chooses the six most important and places them in a basket. The researchers then ask the groups to stick the cartoons in order on a large card, along with a pre-cut circle for each, to show relative importance. (Remember, such drawings may have little meaning somewhere else. The cartoon marked '3' might be 'read' as a big house and a tiny house.) You can see some of the cartoons later in this chapter.

Each group also discusses the causes of each problem, what they are doing about it now, and any other options they can think of that might help to solve it. The researcher writes down the causes, solutions, and so on. Shar's group is finding it difficult to decide, so they use a technique called pairwise ranking, which is also useful for other stages in the research. People are asked, individually or as a group, to compare the first item on the left side of the diagram with the first one running across the top (Figure 14–7). Which is more important? Write that one in the box. Then move on and compare the first item, left side, with the second item running across the top, and so on. The preferred items can easily be counted directly from the boxes.

Another way, which allows each person in a group to choose independently, is to mark the various problems on a wall using words or other symbols. Bags can be hung on the wall under each problem and people can put seeds into the bags according to their priorities.

Now the groups are finished with the cartoons and pairwise ranking. They convene in the village center. A representative of each group will explain the group's chart. Before any of the researchers realize what's happening, the older men, who finished first, have taped their chart to the side of a van, and are holding forth, at length. This is a big mistake. People begin holding their heads and looking intimidated. Fortunately, the younger women, when their turn finally comes, are led by a very strong-minded girl who is prepared to speak up, but this is a piece of luck. In fact, they almost miss their turn, because the other three groups send them off to fetch benches from the school so that everyone might sit comfortably.

When all is said and done, the old men have very different views from the young women and girls. They are worried about girls losing their traditional

Figure 14–7 Pairwise ranking matrix

PROBLEMS	Lack of facilities	Pregnancy	School fees	Losing traditional values	Distance from home	Early marriage
Lack of facilities		Pregnancy	Lack of facilities	Lack of facilities	Lack of facilities	Early marriage
Pregnancy			Pregnancy	Pregnancy	Pregnancy	Pregnancy
School fees				School fees	School fees	Early marriage
Losing trad-itional values					Distance from home	Early marriage
Distance from home						Early marriage
Early marriage						

Score:	3	5	2	0	1	4
Rank	3	1	4	6	5	2

Pairwise ranking

To prepare a pairwise ranking of opportunities (or problems) use the sample ranking table as the model. Prepare separate tables for the set of options for the three to five most important problems. The options for each problem are listed on the top and left side of the matrix. Each open square represents a paired comparison of the points listed at the top and extreme left. For each comparison, ask the group which option is more likely and why. Record the most likely option in the square and develop a list of reasons for the selections. When the chart is completed, add up the number of times each item was identified as more important than the rest, and arrange them in appropriate order. Repeat the exercise for the other major problems and options.

values and getting pregnant. The younger women and girls are more worried about school fees, other school expenses, and distance from home.

The group as a whole is then asked to select six problems that the community might do something about, using largely its own resources, plus, perhaps, some technical advice. This they do, after a lot of discussion, choosing the following: school fees, girls getting pregnant, distance from school, lack of school facilities such as furniture and toilets, early marriage, and girls losing their traditional values (Figure 14–8).

Figure 14–8 Ranking of problems in order of importance

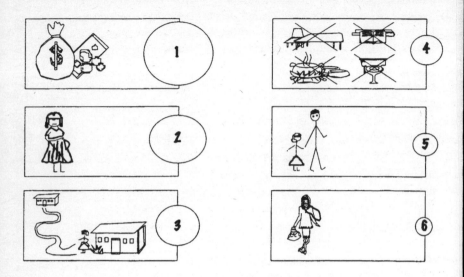

Even though the views of older men usually prevail in the community and the voices of young women and girls are not commonly heard, no group 'won' or 'lost' in this exercise. The final chart was quite different from any of the four individual charts, although older men did manage to get more of their concerns (but not in their original order) on the chart.

If the discussion is going to be contentious or if one group is going to be reluctant to speak up in the larger setting, you will have to develop a strategy to ensure that their voices are heard. If it is unacceptable for both sexes to convene in one place, an agreed person may have to act as a go-between, presenting each side's case to the other.

Sometimes the problems and solutions selected can be handled entirely through community discussion and mobilization, guided, perhaps, by the local committee or some other association. Others require negotiations with bodies outside the village — for example, can the school have more women teachers to improve girls' security and act as role models? They will need to approach the ministry of education. Yet others require technical advice or skills input, sometimes from inside the community, sometimes from outside. The community needs better school facilities, especially school furniture and a bigger kitchen. What will this involve in terms of time, materials, skills, and money? Will it come from donors, from the

Table 14–3 Villagers' ranking of school fees option

Option	Time	Costs	Feasible	Fair	Sustainable	Village	Score
Pay fees at the end of harvesting season	3	1	3	3	3	3	16
Improve women's gardens/fences/storage of vegetable pesticides	1	2	3	3	3	3	15
Sponsors for girls' education	1	1	3	3	3	2	13
Income generation program for young men's carpentry workshop	1	1	3	3	3	1	12
Government to reduce fees	1	1	2	3	3	1	11
Educate girls whose income will pay next generation's school fees	1	1	3	3	3	2	13

community, or from a combination of the two?

Technical experts, such as school heads, inspectors, and district education officers, either on the team or available to it, often come into the picture now. A variety of experts may be needed. One part of the solution to prevent girls from seeking lunch money from older men and boys would be to improve income from gardening, which might require better fencing and insect control. Here an agricultural expert may be more useful than an official of the ministry of education.

Ideally, for each problem, the team should cost several strategies in terms of resources required. In many projects, however, costs may be less tangible, or more local human resources may be called into play. In your project, the options involve attitude changes, values, and power relations.

The next task is to invite all the interested parties (community residents, PLA team, non-governmental organization representatives, and appropriate technical experts) to assemble, usually in a large indoor or sheltered setting. The aim is to discuss and assess the alternative options for each problem. People may want to make additional suggestions or corrections. Assessment depends on having some criteria for making an evaluation. In the example shown in Table 14–3, in assessing the options for paying school fees, the people of Katama decide that they wanted to take time, costs, feasibility, fairness, and other factors into account. They rank each of the options. Paying fees at the end of harvesting season scores highest, and improving women's gardens is a close second. When scoring, you will notice that 'high cost' gets a low score because it is considered of negative value, while 'low cost' gets a high score because this is positive.

Other ways of selecting options are available — for example, voting for or 'buying' options (see National Environment Secretariat, Kenya, 1989, p. 67).

Preparing an action plan

Once priorities and strategies for action have been identified for each problem, the community, through an association or committee, can begin to prepare a community action plan, decide which options to tackle first, determine how to assess their resources and how to coordinate actions, and work out how to monitor and evaluate progress. Table 14–4 presents part of the action plan that emerged from Katama. Note that for each problem, people identified several strategies or 'best bets' and decided to act on several of the more important ones.

Assessing resources

Participants now need to discuss how to get the resources needed to carry out the options. Do they involve non-governmental organizations, government departments, international agencies, bilateral donors, religious bodies, the local council, business, or industrial bodies? What kind of information do these entities require? How should they be approached? Having the assistance of representatives from these bodies to help with questions like these would be very helpful, both at the community meeting, and over the longer term. If outside funding is being sought, the development of a clear action plan may make the community's applications more attractive to funding bodies, because it shows that people have reflected realistically on their priorities and options.

For internal resources, the committee can look at local institutions and associations, non-governmental organizations, and so on, and try, using a matrix perhaps, to relate them to the resources required. List the organizations down one side of the matrix, the resources required across the top, and ask people to distribute seeds or mark numbers as before. Individual- or household-based local resources, such as labor, skills, time, building materials, money, land, and professional services, will almost certainly be required. Taking each participating household, the committee, possibly working with the team, might rank them on their ability to contribute, on a scale of 0 (low potential for contribution) to 3 (high potential for contribution). This procedure may, however, require sensitive information, and could be quite disruptive. One of the challenges of PLA is working out with local people how to handle situations like this.

Table 14–4 Part of a community action plan

Problem: School fees
Best bet: Sponsors
Score: 13
Action: It has been agreed that each head of household, male and female, will contribute one dalasi to a fund to inquire into sponsorship for girls' education. The fund will be collected on a continual basis. The money will be banked, not left in the care of any individual. More discussion is required on this before responsibility is assigned.

Problem: School fees
Best bet: Upgrade gardens
Score: 15
Action: Fencing and pesticides are needed. Seek materials from outside. Villagers willing to contribute labor. First step: organize a village meeting. The Kambeng kafo, which includes members from nearby villages, will be responsible for this initiative. The key contact people are: Omar Faye (m), Aminatta Sambu (f), Makaddy Touray (f), Kaddy Bah (f), Abdou Jarju (f).

Problem: Early marriage
Best bet: Insist girls finish education
Score: 20
Action: This is everyone's responsibility. Much is invested in girls' education and it should not be ignored when it comes to talk of marriage. The school committee will take special responsibility for talking to parents. Girls should get the chance to finish their education, then marry.

Problem: Early marriage
Best bet: Educate parents about the value of girls' education
Score: 19
Action: There are government programs available. A follow-up sensitization program is planned for next year. We can ask the headmistress to arrange this for us. The school committee can discuss this with the headmistress.

Completing the process

The village committee or other organization continues to work when necessary with representatives of donor agencies, government officials, and technical experts. As people become experienced in the PLA process and learn how to approach and work with donor agencies, they should be able to continue the self-help process and apply it to other problems.

Advantages, Disadvantages, and Dangers of RRA and PLA

Some of the advantages of RRA are obvious by now: working with and learning from local people and obtaining relevant information in a timely, cost-effective way. RRA also has a variety of disadvantages. Michael Cernea, a supporter of rapid assessment procedures, has pointed out that 'shortcuts are not beaten paths. They may be strewn with obstacles, confront slippery slopes, and hide methodological dangers' (Cernea, 1992, p. 16). Here are some possible problems. First, in relation to the researcher, you can only do something fast and well after you have learned the fundamentals. When you are taking research shortcuts and accepting 'appropriate imprecision', you have to know enough about research and about the situation you are studying to know what tradeoffs you are making. How much imprecision is too much, for example? You can end up with a partial picture based on overgeneralization from too little or inadequate information. For instance, you might choose inappropriate indicators, rely on too few key informants, and obtain a snapshot picture of the situation rather than an understanding of systems and processes.

Second, there are dangers in relation to the process itself. RRA is excellent for getting locally meaningful information, particularly in relation to shared group ideas and perceptions, but, as a consequence, combining the results of separate studies to get a broader picture can be more difficult. Indeed, no one community may have the picture that you seek. Cernea describes as effective a conventional study in which the male circumcision practices of 409 African ethnic groups were related to HIV seroprevalence statistics. RRA would not have been as useful here. A group can tell you about its circumcision practices, and possibly about its incidence of HIV-related deaths, but doing this 409 times through RRA is not an efficient way of establishing the relationship. Also, when relationships can only be understood through detailed information collected over a period of many years, for example, following a cohort or group of individuals through a series of events over a period of years to see what happens to them and why, rapid research is not satisfactory. As with all research approaches, knowing what they were intended for and understanding their strengths and weaknesses is the best protection against misuse.

Third, there are practical dangers that arise from not carrying out the processes properly: choosing the wrong team; not involving local people at all stages of the work; falling back on the comforting security of questionnaires, 'instruments', and statistics when the process seems too chaotic; preaching and lecturing rather than listening to local people; assuming that your discipline is the only one with anything to contribute; and ignoring people who make you uncomfortable (or whom you make uncomfortable), such as women, the poor, the homeless, or other less powerful segments of the community.

Arrogance — cultural, professional, class, or sexual — is one of the two biggest sins in RRAs. The second is betrayal of community trust: raising people's expectations without taking responsibility for the practical follow-through. RRA is not simply a way of finding things out. It is a way of getting things done. Few other approaches get local people as enthusiastically involved as RRA does, and the letdown if nothing useful comes of it is all the more serious as a result.

The advantages of PLA are also obvious: it is excellent for enabling local communities to identify and address their own problems on a continuing basis. However, addressing some of the problems may be difficult if they require interventions that the community itself cannot provide or the provision of which it cannot easily influence. Such a situation can arise if the problem cannot be handled at the local level — for example, policy changes, or ministry or organizational restructuring. RRA teams may encounter this situation as well, but such teams are often commissioned by institutions that can create or influence change at the non-local level. However, many problems can be dealt with at the local level, and people have better grounds for making a case for external change if they have clearly identified what is wrong and how it might be rectified.

The Philosophical and Ideological Foundations of RRA and PLA

If you read Chapter 2, you may wonder where PLA fits in the philosophical scheme of things. Now that you have accompanied Shar, Mengeh, Graf, and the other team members through a PLA process, you can probably see that RRA and PLA represent an interesting mix of phenomenology, critical theory, and postpostivism. They take a holistic and dynamic systems approach, one which recognizes that human behavior and motivation function in a changing, adaptive way in the context of biological, physical, environmental, and cultural systems; and they recognize, too, the existence of multiple perspectives on a situation or problem. This comes from phenomenology. Influenced by critical theory, they attempt to address these perspectives and antipoverty biases through a series of reversals of perspective and focus. Finally, many projects are shaped by a research plan, which, although always open to adaptation, does make certain assumptions about what topics are important and what sub-topics these involve, much in the manner of a postpostivistic approach. For an excellent discussion, see Jamieson (1987).

How You Can Use RRA and PLA as Part of a Larger Study

Because each community is unique, RRA and PLA work best at the local level. Sometimes, however, combining the results of many communities is possible, to get a picture of a region. For example, mapping has been used in 130 villages in Nepal, covering 6,544 households. Five maps on separate topics were made for each village (ActionAid, Nepal, 1992). Work such as this can be done in a participatory mode locally, and the results analyzed for use on a larger scale as well.

Both can be used in towns and in rural areas and within organizations. They can become part of national or regional research strategies. For example, using RRA and PLA at the local level, you can create meaningful questions for national surveys. You can then explore the findings of the survey in more detail by going back to do local research. You can also study the feasibility of projects at the local level and create more realistic policies. Finally, you can see how they are working out by monitoring and evaluation through RRA and PLA.

You have probably already thought of ways to improve the methods discussed in this chapter. You may want to try applying them to a new area of inquiry, so try out your ideas and let others know how they work. And do profit from the experiences of others. Try to read some of the works listed at the end of the chapter, which tackle a lot of issues not covered in this limited introduction to the subject.

PLA Sources and Contacts

The International Institute for Environment and Development publishes much of the material on RRA and PLA, including *PLA Notes* (available from *PLA Notes*, 3 Endsleigh Street, London WC1H 0DD, England), formerly *RRA Notes,* which provide examples of applications, lists of free materials, contacts for field learning experiences and manuals for a variety of techniques. For information on PLA in particular, see *RRA Notes* Number 13 and *PLA Notes* Number 22. Chambers (1994a, b, c) provides the most comprehensive account of the history and practice of PRA/PLA and of some of the theoretical issues and challenges facing it.

References and further readings

ActionAid The Gambia. 1992. 'From Input to Impact: Participatory Rural Appraisal for ActionAid The Gambia.' London: International Institute for Environment and Development.

Cernea, Michael M., ed. 1991. *Putting People First: Sociological Variables in Rural Development*, 2nd ed. New York: Oxford University Press.

Chambers, Robert. 1981. 'Rapid Rural Appraisal: Rationale and Repertoire.' *Public Administration and Development* 1:95–106.

———. 1983. *Rural Development: Putting the Last First.* London: Longman.

———. 1991. 'Shortcut and Participatory Methods for Gaining Social Information for Projects.' In Michael M. Cernea, ed., *Putting People First,* 2nd ed. New York: Oxford University Press.

———. 1992. *Rural Appraisal: Rapid, Relaxed and Participatory.* Discussion Paper No. 311. Brighton, UK: University of Sussex, Institute of Development Studies.

———. 1994a. 'The Origins and Practice of Participatory Rural Appraisal.' *World Development* 22(7):953–969.

———. 1994b. 'Participatory Rural Appraisal (PRA): Analysis of Experience.' *World Development* 22(9): 1253–1268.

———. 1994c. 'Participatory Rural Appraisal: Challenges, Potentials and Paradigm.' *World Development* 22(10):1437–1454.

Geertz, Clifford. 1983. *Local Knowledge: Further Essays in Interpretive Anthropology.* New York: Basic Books.

Jamieson, Neil. 1987. 'The Paradigmatic Significance of Rapid Rural Appraisal.' In Proceedings of the 1985 International Conference on Rapid Rural Appraisal. Khon Kaen, Thailand: University of Khon Kaen.

Kane, Eileen and Mary O'Reilly-de Brún. 1993. 'Bitter Seeds: Girls' Participation in Primary Education in The Gambia.' Washington DC: World Bank, Africa-Sahalian Department, Population and Human Resources Division. Draft.

Scoones, Ian and Jennifer M. McCracken. 1989. 'Participatory Rapid Rural Appraisal in Wollo, Ethiopia.' London: International Institute for Environment and Development.

Theis, Joachim and Heather M. Grady. 1991. *Participatory Rapid Appraisal for Community Development.* London: International Institute for Environment and Development.

Hancock Towers Newsletter

December 7, 2001

Apology to Mr H. Hussein and Mrs S. Braithwaite

The Association ('Always at Your Service') wishes to apologize to the above-named for any inconvenience caused. It appears that when the Association arranged to send two residents on training of trainers courses in Brighton, there was a mix-up in the coaches. Mr. Hussein was sent on the one bound for 'Empowering Women Through Boxing and Wrestling Skills' and Mrs. Braithwaite on the one for 'Beginning Arabic for Children'. Mr. Hussein said he had not noticed anything strange. It was true that all the other trainees were women, but he himself was a New Man. 'I know one end of a nappy from another,' he told this reporter. Mrs. Parveen Rashid of the Grannies' Club will take over the course, having won two falls out of three in the last session.

Mrs. Braithwaite thanked those who had begged her to continue teaching her course, but said that in fact, most of her 'Postman Pat' song had been in Irish rather than Arabic. Irish is her first language, and in fact, she has been teaching the children Irish ever since.

When he recovers from his recent fall, Mr. Hussein will take over the helm of Beginning Arabic.

Local man freed

Mr. Kevin Darwin, 14-A, has been released early from Glasheen Prison in Dublin. He expressed his thanks to Dr. Dermot O'Connor, one of our Kensington neighbours and a friend of Mr. Darwin's sister Shar. Dr. O'Connell sits on many tribunals dealing with insanity in British prisons. 'I did nothing,' said Dr. O'Connor, modestly. 'I am not licensed in Ireland. I just visited Kev one day, along with his mother and wife Rose. Kev was cooking in the staff dining room, serving dishes such as candied eels flambé with a peanut butter coulis. The governor begged me to help make a case for his release on the grounds of insanity, whose, I am not entirely certain.'

Dr. O'Connell has found a job for Mr. Darwin in Stringvest's restaurant as a chef.

Owing to a misunderstanding, previous issues of this newsletter gave a different account of Mr. Darwin's whereabouts. Ed.

No time for a pet? Love to cook? Make a light blue aspic in a fishbowl and chill some whitebait in it. Lovely terrarium effect, and no feeding or cleaning required.

15 ORGANIZING YOUR QUALITATIVE INFORMATION

Summary

This chapter shows how to record information that you get from a variety of qualitative techniques. *Written notes, tape recording,* and *video* are possible ways.

Some kind of recording method is essential. If you rely on memory alone, you will forget a large part of what you learned.

An organized retrieval system will help you to keep track of what else you need, and is necessary for the next stage in your research, which is analysis.

Well, Laurinda is still looking for that reference she lost when she went to the library in Chapter 8. The old librarian has retired, and the new one doesn't know what Laurinda is talking about. Laurinda has also had the inside door panels removed from her car, in the hope that the slip containing the reference might have fallen down behind them. So this is as good a place as any to talk about the importance of keeping your notes in such a way that you can get at them.

Most people imagine that a research project has just two parts: collecting the material and writing up the results. But there are other 'invisible' parts of the research process which are just as important — planning the research, and recording and organizing the information you collect. Most people want to spend as much time as possible interviewing people, reading new material, or observing something interesting. That, after all, is what they consider research to be. Few want to spend time psychoanalyzing themselves ('What do I *mean* by community art-in-progress?' 'What do I *mean* by successful women?' 'What do I *really* want to study?'), which is what you do in the planning phase. Even fewer people want to go through the boring job of recording and organizing the information they collect. But these two tasks, the initial planning, and the recording and organization of your data, take up at least as much time as collecting the information, and unfortunately they are not nearly as interesting.

Written Notes

Taking notes is discussed in this part of the book, which deals with qualitative methods because quantitative methods often have their own recording forms, such as a questionnaire, an interview schedule, or a standardized scale. As you saw in the previous chapter, RRA and PLA have many recording features built into the research process itself: historical profiles, pie charts, maps, matrices, calendars, and so on are recordings in themselves. They are transferred to paper as part of the RRA/PLA analytical strategy, to enable people to share and assess information, crosscheck and strategize. Chapter 12 showed some ways to record specific types of observations.

But when information is coming at you from all angles — people talking, people doing things, and events happening all at the same time — how can you record it all? Some people scribble notes on old bills, odd bits of paper, and even on the palms of their hands if they are desperate. When the time comes to try to pull the information together, they have hundreds of bits of battered paper. The usefulness of notes like this is very limited.

Most of us have other demands on our time, so we tend to think that what little time we have should be spent on the 'meat' of the project, collecting the information. No need to write it down in any great detail. It wastes research time, and anyhow, you will remember it. Take a few rough notes and catch up later, right? Wrong. There are some hard truths in life: you will not remember it and you will never catch up. Robert Rhoades (1987, p. 121) has estimated that researchers forget 50 per cent of the details of an interview within 24 hours, and more than 75 per cent by the end of the second day.

We tend to remember the unusual and the things that confirm our expectations or fall into patterns we have already identified. A lot of the rest gets lost. It is not a question of bad memory, but of your brain being overloaded. New information keeps coming in, day after day, perhaps in settings in which everything is new to you — the people, the place, and maybe even the customs — and you are constantly trying to make sense of each bit of it while remembering dozens of new names, road directions, where you left your notebook, and so on.

So when you begin to plan your research, allow time for recording and organizing. Depending on the method you use and the content of your material, for every hour's worth of information you collect, you may need three or more hours of recording and organizing time. Questionnaire forms, once prepared, take less time, but certain specialized kinds of information, such as recording of body movements and gestures, take more. This may seem like a lot of time, particularly for a part of the research you may not have known existed, but proper recording, in addition to its more obvious benefits, will save you weeks, or even months, of time when you start to analyze and write up the work. In some cases, it has been known to make the difference between completing a research project and not.

A number of ways of recording information in written form are available. The one you have probably seen most often is the questionnaire, which is not only a guide for getting information, but also a form for recording it. You can also develop a similar form to record interviews when you are going to ask the same questions of a number of people.

But what if your interviews involve putting different questions to each person, observing, and looking at records? You may remember that an issue in Hancock Towers in London is early marriage, found in almost any ethnic group, but just now in the Towers a particular problem among some ethnic groups. A research team from the Towers is concerned about some young girls who are taken out of school at fifteen or sixteen to undergo initiation rites and perhaps to marry men not of their choosing. Are any of them still in school? How many are married? What do members of their families feel about early marriage?

The team:

- Mavis Darwin
- Rose Darwin
- Septus McCardle
- and you

You can begin by checking the records at the local school. You discover from looking at school records and talking to teachers that two years ago class 4A had seven girls from an ethnic group which practices these customs. You would like to know how many of the seven are still at school, and of the ones who are not, why they left and what they are doing. The school records show that two of them are still enrolled and are in their final year at school. The remaining five left. The records don't tell us where these girls went, or where they are now. But the students might know. You find that there is little change in class groups, and most of the girls in the current 6A class were together in 4A. You can create a standard chart to record the information they offer (see Box 15–1 below).

No.	Name of Student	Age in 4A	Date left	Reason for leaving	Where now?	Doing what?
1	Mariama	15	Sept 1999	Marriage	Husband's place, Acacia Gardens	Unknown
2	Fatou	16	Nov 1999	Marriage	Hancock Towers	Works from home, sewing
3	Maria	15	Sept 1999	Marriage	Hancock Towers	At home
4	Isatou	15	Oct 1999	Unknown	Unknown	Unknown
5	Therese	16	Oct 1999	Marriage	Hancock Towers	At home

If the team simply wanted to fill in the chart and count the answers, you would not need to make detailed notes. But you want to find out what happened to these young women, so we conduct detailed interviews with people. You discover that although Mariama has left the district, her grandmother lives in Hancock Towers. She, with others, has formed an Action Group to ensure that sensitization programs concerning female genital mutilation are provided to the local community. You interview the two young women who remained in school to see what made it possible for them to do so. How do you record this? Some of the questions we ask the grandparents, the young women still in school, and those now married, will be the same for all, but many will differ, and will be determined by what the person tells you.

While interviewing the Grandmothers' Action Group in Hancock Towers, you discover that some of them believe their granddaughters should and could go back to school and still manage their household duties. Others disagree. The team would like to know what Mariama spends her time doing, but just asking may not be enough. Researcher Richard Anker has pointed out that people who are not working in paid employment may not need a precise sense of time, may under-report activities that take a short time, and generally under-report all their activities. Parents tend to under-report the economic activities of their children and men of their wives. He concludes that observation is better than questionnaires (Anker, 1981, pp. 8–10). How might the team record this observation?

Many methods for recording information are available, including computerized systems such as LISPQUAL, QUALPRO, ETHNOGRAPH,

KWALITAN, CODETEXT, NUD*IST and a variety of others that allow you to categorize and retrieve information quickly, but they are all based on a process similar to the one described here. (See Miles and Huberman, 1994, pp. 311–317.) If you can think of a better one, use it (and please tell other researchers about it).

The following method can be used to record:

- observations of people, processes, and events;
- interviews;
- material taken from records, books, and other written sources.

We will use an observation situation for the first example. Suppose that the Hancock Towers Grandmothers' Action Group and the local council have had a number of disagreements on how to run gender and health sensitization courses, particularly because of the sensitive nature of related issues like female genital mutilation and early marriage. The Grandmothers' Action Group thinks the programs won't be effective, because the council has chosen inappropriate people who just use the courses as a way to make extra money and don't understand the cultural issues at stake. This is not helping the situation, they think. The council officials think that the Action Group is resistant to the sensitization courses and is bent on making it impossible to get them off the ground. The team studies these differences as they relate to specific issues that they have found to be important in the Grandmothers' Action Group (Box 15–2).

Box 15–2 Points of disagreement (I) between Grandmothers' Action Group members (II) and council officials (III) in X district (IV)

1. **Points of disagreement**

A. On the part of the Grandmothers' Action Group
1. Selection of too few local target groups
2. Selection of inappropriate course lecturers
3. Suspicion of council officials

B. On the part of the council officials
1. Non-cooperation of local residents (grandmothers)
   a. Refusal to participate
   b. Failure to provide local information that would make the courses more successful (etc.)

The team decides that one of the techniques that will give information on point A.3., 'suspicion of council officials', is to observe Grandmothers' Action Group meetings at which this issue is frequently discussed. You get permission to attend the first meeting and you take notes in as much detail as possible. You now have a set of rough notes. The aim is to convert them into as detailed a record as possible in a form that will allow you to retrieve and use the information when you need it. A number of steps and materials are involved: *Step 1* is to have as accurate an account as possible of what occurred in the observation, where, under what circumstances, and in what sequence. For this, you will need a hardbound notebook with sheets sewn in to keep notes secure and in chronological order.

Using the notebook

Use only the pages on the right-hand side of the book. Don't write on the backs of the sheets or on the backs of any other sheets you use. Take all your rough notes in this notebook, including notes of interviews, observations of events, rough diagrams, and notes from books or documents. Avoid using other paper of different sizes, loose sheets, old envelopes, and so on, except in cases where a notebook would be inappropriate or impossible. Each notebook is numbered with a Roman numeral (I, II, III...) and each page in the notebook with an Arabic number (1, 2, 3...). *Step 2* is to add details and information on circumstances, physical features, and background, as well as factors that may have influenced the type and quality of the information.

After the meeting, re-read your rough notes and add anything that you didn't have time to write during the meeting. Do this as soon as possible after the meeting. At the end of the notes, add any of the following, if relevant:

- Circumstances and background. How you came to attend the meeting (who suggested it or invited you, or whose permission you got). This is important. If the person who sent you or gave you permission is disliked or suspected by the people at the meeting or by an interviewee, you may not be aware of it at the time, but it may help to explain later why a particular meeting or session went the way it did.
- Physical description of the setting, descriptions of the participants, their placement, movements from these positions, and so on. A floor plan or diagram may be useful. Maybe all the people on one side of the issue sat in a corner on the left. You won't know this until you are more familiar with the situation, but if you don't record it now, you will never be able to look back and discover it.
- Any background information on the participants or the event that you are aware of. This may include whether they have already had a sensitization course, whether their granddaughters have married early or not, whether they are supportive or not of initiation rites, and anything else that might be helpful, but which you did not learn during the course of the meeting. For example:

> *Mrs. Gomez left the Residents' Association several months ago to head up this new Action Group. Maria is her granddaughter; Maria left school early to marry, and lost her first baby two months ago, due to complications arising because of initiation rites she had undergone last year, prior to her marriage to Abdul Touray.*

or

> *A meeting of this organization is held every month. According to the membership rules, only grandmothers are permitted to attend, but today the researcher and two representatives of the council are present.*

- Record anything that you think may have affected the quality of your notes. Perhaps you suspect that people were inhibited in your presence, or the presence of others. Perhaps you were a participant yourself, and possibly restricted in what you could observe; or possibly you could not take any notes during the meeting itself and are writing entirely from memory.

Step 3 is to extract the material from your hardbound notebook in such a way that you can retrieve the information later and write up your report. For this you will need a typewriter or computer (good, but not essential); paper; carbon paper (if not using a computer), and file folders. The paper should be roughly eight inches by five inches. Use standard typing paper or whatever other paper you can get, cut in half. You can also use specially treated paper that allows you to make copies without using carbon paper.

Now type or rewrite the notes from your hardbound notebook onto the half sheets of paper. Make an original, or top copy, and three or four copies of each sheet. Begin the first sheet and every sheet with these headings in the upper right-hand corner:

1. Topics
2. Event observed or interviewee's name
3. Place of event or interview
4. Date

When you complete the circumstances and background, which may take several pages, begin on the notes proper from the hardbound book. As you finish transferring each page from the notebook to the half sheets, cross out the page in the notebook. If for any reason you do not use material from the notebook (it may seem irrelevant at the time, perhaps), put an 'X' or other obvious mark beside it. From time to time, you should check back through the notebook to see if this marked material is still not useful.

Number each half sheet when you type it. You can number the sheets consecutively through all your notes, or simply begin again at one for each day's notes. You may also wish to give the number on each typed page of the notebook and notebook page from which you are typing in case you ever need to go back to the original rough notes. Having numbered each notebook with a Roman numeral, and each page of the notebook with an Arabic numeral, list them in one corner of the half sheet, for example: 'III:36'.

When you have the entire observation written up on half sheets, go back over each sheet and fill in the headings. Numbers 2, 3, and 4 will be easy. Here they are for our sample half sheet:

1. Topic(s)
2. Grandmothers' Action Group Meeting
3. Community Room, Hancock Towers
4. December 10, 2000

Circumstances and background

Begin here with the material you wrote at the end of your hardbound notebook account. It will read something like the page shown in Figure 15–1. Then write out the substance of your observation, as shown in Figure 15–2. Mark comments of your own, impressions, reminders to yourself, questions you want to pursue, and so on between slashes to separate them from the rest of the text, that is, what you actually saw and heard.

Back to our headings. Point 1, if you remember, is topics. Get the topics by scanning each sheet and deciding what subjects are covered. For your Grandmothers' Action Group Meeting, the topics could be:

1. **Topics: circumstances, composition of meeting, grandmothers' concerns about confidentiality, methods of handling dissension.**

Your notes are likely to run for several pages, so proceed to the next page and do the same thing: fill in all the points and get the topics by reading that page. Your topics may remain the same for several pages or may change for each page. Nevertheless, put all four points on each page even if you are repeating the same points. The meeting you observed was a short one, but if it had continued, the next page's topics might include 'voting in of Vice-President', 'alternative outline for culturally-sensitive programs', and 'role of facilitator in peacemaking between grandmothers and council members'.

You may have one topic on the page, or three or four. If you are using your research outline to collect your information, your notes will reflect the points in your outline and your topics will be similar, if not the same, as your research outline points. If they have very little relationship, you should try to figure out why.

Notice that this approach is both deductive (using the research outline points to decide what to observe) and inductive (allowing other things to emerge, including them in the notes, and giving them topic headings). After some practice, your rough-note taking, organization, and memory

Figure 15–1 First page of field notes

1. Topic(s)
2. Grandmothers' Action Group Meeting
3. Community Room, Hancock Towers
4. December 10, 2000

I went to the Grandmothers' Action Group Meeting at 8.00p.m. with Mrs. Rashid. There were seventeen people present: fourteen grandmothers (numbers 2–15), two council members (1, 17) and myself, (18). There were three speakers on the platform: Mrs. Gilligan (1) Mrs. Gomez (2), and Mrs. Wakefield (3). They were seated in the room according to the diagram below (the box represents the platform).

```
          ┌─────────────┐
          │  1   2   3  │
          └─────────────┘
        4   5   6   7   8   9
    10  11  12  13  14  15  16
                    17
                18
```

(Scale: 1 inch = ___ feet)

will improve, and you can stop filling in all the details in your hardbound notebook, but, of course, you still have to record them on your half sheets.

Step 4 is to file the half sheets so that you have one complete account of the observation or interview and a file folder for each topic that appears in your notes. For this you will need the half sheets, a stapler or paper clips, and file folders.

When you have finished writing up your entire observation on the half sheets, let us imagine that you have filled up ten half sheets. If you made three carbons or copies of each, you now have forty sheets of paper: the ten originals or top copies and thirty carbons. Take the ten originals or top copies and staple or clip them together, from page one to the last page. This means you now have one complete copy of the observation or interview if you ever need to read the whole thing in proper order from the beginning to end.

Now you have in front of you ten piles of carbon copy half sheets with three sheets in each pile. Take the first pile. Read the first topic listed at the top of the page, for example, in this set:

1. **Costs of council programs; inappropriate personnel; benefits of council programs**

costs of council programs comes first. Make a file folder called 'costs of council programs' and put the first sheet in the first pile into it. Now take the second sheet in the same pile. The second topic is 'inappropriate personnel'. File it under that heading. Take the third sheet and file it under

Figure 15–2 Notes on Grandmothers' Action Group meeting

1. Topic(s)
2. Grandmothers' Action Group Meeting
3. Community Room, Hancock Towers
4. December 10, 2000

Observation:

At 8.05p.m. Mrs. Gomez stood up from her seat on the platform and said, 'You are all very welcome to this meeting of the Grandmothers' Action Group. We welcome our visitors from the council, Mrs. Gilligan and Ms. Touray. We warmly welcome Mrs. Mavis Darwin, who seems to be following in her daughter's footsteps by taking up research, participatory research, isn't it, Mavis? Well, you all know we have a full program this evening. We are here to discuss the council plans for sensitization programs, and we intended to develop our alternative plan. I would like to think that everyone here is free to speak her mind. We should not be suspicious of each other — after all, no-one is taking notes or anything like that. Let's try to discuss only positive constructive things.' /I put away my notebook at this point./ For approx-imately sixty seconds, no-one spoke. A woman in the front row, Number 7, waved her right arm at full length, but Mrs. Gomez did not call on her. /Later, I learned that this woman had refused to meet the council members when they first arrived./

One woman, Number 10, said, 'I don't know, I don't feel too comfortable at this meeting. I can't imagine discussing our business with the council members sitting on our backs. Are you all convinced that what we say here is confidential? No, sir. I think they'll go right back to the council and report us. Now you tell me, whatever happened to that nice Mrs. Njie — remember, she came to the first few meetings, then she had trouble with the council over her washing hanging out on the balcony? She never come back, I don't even see her no more at the Grannies Club. I think she's frightened.'

At this point, a council member (No. 1) stood up and said, 'I'd like to assure you we are here to listen and understand your views. Not to spy on you, or your plans.'

'What's that bulge under your jacket, then?' asked No. 4. 'From where I'm sitting, it looks like a small tape recorder.' There was general dismay at this. No. 1 sat down abruptly, shaking her head. /She reddened, perhaps embarrassed?/

No. 13 said, 'And the other one is Abdul Touray's cousin, and you know what happened to his wife, Mariama. It's a disgrace. She shouldn't be allowed in here!' No. 17 walked out.

/Check out the relationship between Abdul Touray and this council member — is she really his cousin? Did Mrs. Gomez know this when she opened the meeting? How close are family ties in this ethnic group — would she be acquainted with her granddaughter's husband's cousin?/

The meeting broke up in disarray at 8.17p.m.

the third topic, 'benefits of council programs'. So far, all you have done is file copies of the same page.

Now move on to the second pile (page 2) and do the same, filing one copy under each of the topic headings listed on that page. If the page has as its topics:

1. Disruption of work; benefits of council programs; improving accountability

you do not have to make a new file folder for 'benefits of council programs', because it appeared as a topic before and you already have a folder. Your folder headings correspond to your topics, which in turn correspond to the points in your research outline or other organizational plan. Notice here that there is a definite bias: all the 'benefits' are ending up in one folder, whereas each 'disadvantage' appears to have a file of its own. Presumably this is because you are focusing on disadvantages. You are finding that the grandmothers and council officials agree on the benefits, but it is the disadvantages that are in dispute. However, later you can always combine two or three folders into one or break one up into several.

What if you have only two topics on a page? You have three copies. File the first copy under the first topic, the second under the second, and throw the third one away. What if you have four topics and only three copies? If you see this happening often, start making four copies. If it happens occasionally, file the first three copies under the first three headings, and for the fourth topic put a note in the file folder for that topic saying 'see December 10, 2000, page 6'. When you need to look at that page, go back to your stapled or clipped pile of top copies, which you should keep all in one place, and read page 6 of December 10.

You can continue sentences and topics from one page to the next. It is easier if you do not continue just one line when the topic is going to change, but otherwise, simply type your notes without worrying about your filing system. If a topic continues on a new sheet, that new sheet will contain the topic in its heading, and therefore you will file the two sheets together. You can staple or clip them if you want to ensure that they stay together.

You can now see why you are using half sheets of paper: it limits the number of topics you can get on a page. If you used standard-sized paper, you might get eight or nine topics to a page, and be forced to make as many copies so that you could file a sheet on each.

You can use this recording method for interviews as well as observations, for diagrams and maps, and for material from books and documents. For books use the headings this way:

1. Topic(s)
2. Author's full name, book title, publisher and place of publication, date

of publication

3. Location of the work (this is useful for documents, especially if you are using sources scattered among a number of agencies and offices and wish to find them again)

4. Date (of your note taking)

Write your notes from books or records or draw your maps and diagrams directly on the half sheets. You can also photocopy material, for instance, paragraphs from books, and paste them on the half sheets. This way, any of your information that is not recorded on questionnaires or other standardized forms will appear on these half sheets. When you are finished with your research, you will have one pile of top copies of all your notes from earliest to most recent. You will also have a set of file folders containing your carbon copies. They will correspond to the topics in your research outline or to whatever organizational scheme you are using. If you wish you can number them to match the points in your outline.

From time to time you can go over your outline points or whatever plan you are using to organize your research and check each corresponding file to see that you are getting the information that you need. You may, of course, have to add or cut points in your outline or plan, and your file folders will reflect this. You may also have to re-categorize your material as you gain more understanding.

Suppose you are doing a piece of descriptive research. You just want to know what the grandmothers' concerns about the sensitization program are and the council's concerns about the grandmothers' participation. When you finish your research and want to write it up, look at your research outline to see if you can use it as the outline for your report. Often, you can. Sometimes you have to re-order the points. In our outline for:

Points of disagreement (I) between Grandmothers' Action Group members (II) and council officials (III) in X district (IV)

if you had happened to place X district in the middle or near the end of the outline, you now might want to make it first, because you will probably want to describe the location near the beginning of your report. Then you might want to say something about the Grandmothers' Action Group Members (II) and the council officials (III) — such as who they are — before moving on to the points of disagreement (I), which is the substance of your research.

When you get the outline points in an order suitable for your report, line up your file folders in the same order. Take your first points, read the corresponding folder, analyze or summarize the material in it, and write it up. Sometimes you may have to group points together, but the procedure is the same. Remember, however, that you need two outlines. One is a guide to the information you need to collect, and one is a plan for writing your report. If one serves for the other, fine, but when you are planning your research at the beginning, never work out your research outline as if it were going to be the outline for your report. The research outline is a plan for collecting information. With any luck, the outline for your report will be a bit more interesting.

If you are doing anything more than very simple descriptive research, you will have to perform more analytical operations than this, such as finding patterns and relationships (see Chapter 16). No matter what you do, you need your information in some organized form like this.

Other types of written recording techniques

Other note-taking procedures are available, but most are variations of the one just described. For example, you can use punched cards. Get or make a pack of cards with holes punched around their edges. Number each card, from one on. Record your information. Put items 2, 3, and 4 in the upper right-hand corner, but not the topics. Assign a hole to each topic. If that topic appears on your note card, open the hole out with scissors or a special punch (Figure 15–3). Open the holes for any other topics that appear on the page. When you want to retrieve a particular topic, line up all the cards, run a knitting needle or other thin rod through the hole assigned to that topic, and all the cards containing information on that will fall off (Figure 15–4). For example, we want to get at some sub-categories. First, you want all the cards with information on young women who left school at age fifteen. You assign hole 8 to that topic. These cards fall off the needle. Then you want to look at which of those young women is now married. You have assigned hole 9 to that topic. You run the needle through again, and now you have all the young women who left school at fifteen and are married. (The reason you number the cards, incidentally, is so that you can reassemble them into chronological order again. If you do not want to keep doing that, make one carbon copy of each note and keep the carbons in order in a box.)

Other written recording techniques are available for kinship (*genealogical charts*, see Schusky, 1983) and body movements (*kinesic notation*, see Birdwhistell, 1970). You are unlikely to need these, but if you do, know they exist so you do not have to reinvent them. For other recording techniques, such as grids, classroom observation forms, and matrices, leaf through this book, particularly Chapters 12, 15, and 16, which show various display forms. You can use many of these for recording.

Figure 15–3 Punched cards with hole 1 opened

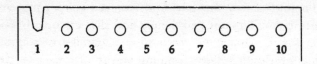

Source: Mitton (1982, p. 83)

Figure 15–4 Selecting cards

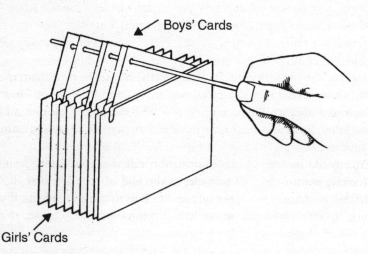

Source: Mitton (1982, p. 84)

Tape Recording

Tape recording is useful if getting the exact words, tones, or music is important, if writing would disturb the flow of conversation, or if you have to be free to do something else during the interview or event. You could also tape record yourself giving a running account of the event.

In these cases, tape recording is simply a substitute for the hardbound notebook. The second stage, putting the material on half sheets, is still necessary. Here are some points to bear in mind if you tape record:

- Many people resent or are frightened by tape recording and, of course, secret tape recording represents a serious ethical breach. Never use a tape recorder without announcing its presence and seeking permission to use it. Keep your tapes confidential, just as you would your written notes. Try both written recording and tape recording to see how each influences the presentation and availability of material.

- Tape recording in itself doesn't produce certain types of information that may be important to your study: 'kinesics', such as body movements and gestures; facial expressions; and the physical characteristics of people and settings. (Written notes do not produce facsimiles of sound, but the caution is necessary, because technical aids sometimes give you a false security of having recorded everything.) Therefore, at the end of the tape recording you must either tape or write the information called for in Step 2: circumstances, physical descriptions, background, and influencing factors, plus the points mentioned above.

- You must transcribe and edit tapes immediately after you have made them. Your research time may be very limited. Perhaps you have had to travel some distance and want to spend all your precious time collecting and wait until you get home to transcribe the tapes. This is usually a serious mistake, because by that time you will have forgotten all the details called for in point 2. You may think that you will not. How could anyone forget such clear impressions? The clear impressions tend to run together, however, and vague recollections will not be good enough in your notes.

- You could include all the information called for in points 2 and 3 by reciting it into the tape recorder at the end of the interview; however, letting un-transcribed tapes pile up can lead to other problems. If you do not have the information on half sheets, classified by topics, it can be difficult to tell how you are progressing, whether you have enough on a particular topic, whether you are unintentionally skipping research points. The sheer volume of work can also present a formidable obstacle when you finally do begin to transcribe.

Video Recording

Filming used to be available mainly to highly trained professionals who could afford expensive, rather unwieldy equipment. The availability of camcorders has changed this. The newer equipment is also less intrusive. The need in the past for lights, big cameras, a crew, and microphones, often produced rather artificial scenes that terrified people.

This discussion is limited to using video as a method of recording research information, not as a visual way of presenting results, conveying meaning, and so on. The principles are the same, however. You still have to get the information into manageable form, and you have to provide information about what is happening. One way of doing the latter, if the situation allows, is to speak while filming or have someone else explain what is happening as you film. If the purpose of your research is to record the intricacies of a process, whether it be children interacting or someone making something, making a video is a good method, particularly if you can show it to other people for interpretation (see Collier and Collier, 1986; Heider, 1976; Hockings, 1975 on the use of videotape in research).

None of the above should deter anyone whose research requires accurate recording of sound or video. It is intended as a cautionary note for those who think tape recording or video offers the easy way out.

Conclusion

All these methods require an investment of time and patience, but are well worth it in the end. Whatever method you choose, the essential thing is that you use it regularly and keep up-to-date. For other systems for doing field notes, including the question of whether they are worth it, see Burgess (1984). Bernard (1994) also offers an alternative system. The only good system is one that works for you, otherwise, you won't keep it up.

Finally, your notes will contain information that may be sensitive or damaging to people. Even if they don't, people often assume that if you have written something down about them, it must imply that they are peculiar or bizarre. Even if you have told people that you are taking notes, they forget after a short while and often get upset at the idea that they have been observed, or had their words written down. If your notes are lost, or somehow made accessible to people who have no right to read them, you are breaching the confidence of people who either a) helped you in good faith or b) didn't know you were studying them at all, and are therefore even more vulnerable. Your entire study can be jeopardized if you lose your notes.

References and further readings

Anker, Richard. 1981. *Research on Women's Roles and Demographic Change: Survey Questionnaires for Households, Women, Men and Communities with Background Explanations.* Geneva: International Labour Office.

Bernard, H. Russell. 1994. *Research Methods in Cultural Anthropology.* Newbury Park, California: Sage.

Birdwhistell, Ray L. 1970. *Kinesics and Context: Essays on Body Motion Communication.* Philadelphia: University of Pennsylvania Press.

Burgess, Robert G. 1984. *In the Field: An Introduction to Field Research.* London; Boston; Sydney: Allen and Unwin.

Collier, John, Jr. and Malcolm Collier, 1986. *Visual Anthropology: Photography as a Research Method.* Albuquerque: University of New Mexico Press.

Heider, Karl G. 1976. *Ethnographic Film.* Austin, Texas: University of Austin Press.

Hockings, Paul, ed. *Principles of Visual Anthropology.* Chicago: Aldine.

Miles, Mathew B. and A. Michael Huberman. 1994. *Qualitative Data Analysis*, 2nd ed. Thousand Oaks, California: Sage.

Mitton, Roger. 1982. *Practical Research in Distance Teaching*. London: International Extension College.

Rhoades, Robert E. 1987. 'Basic Field Techniques for Rapid Rural Appraisal.' Proceedings of the 1985 Conference on Rapid Rural Appraisal. Khon Kaen, Thailand: Khon Kaen University.

Robson, Colin. 1993. *Real World Research*. Cambridge, USA: Blackwell.

Sanjek, Roger, ed. 1990. *Fieldnotes: The Makings of Anthropology*. Ithaca, New York: Cornell University Press.

Schusky, Ernest L. 1983. *Manual for Kinship Analysis*, 2nd ed. New York: Holt, Rinehart and Winston.

PART IV.

MAKING SENSE OF YOUR RESULTS

16 ANALYZING YOUR QUALITATIVE INFORMATION

Summary

Analysis of qualitative data involves getting the information (*collecting*), boiling it down (*reducing*), organizing it in various ways to help you to see patterns and relationships (*displaying*), deciding what you have got (*drawing conclusions*), and satisfying yourself and others that you have found what you think you have (*verifying*).

The entire process involves repetitive loops: what you learn in one stage may send you on to the next stage or back to an earlier stage.

That will teach you to lose your notes.

Now we have reached Step 12 (Box 3–1): analyzing the results. This chapter looks at how to analyze qualitative data, while the next one looks at quantitative data. At the end of the next chapter you will find a discussion of how you might combine the strengths of both to get the best of both worlds.

Words and numbers are two different kinds of symbolic systems, and the techniques for making sense of them also differ. Techniques for analyzing data in numerical or quantitative form are highly developed, as the introduction to the subject in Chapter 17 will show. The main problems in using them are (a) understanding them, (b) collecting your material in such a way that it is suitable for such analysis, and (c) choosing the correct techniques. These are not trivial problems, as anyone who has used quantitative techniques will tell you.

Until recently, however, the analysis of material in words — qualitative data — seemed even more difficult. Your interviews, observations, and quotes might be extremely moving and very telling, but telling what? How would you know if your material was significant? How could you identify patterns? You think what you have is valid, but will anyone else? In short, is human thinking good enough as a mode of analysis?

All analysis, of course, including quantitative analysis, is founded on human thinking. Sometimes when we see something like this:

$$\Sigma = \frac{\Sigma - 1}{x \ (>2)}$$

we think it came from the Almighty. We forget that a human developed it.[1]

In quantitative analysis the thought processes are certainly more formalized and codified than in qualitative analysis. Much of the work has already been done by statisticians. You just apply their procedures. What rigorous procedures can you apply to qualitative materials? Or is it all an art? And is rigor what is wanted in qualitative analysis? Many sociologists and anthropologists, including Bernard (1994), Geertz (1973, 1983), Glaser and Strauss (1967), Pelto and Pelto (1978), and Wolcott (1994), have been wrestling with these kinds of problems for years.

Ways to Look at Your Material

In Chapter 2 we looked at various ways of approaching material. We return to two of these now as we try to make sense of our information.

Working from the top down: deductive approaches

The human brain appears to be programmed to put order on chaos. The chaos in this case is your material. Some kinds of order seem to be universal (see Berlin, Kay, and Merrifield 1985, for example, for color orders), but others are culturally established. In addition, material has many kinds of patterns. Don't assume that if a pattern or theme appears to spring out of your material that this is the 'natural' way to organize it. It's even more important to remember this if you are studying people who are culturally different from yourself; your way of organizing and interpretating may be quite different to theirs, although both may be valid.

If you took a *deductive approach* to your research, your data have already been molded by the time you reach this chapter. You chose the problem you were going to study, and you determined exactly what you wanted to know about it. This then gave you the categories of information to be collected, and you created the questions for your survey or the treatments in your experiment. You ignored material that did not fall into these categories. In

[1] Actually, we developed it just now and it doesn't mean anything.

Chapter 4, you may recall the study you conducted about women entrepreneurs working in the repair/construction business in Hope And Glory. You decided that the height of women entrepreneurs was not relevant in that particular study, so you didn't collect information on it. But maybe height turns out to be important. What you didn't know was that women who are taller than the average male in Hope And Glory actually find it easier to get positive responses when they go to shops to order materials or when they deal face-to-face with suppliers. Short women have a terrible time. Six months after the completion of the research, you hear that almost half of the women have abandoned their businesses. You are curious. Is there any common characteristic the women shared that you missed? A characteristic that might explain, in part at least, why they abandoned their businesses? You return to Hope And Glory. You talk to all the successful women and notice in passing that they are all looking down at you. This is a serendipitous or accidental discovery that you can then pursue. (This might sound a bit slipshod to you after all the work you put into your research outline, but some of the most important scientific discoveries of the past two centuries have been serendipitous. The story of how Alexander Fleming discovered antibiotics is a famous example, but too disgusting to mention here.)[2]

Working from the bottom up: inductive approaches

In *inductive analysis* you allow the categories or patterns to unfold or emerge. Instead of getting a theory, converting it into something you can study, selecting the variables to study and collecting the information on them — and only them — you start out with a more open-ended approach — for example, how do some teachers manage to maintain order in a classroom without being disciplinarians? What happens all day in a Citizens' Advice Bureau? What skills do burglars need?

The researcher can detect patterns in inductive analysis, or the people you are working with can have 'built' them into the research. Remember the schoolgirls who were interviewed in Chapter 4? They categorized their classmates as 'poor', 'rough and ready', 'gorgeous', 'snooty', and so on. In Chapter 14, local people classified community members as 'richest', 'rich', 'in between', and 'poor'.

[2] However, it's all right here. Once, when he had a cold, Fleming decided to study his own nasal secretions. Many people probably do this when they have time on their hands. However, in Fleming's case, a teardrop happened to fall onto the laboratory slide containing the secretions. He found that a substance in the teardrop, although harmless to human tissue, destroyed the bacteria. But serendipity is no excuse for sloppy research planning. As Pasteur, another serendip, said: 'Chance favors only the prepared mind.' Fleming's training prepared him to understand what he had found (Roberts, 1989, pp. 65, 160).

Some advocates of inductive analysis talk of letting the data speak for itself. This is not possible. The data are constantly passing through ordering processes that the human brain puts on them, from the moment the first question is formed in your head. (Of course, the results of the ordering may differ, depending on the question you are asking, the theoretical perspective you take, the techniques you used, your cultural background, and the material you have to work with.) Nonetheless, you can try to give the material a chance to say something to you.

Here is one final example of the difference between deductive and inductive approaches. In Chapter 12 we mentioned a study by Whiting and Edwards in which they observed the actions of 137 boys and girls to test stereotypes about boys' behavior and girls' behavior, such as 'boys are more dominant' and 'girls are more nurturant'. Whiting and Edwards defined what they meant by words like 'dominance' and 'nurturance' before the study started. Only those kinds of behaviors were observed. At the end, the researchers simply had to count them. That is a deductive approach. Another possibility would have been to watch the children, record everything they did (probably filming would have been the only practical way), and then figure out what was there. That is induction.

Having the children watch the film and describe *what they saw themselves doing* would have given an emic and participatory edge to the inductive approach. The categories of meaning and analysis they might offer would probably differ quite radically from the categories identified via deduction or the researchers' induction.

Bear in mind that you can use an inductive approach to data collection — informal interviews, participant observation, cards sorts and so on — and still analyze the material deductively, particularly when you are trying to pull the results of the whole lot together.

Taking a deductive approach to data collection and then using an inductive mode of analysis is more difficult. Of course things can emerge or unfold, but there is not as much scope for this to happen, because you have so carefully restricted the possibilities when you were collecting the material. And one of the reasons you were using a deductive approach to begin with was that you had a clear-cut idea about what was important. At this point you probably don't want to start rooting around for new things to spring out at you, even if they could.

Stages of Data Analysis

Most analysis of qualitative data is a tacking back and forth between deduction and induction. The following stages of data analysis are adapted from Miles and Huberman (1994). The order is slightly different for purposes of clarity in a chapter as short as this. You should read their work, and some of the others listed at the end of this chapter, to get a fuller picture. These stages are:

1. **Data collection** of material in words, as discussed in Chapters 11–13.
2. **Data reduction** — structuring, organizing, and streamlining the material.
3. **Looking for groupings and relationships** — trying to figure out what you have.
4. **Using visual data displays** to clarify groupings and relationships.
5. **Drawing conclusions** — pulling it together, and verifying, or satisfying yourself (and others) that your findings are valid.

In other words, collecting your information, boiling it down, laying it out in various ways to help you figure out what you've got, deciding what you've got, and checking it. Remember, the aim is to find meaningful groupings and patterns of relationships (if they are there, of course!).

The process outlined below does not form a one-way sequence. At each stage you learn something that may send you back to a previous stage or stages. Think of it as a board game: at any moment you may be sent back to the beginning. Figure 16–1 shows the luck of the game.

Figure 16–1 The research process as a board game

Stage 1: collecting the data

At this point, you may feel you have finished collecting your data, but remember that the research process is a dynamic system involving repetitive loops. As you are sorting out your material and seeking patterns, themes, and categories, you may find that you need to collect more information to test your ideas. The Hancock Towers research team of Mavis, Rose, Septus, and you realized this when you examined your initial data on forced early marriage among young women in the Hancock Towers area. You recalled the stories about Haddy: how she was in love with a young graffiti artist but was given in marriage to a man not of her choosing, was then seldom seen outside her apartment, declined, and finally took her own life. It wasn't difficult to see how her younger sister, Isatou, might well have decided that 'disappearing' was a much better option.

Mapping of households in the Towers showed that a significant number of young women who were candidates for early marriage were 'missing' from home. Septus's interviews with fathers and brothers in these families revealed that they believed their daughters and sisters simply ran away from home rather than face an early marriage. But no-one knew what happened next. Where did these young women run to? What happened to them? Did they survive? How? Who helped them? This is a sensitive issue, and people who know are not going to volunteer information. The team had to keep going back through their information, getting new insights and collecting more data. Initially they thought that it would be younger women who would be sympathetic toward girls in this position, and who would help them. After they did a survey that showed it was older women who expressed the highest levels of sympathy, they began to think again. And then Septus remembered his bizarre initial encounter with Avril, the dog lady, on page 195. Septus, a newcomer to the Towers, now knew enough to realize that people don't keep packs of clapped-out racing dogs in their flats, so what was Avril hiding? Isatou, of course.

The team then started working more closely with the Grandmothers' Action Group to see what the older women were doing to help. They found that many of them had sheltered runaway girls. The research moved on from there, but it hasn't been a straight-line process.

Working with the Grandmothers' Action Group, the team now plans to collect case-studies, in strict confidence, to show how and why young women and grandmothers in Hancock Towers developed this extraordinary alliance. They will change names and circumstances, perhaps publish one case-study in each edition of the *Hancock Towers Newsletter*, and by inviting written responses, test the current atmosphere in the Towers in relation to early marriage. Then they may be able to bring people together from different sides of the debate to plan some positive action. In the meantime, Septus is setting up focus group discussions in Hancock Towers and the Greater London area for fathers and brothers who are concerned about loss of cultural values if early marriage is abandoned. The women on the team are going to set up similar focus groups with women.

Research is like a detective story — the clues are often there in the data, you just have to figure out what fits where in order for the big picture to emerge. Back to data collection.

If you collect material at a higher, or more general level, you cannot convert it to a more detailed or specific level. For example, in their survey the team asked: 'How do you feel about the tradition of early marriage?' and 70 per cent of people said they were unhappy with it. They cannot convert this to more specific information, and conclude that people are unhappy because the group practicing early marriage gets a bad name, or the marriages don't last. If, during their survey, they had asked people if they were young, middle-aged, or old, they could not then convert this information to 0–30, 31–60, 61–90.

Stage 2: reducing the data

In quantitative analysis you reduce the material by using numbers. Imagine hordes of women tell you in a survey that they would strangle the person who designed their kitchen if they could find him. They now become '98 percent of the respondents'. Very neat and concise.

You can also reduce qualitative data using numbers. You can observe people in a meeting and say: 'It was found that 40 per cent of the speakers were interrupted at least once during their presentations. Female speakers were interrupted 80 per cent of the time, and male speakers 20 percent of the time.'

Other ways of reducing material are also available. You decide to focus on some things and exclude others; when you collect material, you decide what is relevant and what is not, and you record only some things. From the whole world of acts, behaviors, processes, events, and people, you look at and then take instances of some and not others.

You can summarize or group material. In emic interviews you can look for recurring concepts, labels and words that seem to keep cropping up in interviews. Perhaps these are shared concepts, and the bases for groupings. You can also go through categories in your notes, select some and set others aside (meaning you choose to look at all the information on one category and not on another — not that you look at what supports your idea and ignore what contradicts it). To do this you have to have some kind of conceptual scheme; you have to remember what you are studying. Or you can let the patterns leap out at you, if you are very lucky, and concentrate on those. As you do this, you might find some holes in your materials that were not obvious before. This will send you back to data collection.

Stage 3: looking for groupings and relationships

This stage and the next, using visual data displays, have to be considered together. Saying which of these comes first is difficult, because in reality they work together. At a simple level, you might say that in a deductive approach you conceive the display and then see if the material fits. In an inductive approach you would find the pattern and then use the display to illustrate it. The aim in each case, however, is to group the material in a meaningful way. You can use such devices as grids, matrices, taxonomies, maps, flow charts, causal maps, or networks to help you try out various groupings and relationships to see what you have. You can also use them after you have developed some groupings to refine them and see patterns more clearly. And, of course, you can use data displays to discover what is still missing, which sends you back, as you might have guessed, to more data collection. You will probably go back and forth, trying and rejecting, until you find something that makes sense to you.

How can you figure out what you have got? This section presents a number of ways adapted from the sources mentioned earlier, especially Miles and Huberman (1994).

Scanning the material

You should be scanning your material all along to help you come up with refinements, new questions, and so on. Now that you are near the end, you should try to take a fresh perspective. Think back on your material. If you had to tell someone on a bus three or four things that you seem to have learned from your material, what would they be? If you can't think of anything, put it all aside for a bit, or get a friend to grill you: 'What did you find?' 'Do you mean you spent all that time and found nothing?' 'At least tell me one idea you got.' 'What led you to get that idea?' 'Would you say that's generally true for your research?' 'What are the exceptions?' 'Why?' and so on. ('Hard' scientists reading this should not laugh. Remember we social scientists now know about Alexander Fleming, as well as about Newton, Nobel, Friedel, and Crafts, and many of your other heroes. What we are doing here is far more orderly.) The following sections discuss some more specific approaches.

Look for patterns and themes

Do any things seem to go together? Do any things seem rarely or never to be associated? What kinds of exceptions are there to these 'rules'? Does that tell you anything? For example, Rose and Mavis of the Hancock Towers research team are doing some case studies on young women who 'disappeared' from families in Hancock Towers. About half of these young women managed to rebuild a life for themselves; the others finally had to return home. First, what did they all have in common? (All shared a desire to 'escape' the plans their families had for them. They all 'disappeared' into a grandmother's apartment for several days, before being sent on to sympathetic families in distant towns.) What seems never to be found? (None were reported missing to the police. None returned home within the first month.) What did the group who rebuilt a life have in common? (Most had been allowed to have summer jobs, and were familiar with the world of work. Most were raised in woman-headed households. All were sent to families with similar ethnic backgrounds.) What did the 'returned home' group have in common? (Most came from large families, with male-headed households and at least one older sister who had married young. Most were sent to families with a different ethnic background.) What are the exceptions? (About a quarter of them came from small families, about a third had no older sisters, while one fifth were sent to families with the same ethnic background.) And so on.

You begin to think you see a pattern. Now look for examples that don't fit into your pattern. What about young women who rebuilt a life but never had a summer job, or came from male-headed households? How did they manage? You find that these young women were sent to sympathetic households where work, money, and decision-making processes were shared equally by males and females. What about the 'returned home' group? Being sent to families with a different ethnic background seemed to make it more difficult for the majority to rebuild their lives. But one fifth did get to stay in families with similar backgrounds, but still returned to their original homes. What happened? Why didn't they stay? You discover that these young women were sent to homes where they were not encouraged to continue in school, but were sent to work in factories. You still have a lot of work to do to check out these findings, but as you read in Chapter 8, that's what research is about: search and re-search.

Clustering

Clustering is another name for sorting: what things go together, and why? What name can you give them that shows why they go together?

Remember the emic interview in Chapter 11? Kev, the prisoner, was telling the interviewer what kinds of prisoners were in the prison. He clustered or grouped the prisoners into categories: 'Muppets', 'Lifers',

'ODCs', and so on. Card sorts and triads accomplish the same thing. You can also get categories from observing (informal ways in which prison guards reward cooperative prisoners); from community interviews (asking townspeople in the area around the prison what kinds of benefits and drawbacks there are to having a local prison); from story telling (kinds of strategies less powerful prisoners use to gain favor with those who are more powerful); or from any of the techniques described in Chapters 11, 12, and 13, all of which can be used to cluster people, behaviors, events, and processes.

For example, you study how a local community action group wanted to provide drug information courses and sought funding from local government. A lot of things happen, many people are involved. What are the processes the action group went through to get the money? Can you cluster what you found under a set of headings, such as 'making a case', 'understanding what local government can and can't do', 'showing need', 'having the right representative', 'knowing local government language', 'having pull', 'timing it correctly', and so on?

Or you study three local adult education centers, all offering the same courses. The courses are over-subscribed in two centers, and never filled in the third. You studied many possible reasons: distance, transport, course content, but now your research indicates that the tutor's interactions with the students are very important. In the over-subscribed centers, the tutors behave in certain ways that are not as common in the third center. You have watched a lot of instances of tutor-student interaction — hundreds maybe — and now you are grouping them into clusters, such as 'facilitating', 'obstructing', 'ignoring', and 'affirming'.

Having said so much about grouping you may find that sometimes you have over-grouped. Something you thought was one category is actually three. You have a big lump of a category called 'student participation in adult education center activities'. Maybe you should look more closely: perhaps you have three kinds of participants: workers, drones, and queen bees. If you are looking at tutors as 'affirming', 'obstructing', and so on, you might want to look at 'obstructing' more clearly and break it up into 'interrupting', 'ignoring', and 'using negative body language'. Maybe each has a different effect.

Using metaphors, analogies, or models

In Chapter 2, we referred to the view that positivists hold about nature: nature is a giant clock whose pieces can be taken apart and studied separately. That is a metaphor. 'Mr. Pootle is the Romeo of the department,' is another. In both examples, the similarities between two unrelated things are highlighted to give a better understanding, while the differences are ignored.

Romeo, for example, is a dead, fictional, Italian teenager. Mr. Pootle is not.

Analogies are similar. Something is said to be like something else to highlight some essential feature that both share, while ignoring the differences. 'Being in this adult education center at break-times is like putting your head in a washing machine,' emphasizes the noise, pain, and disruption that would be common to both. 'When the coordinator visits, the tutor is like a chicken with its head cut off.' But you can have more insightful analogies. 'This center runs like clockwork,' emphasizes not only timeliness, but regularity, predictability, and efficiency. 'The tutors' meeting is like a battlefield,' emphasizes hostility, lines drawn, weaponry, and winners and losers.

Models are explanations of how something works, borrowed from a different sphere. At a simple level, you might use a model of a factory to illustrate inputs and outputs in an adult education center; or you might compare it to a garden with its planting, nurturing, and harvesting; or to a prison, invoking containment, restrictions, reshaping, and negative re-enforcement. Models highlight the parts of the system that you think are the most important. There are some quite sophisticated modeling systems in the social sciences, some borrowed from organizational theory, information systems, cybernetics, and chaos theory, among others.

It's always wise when working with metaphors, analogies, and models to remember: Don't let them take over and don't push them too far.

Counting

You are allowed to count in qualitative research. Ignore the comments of researchers who claim you are only doing qualitative research because you can't count (Sechrest, 1992, p. 5). Anything, no matter how vague it may seem, can be collected in numbers if you set up the questions or the categories of observations in ways that allow it. For example, you can convert the following observation into numbers in a variety of ways:

The numeracy tutor asked Lalia, 'How much is four times two?'

'Seven,' said Lalia.

'How much is four times two, Oscar?' she asked.

'Eight,' said Oscar.

She asked Therese, 'How much is four plus seven?'

'Leven,' said Therese.

'How many times do I have to tell you, it's "eleven", not "leven". You must say the 'e' at the beginning. Do you say "irteen"? No, you don't. You are so frustrating. Go turn the kettle on. How much is four times nine, Joseph?'

'Thirty-four,' said Joseph.

'Nearly right,' said the teacher. 'Think a little more. It's the same as six times six.'

'Thirty-six,' said Joseph.

'Excellent,' said the tutor. 'Marco, how much is four times seven?'

'Twenty-eight,' said Marco.

'Very good,' said the teacher. 'Let's have our break now. Some of you deserve it.'

Table 16–1 shows one way to collect the results of these interchanges in numbers.

Table 16–1 Tutors' responses to students' answers in numeracy class B7

Response	Females	Males
Ignoring correct answer	1	1
Rewarding correct answer	1	
Constructively helping with correct answer	1	
Negatively responding to incorrect answer	1	

Benjamin White (1984) used a nominal scale to present quantitative data that he had collected in qualitative form by interviewing people on husbands' and wives' roles in household decision-making (Table 16–2).

Table 16–2 Quantitative presentation of qualitative data

Nature of decision	Wife alone	Wife dominant	Equal joint decision	Husband dominant	Husband alone
Production input purchase	0	18	0	54	28
Hired labor recruitment	0	14	11	44	11
Food budget	67	33	0	0	0
Clothing purchase	45	45	0	0	10
Health care	0	33	0	33	33
Social/ceremonial expenditure	0	44	11	44	0
Number of children	0	11	67	22	0

Source: Benjamin White (1984).

Finding relationships

How does what you have found go together? Box 16–1 sets out some possibilities. Things may simply go together. It is not necessarily the case that one causes the other. If you look back at Chapter 5, you will see the requirements for cause and effect: the two things have to go together, the cause has to occur before the effect, and the relationship cannot be spurious (something else causing both of them). In social research, determining which comes first can be difficult, because the process may have been going on for a long time, and you are seeing the effect in one sequence and the cause in the next, essentially in the wrong order. 'The culture of poverty' was a popular sociological topic in the 1960s and 1970s. Does a certain kind of 'culture' produce poverty, or does poverty lead to certain ways of living? In an ongoing process, it can be difficult to tell, and people tend to make their interpretations based more on an ideological basis than on an experimental one.

Box 16–1 Indicating how things go together

1. A+, B+	(both are high or both are low at the same time)
2. A+, B–	(A is high while B is low, or vice versa)
3. A⇧, B⇧	(A has increased and B has increased)
4. A⇧, B⇩	(A has increased and B has decreased)
5. A⇧, then B⇧	(A increased first, then B increased)
6. A⇧, then B⇧, then A⇧	(A increased, then B increased, then A increased some more)

Source: Miles and Huberman (1994, p. 258).

Almost always when you find a relationship in qualitative research, you have to look back at your material (and probably, as you may have guessed, go back to data collection) — to see if the pattern holds. Look for negative instances — where the relationship does not hold, why not? Look for rival explanations — maybe B is causing A, not the other way around. Maybe a third thing is causing both. Maybe they are not connected in any way at all except in your notes.

You can perform what anthropologist H. Russell Bernard (1994, pp. 71–72) calls 'thought experiments' as well, meaning 'what if?' questions. What if you keep one key element of the research as it is, but change another? Would it still work? Have you got any other research material that might tell you? What if you could alter a critical element? Would that be enough? Do you know of any instances where this happened?

Constructing a picture

Educational researchers Guba and Lincoln (1989) have developed a phenomenological approach called constructivism, in which different people's or different groups' 'claims, concerns, and issues' emerge and are resolved through negotiation. In constructivism, you are not performing operations on the data, such as grouping or clustering. Instead you are trying to build up or construct a picture, inductively, just as you would expect phenomenologists to do. This approach shapes the entire research process from the very beginning, not just the analysis.

A constructivist approach involves the following. First, a contract is developed with the client or sponsor, such as an education center board that is concerned with student dissatisfaction with a new curriculum and tutors' worries about how to implement it. What is to be evaluated, how, and the purpose of the evaluation are clarified and undertakings are sought that the client will adhere to and accept the process, which involves sharing power and, if necessary, a willingness to change. Indeed, all the parties involved must agree to this if the process is to be successful. The evaluation team is trained and organizational arrangements made. Stakeholders (agents, beneficiaries, and victims) are then identified. Evaluators try to understand the claims, concerns, and issues of each group by interviewing people, and then discovering variations on those views by asking to be referred to others whose ideas might differ. Once no new information emerges, this round or 'circle' is complete, and the results are compared with other sources such as literature, observation, the views of the other stakeholder groups that are participating, and the evaluator. The results of these are put to the groups, and some claims, concerns, and issues are resolved and set aside. For example, students concerned that their curriculum didn't include basic self-development classes might discover that the board is already planning them. Any unresolved items are prioritized, and more research is done on these. The competing items are presented to each of the groups, along with useful information. Then each group chooses a representative to form a new circle and negotiate the unresolved items, shape a joint construction, and decide upon action. When the process has gone as far as it feasibly can, case reports and stakeholder group reports are prepared. Finally, because unresolved items almost always remain and situations change constantly, the entire process can be recycled. If you are interested in this approach, look at Guba and Lincoln's (1989) work to understand their full line of argument and to get more information on how to proceed. You should know before you begin that the process is time consuming, and getting people to reach consensus is not easy.

Stage 4: using visual data displays

According to sociologists Schlecty and Nobel (1982, quoted in Patton 1990), the task of the researcher is:

- Making the obvious obvious
- Making the obvious dubious
- Making the hidden obvious

and, we might add for thick-headed people who refuse to see the light, making the dubious obvious.

Data displays help to do that. A visual display does not refer just to making a nice chart to illustrate your findings to others. Here it is an analytical tool, something that helps you to see patterns and relationships. That is why it might precede Stage 3, be used in conjunction with it, or follow it.

In Chapter 14 we used some data displays, including a map and several matrices. We will look at these first. Remember, local people can make these visual displays too, during the research.

Maps

You can use maps to represent anything that has a spatial dimension. In Chapter 14, a village mapped its households, showing who was going to school and who was not. Here are some other things that can be mapped:

- Areas showing location of ethnic groups; social classes; areas used by men, by women, and by everyone.
- Change over time by creating two or more maps of the same place.

Some specific examples:
 ⇨ Use of a place at various seasons, or by time of day — for example, are young women prevented from attending classes at night because they can't go to certain areas?
 ⇨ Areas in the building or general neighbourhood where females' security is most at risk.
 ⇨ Use of office space, and its consequences. When the company was small, everyone worked in the open and there was a lot of socializing in the pub after work. Now senior people have more space, which is enclosed, while junior people work in small semi-open cubicles, and people feel awkward about socializing outside their 'level'.

You can probably think of many other possibilities.

People can help you create these maps, or you can draw them after collecting your information and show them to people for feedback and refinement. People in most places like the idea of maps (unless they are dealing with a controversial subject like contested land boundaries), so maps can be used to look at things in a new way.

You can then use the map to try to figure out relationships. Do men steer clear of certain areas considered 'women's space'? Do women go into men's areas only to perform domestic services? Are some areas of the adult education center used only by the tutors, so it is a privilege for students to use them?

Maps can also be used as a kind of quick 'group questionnaire' if you are working with people who know each other. Instead of going house to house to find out whether people within have physical disabilities, you can work with a smaller group to draw a map showing the households, and mark which ones house people with disabilities, and the type of disability. You can add other relevant information for each household, such as whether the people have access to transport, live alone, have necessary facilities nearby, and so on. Sometimes a map like this has a greater impact than a survey would — the group can show the map to transport authorities, merchants, etc., to demonstrate areas of need.

Matrices
Matrices can help people to see relationships, because information 'intersects'. Matrices have categories going down the left axis and across the top. These can be the same categories going both ways (see the grid approach in Chapter 4, for example) or different categories, as in the matrices in Chapter 14.

Flow charts
Flow charts show a sequence of events, processes, or behaviors. What happens first? Then what? And so on. A flow chart at the end of Chapter 1 shows how to use the chapters.

Causal maps are a type of flow chart. Causal maps can be very simple, such as:

A causes B

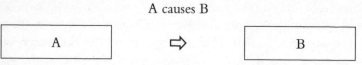

or very detailed, with dozens of variables and arrows going both ways showing the complexity of a process. Figure 16–2 is an example showing factors that prevented women in Hope And Glory from participating in a training scheme for would-be entrepreneurs, and the consequences

Once you have your clusters, patterns, or other groupings and have explored various relationships between them (which causes which, and so on), try showing it visually. Indicate the things that go together — for example, tutors who behave toward students in negative ways, and low enrolment in adult education classes. Indicate by using arrows which way you think the relationship goes. What factors might go in between these or intervene? For example, are tutors overworked and disorganized? Is building in progress at the center? Is there a new board of management? Maybe you identified some causes of disorganization, such as the disruption to classes and tutors because of ongoing building, most tutors underpaid, or failure of the board to approve a new curriculum. These can also be linked to low enrolment as possible causes.

Figure 16–2 Example of a causal map

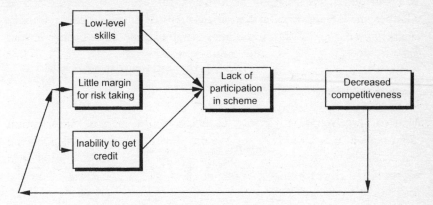

A way of building up such a chart is to consider one case, such as one class of students in the adult education center. Draw it out. Then consider other cases. Do they tell the same story? Do they provide rival explanations or negative cases? Try to find a pattern that explains as many as possible. Find out why the others don't fit, and incorporate all the parts into the chart.

Decision trees

You saw an example of a decision tree in Chapter 5 (Figure 5–2), which helps you to decide what kind of experiment to do under various circumstances. Figure 16–3 is another. How does a parent decide whether to send a child to a religious school? You can track the process through a decision tree. Figure 16–3 shows the beginning of such a tree:

Figure 16–3 Example of a decision tree

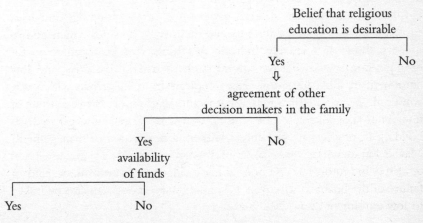

Taxonomies

In Chapter 3, children in a school classified the things teachers did. The resulting table was a taxonomy. One can show taxonomies in several ways (Figure 16–4).

Figure 16–4 Different kinds of taxonomies

1. BOX DIAGRAM

Things Teachers Do At School						
A			B	C	D	

2. LINES AND NODES

A. Things Teachers Do at School

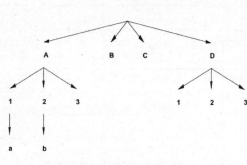

3. OUTLINE

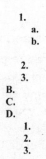

Things Teachers Do at School
A.

   1.
    a.
    b.

   2.
   3.
B.
C.
D.

   1.
   2.
   3.

Source: Spradley (1979, p. 120)

In Chapter 11, we used two of these types of display to show categories of prisoners (Table 11–1 and Figure 11–1).

Componential analysis

When we made a chart in Chapter 4 showing how the girls in a school categorized other girls ('gorgeous', 'snooty', and so on), and another chart in Chapter 11 showing how a prisoner categorized other prisoners in the jail, we were showing componential analysis. A display of this sort (Table 16–5) shows the definitive components or dimensions of a situation as seen by participants in a situation. Once you have a grasp of these dimensions, you too should be able to predict how a new girl (or prisoner, object, or activity) would be classified.

Table 16–3 A componential analysis of 'the girls in this school'

Category	Funny clothes	Money from dodgy boys	Money from boy-friends	Money from parents	Local	Handicapped	West side
Poor	x						
Rough and Ready		x					
Gorgeous			x				
Snooty				x			
Ordinary		x			x		
Handicapped	x					x	
West side		x					x

Stage 5: drawing conclusions and verifying

You have gone from your raw data to patterns. You have tried to relate the patterns and explain them. The purpose of this book is to help you to do basic research in a fairly short time rather than to contribute to academic discourse. If you want to do that you need to be familiar enough with the professional literature to be able to relate the concepts or theories of a discipline to what you have found. This will tie your research to the discipline, relate it to the works of others, and give it a more powerful tool for explaining, because many other people have already thrashed out the theory and tried it in other research. An example of a theory is the one proposed by Robert Park in 1928 in which people classify each other and then behave toward them on the basis of stereotypes that they have about them. Thus, at a party, everybody listens to the mayor's opinions about the World Cup, even though everyone else may know more about the sport. The mayor is an 'important powerful person', and important powerful people have opinions worth listening to. Social workers who think lone teenaged parents don't supervise their children properly and don't notice when they actually do, may try to make them all attend parenting classes, regardless. Tutors who think females are not very good at mechanical drawing may assign them 'simpler' tasks.

You may feel that you are not dealing with theory at your level of work; however, research and the subject matters chosen for research are all shaped by theory, whether you know it or not. You may actually be contributing to theory by offering generalizations, some of which help others to build a theoretical explanation. For example:

- Agricultural modernization may lead to a heavier female workload, so that girls in 'modernizing' societies may be less able to participate in schooling.
- As jobs become more 'technologized', they are assigned to males, even if the work was previously 'female'. (We know this to be true, but why? Males are better at technology? The work is easier? More fun? See Murdock and Provost, 1973.)
- Technological change may lead to redundancy, so that 'redundant' workers may have time, but no money.
- Rural industrialization leads to a more rigid sexual division of labor (Christine White, 1984).
- Librarians have a warped sense of humor and deliberately hide books from deserving people who are desperately looking for them. This is Laurinda's theory — she's still searching for that crucial reference she lost back in Chapter 8.

If you find that people in one community are obstructing plans to build a school in another community, and you have looked at all the things that have happened in connection with this, you might conclude that they are simply jealous or bad-minded. An old theory of George Foster's (1965), which has been the subject of much contention, as theories should be, might help you to get a new insight. Foster argues that in a small, closed community or situation people view all good things — legacies, good luck, good crops, happiness — as existing in a finite (limited) supply, so if you have more, I have less, and you must have some of my share. Imagine yourself at a meeting in which someone passes around a bag of sweets. This is a limited good as there are only so many in the bag. Originally, the bag contained enough sweets for each person to have two. You are at the back of the room, and by the time the bag reaches you, none are left. What do you conclude? You might try this theory on your community findings. Are people afraid that if the next community gets a school they will never get one for their community?

Looking at this theory again, suppose that one teacher marks students according to what they got on an examination. Let us say a lot of students got almost all the answers right, so they all got high marks. But other teachers grade 'on the curve': 11 per cent get As, 22 per cent get Bs, 33 per cent get Cs, 22 per cent get Ds, and 11 per cent get Fs. Suppose all the students did pretty well, only the highest 11 per cent would get As in this system. (Even if they all did very badly, the top 11 per cent would still get A.)

Suppose you see a lot of tension in a classroom: lack of cooperation among students, who are stealing books and destroying other people's notes, in one school, but not in another. There could be many explanations, but you find the two schools use different grading systems. Does Foster's theory throw any light on what is happening? Or is there a rival explanation? Remember that triangulation — using multiple techniques, sources, and researchers — also includes multiple theories.

A theory will probably send you back to your material looking for things that the theory, if it is useful, will now help you understand. You'll notice that this is an inductive approach. In a deductive approach you start with the theory, convert it into something that you can study, and then see if it holds up in relation to what you found.

Once you start thinking about your findings, you might consult a professional sociologist, psychologist, educator, anthropologist, economist, or expert in another discipline, to see if their fields have any theories that might help you to put your work in a larger context. As you probably know by now, this is an inductive approach to analysis: data first, theory later. Deductive analysis involves putting theory first.

How do you confirm your conclusions? *You* might be convinced by them. As far as you are concerned, any fool could see you were right. But plenty of people who are not fools are going to be asking you some hard questions when they read your results. Would other researchers, working in your situation, come up with the same findings? In other words, are the findings replicable? Are they sound, or valid? Here are some common mistakes or fallacies in research:

- *The ecological fallacy*: collecting information at a higher level and then trying to interpret it at a lower one. For example, you are studying a group of villages in a developing country. The anthropologist H. Russell Bernard explains a problem you could have:

For each village, you have data on such things as the number of people, the average age of men and women, and the monetary value of a list of consumer goods. That is, when you went through each village, you noted how many refrigerators and kerosene lanterns and radios there were, but you do not have these data for each person in the village because you were not interested in that when you designed your study. You were interested in characteristics of villages as units of analysis.

In your analysis, you notice that the villages with the population having the lowest average age also have the highest average dollar value of modern consumer goods. You are tempted to conclude that young people are more interested in (and purchase) modern consumer goods more frequently than older people do. But you might be wrong. Villages with greater employment resources (land and industry) will have lower levels of labor migration by young people. Because more young people stay there, the average age of wealthier villages will be lower. Though everyone wants household consumer goods, only older people can afford them, having had more time to accumulate the funds. It might turn out that the wealthy villages with low average age simply have wealthier older people than villages with higher average age. It is not valid to take data gathered about villages and draw conclusions about villagers (Bernard 1994, pp. 47–48).

Even though this is a survey example, the principle applies to qualitative research, as well.

- *The holistic fallacy*: tidying up your material so that inconvenient bits that don't fit your patterns, groupings, or theories are omitted. Usually this is not deliberate. The human brain, as we said before, tries to put order on chaos.
- *The exotic fallacy*: anything different, unusual, or bizarre (to you) will stand out more, be more likely to be recorded, pondered over, and so on. There is a belief about Ireland, for example, that certain things, usually preposterous ones, 'could only happen in Ireland', like a beggar speaking classical Greek while a professor of Greek is unable to speak a word of it. Visitors, including researchers, are constantly noticing these things, and failing to notice that most beggars know little Latin and less Greek.
- *The going native fallacy*: 'becoming one of the people'. This is the 'my people' syndrome. You lose your perspective, seeing things only the way local people do. You may recall that we discussed this in Chapter

7 along with the next fallacy.

- *The elite fallacy*: talking to the more powerful, more prominent, more educated people and adopting their perspective.

The following sections discuss some ways to try to avoid such fallacies and verify your material.

Checking for bias

You may be biased not only in the people you chose, as we saw in Chapter 7, but in the events and activities that you look at and the perspectives you take.

- *Events, activities*. Is your material representative? Maybe you used a random sample, but the things people talked about were not representative. They may have talked about the ideal instead of the real ('the father of the family makes all the important decisions' may be more of a local ideal than a reality). They may have talked about the most recent events, which stick in their minds, rather than about a pattern over time. They may have talked about the more dramatic rather than the ordinary. In research in Zambia in 1988, one could have concluded that the country was overrun with female pilots. Almost every official who was interviewed listed this as a feasible occupation for girls. There was one, recently appointed, and therefore fresh in everyone's mind.
- *Perspectives*. You may have had a 'blinding light' experience: you had a wonderful idea that can explain everything, and now you see nothing except what it explains. Or you may think people are more concerned about a subject than they actually are: adult education is all they talk about. But adult education is all you talk about. They are just responding.
- *Researchers*. 'Your' community, neighbourhood, or village, if you are studying one, is not a typical community, neighbourhood or village, it's one with a researcher in it. This changes everything. Your job is to figure out what has changed as a result of your presence. Or the reverse may occur: the place you are studying can affect you and you might be seduced into 'going native', or you might conclude, when things get tough, that the local people are engaged in a giant conspiracy to keep you from finding things out, or that people are holding interesting meetings behind your back.

Triangulation

Have you used the right techniques? Did you observe what people did and are now trying to read what people think into your results? Did you use as many techniques as appropriate? Did you use a wide variety of sources, types of people, documents? Did you consult or use other researchers or look at the work of other researchers? If you are aiming at developing theory, did you try various theoretical explanations?

If you are lucky, things fall into place. One approach supports another. If not, you are back (as you might have guessed) to data collection or some other phase of the analysis process. In a study in The Gambia, a map showed, by household, boys and girls who went to school and those who did not. The name of each household was then put on a card and people were asked to sort them into well-being categories. They were then asked to comment, for each category, on the school attendance of its boys and girls. In every category, they overestimated (according to the information they had provided earlier for the map) the number of girls being sent to school, and also said that the poor sent almost no children, boys, or girls. Which of these findings was right, if either? To make matters worse, interviews around the village showed that each village had about 25 per cent of their girls missing from the map. They were not considered to be of school age for a variety of reasons.

Another difference surfaced based on documentary material. An International Labor Organization study (Ahmed and others, 1992, p. xii) had grouped people in the same Gambian community into 'non-poor', 'borderline poor', 'very poor', and 'ultra poor', while the same villagers were calling themselves 'very rich', 'rich', 'in-between', and 'poor'.

In fact, reconciling the material 'factually' was unnecessary. Each piece of information told us something different. Once the 25 per cent of missing girls was put right, the village maps reported the situation 'as it was' in the school; the card sort told us about the way people thought it was, or should be; the International Labor Organization study looked at income and food security; while the villagers looked at a broader conception of security, comfort, and well-being.

Looking at exceptions
What doesn't fit in? What can it tell you? Extreme cases are a form of exception: looking at the poorest, the best students in class, the strongest tutors may give you some insights about the others who don't fall into these categories. When you are using data displays, these may stand out.

Negative cases
Some modes of verification are borrowed directly from quantitative research in the natural sciences: if you read about experiments in Chapter 5, you may recall that you cannot prove a hypothesis, but you can disprove it by getting a result that shows that what you thought was the cause did not produce the effect that you expected. You can do something similar

in qualitative research. Your material suggests a pattern or relationship. Look for negative cases among your interviews, case studies, and observations that don't support it or that contradict it. Can they help you to refine the pattern? Suggest a new one? Or perhaps there are several patterns. Under certain circumstances one thing happens or people behave one way, and under others something else happens. These negative instances may help you to figure out what such circumstances might be. Remember, of course, that there may be no pattern. You just imposed one on the material.

Ruling out spurious relationships

We have discussed spurious relationships before: A and B are related, but a third factor causes both of them. Children in many Western countries used to be told that the stork brought them. In places that have storks, a correlation does appear to exist between the numbers of storks and the numbers of human births: when one rises, so does the other, so they co-vary. And let us say that the number of storks rises before the number of human births does, so we have the right time order. So do storks cause babies? Maybe a third thing caused both, such as the right ecological conditions. Maybe in bountiful times, people not only survive and have the right circumstances for reproducing, as do storks, but perhaps now people don't need to eat storks.

In qualitative research you have to work these things out for yourself. Look at other cases, other instances, other groups or communities, where the two things don't go together (negative cases) or where they do, but some other evidence might suggest what the connection is. Or do a thought experiment. As a result of research which you are doing, you think that shops that have owner-managers have better interpersonal relationships with customers than shops where managers have been specially hired to do the job. 'If I were able to give all managers that sense of ownership, would it lead to better customer relations?' But maybe owner-managers tend to have small, less impersonal shops or serve specific neighborhoods or cater to a particular clientele, and one or more of those factors is why they have better relationships with customers.

Or in schools with good sports facilities, the children do well at their studies. Maybe sports relieve tension, increase teamwork. 'If I were able to provide a sports program in other schools, would the children's academic performance rise?' Maybe wealth is the cause of both: schools with sports programs also have better learning facilities, attract better teachers, and so on.

Within a particular adult education center, students who do badly at self-development courses also do badly at language classes. 'If I could improve one, would the other improve?' Think again. Maybe the students are just tired.

Checking rival explanations

Thinking about these things might lead you to look for other explanations — larger ones, as in the examples above, or just different ones. Much of the advice given so far can help you to identify rival explanations — negative instances may suggest them. Ask colleagues for ideas. Try your ideas out on local people and see if they have other explanations. But now is really not the time; you should have been thinking of rival explanations all the way through your research. If you have not and you are trying to check some now, this takes you back to — guess where — more data collection.

Replicating evidence

Would someone who repeated your study find what you did? Would you? We are not talking here about precision, coming up with the same numbers, for example, but coming up with the same patterns, relationships, and conclusions. You can try to replicate your findings by looking at some new instances: another neighbourhood, another tower block, another set of grandmothers. Does your idea explain what is happening there, does the pattern hold true? (Of course, some things are true only for the particular place or people studied, but you can still try to check your findings against new examples in this place or with these people.) Checking for replication calls for some ruthlessness on your part; by now your findings are almost as close to your heart as your own child. Picture your worst enemy. If you are lucky enough not to have any enemies, make one up. This person is going to do your study over again, trying to prove you wrong. Where will the weaknesses be? Look at them again.

Finally, sharing your ideas with the people who participated in your study is one of the most powerful ways of verifying conclusions. As you get ideas, make connections, see patterns, ask people: 'Does it ring true?' Do they know of cases where your pattern does not hold? Can they identify people, situations, or places you should look at that would confirm your results or change your mind? Have they got better ideas?

No-one follows all these procedures. Sometimes, some of them can't be used. There is also a practical element: you want to finish your study in your lifetime. In situations where urgent action is needed, you want to finish it a lot faster. The non-literate teenagers in your study have grown into adults, and you continue to mess around with variables while they still can't read and write. But using as many procedures as you can, like any form of triangulation, strengthens your research, and knowing that good research should meet these standards helps keep you from going off the straight and narrow while you are collecting the information and analyzing it.

Computer Programs for Qualitative Analysis

Computer programs, such as LISPQUAL, QUALPRO, ETHNOGRAPH, KWALITAN, CODETEXT, NUD*IST, and SYSSTAT, are available for analyzing certain kinds of qualitative data (see Pfaffenberger, 1988; Weitzman and Miles, 1995). These can help you to code, search for, and retrieve material, use networks, create matrices, and build theory. Some are more complicated than others, some have more features. See Miles and Huberman (1984, pp. 311–317) for an assessment of 22 programs and addresses where you can get them.

What Next?

Now that you have all of your material organized, how do you put it together to produce a report or study?

Shar, back from her African trip, is facing this problem right now. You may recall from Chapter 11 that she organized some focus groups to help Kensington residents such as Dr. Dermot O'Connor deal with the loud noise from nearby restaurants, and to help the restaurant owners deal with the ensuing noise from Dr. O'Connor. Dermot is delighted with the successful outcome of the focus groups, and Shar now wants to prepare a written report on her study and publish it. Fame beckons. She bursts in on Dr. O'Connor, who is having tea with an old friend, George.

'Rather inchoate,' says George, after leafing through the first several hundred pages. 'What you require is a form.' He outlines an hourglass with his hands.
'Here, you,' says Shar. 'I'll have you up. There's a name for the likes of you.'
'No, no, my dear, I simply meant that a good report often takes the shape of an hourglass.'
'Shar, dearest one,' said Dermot. 'Calm yourself. George is a distinguished Professor of Classics. Honorary librarian of the Academy. Author of many inscrutable works of scholarship. Not, of course, that that is any guarantee these days. Sharon, Professor George Darwin. George, Sharon Darwin.'
'Did your grandad have something to do with monkeys?' asks Shar.
'Something like that,' says George. 'Did yours?'

If you have some numbers in your report which need to be analyzed, read Chapter 17. If not, go to Chapter 18, and learn more about the hourglass model and how to shape your report.

References and further readings

Ahmed, Iqbal, Arne Bigsten, Jorge A. Munoz, and Prem Vashishtha. 1992. *Poverty in The Gambia*. Geneva: International Labour Organisation.

Berlin, B., P. Kay, and W. Merrifield. 1985. 'Color Term Evolution.' Presented at the annual meeting of the American Anthropological Association.

Bernard, H. Russell. 1994. *Research Methods in Cultural Anthropology*. Newbury Park, California: Sage.

Caracelli, Valerie J. and Jennifer C. Greene. 1993. 'Data Analysis Strategies for Mixed Method Evaluation Designs.' *Educational Evaluation and Policy Analysis* 15(2):195–207.

Carspecken, Phil Francis and Michael Apple. 1992. 'Critical Qualitative Research: Theory, Methodology and Practice.' In Margaret D. LeCompte, Wendy L. Millroy, and Judith Preissle, eds., *The Handbook of Qualitative Research in Education*. San Diego, California; London; Tokyo: Academic Press.

Eisenhart, Margaret A. and Kenneth R. Howe. 1992. 'Validity in Educational Research.' In Margaret D. LeCompte, Wendy L. Millroy, and Judith Preissle, eds., *The Handbook of Qualitative Research in Education*. San Diego, California; London; Tokyo: Academic Press.

Eisner, E. 1991. *The Enlightened Eye: Qualitative Inquiry and the Enhancement of Educational Practice*. New York: Macmillan.

Foster, George. 1965. 'Peasant Society and the Image of the Limited Good.' *American Anthropologist*.

Geertz, Clifford. 1973. *The Interpretation of Cultures: Selected Essays*. New York: Basic Books.

Glaser, B.G. and A.L. Strauss. 1976. *The Discovery of Grounded Theory: Strategies for Qualitative Research*. Chicago: Aldine.

Guba, Egon G. and Yvonna S. Lincoln. 1989. *Fourth Generation Evaluation*. Newbury Park, California: Sage.

Miles, Matthew B. and A. Michael Huberman. 1994. *Qualitative Data Analysis: An Expanded Sourcebook*. Thousand Oaks, California; London; New Delhi: Sage.

Murdock, G.P. and C. Provost. 1973. 'Factors in the Division of Labor by Sex.' *Ethnology* 12(2):203–225.

Patton, Michael Quinn. 1990. *Qualitative Evaluation and Research Methods*. Newbury Park, California: Sage.

Pelto, P. and G. Pelto. 1978. *Anthropological Research: The Structure of Inquiry*. Cambridge, U.K.: Cambridge University Press.

Pfaffenberger, Bryan. 1988. *Microcomputer Applications in Qualitative Research*.

Newbury Park, California: Sage.

Pittman, Mary Anne and Joseph A. Maxwell. 1992. 'Qualitative Approaches to Evaluation: Models and Methods.' In Margaret D. LeCompte, Wendy L. Millroy, and Judith Preissle, eds., *The Handbook of Qualitative Research in Education*. San Diego, California; London; Tokyo: Academic Press.

Sechrest, Lee. 1992. 'Roots: Back to Our First Generations.' *Evaluation Practice* 13(1):1–7.

White, Martin King. 1980. *The Status of Women in Pre-Industrial Societies*. Princeton, New Jersey: Princeton University Press.

Park, Robert 1928. 'The Bases for Race Prejudice.' *The Annals* 140:11-20.

Spradley, James P. 1979. *The Ethnographic Interview*. New York: Holt, Rinehart and Winston.

Strauss. A. and J. Corbin. 1990. *Basics of Qualitative Research: Grounded Theory Procedures and Techniques*. Newbury Park, California: Sage.

Weitzman, Eben A. and Matthew M. Miles. 1995. *Computer Programs for Qualitative Data Analysis*. Thousand Oaks, California: Sage.

White, Benjamin. 1984. 'Measuring Time Allocation, Decision-Making and Agrarian Changes Affecting Rural Women: Examples from Recent Research in Indonesia.' *IDS Bulletin* 15(1):1–5.

Wolcott, Harry F. 1994. *Transforming Qualitative Data: Description, Analysis, Interpretation*. Thousand Oaks, California: Sage.

Youth nuisance

The Towers has seen a resurgence of juvenile yobbos breaking lights, painting graffiti and being cheeky to the elderly.

In the latest incident, Mrs. Parveen Rashid reports that her upper plate was lifted when she removed it to play bingo in the Comm-unity Room last night. 'After I lost the lower plate during the recent unpleasantness at the Grannies' Club, it is easier to shout out during the bingo if I wear no teeth at all.'

Now Mrs. Rashid has received an anonymous ransom note, signed 'The Fang', demanding 50 quid for their return.

Asked if she was frightened by the note, Mrs. Rashid said 'Note, smote, I would not pay tuppence three farth-ings for them now. God knows who's been wearing them since.'

Letters on Sir Evelyn's plans for the Towers

In our October 26 issue, we reported that Sir Evelyn Pettigrew, chair of the British Heritage Council, has recommend-ed that Hancock Towers be preserved as an 'excellent represent-ation of 1960s British architecture. They are a magnificent pair,' he said. We asked for your responses, and here are some:

'I invite the Sir to make a State Visit to my lav. There is no hot water and when next door flushes their loo it comes up in my bath.'

'It's a pity we working class don't stand up for our building rather than rely on toffee-nosed twats. I propose the Association erect a monster sign on the roof saying hancock towers: if you lived here you'd be home now. Show our pride, like.'

'It's all very well to say my lav goes into next door's bath. His flushes into my kitchen. I got three goldfish the other day.'

'I like Hancock Towers just as it is. If I hear another word about all this, my next letter shall contain details of frequent visits by a dignitary to a married lady on my floor when her husband is working. A "magnificent pair", in-deed!'

17 ANALYZING YOUR QUANTITATIVE INFORMATION
by Richard Scaglion[1]

Summary

This chapter discusses statistics that are appropriate for analyzing samples, although some can be used for universes or populations as well. A number of computer programs are available to make your analysis much easier, but you can also do statistical calculations by hand.

Univariate analysis involves analyzing one variable at a time.

Frequency distributions show the numbers and percentages of people or items that fall into different categories.

Categories can be *nominal*, *ordinal*, *interval*, or *ratio*.

The *mean*, *median*, and *mode* are measures of central tendency, that is, different ways of finding a 'middle point'.

The *standard deviation* tells you to what extent your data are spread out or clumped around the mean.

Indices of *skewness* and *kurtosis* tell you what your information would look like if plotted on a graph.

[1]Richard Scaglion is professor of anthropology at the University of Pittsburgh

Bivariate analysis helps you to understand association and correlation between two variables.

Tests of *association* show how likely it is that a relationship between variables in your study is due merely to chance.

Statisticians have established *levels of significance* to help interpret tests of associations between variables in your study.

Statistics for computing the probability of the difference between what you found and what might be expected by chance are available. *Chi square tests* are appropriate for nominal data. Other tests are available for ordinal, interval, and ratio data.

Measures of *correlation* examine the strength of an association between two variables. The *phi coefficient* and *Cramer's V* are two such measures. Correlation does not prove causation, however. Just because two things go together does not mean that one causes the other.

Multivariate analysis explores relationships among a number of variables.

You will need all your strength for this chapter. One way to read it is to go through it for a basic understanding, and then come back to relevant parts when you are doing your analysis. Another is to put your hands over your face and read it between your fingers.

Here we show you another way of tackling Step 12 (Box 3–1): analyzing the results. No matter how you have organized your data, remember that, like the write-up, data analysis is simply telling a story. You start out with a general description or idea of what you have observed. You then go into more detail, giving examples to illustrate your points. At the conclusion, you summarize your main findings. In a purely qualitative study, you would do these things using words alone. The evidence you would give to support your observations would be in the form of statements and illustrative descriptions. By adding quantitative data, however, you can provide more support for your conclusions.

Think about the following statements: 'Many older people in the Towers are concerned about security,' and 'More girls than boys pass the mathematics paper in the final examination.' What exactly did the authors of these statements mean by many and more? What is the basis for their statements? Is it intuition, observation, or what? Would we share their opinions? Suppose the first sentence read: 'Out of 100 older people, 25 said security was their biggest worry.' In this case, one might not consider 25 of 100 people to be many, But what if the sentence had read: 'Out of the 100 older people, 93 said security was their biggest worry'? This is much more convincing — the reader is more likely to believe that many older people really are worried about security.

Don't think of quantitative analysis as a mysterious process in which numbers are fed into a machine that digests the information, analyzes it for you, and spews forth numbers that are incomprehensible to the average person. You do the analysis. Even if you use a computer, it only does what you tell it to do. Basically, the computer is a counting device that saves you the time and trouble of counting yourself. However, you do not have to have a computer. In the examples above, you could count up the older people that you interviewed and sort them into those who were concerned about security and those who were not. Similarly, you could count up the number of children who pass the mathematics paper in the final examination and sort them by sex. However, when you have many variables, sorting all these data into so many categories by hand becomes tedious. Of course, this is what researchers did before computers were invented, and you can do it now if necessary.

We need to ask many questions in the two examples cited. What is the general rate of concern among older people in the community that we studied? Why are some people concerned and others not? What factors are associated with girls' better performance on the mathematics paper? Is it because they are getting extra classes, or have new gender sensitive textbooks, or spend more time studying, or because of some combination of these factors? The computer helps us to look at all these relationships and more. Whether it is done by computer or by hand, quantitative analysis helps us to be more precise in our descriptions.

In reading this chapter, you should be aware of a distinction that statisticians make between a *sample*, on the one hand, and a *universe* or complete *population* of people or items, on the other. We have already mentioned this in Chapter 6, as part of our discussion of sampling. This chapter is written from the perspective of analyzing a sample, because most of our data involve samples. If you are working with a universe, you should be careful because certain quantitative measures such as the standard deviation have slightly different formulas depending on whether a sample or a universe is being described.

Generally speaking, investigators use the *statistical tests of association* (listed later in the chapter) to draw conclusions from a sample only, although many of the other quantitative measures described in this chapter, such as the *measures of central tendency* and *dispersion*, are useful ways of expressing results whether they have been derived from a sample or from a complete population. If you are working with a universe, you might want to consult a standard statistics text such as one of those listed at the end of this chapter.

One of the concerns of parents in Hancock Towers is that their children are being exposed to drugs. This is a serious enough worry with teenagers, but now even children as young as five years old are hearing about drugs from their friends and classmates. Parents would like to develop some programs to help deal with this, and they have decided to do a survey of all Tower residents who have children between 5 and 17 years old. They want to know how many children there are, their ages, what concerns they have, who might be able to help them, etc. In this chapter, we will work with them to see how we can use quantitative analysis to get a picture of what is going on.

Univariate Analysis: Frequency Distributions

Suppose we have planned your study, collected your data, and coded it for analysis as we described in Chapter 9. What do we do next? The first step is to get an overall idea of what is happening. We should look at each variable in turn to see how it is distributed. The researcher-parents in the Towers will be looking, among other things, at the children's ages, what schools they attend, and the language spoken in their homes. They may also want to know the marital status of the parents, their occupations, and their levels of education. Each of these is a variable. We want to find out how many people or things in our sample fall into each category of each variable. For example, how many children are in state schools, how many in private schools, and how many have left school altogether? This type of analysis is called a *frequency distribution*, because we want to know about the distribution of each variable, that is, how many children fall into each category of our variable 'type of school'. It is also called *univariate analysis* because we are looking at only one variable, in this case, what type of school, if any, the child is attending.

When we do a study, some of your data will fall into *non-numerical* categories: marital status, ethnic group, and sex are variables of this type. Other data will be *numerical*: age, number of years of school attended, examination scores, weight, height, and so on. In the non-numerical or grouped data, categories should be exhaustive (everything fits into some category) and mutually exclusive (nothing fits into more than one category). In some cases, the categories fit into some sort of order (primary education, secondary, third level), and in some cases they do not (like single, widowed, married, divorced). When there is no inherent rank ordering of categories, that is, where each category is on the same level, we call the data *nominal*. An example is color. We cannot say that red is 'higher' or 'above' green, they are simply different things. *Ordinal* data are similar to nominal data, except that ranking is present. We know that cool is below hot on a temperature scale. Number-based scales form *interval* data. Here we know more than a rough ordering, we know how much higher or lower one number is than another. In the temperature scale, for example, we know that fifteen is five degrees lower than twenty. We can perform numerical computations with interval scales. We can say, for example, that five degrees plus five degrees is equal to ten degrees. We cannot do that with ordinal data: saying that cold plus cool equals hot is absurd. Yet researchers sometimes make such statements.

People who use computers a lot use an abbreviation to describe what happens when one is not careful with data analysis: GIGO, or garbage in, garbage out. Consider an occupational status code like the following:

Unemployed	1
Self-employed	2
Employee	3
Working at home	4

Now suppose that the researcher-parents, as part of their survey, asked about the occupational status of the parents of these children. If we looked at the distribution of this variable it would look something like Table 17–1.

Table 17–1 Occupational status of parents

Category	Code	No. of parents
Unemployed	1	10
Employee	2	20
Self-employed	3	10
Working at home	4	10
	Total	50

We could ask the computer to find the average of the variable occupational status. It would compute the *mean* or average using the code numbers we have given it, and would find a mean of 2.5. Does this mean that the average parent of a child in our study is halfway between being an employee and self-employed? Of course not. This is an example of GIGO. We gave the computer meaningless data and we received meaningless results.

However, suppose we still want some sort of measure of where the average school child's parent stands in terms of occupational status. Statisticians call such indices *measures of central tendency*. Table 17–1 contains nominal data, and the measure of central tendency most commonly used for such data, called the *mode*, is rather obvious: it is simply the most common category. Here the mode is 2, because more parents fall into this category than into any other single category.

Suppose we asked the parents about their level of education, and produced the frequency distribution (for ordinal data) shown in Table 17–2.

Table 17–2 Level of schooling

Category	Code	No. of parents
Primary school	1	25
Middle school	2	19
Second level	3	10
Third level	4	6
	Total	60

Again, the mean or average is meaningless. The mode or most common category is primary education. For ordinal data like this we have an additional measure of central tendency: the *median* or middle value. For ordinal categories, the median category is the category at the half-way point. In the example in Table 17–2 we have a total of 60 parents. Half of this number is 30. There are 25 in the first category and 19 in the second, making a total of 44 who have a middle school education or less. The midway point has been passed; thus, middle school is the median category, and is a good measure of central tendency for this sample.

What about interval data? What measure of central tendency should we use? Actually we can use all three we have mentioned, although the mean is usually the most efficient. Consider Table 17–3.

If we multiply each age by the number of children who are that age, repeat the process for each age, add up the results, and divide by 129, we will get the mean, which is 10.3. The mode, or most common category, is ten, and the median age is also ten. All these measures of central tendency show that the average child is around ten. Which is the best measure? The mean is a little high because of a few older children, but all are fairly close. We could report any or all of these measures.

You may have noticed that for the nominal (occupational status) and ordinal (levels of schooling) data, the tables were interesting and useful, but

Table 17–3 Ages of children

Age	No. of children	
5	6	30
6	8	48
7	10	70
8	12	96
9	15	135
10	17	170
11	16	176
12	14	168
13	11	143
14	9	126
15	6	90
16	2	32
17	3	51
Total	**129**	**1335**

the measures of central tendency were not so revealing. For the interval data, the table was rather long, and we really would not have had to look at all the numbers. We could have just looked at the measures of central tendency. This is because for interval measures we can summarize our findings using descriptive statistics, that is, statistics that describe how the variable is distributed.

As you can see, measures of central tendency give us some idea of where the mid-point or 'average' of the sample lies. However, that is not enough. What do the rest of the data look like? For example, in Table 17–3, we can see that the data are clumped around nine, ten, and eleven, but a little bit spread out for the older children. In other words, most of the data are fairly close to the mean. The standard deviation is a measure that will help us to get a picture of the closeness or distance of the data from the mean. It tells us how far from the mean the data are dispersed.

To get a better picture of the standard deviation, and of some terms that will be introduced later in the chapter, look at a *normal curve of distribution*, shown in Figure 17–1. In this curve, the mean, the median, and the mode coincide. The central axis is marked XY. Notice that there are two points where the curve changes from concave to convex. These are called *points of inflection*. If you drop a line from these points to the baseline, you will have one unit of distance, or one standard deviation on either side of the central axis or mean. On a normal curve, 68.26 per cent, or a little more than two-thirds of all the children would fall into these two

Box 17–1 How to read a statistical formula

A formula is a set of instructions, written in shorthand. Here are a few pointers to help you read a formula.

First, you will often see letters such as x, y, and z. These stand for the variables. The symbol Σ tells you to sum up something. As in basic arithmetic, the symbol $+$ tells you to add, $-$ tells you to subtract. However, the symbol for multiplying, x, is usually not used. Instead, you will see instructions such as 'xy', which mean that you should multiply the value of your variable x by the value of your variable y. To show that you should divide, a slash (/) or a horizontal line — is used instead of $\div$.

In some formulas you must square your number (x^2) or multiply it by itself (9^2 is 81). In other cases you must take the square root ($\sqrt{}$) of your number or find the number which, multiplied by itself, yields your number. The square root of eighty-one ($\sqrt{81}$) is 9. When you see 'n' in a formula, it refers to the number of cases you are dealing with, for example, the number of children in Hancock Towers. A bar over a symbol refers to the mean of whatever the symbol stands for. If 'x' refers to children's ages, then a barred x ($\bar{x}$) tells you to get the mean of their ages.

The formula is usually written in a way that tells you the order in which you should perform the calculations. For example

$$\frac{x}{y} + 3$$

means divide x by y, then add 3.
If the formula says

$$\frac{x+3}{y}$$

add 3 to x, and then divide by y.
If the formula is not clear, do your multiplication and division first, then your addition and subtraction.
If the formula contains brackets ( ), do the work inside the brackets first. For example,

$$x - (y + z)$$

tells you to add y and z, then subtract from x.
Here is the formula for calculating the mean. The procedure for calculating chi square (χ^2) is shown later. The mean:

$$\bar{x} = \frac{\Sigma x}{n}$$

con't.

Let us say we are looking for the average work hours of four mothers:

	Hours worked
Mother A	8
Mother B	6
Mother C	4
Mother D	6

This formula says, 'To get the mean ($\bar{x}$), add together (Σ) all the values of the variable x (hours worked) and divide by the number of cases (four mothers).' So we have:

$$\bar{x} = \frac{8+6+4+6}{4} = 6$$

The example of children's ages in Table 17–3 will require an additional procedure. We have a number of children in each age group, so we must multiply the number of children by the age in each category, add them all, and then divide by the total number of children, in this case 129.

central areas, that is, between −1 and +1. If you move out two standard deviations from the mean, between −2 and +2, you will expect to find 95.74 per cent of all the children. Between −3 and +3, you will find 99.74 per cent of all the children.

Figure 17–1 Points of Inflection and standard deviation

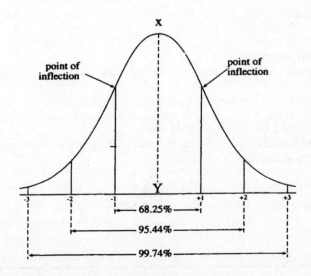

Table 17–4 Standard deviations for three groups with the same mean

from Tower W	Children's ages from Tower X	from Tower Y
10	8	6
10	8	6
10	9	9
10	9	9
10	10	9
10	10	10
10	11	10
10	12	10
10	13	18
S = 0	S = 1.54	S = 3.3

The greater the standard deviation for a group of figures, the more spread out or dispersed the figures are. Table 17–4 shows distributions of ages for three groups of children whose mean average age, ten, is the same. However, standard deviations for the groups show that they are dispersed differently.

In each group the mean is ten, and in Tower W so are the median and the mode. The ages of the children from Tower W show no variation at all, so the standard deviation is zero. (If someone told you that the mean was ten and the standard deviation was zero, you would know the distribution automatically.) Children from Tower X have more variation and, as a consequence, a greater standard deviation, 1.54. Children from Tower Y are unusual in that although the figures cluster together, a few extreme cases cause the standard deviation to be much higher, 3.3.

Computing the standard deviation

Now let's compute the standard deviation. Because we are interested in how far each number (or *variate,* since we are looking at how much they vary from the mean) is from the mean, we must first compute the mean, which is simply the average of the numbers. We have already calculated the mean age to be 10.3 years. We then find the difference between each variate and the mean to get an idea of how far apart they are. For example, an age of 11 is close to the mean (a difference of only 0.7), whereas an age of 15 is far from the mean (a difference of 4.7). If you subtracted the mean from each variate, you would get some negative numbers, for example, $7 - 10.3 = -3.3$, and some positive numbers, for instance, $15 - 10.3 = +4.7$. We would like to add up all the differences between variates and the mean to get an idea of the total amount of dispersion, but the combination of the negative and positive numbers would cause the total to be around zero. To eliminate this problem, statisticians square the differences (multiply each difference by itself) to eliminate the negative signs, and then they add them up. But one problem remains: the bigger the sample, the bigger this sum will be. If we had twice as many children in our study and the sample were to be distributed in exactly the same way, this sum would be twice as big, even though the sample would not be spread out any more than before. To eliminate this problem, we divide the total sum by the sample size (actually, the sample size minus one, for reasons that are not important to this discussion). In mathematical notation, the formula discussed above is as follows:

$$S^2 = \frac{\sum_{i=1}^{n} (x_i - \bar{x})}{n-1}$$

where S^2 is the square of the standard deviation, $\sum_{i=1}^{n}$ is the sum of the quantities, x_i is each variate, $\bar{x}$ is the mean, and n is the size of the sample.

This formula says exactly what we said in words. You read it from the inside out. (For help with how to read formulas see Box 17–1.)

You have already calculated the mean. Now:

1. take each variate and subtract the mean from it
2. square the result
3. add up all the results
4. divide by the sample size, minus one

You may have wondered why the above formula gave the square of the standard deviation and not the standard deviation itself. This is because the square of the standard deviation is a useful *measure of dispersion* (a measure of how spread out the data are) called the *variance*.

Doing the complete calculations for the ages of all 129 children from Tower X would take a lot of space. Although it is easy to do, it becomes rather repetitive. So for purposes of illustration let us compute the standard deviation of a sub-sample of only five of these children, randomly chosen from the rest (Table 17–5). If we were really doing this study, of course, we would use all 129 children. We will see that the mean and standard deviation of the sub-sample will turn out to be different from those of the whole sample.

Of course, we are working with only five children in order to illustrate the process. When we do the calculations for all 129 (Table 17.3) we will find that roughly two thirds of all the cases in our sample of children from Tower X fall within one standard deviation (plus or minus) of the mean. For the data in Table 17.3, the standard deviation is 2.9. Thus, about two thirds of the children are between 7.4 and 13.2 (10.3+ or −2.9).

Table 17–5 Computations for standard deviation

Age	Mean	x_i-x	$(x_i-x)^2$
8	10.2	−2.2	4.8
10	10.2	−0.2	0
11	10.2	0.8	0.6
9	10.2	−1.2	1.4
13	10.2	2.8	7.8
			14.6

$S^2 = 14.6/(5-1) = 3.6$
$S = \sqrt{S^2} = \sqrt{3.6} = 1.9$

There are many other descriptive statistics, each of which has a particular purpose. The intent of this chapter is not to teach you how to compute all of these, but to give you some appreciation of the more commonly used statistics and why we use them. So it is really enough for us to know that the standard deviation is another measure of dispersion, or indication of how spread out the data are. Just by inspection, we can see that the sub-sample of children's ages that we analyzed in Table 17–4 is less spread out than the full sample in Table 17–3. The sub-sample contains no very young or very old children. Thus, although the means are similar, the standard deviation of the sub-sample is less than that of the whole sample.

Some tools for univariate analysis

Keep in mind that our overall purpose is to look at (or describe) the distribution of each of our variables. The most efficient way to accomplish this is to have a computer do it for us. Many computer programs are available to accomplish all sorts of research tasks. Most of these programs have been put together in software packages so that you do not have to do any computer programming or calculations yourself. You have only to define your variables and the categories for each variable, then tell the computer what general sort of analysis you want it to do. You may not have access to a computer, but understanding what the results of a computer analysis look like is still important, so that you will be able to read and interpret them if you come across them in other studies.

Perhaps the most commonly used software package is the Statistical Package for the Social Sciences (SPSS). Researchers who want to use SPSS to do univariate distribution analysis of the sort we have been discussing generally use two routines: *frequencies* and *descriptive statistics*. The first is particularly useful for nominal and ordinal data, the second for interval data. If we had used the frequencies routine to analyze the marital status data for the parents of a sub-sample of children in our survey, our results would resemble those set out in Table 17–6.

Table 17–6 Marital status

Category label	Code	Absolute frequency	Relative frequency (%)	Adjusted frequency (%)	Cumulative frequency (%)
Single	1	11	21.6	22	22
Married	2	28	54.9	56	78
Divorced	3	7	13.7	14	92
Widowed	4	4	7.8	8	100
	0	1	2	Missing	100
Total		51	100	100	

One missing case has been included here to illustrate how such data are handled. A missing case would occur if, for example, an interviewee declined to give her marital status.

The category label has been defined for the computer, as has the code number. The *absolute frequency* gives the number of people in each category. The *relative frequency,* expressed here as a percentage, is simply the percentage each category forms of the total sample (where missing data are included in the total). The *adjusted frequency* is a similar percentage, except that here missing data are excluded from the calculations. The *cumulative frequency* adds succeeding categories of adjusted frequencies. In Table 17–6, for example, 78 per cent of the sample for whom data exist are either single or married. Cumulative frequencies are sometimes useful for ordinal data. For example, if we had a frequencies table for the ordinal variable of level of education desired discussed earlier (Table 17–2), we could use the cumulative frequencies to show the increasing number of parents whose education occurred at a particular level or lower. We could say that for this sample 90 per cent had no more than a secondary level education.

In our final report we would not want to include tables showing the distribution of every variable, but would select only those that were most important. Similarly, we would not want to list all the percentages that the computer calculated for us, but only those that were critical for supporting our main findings. One of the problems facing social researchers who use computer analysis is to sort through the massive amount of information generated and select the most important to report. If you are doing your calculations by hand, you merely concentrate on the most important variables from the beginning.

Software packages like SPSS generate statistics that experts in the social sciences have found extremely useful. The descriptive statistics routine of SPSS, for example, can be used to analyze interval variables. No tables are produced because, as we have seen, these are not really useful for interval variables. Instead, a list of descriptive statistics is produced. If we used SPSS to analyze the data in Table 17–3, we might get something like Table 17–7.

Table 17–7 Ages of children in Hancock Towers

Mean	10.349	Std err (standard error)	0.258	Median	10
Mode	10	Std dev (standard deviation)	2.9306	Variance	8.5884
Kurtosis	-0.6074	Skewness	0.12873	Range	12
Minimum	5	Maximum	17		
Valid cases	129	Missing cases	0		

Each statistic in Table 17–7 has a particular purpose. Each tells something about the distribution of the variable 'ages of children in Hancock Towers'. First are the measures of central tendency, the mean, the mode, and the median. These give us some idea of the average age of these children, which we saw previously was around ten years. The standard deviation and variance, as measures of dispersion, tell us how spread out the data are. We have already noted that about two-thirds of the children are between 8.3 and 12.1 years old (one standard deviation or about 1.9 years either side of the mean, which is about 10.2 years). The *minimum, maximum,* and *range* simply indicate the youngest and oldest children and the difference between them. The standard error is useful for certain statistical tests that need not concern us here.

Skewness and *kurtosis* are two useful indices that provide information about the shape of the distribution of the variable 'ages of children in Hancock Towers'. For certain statistical tests, we are concerned that the distribution of the variable be reasonably normal. By this we mean that we expect most cases to be fairly close to the mean, with fewer and fewer cases the further we go from the mean. Thus, we would expect most children to be about ten years of age and somewhat fewer to be nine, even fewer to be eight, and going in the other direction, somewhat fewer to be eleven, fewer still to be twelve, and so on. When we plot the normal situation (what we would expect) on a graph, the shape resembles a bell, as was shown in Table 17–1. Many statistical tests require that the distribution of a variable be approximately this shape for the test to be valid. Indices of skewness and kurtosis tell us about the shape of our variable's distribution.

Skewness is a measure of symmetry that indicates how lop-sided the distribution of our variable is. The normal curve has a skewness index of zero, because it is perfectly symmetrical. However, positive skewness indicates that the 'hump' in our shape is not in the center, but to the left of center: the cases are clustered to the left (below) the mean, with extreme values found mostly to the right. Consider the distribution of the variable 'ages of children in Hancock Towers' presented in Table 17–3. This distribution would have a slightly positive index of skewness (the actual index is about +0.13) because the clustering is to the left and most of the extreme values (older children) are to the right of the mean. The higher the index of skewness, the more lop-sided the distribution. Negative skewness indicates that the distribution is skewed in the opposite direction, with cases clustered to the right of the mean and most extreme values to the left.

Figure 17–2 Skewed distributions

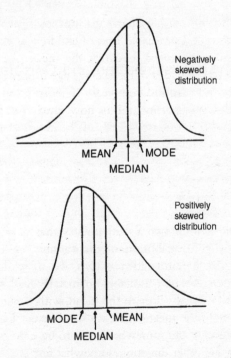

Suppose that in Table 17–3 most of the children were clustered in the older range, with only a few extreme cases below the mean. Our 'hump' would appear at the right of our shape, indicating negative skewness. Figure 17–2 shows how negatively and positively shaped distributions look.

Kurtosis is a measure of how narrow or flat the distribution is. Is our hump shaped like a bell, a finger, or a plateau? Again the normal curve has a kurtosis of zero. A positive index of kurtosis indicates that the distribution is narrower than the normal curve. Such a curve would look tall, thin, and finger-like compared to the bell-shaped curve. A negative index of kurtosis would mean that the curve would look somewhat flat, with no sharp peak. A positive index indicates a narrow curve. The greater the index, the narrower the curve.

As you can see, the various statistics help describe how interval variables are distributed. They provide the statistician with a sort of shorthand in which a quick scanning can convey quite a lot of information and eliminate the need to plot most variables. So long as the variables are reasonably normally distributed, with indices of kurtosis and skewness near zero, relatively small standard deviation, and measures of central tendency that are relatively similar, the researcher can confidently proceed with further analysis. If any of these statistics seems to be very different from what you expected, you can use the tables provided by the frequencies program to provide additional information about the distribution of the variable in question.

Bivariate Analysis: Association and Correlation

You now have a basic description of your data. This was the purpose of our univariate or distribution analysis.

Let us look at what this kind of description tells us. Perhaps we are doing a survey of the area of London in which Hancock Towers is located. We are interested in people's social needs. Are they getting the services they require? Are the services being sufficiently responsive to changing needs? We have collected information on level of education, unemployment, drug use, criminal conviction rate, single parents, older people living alone, and a number of other urban issues. We know how many of our sample of people or things fall into each category of each variable, and we know something about what the average person or thing is like. This will help us to describe our sample. For example, we should now be able to give a clear picture of the population in our study. We know, for instance, how many young people are unemployed, what percentage of these are males/females, how many people have been convicted of crimes, how these are distributed by ethnic group, and so on.

Now we want to carry this analysis one step further. We want to learn about the relationship between two variables. Suppose there is a common belief that people who live in Hancock Towers have a higher criminal conviction rate than those who live in neighboring more affluent communities, such as the grander areas of Kensington, or a new luxury 'gated' residential area, Stockbroker Pastures. Your study includes all three geographical areas. We know that a number of people in Hancock Towers have been convicted of crimes. Are the two connected? That is, if you are living in Hancock Towers and are arrested for a crime, is it more likely that you will actually be convicted than someone living in Kensington or Stockbroker Pastures would be? To answer these types of questions we need to do a *bivariate* analysis, or an analysis of the relationship between two variables.

Table 17–8 Criminal conviction rate in three areas in London

Convicted?	Hancock Towers	Kensington	Stockbroker Pastures	Total
No	33	75	12	120
Yes	33	72	13	118
	66	147	25	238

Once again we need to consider the level (nominal, ordinal, or interval) of the data. Let's say we would like to examine the relationship between conviction rate and area of residence. We can draw a sample of arrest records, examine whether the individual who was arrested was convicted or not, and then correlate this with the area of residence. The variable 'convicted or not' and the variable 'residence' are both nominal variables. To look at this relationship, we need to construct a table with the categories of one of the variables along one axis and the categories of the other variable along the other axis. Such a table is called a *contingency table*. If we actually did such an analysis of the area, we might use hand tallies to construct a contingency table as shown in Table 17–8.

An examination of Table 17–8 does not seem to show much of a relationship between the likelihood of conviction (after being arrested) and area of residence. This distribution is about what we would expect by chance. Contrast Table 17–8 with Table 17–9.

Table 17–9 Criminal conviction rate in three areas in London

Convicted?	Hancock Towers	Kensington	Stockbroker Pastures	Total
No	25	75	20	120
Yes	43	62	13	118
	68	137	33	238

Table 17–9 seems to show some relationship between the variables in

question: for people who have been arrested, more of those from Hancock Towers seem to be convicted than do those from, say, Stockbroker Pastures. One could imagine a situation in which the conviction rate imbalance was even greater than this — a situation in which virtually all those Hancock Towers residents who were arrested were ultimately convicted, for example. Obviously there is some sort of a continuum between what we would expect purely by chance and a 'perfect' relationship (in the statistical sense). We need some sort of measure to indicate where along such a continuum the relationship we are concerned with falls.

It is possible, of course, that no relationship actually exists between conviction rates and residence despite the apparent relationship we observe in Table 17–9. We might have chosen a bad sample where, because of a peculiar situation, a lot of Hancock Towers residents just happened to be convicted more frequently than normal. The first major category of statistical test, a test of association, measures the likelihood that the distributions observed are really due merely to chance.

Suppose that you had a coin with a head side and a tail side, and you wondered whether it was a fair coin, or whether perhaps there was something wrong with it — maybe it was minted improperly so that one side was heavier than the other. If you flipped the coin once, and it came up heads, you would not think your suspicions were justified, because there is a fifty-fifty chance, or 50 per cent probability, that this would happen just by chance. If you then flipped the coin again and got another head, you might begin to suspect something. There is still a 25 per cent probability, however, that this would occur by chance. There is a 12.5 per cent chance of three consecutive heads, a 6 per cent chance of four, a 3 per cent chance of five, a 2 per cent chance of six, and so on. By the time seven or eight consecutive heads had come up, either a very unlikely event had occurred, or else your suspicions about the coin were correct.

Naturally, different researchers would become convinced at different points in the above test. Some people would be convinced after five or six heads, others would wait for ten heads to become convinced. Statisticians have set certain standard *levels of significance*, or probability levels, at which one might become convinced. The lowest of such levels is usually 0.05 or 5 per cent. This means that the observed distribution, or the pattern of heads that we got, might come up 5 out of 100 times purely by chance. Stated differently, there is a 5 per cent chance that this distribution occurred randomly. The next level is 0.01, where the distribution only has a 1 per cent probability of occurring by chance. The last commonly used level of significance is 0.001, or only one chance out of 1,000 of the distribution occurring randomly.

Which level of significance should you use? That is up to you. What are you willing to accept? If you accept the 5 per cent level, 5 percent of the relationships that you report are likely to be due to chance.

Returning to the table of conviction rates and residence, how do we obtain such probability using a statistical test of association? There are many such statistical tests, all of which usually take a similar form. A statistic is computed that is associated with a probability level depending upon the difference between the distribution and what would be expected by chance. For nominal data, the appropriate statistic is called the chi square, written χ^2. To give you an idea of how such statistics are computed, let us look at how we would work out a chi square by hand.

First you need to understand some basic terms. Look again at Table 17–9. You will see that conviction rate forms two rows (rows go across) while residence has three columns (columns go down). Contingency table sizes are named according to a 'rows by columns' format. Thus Table 17–9 is a two-by-three contingency table. The totals in the margins of the table are called *marginals*. We see that 118 is the 'Yes' (convicted) row total. The number in the lower right, in this case 238, is the grand total or total sample size.

The overall strategy in computing the chi square is to figure out what we would expect, by chance, to occur in each box or cell of the table. Then we look at what actually occurs in each cell. The bigger the difference between what is expected and what really occurs, the more likely that a relationship between the variables in question really exists.

How do you figure out the expected value for each cell? Consider the upper left-hand cell, Hancock Towers residents not convicted. How many people would we expect to be in this category by chance? In our sample, 68 out of 238 people live in Hancock Towers, or 28.6 per cent of our sample. If no relationship exists between the variables, we would expect about 28.6 per cent of the people who were convicted to be in this category. As the sample has 118 people convicted, 28.6 per cent, or about 34 of them, would be expected to be Hancock Towers residents. This is very different from the 43 people whom we observed in this category.

A formula for figuring out the expected value in each box is as follows (Mitton, 1982, pp. 252–254):

$$E = \frac{\text{row total x column total}}{\text{grand total}}$$

Using this formula to calculate the expected value in the first box we would have:

$$\frac{120 \times 68}{238} = 34$$

just as we computed above. Once we know that 34 of the 68 Hancock Towers residents would be expected to be 'not convicted', we know by simple subtraction that the remaining 34 residents would be expected to be convicted. We could, of course, apply the above formula as follows:

$$\frac{118 \times 68}{238} = 34$$

The purpose of this section is not so much to show you how to compute a chi square as to give you some appreciation of how it is computed. The formula for the chi square is as follows:

$$\chi^2 = \Sigma \frac{(O-E)^2}{E}$$

where χ^2 is the chi square, Σ is 'the sum of', O is any given observed value, and E is the expected value. Again, we read the formula from the inside out.

1. Compute the expected value for each cell.
2. Subtract the expected result from the observed result.

3. Square what you get.

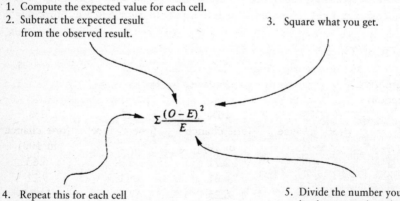

$$\Sigma \frac{(O-E)^2}{E}$$

4. Repeat this for each cell and add up the results.

5. Divide the number you get by the expected result.

If you have followed all this so far, you will realize that the bigger the difference between observed and expected values, the bigger the chi square. That is, when the numbers in the contingency table are very different from what we would expect by chance, we would expect to find a large chi square value. Let us actually compute this chi square. First we letter the cells going across the rows so that the 'not convicted' row has cells a, b, and c and the 'convicted' row has cells d, e, and f. We would compute the chi square as shown in Table 17–10.

Table 17–10 Computations for chi square

Cell	O	E	$(O\text{-}E)$	$(O\text{-}E)^2$	$(O\text{-}E)^2/E$
a	25	34.3	−9.3	86.5	2.5
b	75	69.1	5.9	34.8	0.5
c	20	16.6	3.4	11.6	0.7
d	43	33.7	9.3	86.5	2.6
e	62	67.9	−5.9	34.8	0.5
f	13	16.4	−3.4	11.6	0.7
				$\Sigma = 7.5$	

We still have not yet reached our ultimate goal, which is to translate the chi square statistic into a probability. We do this by determining the *degrees of freedom* (df), which we calculate by using the following formula:

$$\text{degrees of freedom} = (\text{rows} - 1) \times (\text{columns} - 1)$$

You get the number of rows and columns from your contingency table. The df for Table 17–10 is 1 x 2 = 2. We would then look at a chi square table found in most statistics texts. Here is part of one (Table 17–11 below):

Table 17–11

Degrees of freedom	Significance levels			
	20% (one chance in 5)	10% (one chance in 10)	5% (one chance in 20)	1% (one chance in 100)
1	1.64	2.71	3.84	6.63
2	3.22	4.61	5.99	9.21
3	4.64	6.25	7.81	11.34
4	5.99	7.78	9.49	13.28
5	7.29	9.24	11.07	15.09

We can see from Table 17–11 that with two degrees of freedom, a value of 7.5 for χ^2 would be significant at the 5 per cent level, being bigger than 5.99, but it would not be at the 1 per cent level, being smaller than 9.21.

Thus the observed distribution would occur less frequently than 5 per cent of the time due to chance alone. Given such a finding, we can be reasonably confident that a relationship really exists between conviction rates and residence patterns.

At this point, you will perhaps be relieved to know that the chi square is the only statistical test of association to be computed in this chapter. Although the above calculations may seem tedious, they do not really take long to work out once you are familiar with them. And, again, if you have access to a computer it can make short work of these sorts of computations. A computer software package called the Statistical Package for the Personal Computer checked the foregoing calculations in an instant.

Each type of statistical test takes basically the same form, where the final figure is a probability. Thus, even when you are unsure as to how a statistic is actually calculated (as you may still be unclear about the chi square), so long as the statistic is appropriate, the results are not difficult to interpret, that is, they indicate the probability of the observed distribution occurring by chance or through sampling error. The smaller the probability, the more confident you can be of your results. Generally, the probability should be *less than* .05 for you to believe that some relationship exists between your variables.

Naturally, the smaller our sample size, the greater the probability that the distribution is due to chance. In other words, if we had only recorded the conviction rates and residence patterns of twenty or thirty people, even though the proportions of conviction rates might be exactly the same as reported in Table 17–9, it is more likely that we might have selected an unusual sample. As the numbers involved are smaller, the chi square would be smaller, and the probability would be greater that the distribution was due to sampling error. This is why social scientists are so enamored of large samples.

Because of this problem of sample size affecting probabilities, statisticians have devised another type of statistic, *measures of correlation*, which measures the strength of the association regardless of sample size. Think again of the example of flipping coins. If you get three heads in a row, you have got nothing but heads. This is a very strong association — perfect in fact — but it might easily happen by chance. By contrast, getting 100 heads in a row, followed by one tail, followed again by 100 heads, would actually be a weaker association (it wasn't perfect), but it probably would not have happened purely by chance, because the sample size (number of flips) is so large. Thus, probabilities together with measures of the strength of associations help us to make up our minds about bivariate relationships. We can feel confident that a relationship really exists when probabilities are low and strengths are high.

For a two-by-two contingency table (one with two rows and two columns), the measure of correlation associated with the chi square statistical test is called the *phi coefficient*. Phi is computed by dividing the chi square by the sample size (thus controlling for sample size), and then taking the square root ($\sqrt{}$) of this number. For tables other than two-by-two, a related statistic called *Cramer's V* is computed.

Just like statistical tests of association, measures of correlation all take the same form. Thus, without knowing exactly how such indices are actually computed, you can successfully interpret them once you know a few basic principles. Measures of correlation generally range between −1 and +1. A correlation coefficient of zero means that there is absolutely no relationship between the variables. Positive measures of correlation indicate positive relationships. This means that as one variable increases, the other also increases. An example of such a relationship would be height and weight. Generally speaking, the taller a person is, the more she or he will weigh. Of course, the relationship is not perfect, because some people are short and stout and some are tall and thin, but the relationship generally holds. If the relationship were perfect, the correlation coefficient would be +1. The greater the measure of correlation, the stronger the relationship.

Sometimes variables may be related in a *negative* direction. An example might be the relationship between income and missing teeth. As income increases, people are more likely to be able to spend more on professional dental care, preventing tooth decay and replacing missing teeth, so that as income level rises the number of teeth missing declines. In this case, we would expect a negative index of correlation, the more negative, the stronger the relationship. The *absolute value* of a number is the size of a number if we ignore the sign (+ or −) of the number. We could then say that the greater the absolute value of the measure of correlation, the stronger the relationship between variables. The sign merely tells us whether the relationship is positive or negative.

To summarize our discussion, for each bivariate relationship two classes of statistics might be useful to evaluate the relationship:

- A *statistical test of association* that will be expressed as the probability of the relationship being due to chance (such as sampling error). We generally consider relationships that have less than a 5 per cent probability of occurring by chance ($p < 0.05$) as being significant. In contrast, probabilities of about 0.3 (three chances out of ten of being randomly distributed) are not.

- A *measure of correlation* between −1 and +1 that tells us about the strength of the relationship. We consider relationships with correlation coefficients having absolute values of about 0.7 or 0.8 as being strong. Correlation coefficients of 0.1 or 0.2 are not thought to indicate much of a relationship between the variables of interest.

Table 17–12 summarizes the types of data we have discussed together with the names of the tests of significance and measures of correlation most commonly used. See almost any introductory statistics text (such as those listed at the end of this chapter) for further discussion of these tests and measures.

Table 17–12 Common tests of association and measures of correlation

Type of data	Statistical tests of association	Measures of correlation
Nominal	Chi square	Phi
	Fisher's exact test	Cramer's V
Ordinal	Wilcoxen U	Gamma
	(Mann Whitney U)	Kendall's tau
	Spearman's r	
Interval	Student's t	Pearson's r

One word of caution concerning Table 17–12. It is based on the assumption that we are comparing nominal data with nominal data or ordinal with ordinal. In some cases we might need to compare data of different levels, nominal with ordinal, for example. We might try to relate marital status of women (nominal data) with level of completed education, such as primary, middle, or secondary school (ordinal data). In this case, we must use the tests and measures of correlation associated with the data of the *lower order*. So when we are comparing nominal with ordinal data, we must use the tests for nominal data. This is because ordinal tests are based on the order of the data; we want to know whether, as one variable increases, the other either increases or decreases. For nominal data the order is meaningless, so we are only seeking to find out whether there is an association of any type between the variables in question.

Researchers who use SPSS or a similar statistical package to analyze bivariate data will find three routines particularly useful. Depending on the package used, these routines will be named something like 'cross-tabulation', 't-test', and 'scattergram'. The cross-tabulations (crosstabs for short) routine is generally used for nominal or ordinal data, while the other two are used when at least one variable is interval. The crosstabs routine produces contingency tables together with associated statistics. Let us look at such a table for one of the relationships we might like to examine.

Some researchers have noticed a pattern in which male teachers seem to have pursued higher education more than female teachers, and males also seem to teach at higher levels more frequently — for example, at the secondary level. Suppose that we want to examine this pattern for a large sample of teachers from our study area. We collect our data, divide our sample by sex and level of education, use our computer software to provide us with a cross-tabulation or contingency table comparing these two variables, and get results similar to those in Table 17–13. (A real crosstab table will have the items presented in the heading section of Table 17–13; it will not have the words 'count', 'row %', and so on alongside the actual figures in the body of the table. They appear here for the sake of clarity.)

Table 17–13 Level of teacher training by sex

Sex	Count Row% Col % Total %	Training None (Code) 1	Some 2	Program 3	Degree 4	Row total
Females	1 (Count)	62	33	36	16	147
	(Row %)	42.2	22.4	24.5	10.9	38.5
	(Col %)	57.9	34.7	37.9	18.8	
	(Total %)	16.2	8.6	9.4	4.2	
Males	2 (Count)	45	62	59	69	235
	(Row %)	19.1	26.4	25.1	29.4	61.5
	(Col %)	42.1	65.3	62.1	81.2	
	(Total %)	11.8	16.2	15.4	18.1	
	Column (Count)	107	95	95	85	382
	Total (Row %)	28	24.9	24.9	22.3	100

Kendall's tau c = 0.28768   Significance 0.0000   Gamma = 0.39632

The first thing you probably notice is that there are a lot more numbers in the cells than when we looked at similar contingency tables produced by hand (Tables 17–7 and 17–9). For the moment, focus your attention only on the top numbers in each cell: these are the frequency counts indicating how many are in each cell. If the other numbers are ignored, this contingency table is the same as the others we produced. The rest of the numbers in the cells are percentages to help you in your descriptive discussions of the data.

In the upper left-hand corner of the table is a guide to the numbers in each cell. First is the *count*, which we have already described. Next is the *row* %, or the percentage found in each cell for that row. For example, the first row consists of the 147 women teachers. The row per cent in the first cell is 42.2 per cent, indicating that 62 out of 147, or about 42 per cent, of women teachers had no training at all. Next is the *column* %, which in this case tells us that 57.9 per cent of all of the teachers who had no training at all were women. Both of these numbers support our hypothesis, but percentages can be deceiving, as we have seen. (The fourth number is the *percentage* that these untrained women represent out of the total 382 people.)

Statistical measures have been devised to put more 'objectivity' into data analysis. For this reason, we need to examine the measures that accompany the table. Both the Kendall's tau and the Gamma coefficients have positive values, indicating a positive relationship between the variables. This is in the direction we predicted. The relationship is not strikingly strong, however, because these coefficients are not very large. However, the sample size is large. The Kendall's tau statistic has a probability associated with it that appears simply as 0.0000. This means that the probability of a relationship of this type occurring by chance in this large a sample is so small as to be nearly zero. We would thus have good support for our hypothesis about the relationship between sex and teacher training. We have used ordinal measures to examine this relationship, because the categories of 'sex' could be considered either as nominal (different categories) or as ordinal (ranked according to 'femaleness', with 'male' being seen as 'less femaleness'. Alternatively, we could take 'maleness' as the standard). Because the category level of teacher training can also be considered as ranked or ordinal data, ordinal statistics are appropriate for us to use.

As we pointed out earlier, the computer is a slave to your instructions. We know from Table 17–12 that Pearson's r is inappropriate for ordinal data. It should be used for interval data only, because the nature of the computations for Pearson's r require actual measurements of some sort, but the computer will compute Pearson's r for table 17–13 if you ask it to, again illustrating the GIGO principle. This would be rather like averaging ten apples and five oranges and getting apple-and-a-half. For this reason, if you do use a computer, you should be careful to give meaningful instructions so as to produce appropriate statistics.

For interval data, the crosstabs routine is not very useful. There are generally so many categories for each interval variable (because nearly every measurement is slightly different) that we get an enormous contingency table that is extremely hard to read, much less interpret. We need to turn to other types of analysis.

When we have an interval measurement as one of our variables (for example, test scores or IQ scores) and the other variable consists of a few categories (males and females, for example), we can use the *Student's t* test to examine whether there is a difference between any two categories. By comparing the mean or average scores of males and females, for example, we could see whether any difference we observe is significant.

For example, let's say we gave an examination to the students in a mathematics class. The girls in the class had an average score of 91, whereas boys averaged 86. We could use the t-test to determine the probability of a difference like this being due to sampling error or chance. If we arrive at a final probability of 0.02, suggesting that the observed distribution would occur by chance only 2 per cent of the time, we could well conclude that there really was a difference between the girls and the boys. If, however, the t-test indicated a probability of 0.8, we would conclude that the observed distribution had an 80 per cent chance of being random. This would mean that if we had tested two randomly chosen groups of similar sample size in which each group consisted entirely of girls, we would find a similar difference in test scores about 80 per cent of the time. In this case, we would decide that there was no important difference between girls and boys on the test. Again, SPSS has a routine for researchers to compute the t-test.

As you are now aware, the type of data you have determines the type of bivariate analysis you undertake. In the crosstabs example (Table 17–13), we used a contingency table because the variable 'level of teacher training' was an ordered (ordinal) variable, but suppose we had gathered the exact amount of teacher training in years. Here, teacher training would be a more exact measurement: an interval level variable. We could use the t-test to compare the mean or average years of training for men and women.

At times you might want to examine or report the strength of the relationship between two interval variables — height and weight, age and income, family size and income, and so forth. SPSS has another routine that computes Pearson's r, the appropriate measure of correlation. Another useful routine, *scattergram*, not only computes Pearson's r, but also provides a plot of the two variables. Figure 17–3 provides an example of such a plot.

Figure 17–3 plots the distribution of two interval level variables in a study of education in various countries. It is meant to illustrate the relationship between male life expectancy and primary school enrolment: as the life expectancy of the citizens of a particular country increases, the primary enrolment rate also increases. Each o on the table represents a data point or country. You will notice that a line extends from the lower left across the figure to the upper right. This line would not always be plotted on the print-out, but has been added for illustrative purposes. This line, which best approximates the *linear* or straight-line relationship between the two variables, is called a *regression* line. Pearson's r is computed by measuring how far the data points are from this ideal line. Here, the Pearson's r is 0.75095, indicating a strong positive correlation.

A word of caution concerning linear regression analysis. This type of analysis, together with Pearson's r and associated statistics, is only meant to

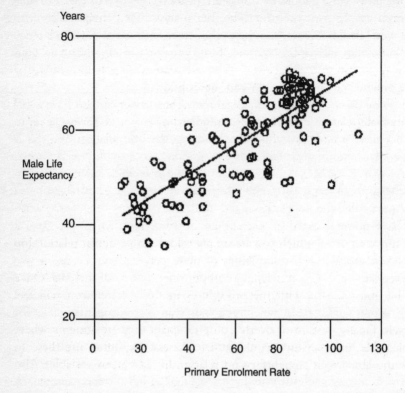

Figure 17–3 Example of a plot of Pearson's r generated by the scattergram routine.

test or examine variables that are associated in a simple straight-line fashion. Such relationships could be roughly expressed in the form: the more of A, the more (or less) of B. But interval variables could be related in other ways, for example, where the plot looked like a curve that increased and then decreased. Such a relationship might be described as: the more of A, the more of B up to a point, after which the less of B. Quantitative techniques for describing such relationships are available, but they become somewhat complicated and are beyond the scope of this discussion. In basic descriptive social research, we are interested in illustrating straightforward relationships. If, for some reason, a complex bivariate relationship between interval variables became critical to your discussion, you could simply show the scattergram plot to allow the reader to examine the relationship visually.

Using Descriptive Statistics

We are now at a logical point to conclude our discussion of how data analysis can help you provide support for your descriptive research. The first step is to look at the distribution of each important variable to understand the make-up of your study population. You probably will have an intuitive feel for how many people or things are in each category of each variable just from having done the study. The data analysis merely helps to confirm what you already know. You may choose to include a few frequency distributions or descriptive statistics from your univariate analysis in your write-up to clarify the nature of your population. This helps you to be more precise and convincing in your description.

In doing descriptive research, social researchers generally also have a feel for bivariate relationships. If, indeed, residents of Hancock Towers seem to be convicted at rates exceeding that of the general population, and this is the general topic of your research, you are likely to know it, or at least to suspect that this is true. Again, bivariate analysis helps to confirm what you already suspect is true. Including contingency tables and statistical tests in your write-up helps to convince the reader that you are being objective and have nothing to hide. You should be suspicious when you read a descriptive report in which you are simply told that a particular relationship exists. You should also be suspicious of mere percentages, because, as we have seen, these can be misleading without reference to all the data. Once you become familiar with the procedures in this chapter, you will feel much more comfortable when you can scan a contingency table for yourself. Finally, beware of overly complex quantitative treatments where simple tables and statistics would suffice. Researchers often use these to mask the absence of straightforward relationships between variables. Also beware of statements that *sound* statistical but aren't — for example, 'A statistically-oriented projection of the significance of these findings' usually means 'a wild guess'; 'the results are correct within an order of magnitude' usually means 'wrong'.

In this chapter we have discussed what, for the most part, is called *descriptive analysis*. As more variables become involved, they begin to affect one another in complex ways, and you lose the feel for the data that you had in univariate and bivariate analysis. *Multivariate analysis* is used to explore the relationships among a number of variables. Such analyses are generally called *exploratory statistics*. You are less interested in confirming relationships already suspected than in revealing relationships obscured by the complex interaction of variables. While such analyses can be of use in descriptive research, they take us somewhat beyond the bounds of basic social research and are beyond the scope of this chapter.

A final word of caution: just because two variables are associated, do not assume that one causes the other. Correlation makes no statement about causality. Consider Table 17–14, a contingency table.

Table 17–14 Relationship between fire trucks and fires in Hope And Glory, Ohio

	Fires	
Fire trucks	Present	Absent
Present	20	2
Absent	0	30

These data might be based on a number of observations in Hope And Glory. The fire department is apparently efficient: whenever fires occurred, a fire truck was on the scene. If you were not careful, you might conclude that the fires were caused by the fire trucks. Obviously this is stupid, but researchers who ignore the fact that correlation is not causality often arrive at equally stupid conclusions.

You should also keep in mind that you are never proving that any relationship exists, you are only showing that it is more or less likely. If someone flips a coin that comes up heads 100 or 1,000 times in succession, you would be inclined to suspect that something was wrong with the coin. However, the laws of probability tell us that it is possible, although extremely unlikely, to get 100 straight heads just by chance. For this reason you should avoid statements such as: 'This proves that…' or even 'This shows that…' You can say something like: 'This suggests that…' or 'This supports the idea that…'

Finally, don't worry if you are not quantitatively oriented. Remember that data analysis is just a tool to help you be more convincing and to make your work easier. You can use data analysis at a variety of levels. If you just have a few variables that you want to describe or want to show how strong one or two relationships are, you might consider doing a few simple statistical tests by hand. Basic statistics texts will help you to do this. You may actually save time by not coding your data or doing computer analysis, but if you plan to look at a relatively large number of variables and you have access to a computer, consider computer analysis. It really is not difficult. So many convenient programs are available that it is really only a matter of defining your variables and requesting the appropriate statistics. You need only to put aside your fears, tabulate some of your data, and use it to make your final report that much more precise and convincing. But whether you do your computations by hand, by computer, or not at all, the material in this chapter will help you to make sense of research reports that do use quantitative analysis.

Integrating Qualitative and Quantitative Data

Can you use the quantitative analytical approaches in this chapter and the qualitative ones described in Chapter 16 together? You may remember that we have discussed triangulation — using multiple methods, sources, researchers, or theories on a problem — several times in this book. Triangulation can also be used for analysis by combining different ways of figuring out what you have got.

The few researchers who use both qualitative and quantitative data in the same study tend to present one kind of material and then another, without integrating them. Researchers Caracelli and Greene (1993) have reviewed a small number of successful instances in which researchers in the field of educational evaluation have managed to combine their material more successfully:

- *Data transformation*: you can convert qualitative data to quantitative data or vice versa so that you can analyze them together. To do this, you code the qualitative data, using numbers in the same coding categories that you have used for your quantitative data. Alternatively, you convert your quantitative data into words and look for named patterns, themes, and groupings, just as you would with qualitative data.

- *Typology development*: you can use one type of data and develop a typology or set of categories. Use these categories to analyze the data collected the other way.

- *Extreme case analysis*: you can identify extreme cases, for example, analysis of a questionnaire shows a small number of girls who do not intend to go on to secondary school, but who seem to have all the characteristics that usually lead girls to continue on. Qualitative data can probe this. Alternatively, you come across such girls in interviews. How widespread is this situation? Do any other characteristics explain your findings? A questionnaire can help here. The analysis of each kind of material will refine your understanding.

- *Data consolidation or merging*: putting both kinds of material together, as in data transformation, to create new variables (not simply transformed ones) that you then investigate or analyze.

As a beginning researcher, you are probably most likely to use extreme case analysis, learning from one type of analysis and testing it or exploring it further through another type of analysis.

References and further readings

Statistics

Bernard, H. Russell. 1994. *Research Methods in Cultural Anthropology.* Newbury Park, California: Sage.

Blalock, Hubert M., Jr. 1979. *Social Statistics*, revised ed. New York: McGraw Hill.

Fitz-Gibbon, Carol Taylor, and Lynn Lyons Morris. 1987. *How to Analyze Data.* Newbury Park, California: Sage.

Irvine, John, Ian Miles, and Jeff Evans, eds. 1976. *Demystifying Social Statistics*. London: Pluto Press.

Kenny, David A. 1987. *Statistics for the Social and Behavioral Sciences*. Boston: Little Brown.

Mitton, Roger. 1982. *Practical Research in Distance Teaching*. London: International Extension College.

Computer Applications

Couper, Mick, ed. 1998. *Computer Assisted Survey Information Collection*. New York: John Wiley.

George, Darren and Paul Mallory. 2000. *SPSS Windows Step by Step: A Simple Guide and Reference*. London: Allyn and Bacon.

Morgan, George A. and Orlando V. Greigo. 1998. *Easy Use and Interpretation of SPSS for Windows: Answering Research Questions with Statistics*. Mahwah, New Jersey: Lawrence Erlbaum Assoc.

Hancock Towers Newsletter

December 21, 2001

Moving family reunion in Community Room

In a surprise 'This is Your Life' party for Kev Darwin in the Community Room last week, the Darwins of 14-A met a long-lost relative. Shar introduced her family to Professor George Darwin, Professor of Classics at the University, and author of many scholarly works.

'Actually, this was supposed to be an encounter session for Kev so relatives could confront him with the awful consequences of his actions,' said Shar, 'but there was a bit of a mix-up. Dr. O'Connor thought it was a 'This is Your Life' party and invited George. Anyhow, all's well that ends well.'

Professor Darwin said he was delighted to meet long-lost relatives and has now agreed to write a series of 32 articles on kinship terminology in the Mogul Empire for the Association Newsletter ('Always at Your Service!') and is now helping Kev to publish a prison memoir-cum-cookbook, *Grilling with Gangsters*. Professor Darwin said this genre was new to him but he was certain that the public would find it not unattractive.

Dr. O'Connor offered to do a section for the Newsletter on household hints. He himself often dressed as a housemaid, he said.

Mrs. Jennie Richards, chair of the Residents'

Association President hands over to replacement

Association, has resigned in order to take a lectureship in international company law at Richard Branson University. Mrs. Rose Darwin was elected in her place.

The Association thanked Mrs. Richards for all her work.

More letters on Sir Evelyn's plans for the towers

'In your last issue you said I sent an anony-mouse note. I did not. I changed my name by deed poll from Thomas Brown to The Fang. It is all legal.
Signed, The Fang'

From Sir Evelyn Petti-grew: 'Upon reflection, I believe the Heritage Council has too much on hand just at the moment and I am therefore withdrawing my rec-ommendations in rela-tion to the Towers.'

MORE INSIDE!

18 SHARING YOUR FINDINGS

Summary

Sharing your results is an essential part of the research process. How you do this depends on your audience and your purpose. Your presentation may take a variety of forms: written or verbal reports, a videotape, workshops, and so on. Shorter is better. Clear language is essential.

Your presentation will probably contain some description of what you found, some analysis, and some interpretation. Applied research will also contain recommendations. This chapter shows several ways of organizing each of these.

Different audiences require different formats. Writing for an academic audience, for example, means using a fairly standardized format. Organizations may have their own preferred forms. The needs of other audiences may require that you develop a format specifically for them.

To make your research useful, you should work from the beginning with the people involved so that your recommendations are practical, realistic, and have genuine possibilities for being implemented.

We are now at the point where you must present your results. A major problem in research is that once it is completed the people who participated may never hear from the researcher again. Officials who helped to locate statistics, local organizations that got involved, and local people who took time from their work to help are all left in the dark. What did the researchers find? Will anything useful come out of it? Will the participants — the organization, householders, or factory workers — bother to help the next research team that comes along?

Selfishness, arrogance, and inefficiency are the three most common reasons for failing to share and use research findings. Researchers may think that advancing their careers by publishing the results in an academic journal or circulating them to colleagues in an organization is more important. Or perhaps they think that the people who participated do not really count. If the results are going to have an impact on their lives, they will find out about them eventually. Finally, researchers may be so disorganized or may have collected so much information that determining the results takes years, at which point no-one is interested any more.

Your frame of mind is important here: are you *using* people or are you *working with* them? Taking up people's time, raising their expectations, and then disappearing is unethical. You will have been careful, of course, not to promise anything that you cannot deliver, but even so, it is reasonable for people to expect that even if nothing more practical comes of the research, they will at least be able to share your findings, discuss them, and perhaps gain some insights.

From the researcher's point of view, also, skipping this stage is foolish. People's comments can help you to correct mistakes, refine your work, and consider other interpretations. Finally, it is unwise on a practical level too. People will not help you again, and they may not help anyone else either.

So you will present something, but what? The answers to these questions will help you to decide:

- What is the purpose of the research? Are you supposed to provide a basic picture? Are you supposed to explain something? Are you supposed to evaluate? Are you supposed to come up with a plan of action? Are you facilitating local people to develop their own plan of action?

- How will the research be used and by whom? Perhaps your research will lead to a set of questions that project planners should ask themselves before starting a new project. Perhaps local development authorities will use it to create a slide show to help inform local people about new opportunities for setting up small businesses. Perhaps the research will provide detailed case studies to show a government department or non-governmental organization (NGO) why a particular intervention did not encourage women to set up small businesses, and how it might be improved. Perhaps you will have twenty minutes to convince busy officials that the expensive, newly published guidebooks for small-business enterprise are seriously gender-biased. Each of these uses will require a different format.

- Has your research been commissioned? Before you begin your research you must find out exactly what the sponsor expects and needs.
- Who are the participants or stakeholders in your research: government officials, local business people, the staff of an enterprise center, a Grandmothers' Action Group, members of an NGO? What you prepare for each of these may differ, because their needs and conventions for communicating differ.
- What are your obligations, contractually and morally, to each stakeholder?
- What will each expect of you?
- What information does each need?
- What is the best way to get it to them?
- What is the best way to do what you can to see that it is used?

Report, Talk or Workshop?

First decide whether your presentation will be a report, a talk, or a workshop. Often, the people who will have a role in deciding what to do with your results may need to study the findings, incorporate them into the work of others, or have something in hand to support a case they are going to make. In such situations, a written report is necessary.

Sometimes, however, people may not have time to read, or the situation may be moving so fast that they just want results and recommendations quickly. If these people commissioned your research, you should know what they expect from the beginning, so that you do not waste everyone's time by settling in to write the study of the century. A well-planned briefing may be the best approach here. Try to allow for about twenty minutes to present your results and about forty for questions. Six to ten simple charts, slides, or transparencies may help to get your points across. Any more leads to something professional presenters call 'death by transparency'. Give people individual copies of your charts, a short report with an executive summary, or anything else you think will help.

If you have taken a participatory approach, now is not the time to take all the glory yourself. Try to arrange for local people to be invited to present their findings. Not only is this fair, it can also be far more effective. Decision makers get an opportunity to meet people whose lives they affect. They can also see that local people are well able to analyze their own situation and make their case.

In other cases, people don't have access to written materials — copies may not reach them or they may not be able to read. This doesn't disqualify them from knowing about and considering what you found. Once again, a verbal presentation is probably the best. For a local community, try to find a way that all the kinds of people concerned, regardless of sex, power, age, location, and so on, have a chance to hear and discuss what you found. While you are doing your research, discuss with people how you might develop a reasonable plan for sharing your results and for getting feedback. If you cannot meet all the groups yourself, pre-arranged community meetings chaired by someone who understands the research and can be relied upon to communicate it responsibly may work. The community may also want a written copy to show to agencies, other researchers, and so on.

So writing something is still probably a good idea, even if your main mode of presentation is a talk. The report may be useful to you later or to other researchers, people can use your results to plan other research, or it may save someone else from having to repeat your study.

Of course, you don't have to restrict yourself to a report or a talk. Your findings may be more effectively presented in a video, or even in a literary work, such as a play or a short story. If you are convinced of the value of your work, you might try several ways of getting the message across. Whatever mode you use, remember that the material may have to be translated, sometimes into several languages, to reach all the people concerned.

Length

Ten to 20 pages, including charts, diagrams, and other elements, are about as much as you can expect people to read. Any information that is needed to understand your findings, but which would interrupt the report too much, should go into an appendix. This can include an essential table, an organizational diagram, calculations showing how you arrived at costs, a short explanation of your methods, a copy of your survey form, or anything else the reader needs to know. However, writing ten pages and attaching 100 pages of appendices is pointless: people's hearts will quake at the size, and they may never look at the ten pages.

Balancing the Emphases in the Report

All research involves description and analysis, and most research reports also include some interpretation. Description tells what happened (see Wolcott's 1990 'telling the story'); analysis tells the relationships and patterns you found; and interpretation tells what you or others think the research means and how to use it.

How much space should you give to each part of your presentation? Each report differs. If little is known about the situation or what is known turns out to be incorrect, your real contribution is description, so that section will take up a greater proportion of your research. What is life like for sexual offenders in Glasheen Prison? Description is also useful to show

how all the pieces fit together, that is, to present a holistic picture of a situation. When bullying goes on in a school, who is affected? What role do parents play? What are the consequences for the victims? How are the perpetrators handled? What does the school administration do? Does the law come into it? Do social workers, or psychologists?

Traditionally, anthropologists have focused more on description than most other social scientists because they studied people whose way of life was largely unknown to the rest of the world. More recently, other researchers took up this idea of descriptive *ethnography* to get a better idea of what really happens in people's lives and of how any particular experience fits into the broader picture.

If the facts are clear enough, but people do not know how to relate them to one another and make sense of them, your biggest contribution will be analysis, and that will form the major section of your report. Traditionally, 'quantitative' research provided a lot of material for analysis and convenient statistical tools for doing it, so 'quantitative' researchers gave this part of the report a greater emphasis, but 'qualitative' researchers can do this as well by boiling down data into categories, patterns, typologies, and so on as we saw in Chapter 16.

If people want to know what you or others who are participating in the research think the analysis means, you will spend more time on interpretation. People who take an interpretive philosophical approach will emphasize this section, and examine the perspectives of all those involved and the meanings they attach to them. Senior researchers, educators, administrators, and others often feel freer to move into the interpretive realm, because even with scanty data they bring a lot of experience and insights to bear in reaching beyond the material at hand to speculate, suggest implications, and challenge theory. People are more inclined to listen to them than to a novice.

Recommendations are a form of interpretation. Description and analysis will take you only so far on the road to recommendations. Practical constraints, ideological and political considerations, diplomacy, and common sense also enter into the process of forming recommendations. Analysis may show a finding to be statistically significant, but that has nothing to do with it being important. All it shows is that a difference, which is unlikely to be the result of chance, exists between two groups, or before and after an experiment, and if you are studying a large sample, say 2,000, even tiny differences can be statistically significant. You still have to decide whether they really mean anything, and what, if anything, should be done.

This is purely a matter of judgment. You need to know whether a recommendation you are considering falls within the powers of the organizations that are interested in your research. You also need to know whether the community can sustain the recommendation — keep it going over the long run. If the recommendation makes great sense and everyone but the bosses in the company favor it, think again. And think again if a similar idea failed, even under completely different circumstances, in a neighboring community; or if the problem is low on the list of community priorities; or if it will cost too much in time or money; or if it will result in undesirable social or technical side effects. All these issues and many more require you to place your facts and analysis in a bigger context and to interpret them in that light.

When you finish your research, you may be overwhelmed. You have all this wonderful information, each bit is like gold, and all of it must go into your final presentation. Wolcott (1990, 1994), who specializes in helping educational researchers to present their results concisely, calls this mistake — one that beginning researchers often make — the 'heap' approach. He offers two simple instructions for planning the bare bones of your research findings:

- Tell the story.
- Then tell how it happened to be the way you told it.

For action-oriented research we could add another piece of advice:

- Then tell what should be done about it. (Of course, if you are working in a participatory project, at this point you will be asking people what *they* think should be done about it.)

Your material may help you. Perhaps when you began your research you had an idea of the kind of report you wanted to write. Now that you have finished, the material clearly falls into place some other way. You are very lucky. Do it that way. But if that does not happen, consider the following ways of organizing, some of which Wolcott (1994) develops in more detail.

Organizing the findings

Here are some options for organizing your findings:

1. Use your research outline, if you made one. Place the problem or issue in its place and time, then focus on the central points or the core of your research.
2. Organize the report around the participants' perspectives: the key concepts or categories that emerged from an emic approach.
3. Be guided by what you found in the analysis. Take the central charts,

diagrams, and statistical findings and use them as the skeleton for the text of your report.

4. Ask people who are concerned with the issues what they need to know. Write the report that way.

If you are reviewing or evaluating a project, present:

- the situation or problem;
- the purpose the project was intended to meet;
- an explanation of how the current situation came to be as it is;
- which (and whose) needs are currently being met and which are not;
- who is involved;
- what facilities are involved;
- what resources are involved;
- what the consequences of the current situation are;
- what coping strategies are being employed;
- what options are open;
- what constraints have to be taken into account.

5. Present your findings in chronological order. O'Reilly-de Brún (1994), in a participatory rural study in The Gambia, used this approach. She based each stage of the research on what she had learned in the previous stage, and reported it this way. The process and the findings would have been obscured in another format.

6. Present the material from various perspectives: different people, different organizations, different levels of administration, different disciplines as reflected by members of the team, different players in the event. Literary authors often do this, and if you are taking an interpretive approach, this way makes sense.

7. Take a central event and show how other things fed into it or related to it in some way.

8. Take a life history and show how it reflects and brings together in one human experience the points you want to make.

9. Use a case study to show how all the factors that interest you come together in a situation.

10. Take a day, a week, or whatever period seems best and chronicle the events.

11. Take the people or the groups concerned and show the interactions and inter-relationships among them.

12. Take the outcome and show what led up to it.

Organizing the analysis

The procedures suggested in Chapters 16 and 17 should help you to identify concepts, patterns, and relationships when organizing the analysis. Present the ones you think are important. Relate what you found to other people's studies, to ideas from other disciplines, to what researchers found somewhere else, to a theory if this is useful. If it is not, leave your results to stand on their own, do not dress them up needlessly. Use just enough evidence and supporting material — in the form of tables, graphs, diagrams, case studies, and quotes — to clarify and substantiate your analysis. You are not on trial for your life, mustering every shred of evidence; you are trying to present a modest piece of work that is readable (or 'listenable'), creditable, and convincing. If people want more information, they can ask you questions or write to you.

Organizing the interpretation and recommendations

Start by organizing your interpretation.

- Tell how you read the findings. What do they mean, what are their implications, why are they important, where do they lead?
- Tell what your study does not show. What else needs to be known?
- Tell what went wrong and how you would do the study again if you had the chance.
- Point out anything interesting that you came across but could not study, for whatever reason. Maybe this will help someone else.

What recommendations arise out of your analysis and interpretations?

- Recall your brief. What are your recommendations supposed to cover? Don't try to reform the world and don't venture into areas about which you know nothing or have no research to back you up, or your other recommendations will be discredited. For example, if you were asked to cost your recommendations, you should have. If you were not and do not know how, don't try now.
- Tell what is really needed. 'As the analysis shows, all the guideline texts are gender stereotyped and should be replaced.' Then tell what, in your estimation, is practicable. 'A phased program should be put in place to rewrite the *Guide to Small Business* for use in the enterprise center and community in twelve months' time.'
- Tell what you think the implications of the recommendations will be. What should people expect? 'As a result, the predominance of

businessmen in the enterprise center may decrease: more women may apply for space in the 'start-up' units and this may, in the long term, affect the distribution of economic power in the community.'

- If you are reviewing or evaluating a project, look back at the pertinent points in the section on organizing the findings. What will be the consequences of each option? How can they be implemented?

Try to identify one, two, or three simple and clear tables that reflect the core of your findings and put them at the front. These are what people will remember.

Format

What should your presentation look like? Policy makers, local government officials, organizations, project managers, community leaders, field officers, and local people may each have different pictures in their heads of what your work will look like when it is finished.

Reports

To be effective, you may have to prepare more than one report, each tailored to a specific group. Academic writing, which is discussed later, has some conventional patterns. In the case of other audiences, ask to see examples of reports or papers that are considered clear and well-organized. Generally, a report will contain:

- a title;
- a table of contents;
- an executive summary (of the next four parts);
- an explanation of what you studied and why;
- a brief account of how you carried out the study;
- the findings and analysis;
- the recommendations, if you are making any;
- any references (books, articles, reports) you used.

In the case of surveys, under the section describing how you did the study, you will be expected to explain your sampling method, the numbers, and the response rate (and what kinds of people did not respond); to describe how you carried out the survey; to evaluate the effects of any sampling and non-sampling errors; and to explain what statistical tests you applied and the levels of significance you used. Do this as simply and briefly as possible, or your readers will skip it. If complications affected the research, say so, but try to put any extended explanation in an appendix.

Academic papers

Traditionally, academic papers are constructed according to a fairly common pattern — what researchers Judd, Smith, and Kidder (1991) call the hourglass shape of the report, as shown in Table 18–1.

In other words, the report includes the preliminary materials (the general background of the problem, the specific problem you are studying, what other authors have said) and your own research (your specific research focus, how you studied the problem, your results, and your interpretations). The closing materials (a summary, a list of the books and articles you used, and any appendices) will conclude the report. In some cases, a summary of about 100 to 150 words appears at the beginning and is called an abstract. If you look at conference papers and articles in professional journals, you will see that most follow a pattern like this.

This plan is not shown to suggest that you write an academic paper. Indeed, people who are in the habit of writing academically often find that soon they are incapable of communicating with most of the rest of the human race. It is possible, however, that your research is of interest to professional researchers, and currently it is unlikely to be published in a journal unless you follow the rules.

Language

Fortunately, obscure jargon-laden writing is becoming less acceptable, even in academic journals. Try to aim for 'parsimonious elegance'. This means writing simply, attractively, and to the point. It requires discipline and a ruthless approach to your own writing, particularly if you have a civil service or academic background and have to unlearn an arcane writing style. At the other extreme, try to avoid a tabloid journalistic style: sensational, too many judgmental adjectives, language that is too flowery, too many exclamation marks, and so on.

Consider writing in the first person ('I' for an individual, 'we' for a team), but use the terms sparingly. Once you choose, do not switch and suddenly start calling yourself 'the author'. Use the active voice: 'Many people thought...' rather than: 'It was thought by many people...' Do not use jargon unfamiliar to readers, but use correct professional terms when writing for professional readers. Watch for gender-stereotyped language: do not use 'he' or 'him' when you mean both male and female, say 'husband and wife' or 'wife and husband' rather than 'man and wife'. Do not use language that assumes that females are always defined by their relationships to males or are always helpers, such as 'the farmer and his wife'. The wife may be a farmer too, or the farmer.

Table 18–1 Pattern of the typical academic paper

The report	*Examples*
The report begins broadly:	'Investment in small business enterprise yields broad economic benefits to a community.'
It becomes more specific:	'Investment in encouraging women to enter the small business market is a significant factor in the improvement of a community's economic status and standard of living.'
And more so:	'Yet many communities have business enterprise systems that are not designed to meet the needs of women.'
And more so:	'O'Connell has shown that gender bias in guidelines and texts designed for use in the small business market is an important example of this failure to meet business women's needs.'
Until you are ready to introduce your own study in conceptual terms:	'Guidelines and texts used in business enterprise centers in 20 urban and rural communities in X country were examined for gender bias.'
The method and result sections are the most specific, the 'neck' of the hourglass:	Three separate coding teams analyzed the texts using a scoring system based on eighteen criteria established by O'Connell. Table 1 shows that, with the exception of fire regulations text, all texts were seriously biased on all eighteen criteria.'
The discussion section begins with the implications of your study:	'These results show that most women are being exposed to business enterprise guidelines that have little relevance to their experience or needs.'
It becomes broader:	'Clearly, the Department of Trade & Enterprise must recognize the importance of making "small business" information and guideline reference materials meaningful for both sexes.'
And more so:	'Only then can the potential contribution of both males and females to small business enterprise be realized.'

Source: Adapted from Judd, Smith, and Kidder (1991, p. 456)

Tables and diagrams

Ask yourself: 'What am I trying to convey in my tables and diagrams?' and then set them up in the simplest way you can. Do not clutter the report with tables just because you had to prepare them to understand your material. Use only the ones you need to make your points. Keep them simple: if they are too detailed, the picture may be lost. Do not insert the results of statistical tests under the table or chart just because the computer performed them. Many of them may be meaningless, as we saw in Chapter 17, and many of them may be meaningless to your readers even if they are legitimate and necessary. Consider how to say what they mean in plain language. For non-technical readers, instead of saying: 'The chi square (1, N = 58) = 4.50, p = 0.05 showed a statistically significant difference between the two sexes,' you can say: 'Women were significantly more likely to say that they intended to expand their business within the first three years of trading,' and many people will take your word for it. Of course, in a report for a technical audience, you may want to give the statistical results.

As we saw in Chapter 5, if you know what your independent variable (the cause) is, you should lay out tables so that the independent variable is on the left axis of the table and the dependent variable across the top, so that percentages show how much of the independent variable is reflected in the dependent variable. If you are testing a hypothesis, an incorrectly laid out table will not give you the information you need.

Even if you are not testing a hypothesis, consider how you want to express your results. Suppose you have done a study of a small company that revealed gender bias on the part of management personnel against female employees in the workforce. The study shows that gender-conscious women resented management, while women unaware that they were being discriminated against had a less fraught relationship with management personnel. If you want to say 'of the gender-conscious women, 40 per cent were younger and 60 per cent were older,' put *younger women* and *older women* on the left axis (Table 18–2) and *gender-conscious* and *not gender-conscious* across the top. If you want to say 'of the younger women, 57 per cent were gender-conscious and 43 per cent were not,' put *gender-conscious* and *not gender-conscious* on the left axis (Table 18.3). Look at the tables, which show the results for 150 women. They *do* come out differently, even though the actual results do not change.

Notice that the tables use percentages. You can include the actual number before each percentage, but be sure to give the percentage as well, because it makes the pattern much clearer. Give the actual numbers in the total. Most researchers show the latter in parentheses.

These tables are two-by-two: two variables on the left axis and two on the top, so that there are four cells or boxes within the table. You can have more extensive tables, four-by-three, for example, giving you twelve cells.

If you have too many cells in your tables, people will lose sight of patterns. Consider combining some of the cells if you can.

Table 18–2 Women's age by gender consciousness (per cent)

Women's age	Gender-conscious	Not gender-conscious
Younger women	40%	20%
Older women	60%	80%
Total number of women	(60)	(90)

Table 18–3 Women's gender-consciousness by age (per cent)

Gender-consciousness	Younger	Older
Gender-conscious	57%	33%
Not gender-conscious	43%	67%
Total number of women	(42)	(108)

This book has used various kinds of data displays, and some of them might help your readers to understand your material, just as they helped you. You can, for example, use pie charts to illustrate percentages (Figure 18–1).

Figure 18–1 Destination of women who abandoned business enterprise at end year.

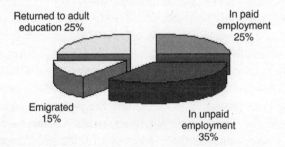

Figure 18–2 Observation test scores by women's groups using two scales.

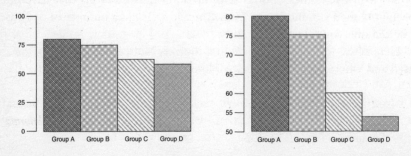

Your percentages should add to 100 per cent. The pie chart is 360 degrees. To work out how much of the pie should be given to the 35 per cent of women at home, multiply 360 by 35/100, which gives you 126 degrees. To draw a slice representing 126 degrees, use a protractor (a clear plastic device for measuring angles, usually available in places that sell school supplies).

If you are illustrating two variables, such as the relationship between women's groups and scores on an observation test, you can draw a bar chart (Figure 18–2). Try to draw the chart within an invisible square. If you make it taller than wide or wider than tall, the results will be distorted. Make sure that you show the scale you are using along the left side. Drawing only a section of your scale can also be misleading — for example, see how group D's performance seems to deteriorate when you change the scale.

References

If you draw upon someone else's work, such as a book, an article, or a paper, you must recognize the fact by giving the reference or citation. Throughout the text of this book you will have noticed insertions such as (Hartnett and Heneveld, 1994, p.12). This tells you that the idea or quotation was taken from page twelve of a book or article written by Hartnett and Heneveld and published in 1994. To find the title, look at the reference section at the end of the chapter or the end of the book. In a short report, you will not have chapters, so put the references at the end, which is the usual approach unless chapters are written by different authors.

Large organizations, universities, journals, and publishing houses have style rules about how references should look. You can ask for these. You can also get books on standard styles from your library or from the Internet (see Chapter 8). The style used in this book is known as Chicago style (see below). Writers of British English follow Rees (1970) or *The Economist Pocket Style Book* (1986). If you are doing the research for an organization, see if there is a preferred style. Whatever system you use, be consistent. You can consult books such as the University of Chicago's *Manual of Style* for correct forms for all the different kinds of problems you might run across: books with five authors, books with no author, manuscripts that have not been published yet, and so on. Even Chicago style has a number of options. Use the one you select consistently.

Here is the form for an article in a journal. Notice what punctuation is used and where. Notice also that all lines after the first are indented.

Hoxeng, James, Carlos Rojas, and Eduardo Velez. 1999. 'Sexual Responses of Women Toward Bearded Men.' *Journal of Abnormal Phenomena* 62(4):239–256.

This article has three authors. Only the name of the first author is reversed (but some publishers reverse all of them). The work was published in 1999, and in this style the title of the article is in quotation marks. The name of the journal is in italics. This article appeared in volume 62, number 4 of the journal, starting on page 239 and ending on page 256. This, of course, is the lost reference Laurinda has been looking for since Chapter 7.

Here is the form for a chapter in a book:

Gel, Susan. 1991. 'Between Speech and Silence — the Problematic of Research on Language and Gender.' In Micaela Di Leonardo, ed., *Gender at the Crossroads of Knowledge*. Berkeley: University of California Press.

Here is the form for a book:

Robson, Colin. 1993. *Real World Research*. Oxford: Blackwell.

Another common form you will find is the date in parentheses (1982). Or sometimes the date is placed after the publisher's name: Oxford: Blackwell, 1993.

Other ways of citing references are possible, such as handling each as a footnote, giving all the details at the bottom of the page on which they appear, but then you still have to write them all out again in the references at the end. The system described in this chapter is probably the simplest.

If you need to, you can put a content footnote at the bottom of a page of text. This is something that you think the reader should know, but which would interrupt the discussion if you put it in right there. For example, you are discussing an adult education course taught by Ms. Slavin.[1] You want people to know that this is not her real name and that, in fact, you have changed all the tutors' names, but not the names of colleges. See the way the footnote at the bottom of this page handles this.

Circulating the Study

Once you have a finished draft of your report, ask other people for their comments. You may be so involved that you have taken certain things for granted or have missed something. If you do not know who should be reading or hearing about your work, you probably should not have started the study to begin with. It means you do not know who is involved, what else has been done, who might do something with your results, and so on.

---

[1] The names of individual tutors have been changed, but not the names of colleges or districts. (This is an example of a content footnote.)

And who reads your study will have some bearing on what you say. If it is for internal circulation only, you can say things that you might not say if it were reaching a wider audience or the general public. Even then, you have to be diplomatic if you want people to be receptive to your analysis and recommendations.

If your report is being widely circulated, you have to be even more careful. People do not want themselves, their organization, their policies, or their community to be seen in a bad light. What constitutes a bad light in their eyes and yours may be two entirely different things. People have written books on the consequences of researchers portraying what they thought was a rather neutral account, only to find that the people involved in the study felt outraged and betrayed. That is why all the participants should be involved in every stage of the study. Even that will not please everyone, and in the end, you will have to make decisions, sometimes difficult ones, yourself.

If an organization or group has commissioned your study, they may control its circulation. Try to work out the circulation group in your initial planning discussions. If the organization has no intention of circulating the study to the people who participated in it, try to negotiate their inclusion.

Circulating drafts will help you to see if the audience you are trying to reach understands it. Ask for comments. You will discover various kinds of 'reviewers' — for example, the punctuation-only reader, who ignores the substance of your report to look at the commas; the destructive reader, who may resent a newcomer to the field, is jealous, is intolerant of approaches other than her own or annoyed that her name or the name of her book does not appear in your study; and the surprise! reader, who says nothing about your draft, but waits to attack the final product. When you encounter any of these, you may be heartened to know that the true greats in many fields tend to be supportive, constructive, and genuinely anxious to help. There are also ordinary people around who will look at your draft in this spirit. Try to learn from comments, and do not give up.

When your study is finished, the widest form of circulation is publishing in a journal or book or presenting a paper at a professional conference. Remember that only a small proportion of papers submitted to journals by trained academics, people whose careers may depend upon publication, are published the first time around. If you still want to try, remember that no matter how good your work, a journal will not publish something that is outside its area or that does not follow its style. Learn what the journal publishes by reading its articles. Read the instructions to authors, usually found somewhere in the issue. If your article is rejected, but returned with comments, see if they can help you to improve it. Resubmit it or try another journal. Remember, however, that all of this can take a very long time. Do not overlook local journals and magazines. The people you are trying to reach may be more likely to read them.

However, you don't need to publish in a professional journal to get a wide circulation. Here is a set of steps that will help you to get your message across. We are indebted to Robert Chambers for this advice.

- Ensure that a large number of copies are made.
- Send copies with a short covering letter giving the main findings to key people and ask for an appointment to come and discuss them.
- Condense the findings and send them to newsletters. There are many newsletters now that have both international and national circulation. They can be an effective way of communicating.
- Spend time on address lists and on finding out who key people are.
- If the report has to go to the top of a hierarchy but you feel it would be useful for people at different levels to receive the report, send enough copies for full distribution within the hierarchy, and if possible copy your letter to people at different levels who may expect to receive copies. Often reports get stuck at the top or near the top. If those lower down know the report exists and where it is, they may be able to ensure that they receive copies.
- Make translations into appropriate languages.
- Consider articles in newspapers, either by yourself or by a journalist who interviews you.
- A broadcast can also be most effective. Television interviews are also worth considering.

Using the Results

Most readers of this book will be doing a piece of research that they hope will be useful to others. Despite your best efforts, all kinds of things can prevent this from happening. For example, the person who commissioned your research may be transferred to a new job, and her replacement is not interested in what you worked on. Or maybe what you discovered can't be dealt with at the level to which you have access. Suppose local businesswomen have stated that without government-sponsored crèche facilities, they will not move to the purpose-built enterprise center in town. This presents a problem. It would be unusual for this to be solvable at the local level. If the community you worked with is unusual in holding this view, you may find that official programs may not be flexible enough to make an exception for it. If, however, you think that this view on access to government-sponsored childcare is more widespread, information from your one community will not be enough to convince decision makers. You may need to do more extensive survey research or convince others to do the research. Or perhaps you find that your recommendations cross a number of agencies or departments, and it is difficult for them to cooperate.

These and many other circumstances can lead to your study having little or no effect. You cannot foresee all of them, but you can reduce the possibility of all your work being wasted by remembering the following points:

- Your work does not have to be perfect. You can and should admit to mistakes you made and problems you encountered, but it does have to stand up to critical scrutiny. Hit and miss sampling, badly designed experiments, poor questionnaires badly administered, or ignorance of what is already known on the subject will weaken your credibility.
- People have to understand your findings. Write clearly.
- Your recommendations have to relate to something that is achievable. Recommendations that are too broad, expensive, or impractical; that are politically impossible; or that fall outside the brief of an organization or department will be ignored. Also, if you are doing a participatory research action project that is going to depend entirely on local resources, it should not concentrate on initiatives that require external support or funding.
- Keep all the stakeholders, including any sponsoring organizations, informed throughout the research. People's comments can help to make your recommendations more workable. If your research is not commissioned, try to find out what agencies and groups would be interested in the kind of work you are doing and what kinds of activities they support.
- Try to be aware of whom your research will offend, whom it will support, and who will use it for their own purposes. Local researchers are more likely to be aware of these difficult issues. Research results can be presented in many ways. If you are doing an evaluation of something, be positive and diplomatic in presenting your result; people or organizations invest a lot of themselves, as well as of their money, in their endeavors, and thoughtless negative comments can be hurtful and unproductive. Consider to whom you should send drafts of evaluations. People will not be pleased to find criticisms, no matter how constructive, being widely circulated.
- In the end, it is up to you to show people how they can use your results. To do this, you need to understand who will be involved and how things work. For example, if yours is a community-level study, you need to understand the local authority structure and various

features of social organization. Will the mayor feel she is being bypassed? Will all the women's groups in the area work together? If you are working with an organization, you need to know something of its corporate culture, that is, how it works (both in principle and in practice), who is responsible for what, its internal politics, and so on.

References and further readings

O'Reilly-de Brún, Mary. 1994. 'Tender Shoots: A Case Study of Community Mobilization and Response to Problems of Girls' Education in Gambia.' World Bank, AF5PH: Washington, D.C. Draft.

Economist Publications. 1986. *The Economist Pocket Style Book*. London.

Judd, Charles M., Eliot R. Smith, and Louise H. Kidder. 1991. *Research Methods in Social Relations*, 6th ed. Fort Worth, Texas: Holt Rinehart and Winston.

Rees, Herbert. 1970. *Rules of Printed English*. London: Longman and Todd.

University of Chicago Press. 1993. *The Chicago Manual of Style*, 14th ed. Chicago, Illinois.

Wolcott, Harry. 1990. *Writing Qualitative Research*. Newbury Park, California: Sage.

——. 1994. *Transforming Qualitative Data*. Thousand Oaks, California: Sage.

The Hope and Glory Vindicator

Volume 183 Issue 1   January 5, 2002

Town welcomes war bride

Mr. and Mrs. Septus McCardle have arrived from London, England. Mrs. McCardle, the former Mavis Darwin, met Septus when he went to England to do some research. Folks here might recall Mrs. McCardle's daughter, Sharon, who worked here as a researcher herself earlier this year. Mrs. McCardle is a descendant of the famous monkey-trainer Charles Darwin. 'It was love at first sight,' said Mrs. McCardle, 'the minute I saw that beard.'

The lovebirds plan to live in a luxury condo at The Mill at Ye Foxxe Hunt, which used to be the boiler factory.

New company

Mrs. Juanetta Wilcox has joined forces with the Mormon ladies who used to live behind the boiler factory to form an all-female repair and construction business. 'We are operating on a shoestring,' said Mrs. Wilcox, 'so we bought a pick-up from Dick's Construction Co. — it went belly-up a while back. We can't afford fancy signpainting, and Dick didn't want us using his company name, so we just put "No" in front of the sign, and it looks real good.'

Court News

Sylene DeWitt has sued Skip Anderson for breach of promise. Skip said he pulled out because there was something wrong 'but I just can't put my finger on it.' Skip is now engaged to DeeDee Whump Grey Wolf-Anzivino, who divorced her husband Tony after discovering he was not an American Indian.

INSIDE THIS ISSUE

Hancock Towers Newsletter
January 4, 2002

African researchers arrive

A few months ago, four researchers from Hancock Towers went to a village in Africa to look at issues of early marriage and female genital mutilation, which were the source of some controversy in Britain. They hoped to study the issues in their local cultural context.

Now, two women from the village, members of a women's group, have arrived to work with the Tower researchers. Amy Dibba and Mariama Faye were shown how to do participatory research by the Towers team, and are now here to study the problems of first-generation immigrants to Britain. 'One of the messages we would like to get across to people is that nothing in their religion requires early marriage,' said Ms. Dibba. 'We can be true to our religion and our heritage without that.'

Yank starts business

Tony Anzivino, one of the researchers who accompanied Shar Darwin when she returned from the States, is staying here and starting his own business. He had thought of setting up a research consultancy, or working as a securities trader, but decided in the end to fall back on some training in chimney sweeping, and set up a business.

Tony, who will trade under the name Chief Myron Grey-Wolf III, already has his motto painted on his van: 'You've tried the Cowboys... Now try the Indians!' Good luck, Tone!

Towers boy wins in Dublin

Little Abdullahi Osman El-Salim of #22-A won first prize in oral Irish in Dublin last week. Abdullahi was a pupil in Mrs. Braithwaite's Beginning Arabic course.

APPENDIX: GRID FOR ASSESSING A PROBLEM

	1 Reasons	2 Activity	3 Needs	4 Processes	5 Resources	6 People
A Reasons	WHY HAS THIS SITUATION COME ABOUT?	Why was this activity chosen?	Why have these needs arisen?	Why were these processes chosen?	Why were these resources chosen?	Why are these people involved?
B Activity	Why these activities?	WHAT ACTIVITIES ARE INVOLVED?	How does the activity meet needs?	How does the activity relate to the processes?	How do the activities relate to the available resources?	What activities do people carry out?
C Needs	Why these particular needs?	What needs are these activities meeting?	WHAT ARE THE NEEDS IN THIS SITUATION?	How do needs relate to the processes employed?	How do needs relate to resources?	What needs do the people meet? What are their needs?
D Processes	Why are these processes being used?	How are processes related to activities?	What processes are being used to meet needs?	WHAT PROCESSES ARE BEING USED?	What processes are used in getting resources?	What processes do they employ?
E Resources	Why are these resources being used?	How are resources related to activities?	What resources are being used to meet needs?	What resources are needed to carry out the processes?	WHAT RESOURCES ARE INVOLVED?	What resources do people control/use?
F People	Why are these people involved?	Who is involved in the activities?	Who is meeting those needs?	How do the people carry out the processes involved?	Who controls/ uses the resources?	WHO ARE THE PEOPLE INVOLVED?

7 Places (locations, sites, institutions)	8 Consequences	9 Time/Change	10 Identification of Options	11 Assessment of Options	12 Recommendations	13 Prediction
Why this place or these places?	Why have these consequences come about?	Why has the situation changed? Why will it change?	Why have you identified these particular options?	Why have you made this assessment?	Why do you make this recommendation?	Why do you predict this outcome?
What happens at each place?	What is the impact on activities?	Have the activities changed? Will they change?	What are the options in relation to activities?	How does each of the options relate to desired activities? How will these options affect activities? What activities will they require?	What recommendations do you make in relation to these activities?	What will happen if the current activity or the activity as it is projected, continues? What will happen as a result of your recommendation?
What needs are being met at each place?	What is the impact on needs?	Have the needs changed? Will they change?	What are the options in relation to needs?	How does each of the options relate to identified needs? How will these options affect needs? What needs will they meet?	What recommendations do you make to meet these needs?	What will happen if current needs continue to be met as they are, or as it is projected they will be met? What will happen as a result of your recommendation?
What processes are being used in each place?	What is the impact on processes?	Have the processes changed? Will they change?	What are the options in relation to processes?	How does each of the options relate to desired processes? How will these options affect current processes? What processes will they require?	What recommendation do you make in relation to processes?	What will happen if the processes in current use are continued?
What resources are available in each place?	What is the impact on resources?	Have the resources changed? Will they change?	What are the options in relation to resources?	How do each of these options relate to resources? How will these options affect resources? What resources will they require?	What recommendation do you make in relation to resources?	What will happen if resources continue as they are, or as they are projected to be? What will happen as a result of your recommendation?
Who is in each place?	What is the impact on personnel/ beneficiaries?	Have the personnel/ beneficiaries changed? Will they change?	What are the options in relation to personnel/ beneficiaries?	How will these options affect personnel/ beneficiaries? What personnel will they require?	What recommendation do you make in relation to personnel/ beneficiaries?	What will happen if the personnel/ beneficiaries remain as they are or are projected to be? What will happen as a result of your recommendation?

	1 Reasons	2 Activity	3 Needs	4 Processes	5 Resources	6 People
G Places (locations, sites, institutions)	Why have these locations been chosen?	Which places are used for which activities?	Where are the needs being met?	How do the places relate to the processes?	Where are the resources being used?	Where are the people involved?
H Consequences	Why have these consequences occurred?	What are the consequences of this activity?	What are the consequences of these needs? Of being met? Of not being met?	What are the consequences of these processes?	What are the consequences of these resources?	What are the consequences of these people being involved?
I Time/Change	If the situation has changed, or will change, why?	Have these activities changed over time? Do you anticipate change?	Have these needs changed? Do you Do you anticipate change?	Have the processes changed over time? Do you anticipate change?	Have these resources changed? Do you anticipate change?	Have the personnel/ beneficiaries Do you anticipate change?
J Identification Options	Why have these options been identified/ selected?	What options are there in relation to these activities?	What options are there for meeting these needs?	What options are there for other processes?	What options are there for resources? For different use of resources?	What options are open to the people involved? What personnel/ beneficiary options are there? What do you think of your options?
K Assessment of Options	Why has this assessment been made?	What is your assessment of these activities?	What is your assessment of these options for meeting needs?	What is your assessment of these options for using other processes?	What is your assessment of these options for using other resources or using resources differently?	What is your assessment of the options in relation to personnel/ beneficiaries? What is their assessment?
L Recommen- dation	Why these recommend- ations?	What do you recommend in relation to these activities?	What do you recommend to meet these needs?	What do you recommend in relation to these options?	What do you recommend in relation to these resources?	What do you recommend in relation to these options?

7 Places (locations, sites, institutions)	8 Consequences	9 Time/Change	10 Identification	11 Assessment	12 Recommendations	13 Prediction
WHAT ARE THE PLACES, SITES, LOCATIONS?	What is the impact on locations?	Have the locations changed? Will they change?	What are the options in relation to locations?	How will these options affect locations? What locations will they require?	What recommendations do you make in relation to locations?	What will happen if locations remain as they are, or as they are projected to be? What will happen as a result of your recommendation?
What are the consequences of using these locations?	WHAT ARE THE CON-SEQUENCES OF THE CURRENT SITUATION?	Have the consequences changed? Will they change?	What are the options, having considered the consequences identified so far?	How will these options affect the consequences of the current situation? What are the consequences of these options?	What recommendations do you make, taking all identical consequences into account?	What will happen if the current consequences, or projected consequences, continue? What will happen as a result of your recommendation?
Have the locations changed over time? Do you anticipate change?	How have the impacts changed? How will they change?	HAS THE SITUATION CHANGED OVER TIME?	What are the options, in view of past and projected change?	What changes will these con-sequences bring about? What changes will they require?	What recommendation do you make, taking into account past and anticipated changes?	What will happen if change, or projected changes occur? What will happen as a result of your recommendation?
What options are there in relation to location?	What are the consequences of the options which have been identified?	Have the options changed? Will they change?	WHAT ARE THE POSSIBLE OPTIONS?	What options have you chosen to assess?	What recommendation do you make in relation to each identified option?	What will happen if the proposed options are not implemented? What will happen as a result of your recommendation?
What is your assessment of the suitability of this place?	What are the consequences of your assessment?	What is your assessment of the impact of change?	How will you identify the options?	WHAT IS YOUR ASSESSMENT OF EACH OPTION?	What recommendation do you make about how to assess options in future?	What will happen if assessments are not made in the future? What will happen as a result of your recommendation?
What do you recommend in relation to these options?	What do you recommend, knowing the consequences?	What do you recommend as a result of this assessment?	How do you recommend the options be assessed?	What recommendations do you make in relation to each option?	WHAT ARE YOUR RECOM-MENDATIONS?	How do you recommend that assessment of options be made in future? What will happen as a result of your recommendation?

INDEX